PRIMARY SOURCES FOR ANCIENT HISTORY

VOLUME I: THE ANCIENT NEAR EAST AND GREECE

by Gary Forsythe

DORRANCE
PUBLISHING CO
EST. 1920
PITTSBURGH, PENNSYLVANIA 15238

Dorrance Publishing Co
585 Alpha Drive
Pittsburgh, PA 15238
Visit our website at www.bookstore.dorrancepublishing.com

ISBN: 978-1-4809-5425-0
eISBN: 978-1-4809-5401-4

CONTENTS

Preface ix

Part I, Early Mesopotamia and Egypt 1
1. The Sumerian King List 3
2. The Epic of Gilgamesh 9
    A. The Coming of Enkidu 10
    B. Heroism, Death, and the Underworld 11
    C. Gilgamesh's Quest for Immortality 12
    D. The Flood Story 13
    E. The End of the Poem 17
3. Gilgamesh and Agga 19
4. War Between Lagash and Umma 23
5. The Legend of Sargon 27
6. The End of the Sargonid Dynasty 29
7. King Shulgi of Ur 37
8. The Law Code of Hammurabi 41
    A. Administration of Justice 42
    B. Damage to Crops 43
    C. Debt Servitude 43
    D. Marriage, Divorce, and Adultery 43
    E. Disowning and Acknowledging Children 46
    F. Personal Injury 47
    G. Damage to Property 49

9. Egyptian Book of the Dead 53
10. An Egyptian Tale of Magic 59

Part II, The Late Bronze Age 63
11. Egyptian Defeat of the Hyksos 65
12. Suppiluliumas and the Egyptian Queen 69
13. The Battle of Kadesh 75
14. Treaty Between the Egyptians and the Hittites 85
15. Ahhiyawa in the Hittite Texts 91
    A. The Indictment of Madduwatta 91
    B. The Tawagalawa Letter 98
16. The Last Days of Ugarit 105
17. Ramesses III and the Sea Peoples 107

Part III, The Great Empires and the Hebrews 109
18. The Veiling of Women in Ancient Assyria 111
19. The Royal Annals of Ashurnasirpal .113
20. Sennacherib's Siege of Jerusalem 119
    A. The Assyrian Royal Annals of King Sennacherib 120
    B. The Biblical Account 120
21. The Old Testament 127
    A. The Two Accounts of Creation 128
    B. The Garden of Eden 131
    C. The Biblical Flood Story 132
    D. The Exposure of Moses 138
    E. The Miracle of the Burning Bush 139
    F. The Ten Commandments 140
22. Cyrus the Great 145
    A. The Babylonian View 145
    B. The Biblical View 148
    C. The Account of Herodotus 149
23. Persian Religious Toleration 163
    A. The Egyptian Goddess Neith 163
    B. The Cult of Apollo at Magnesia .165
24. Darius' Building of the Palace at Susa 167

Part IV, The Greek Archaic Period 169

  25. Homeric Society 171

    A. The Quarrel Between Agamemnon and Achilles 171

    B. Odysseus and Thersites 178

  26. Greek Colonization 187

    A. Greek Colonization of Sicily 188

    B. The Foundation of Cyrene 191

  27. The Greek Tyrants 197

    A. Aristotle on Tyranny 197

    B. How to Become a Tyrant 198

    C. Cylon of Athens 201

    D. Cypselus and Periander of Corinth 203

    E. Cleisthenes of Sicyon 206

  28. Contrasting Views of the Spartan State 211

    A. Xenophon 211

    B. Aristotle 216

  29. Aristotle on Early Athens 223

  30. Early Greek Lyric Poetry 239

    A. Archilochus 239

    B. Tyrtaeus of Sparta 240

    C. Sappho of Lesbos 242

    D. Semonides of Amorgos 243

    E. Xenophanes of Colophon 246

Part V, The Classical Period of Greece 249

  31. Herodotus and Xerxes' Invasion of Greece 251

    A. Preface to the History 252

    B. Debate of the Persian Nobles 252

    C. Despotism of the Persian King 256

    D. The Battle of Thermopylae 258

    E. The Battle of Salamis 266

  32. From Delian League to Athenian Empire 273

  33. The Workings of the Athenian Empire .283

    A. Athenian Decree Concerning Erythrae 283

    B. The Coinage Decree 285

    C. Measures for Collecting the Tribute 286

    D. Settlement of Affairs in Chalcis 287

34. The Old Oligarch 291

35. Thucydides and the Peloponnesian War 301

    A. Thucydides' Methods of Research and Writing History . . .301

    B. Sparta Declares War on Athens 302

    C. Pericles' Last Speech 307

    D. Athens Decides the Fate of Mytilene 313

    E. The Melian Dialogue 324

    F. Nicias' Letter to the Athenian Democracy 331

    G. Athenian Utter Defeat in Sicily 335

36. The Thirty Tyrants of Athens 347

37. Thebes Liberated from Sparta 359

38. Philip of Macedon 369

    A. Philip's Astonishing Accession to the Throne 369

    B. Demosthenes and the Battle of Chaeronea 373

    C. Philip's Polygamy and Last Disastrous Marriage 377

    D. Philip's Assassination 378

39. Alexander the Great 383

    A. The Smartness and Effectiveness of the Macedonian Army .383

    B. Alexander's Visit to Siwah 388

    C. Alexander before the Battle of Gaugamela 389

    D. The Murder of Cleitus 390

    E. Mutiny and Reconciliation 393

Suggested Modern Readings 399

    A. Before 1100 B.C. 399

    B. The Great Empires and the Hebrews 402

    C. Archaic and Classical Greece 404

Cover Caption: Painting by the French artist Charles La Bran (1665), entitled "Entry of Alexander into Babylon".

PREFACE

This two-volume collection of ancient historical primary source material in English translation is intended to be used in introductory college courses that survey the history of the ancient Mediterranean world. Since it is a common practice to cover the ancient Near Eastern civilizations and Greek history to the end of the Classical Period in one semester and to cover all of ancient Roman history in another, these readings have been organized into two separate volumes. Of course, as collections of primary source material, these volumes are not designed to serve as the fundamental textbooks for such courses, but they are to be used alongside narrative survey histories written by modern scholars; and these readings should serve as important supplements in providing undergraduates, who have little or no previous background in ancient history, with an introduction to the rich and varied nature of our surviving ancient historical sources, to many of its important writers, and to many of the basic problems and questions that have become a standard part of modern historical inquiry into the ancient Mediterranean world. Consequently, since it is assumed that students will be reading some modern narrative survey as their basic textbook, the introductions to the various readings are kept brief and to the point, the expectation being that an assigned textbook and course instructor will provide students with the additional necessary context and guidance for greater understanding.

No selection of ancient source material can possibly please all instructors. Indeed, the reason why the present author has undertaken to compile this collection of material resulted from his own dissatisfaction with currently available readers of this sort. It is hoped that these two volumes will provide instructors with more choices in what they can use in introducing the history of the ancient Mediterranean world to their students. There should be rather little debate over the choice of readings for the periods of Archaic and Classical Greece, but the situation is likely to be far different regarding the ancient Near Eastern readings: for much of our surviving primary sources from these civilizations is not easy for beginning students to digest. The author has striven to present for every major period of ancient Near Eastern history at least one reading that is readable, understandable, and revelatory in some important way or ways. Moreover, some of these readings have the additional advantage in shedding important light on how certain aspects of The Old Testament were adaptations of well-established features of ancient Near Eastern thought, literature, and culture.

In an attempt to make these volumes as affordable as possible, the translations, whenever feasible, have been excerpted from works no longer under copyright and thus requiring permission from and payments to publishers for reproducing copyrighted material. Since, however, many of these older translations often employ wording and styles of punctuation that many undergraduate students today may find unfamiliar or perplexing, I have carried out a systematic and careful proofreading and editing of all the texts. This has resulted in the occasional replacement of an archaic word with a more modern one, frequent slight adjustments in sentences in order to make them more understandable, and countless changes in the punctuation of complex sentences in an effort to render these selections more easily readable for today's college students. Moreover, I have avoided altogether the use of footnotes to explain occasional oddities in the ancient texts. Instead, I have simply enclosed within brackets brief explanatory phrases in the texts themselves. Bibliographies of modern works have been placed at the ends of both volumes to serve as aids to both instructors and students for pursuing their interests into the fascinating history of the ancient Mediterranean world.

PART I
EARLY MESOPOTAMIA AND EGYPT

READING 1
THE SUMERIAN KING LIST

The following is a Mesopotamian text that was composed during the period of the Old Babylonian Kingdom (ca. 1900-1600 B.C.). It has survived in several different versions, and modern scholars have succeeded in piecing together a relatively complete text from the various surviving fragments of these different copies of this document. It is a list of Mesopotamian rulers, beginning with earliest mythical times and coming down to the eighteenth century B.C. The kings listed from the late Sumerian period (ca. 2500 B.C.) onward are historical, and their reigns are likely to be accurately recorded. That material therefore is important in helping to establish a basic chronology from that point forward; but for the preceding period the names of the kings cannot be verified. The text exhibits three basic features of Mesopotamian thought: (1) that the institution of kingship was of divine origin; (2) that in early times leadership within Mesopotamia was exercised at different times by different city-states; and (3) that as shown by the decreasing lengths of the kings' reigns, the Mesopotamians generally regarded human history as moving along a downward slope of gradual decline, unlike our modern assumption of scientific advancement, technological progress, and sustained economic growth. Notice that for the earliest kings, to whom extraordinarily long reigns are attributed, the years of their reigns are multiples and sums of 60, 600, 3600, and 6000 in conformity with the Mesopotamian mathematical system based on 60, not 10.

(Taken from pp. 328-331 of The Sumerians: Their History, Culture, and Character, by Samuel Noah Kramer, U. of

Chicago Press, copyright 1963, reprinted with the permission of the publisher)

After kingship had descended from heaven, Eridu became the seat of kingship. In Eridu Alulim reigned 28,800 years as king; Alalgar reigned 36,000 years. Two kings reigned 64,800 years. Eridu was abandoned, and its kingship was carried off to Badtibira. In Badtibira, Enmenluanna reigned 43,200 years; Enmengalanna reigned 28,800 years; Dumuzi, the shepherd, reigned 36,000 years. Three kings reigned 108,000 years. Badtibira was abandoned, and its kingship was carried off to Larak. In Larak, Ensipazianna reigned 28,800 years. One king reigned 28,800 years. Larak was abandoned, and its kingship was carried off to Sippar. In Sippar, Enmeduranna reigned 21,000 years as king. One king reigned 21,000 years. Sippar was abandoned, and its kingship was carried off to Shuruppak. In Shuruppak, Ubartutu reigned 18,600 years as king. One king reigned 18,600 years. In five cities, eight kings reigned 241,200 years. The Flood then swept over the land.

After the Flood had swept over the land, and kingship had descended from heaven a second time, Kish became the seat of kingship. In Kish, Gaur reigned 1,200 years as king; Gulla-Nidaba-annapad reigned 960 years; Palakinatim reigned 900 years; Nangishlishma reigned ... years; Bahina reigned ... years; Buanum reigned 840 years; Kalibum reigned 960 years; Galumum reigned 840 years; Zukakip reigned 900 years; Atab reigned 600 years; Mashda, the son of Atab, reigned 840 years; Arurim, the son of Mashda, reigned 720 years; Etana, the shepherd, he who ascended to heaven, who made firm all the lands, reigned 1,560 years as king; Balih, the son of Etana, reigned 400 years; Enmenunna reigned 660 years; Melam-Kish, the son of Enmenunna, reigned 900 years; Barsalnunna, the son of Enmenunna, reigned 1,200 years; Meszamug, the son of Barsalnunna, reigned 140 years; Tizkar, the son of Meszamug, reigned 305 years; Ilku reigned 900 years; Iltasadum reigned 1,200 years; Enmebaraggesi, he who smote the weapons of the land Elam, reigned 900 years as king; Agga, the son of Enmebaraggesi, reigned 625 years. Twenty-three kings reigned 24,510 years, 3 months, and 2 days. Kish was defeated in battle, and its kingship was carried off to Eanna [a sacred precinct of Uruk].

In Eanna, Meskiaggasher, the son of the sun-god Utu, reigned both as priest and king 324 years. Meskiaggasher entered the sea and ascended the mountains;

Enmerkar, the son of Meskiaggasher, the king of Uruk who had built Uruk, reigned 420 years as king; Lugalbanda, the shepherd, reigned 1,200 years; Dumuzi, the fisherman, whose city was Kua, reigned 100 years; Gilgamesh, whose father was a nomad(?), reigned 126 years; Urnungal, the son of Gilgamesh, reigned 30 years; Udulkalamma, the son of Urnungal, reigned 15 years; Labasher reigned 9 years; Ennundaranna reigned 8 years; Meshede reigned 36 years; Melamanna reigned 6 years; Lugalkidul reigned 36 years. Twelve kings reigned 2,310 years. Uruk was defeated in battle, and its kingship was carried off to Ur.

In Ur, Mesannepadda reigned 80 years as king; Meskiagnunna, the son of Mesannepadda, reigned 36 years as king; Elulu reigned 25 years; Balulu reigned 36 years. Four kings reigned 177 years. Ur was defeated in battle, and its kingship was carried off to Awan.

In Awan, there were three kings who reigned 356 years, [but their names are destroyed in large part; and then the text continues.] Awan was defeated in battle, and its kingship was carried off to Kish. In Kish ... reigned (more than) 201 years as king; Dadasig reigned ... years; Mamagal reigned 420 years; Kalbum, the son of Mamagal, reigned 132 years; Tuge reigned 360 years; Mennumna reigned 180 years; Lugalmu reigned 420 years; Ibbi-Ea reigned 290(?) years. Eight kings reigned 3,195 years. Kish was defeated in battle, and its kingship was carried off to Hamazi.

In Hamazi, Hadanish reigned 360 years. One king reigned 360 years. Hamazi was defeated, and its kingship was carried off to Uruk. In Uruk ... reigned 60 years as king; Lugalure reigned 120 years; Argandea reigned 7 years. Three kings reigned 187 years. Uruk was defeated, and its kingship was carried off to Ur.

In Ur [the names of the rulers of the Second Dynasty of Ur, who were four in number and probably reigned 116 years, are destroyed]. Ur was defeated, and its kingship was carried off to Adab. In Adab, Lugalannemundu reigned 90 years as king. One king reigned 90 years. Adab was defeated, and its kingship was carried off to Mari. In Mari, Ilshu reigned 30 years as king; ..., the son of Ilshu, reigned 17 years; ... reigned 30 years; ... reigned 20 years; ... reigned 30 years; ... reigned 9 years. Six kings reigned 136 years. Mari was defeated, and its kingship was carried off to Kish.

In Kish, Ku-Bau, the innkeeper, she who made firm the foundations of Kish, reigned 100 years as "king." One king reigned 100 years. Kish was defeated, and its kingship was carried off to Akshak. In Akshak, Unzi reigned 30 years as king; Undalulu reigned 12 years; Urur [or Zuzu] reigned 6 years; Puzur-Nirah reigned 20 years; Ishu-Il reigned 24 years; Shu-Sin, the son of Ishu-Il, reigned 7 years. Six kings reigned 99 years. Akshak was defeated, and its kingship was carried off to Kish.

In Kish, Puzur-Sin, son of Ku-Bau, reigned 25 years as king; Ur-Zababa, the son of Puzur-Sin, reigned 400 years. Simudarra reigned 30 years; Usiwatar, the son of Simudarra, reigned 7 years; Ishtar-muti reigned 11 years; Ishme-Shamash reigned 11 years; Nannia, the stoneworker, reigned 7 years. Seven kings reigned 491 years. Kish was defeated, and its kingship was carried off to Uruk.

In Uruk, Lugalzaggesi reigned 25 years as king. One king reigned 25 years. Uruk was defeated, and its kingship was carried off to Agade. In Agade, Sargon, whose father was a gardener, the cupbearer of Ur-Zababa, the king of Agade who built Agade, reigned 56 years as king; Rimush, the son of Sargon, reigned 9 years; Manishtushu, the older brother of Rimush, son of Sargon, ruled 15 years; Naram-Sin, the son of Manishtushu, reigned 56 years; Sharkalisharri, the son of Naram-Sin, reigned 25 years.

Who was king? Who was not king? [meaning a period of anarchy] Igigi, the king; Nanum, the king; Imi, the king; Elulu, the king. The four of them were kings but reigned only 3 years. Dudu reigned 21 years; Shudurul, the son of Dudu, reigned 15 years. Eleven kings reigned 197 years. Agade was defeated, and its kingship was carried off to Uruk. In Uruk, Urnigin reigned 7 years as king; Urgigir, the son of Urnigin, reigned 6 years; Kudda reigned 6 years; Puzur-ili reigned 5 years; Ur-Utu reigned 6 years. Five kings reigned 30 years. Uruk was smitten with weapons, and its kingship was carried off to the Gutium hordes. In the Gutium hordes, first reigned a nameless king; then Imta reigned 3 years as king; Inkishush reigned 6 years; Sarlagab reigned 6 years; Shulme reigned 6 years; Elulumesh reigned 6 years; Inimbakesh reigned 5 years; Igeshaush reigned 6 years; Iarlagab reigned 15 years; Ibate reigned 3 years; ... reigned 3 years; Kurum reigned 1 year; ... reigned 3 years; ... reigned 2 years; Irarum reigned 2 years; Ibranum reigned 1 year; Hablum reigned 2 years; Puzur-Sin, the son of Hablum, reigned 7 years; Iarlaganda reigned 7 years; ... reigned 7 years; ... reigned 40 days. Twenty-one kings reigned 91 years and 40 days. The Gutium hordes were defeated, and their kingship was carried off to Uruk.

6

In Uruk, Utuhegal reigned 7 years, 6 months, and 15 days as king. One king reigned 7 years, 6 months, and 15 days. Uruk was smitten with weapons, and its kingship was carried off to Ur. In Ur, Ur-Nammu reigned 18 years as king; Shulgi, the son of UrNammu, reigned 48 years; Amar-Sin, the son of Shulgi, reigned 9 years; Shu-Sin, the son of Amar-Sin [an error for "the son of Shulgi"], reigned 9 years; Ibbi-Sin, the son of Shu-Sin, reigned 24 years. Five kings reigned 108 years. Ur was defeated, and its kingship was carried off to Isin.

In Isin, Ishbi-Erra reigned 33 years as king; Shuilishu, the son of Ishbi-Erra, reigned 10 years; Idin-Dagan, the son of Shuilishu, reigned 21 years; Ishme-Dagan, the son of Idin-Dagan, reigned 20 years; Lipit-Ishtar, the son of Ishme-Dagan, reigned 11 years; Ur-Ninurta reigned 28 years; Bur-Sin, the son of Ur-Ninurta, reigned 21 years; Lipit-Enlil, the son of Bur-Sin, reigned 5 years; Erraimitti reigned 8 years; Enlilbani reigned 24 years; Zambia reigned 3 years; Iterpisha reigned 4 years; Urdukuga reigned 4 years; Sinmagir reigned 11 years. Fourteen kings reigned 203 years.

READING 2
THE EPIC OF GILGAMESH

Gilgamesh, a legendary king of Uruk during the Sumerian period, emerged early on as a heroic figure among the Mesopotamians. Many stories were told about him and his supposed great deeds. By the time of the Old Babylonian Kingdom (ca. 1900-1600 B.C.) these stories had been fashioned into a continuous tale that is now generally termed The Epic of Gilgamesh. According to this long narrative poem, Gilgamesh is so full of strength and energy that he wears out his subjects, who then pray to the gods for relief. They in turn instruct one of the goddesses to fashion out of clay a mighty man named Enkidu, whom they send to Uruk to put Gilgamesh in his place. But after the two fight one another to a standstill, they become friends and then go off to perform great exploits, first killing the monstrous guardian of a great cedar forest (named Humbaba) and then slaying the bull of heaven that has been ravaging the land, because Ishtar, goddess of female beauty and sexuality, had offered herself to Gilgamesh, only to be scorned. After Enkidu offers another insult to Ishtar, the gods decree that Enkidu must die. After Enkidu falls sick and dies, the poem describes Gilgamesh's last major exploit, a quest for immortality, so that he would not succumb to death like his friend Enkidu. An important part of this quest involves Gilgamesh sailing off to a mysterious island in the sea, a place called Dilmun, where there live the only two mortals of Mesopotamian myth who were ever granted immortality by the gods. These two people are a married couple: Utnapishtim and his wife, who had survived the great flood that had once destroyed all life on earth. During Gilgamesh's visit on this island Utnapishtim tells him the story of this great flood, whose basic outline was later adopted and adapted by the authors of Genesis in The Old Testament. The two versions of this story, Mesopotamian vs. Hebrew (see below Reading 21C), reveal important differences between the ways in which these peoples viewed the divine.

A. The Coming of Enkidu

When the poem begins, Gilgamesh is ruling arrogantly over the people of Uruk. His most unbearable behavior is that he takes to bed every virgin on her wedding night and enjoys her before her husband. When the people of Uruk pray to the gods for assistance against their overbearing king, the gods instruct one of their number to create Gilgamesh's equal in physical strength in order to check Gilgamesh's oppression of his subjects. Accordingly, the goddess Aruru uses water and clay to form Enkidu, who is huge and powerful with long flowing hair. But initially Enkidu is a wild man, an innocent creature of nature, who roams in the wild with the other wild animals, who accept him as one of their own. He eats grass and drinks water from a watering hole along with them, being devoid of all human knowledge and civilized ways. When a trapper comes upon Enkidu among the other animals and is frightened by him, he reports his presence to Gilgamesh in Uruk; and the latter sends out with the trapper a temple prostitute, Shamhat by name, to seduce Enkidu. This brings about Enkidu's loss of innocence and his acquisition of human understanding; and after the wild animals now fear and run away from Enkidu as they behave toward other humans, Enkidu is then ready and eager to come to Uruk to champion the people of the city against their oppressive king.

(Composed by Gary Forsythe from different translations)

The trapper, taking the temple prostitute Shamhat with him, went on his way. They arrived at the watering hole on the third day, and the trapper and the harlot sat down there. They waited in their places for one day, and then for a second day. Then on the third day the wild animals came down to drink, their hearts rejoicing in the water, and with them to drink was Enkidu, the wild man, born in the hills, who eats grass with the gazelles. She saw him, the savage man, the barbarous man come from the wilderness. "There he is," said the trapper, "now bare your breasts, woman. Have no shame. Let him see you naked. Welcome his ardor. Lie with him, and teach him your woman's arts. As his desire is drawn to you, the wild beasts who have shared his life in the hills shall reject him."

She bared her breasts. She was not shy. She laid aside her robe and welcomed his ardor. He lay upon her, he possessed her, she taught him her woman's arts. For six days and seven nights Enkidu mated with the woman, until he was fully satisfied. He then returned to the wild beasts, but when the gazelles saw Enkidu, they bounded off, the wild animals ran away. He was astonished and tried to follow, but his body was spent, his knees weak, his swiftness gone. The wild animals had left. It was not as before, but he now had wisdom, human understanding.

B. Heroism, Death, and the Underworld

When Enkidu and the prostitute arrive in Uruk, the people are astonished at Enkidu's formidable appearance and regard him as a suitable match for Gilgamesh. When the latter ventures out at night to deflower another virgin on her wedding night, Enkidu is there to bar the way, and the two engage in a mighty struggle, which ends with Gilgamesh throwing Enkidu to the ground. When Enkidu acknowledges and praises Gilgamesh's strength, the two form a lasting friendship. Now that Gilgamesh has found someone as mighty as himself, he abandons his oppressive ways and conceives the idea of the two of them performing a heroic exploit. After traveling a long distance to the Cedar Forest, the two heroes kill its monstrous guardian, Humbaba; and on their return the goddess Ishtar invites Gilgamesh to become her mortal lover. But in a lengthy reply Gilgamesh rejects her offer by pointing out several instances in which Ishtar had offered herself to other mortal men, only to tire of them and to change them into different animals. When Gilgamesh makes it clear that he does not wish to suffer such a fate, the insulted Ishtar ascends in rage to heaven, where she complains to her divine parents of her scornful mistreatment by Gilgamesh, and she demands that she be allowed to seek revenge. She is given the bull of heaven; and when she releases it upon the earth, it proceeds to devastate the land and to kill thousands of people until Gilgamesh and Enkidu show up and kill the bull. This forms the second great exploit of the two heroes, but it also forms the prelude for Enkidu's death: for when, following their victory over the bull, Enkidu offers a grievous insult to Ishtar, the gods decree that he must die; and after falling ill, and while lingering for days on his bed, Enkidu has a frightening dream in which he sees the gloomy conditions of the underworld that await him.

(Composed by Gary Forsythe from different translations)

Enkidu said, "My friend, last night I had a dream. The heavens thundered, the earth replied, and I stood between them before an awful being. His claws were like the talons of an eagle. He fell upon me, he seized me by the hair, he overpowered me. He changed my arms into wings covered in feathers like a bird. He bore me down to the palace of Irkalla, the house of darkness, the place from which no one ever returns, on the road from which there is no way back.

The dwellers there sit in darkness, where dust is their food, and clay is their meat. They are clothed like birds with wings as their garments. They see no light, they sit in darkness. I entered the House of Dust. There I beheld kings and princes who had once ruled the earth, their crowns now put away forever. They had once been viewed as the gods Anu and Enlil, but now they were like servants, fetching and carrying roasted meats and cool water. There in the House of Dust, where I entered, dwell high priests and acolytes, temple servants and prophets. I beheld Etana, the king of Kish whom the eagle had long ago carried to heaven. I saw Sumuqan, the god of cattle; and I beheld Ereshkigal, the queen of the underworld. Before her knelt her scribe Beletseri, reading from a tablet. She lifted up her head, saw me, and asked, 'Who has brought this one here?'"

C. Gilgamesh's Quest for Immortality

When Enkidu finally dies, Gilgamesh mourns for him profoundly and seems lost without his heroic companion. He also becomes fearful of his own death and conceives the idea of achieving immortality by finding Utnapishtim, a man who had survived the great flood of time past, and whom the gods had honored with the unique distinction of granting him and his wife eternal life on a distant island called Dilmun. After searching over a vast extent of forest, Gilgamesh eventually reaches a fairyland of the mountains, where twin peaks guard the rising and setting of the sun. After the guardian of the place, a scorpion man, allows Gilgamesh to enter, the latter travels a long distance through perpetual darkness until he emerges into a paradise called the Garden of the Gods, where he comes upon Siduri, who urges Gilgamesh to give up his futile quest for immortality.

(Composed by Gary Forsythe from different translations)

Siduri said, "Gilgamesh, Whither are you hastening? You shall never find that life which you are seeking. When the gods created man, for him they allotted death, but life they kept for themselves. Gilgamesh, fill your stomach with good food. Make merry every day and every night. Make each day a day of joy. Dance and play every day and every night. Wear clothes that are sparkling clean, and bathe yourself in water. Cherish the child who holds you by the hand, and give delight to your wife with your embrace, because this is the lot of mankind."

D. The Flood Story

When Gilgamesh insists in learning from Siduri how to find Utmapishtim, she warns him that it may be impossible for him to cross over the sea to Dilmun, but she says that he might succeed if he can find Urshanabi the boatman. Gilgamesh does in fact succeed in locating Urshanabi and having him carry him by his boat a long distance over the waters to the island of Dilmun, where Utnapishtim and his wife live forever in quiet ease. During his stay on the island Utnapishtim tells Gilgamesh the story of the flood, and how he and his wife had been given immortality by the gods.

Unfortunately, there is a break in the Cuneiform tablet where there should have been described the reason for the gods bringing on the flood for destroying life on earth. This gap may be filled from another well-documented Mesopotamian story, the myth of Atrahasis. In that tale a man named Atrahasis plays the role of Utnapishtim as the builder of the great boat stocked with animals and craftsmen who survive destruction; and the flood is the third and final way in which the gods try to wipe out mankind. Human beings have become so numerous and create such a terrible clamor that the earth bellows like a bull, and Enlil complains of the unbearable noise and of the fact that he cannot sleep. He first tries to destroy mankind through pestilence; and when this fails, he tries drought and famine; and when they also do not bring about total success, he brings on the flood.

(Taken from pp. 89-101 of Cuneiform Parallels to The Old Testament, by Robert William Rogers, Oxford U. Press 1912, revised by Gary Forsythe)

Gilgamesh said to him, to Utnapishtim, the faraway: "I look upon thee, o Utnapishtim. Thy appearance is not changed. Thou art like me. Thou art not different. Even as I am, thou art. Thy heart is in perfect state to make combat. Thou dost lie down upon thy side and upon thy back. Tell me, how hast thou been exalted, and amid the assembly of the gods hast thou found life?"

Utnapishtim spoke to him, to Gilgamesh. I will reveal to thee, o Gilgamesh, the hidden word. And the decision of the gods will I announce to thee. Shuruppak, a city which thou knowest, which lies on the bank of the Euphrates, that city was very old, and the heart of the gods within it drove them to send a flood, the great gods.... their father Anu, their counsellor the warrior Enlil, their messenger Ninurta, their prince Ennugi. The lord of wisdom, Ea, counselled with them and repeated their word to the reed hut: "reed hut, reed hut, o wall, wall, o reed hut, hearken! O wall, attend! O man of Shuruppak, son of Ubaratutu, pull down thy house, build a ship, leave thy possessions, take thought for thy life, thy property abandon, save thy life, bring living seed of every kind into the ship. The ship, which thou shalt build, so shall be the measure of its dimensions. Thus shall correspond its breadth to its height. Cover it with a roof, like the vault over the abyss."

I understood it and spake to Ea, my lord, "my lord, as thou hast commanded, I will observe; and I will execute it. But what shall I say to the city, the people, and the elders?" Ea opened his mouth and spake. He said unto me his servant, "thou shalt so say unto them: Because Enlil hates me, no longer may I dwell in your city, nor remain on Enlil's earth. Into the ocean must I fare, with Ea, my lord to dwell. Upon you will he then rain abundance, a catch of birds, a catch of fish, rich harvest. A time has Shamash appointed; on an evening the senders of rain shall rain upon you a mighty rain-storm."

As soon as the morning glow appeared [about ten lines missing], the strong one ... brought what was necessary. On the fifth day I set up its form, in its plan 120 cubits high on each of its sidewalls. By 120 cubits it corresponded on each edge of the roof. I laid down its hull, I enclosed it. I built it in six stories. I divided it into seven parts. Its interior I divided into nine parts. Water-plugs

I fastened within it. I prepared a rudder and laid down what was necessary. Three sars of bitumen I poured over the outside. Three sars of bitumen I poured over the inside. Three sars of oil the stevedores brought up. Besides a sar of oil which men use as a libation, the shipbuilder stowed away two sars of oil. For the people I slaughtered bullocks, I slew lambs daily. Of must, beer, oil and wine I gave the people to drink like water from the river. A festival I made, like the days of the feast of Akitu [i.e., of the new year]. I opened a box of ointment; I put ointment in my hand.

At the rising of the great Shamash the ship was finished. The launching was hard. Two thirds was submerged. With all that I had, I filled the ship. With all that I had of silver, I filled it. With all that I had of gold, I filled it. With all that I had of living things, I filled it. I brought up into the ship my family and household. The cattle of the field, the beasts of the field, craftsmen. All of them I brought in. A fixed time had Shamash appointed, saying, "When the sender of rain sends a heavy rain in the evening, then enter into the ship, and close thy door." The appointed time came near. The senders of the rain in the evening sent heavy rain. The appearance of the weather I observed, I feared to behold the weather, I entered the ship and closed the door. To the ship's master, to Puzur-Amurri the sailor, I entrusted the building with its goods.

When the first flush of dawn appeared, there came up from the horizon a black cloud. Adad thundered within it, while Nebo and Marduk went before. They go as messengers over mountain and valley. Nergal tore away the foundations. Ninurta advances, the storm he makes to descend. The Anunnaki lifted up their torches, with their brightness they light up the land. Adad's storm reached unto heaven. All light was turned into darkness. It flooded the land. For one day the deluge raged high, the waters covered the mountains. Like a wave of destruction, they brought it upon men. No man beheld his fellow. No more were men recognized in heaven. The gods feared the deluge. They drew back, they climbed up to the heaven of Anu. The gods crouched like dogs, they cowered by the walls. Ishtar cried like a woman in travail. Loudly cried the queen of the gods with her beautiful voice, "The former time is turned into clay, since I commanded evil in the assembly of the gods. Because I commanded evil in the assembly of the gods for the destruction of my people, I commanded battle. I alone bore my people. And now like the spawn of fish they fill the sea." The gods of the Anunnaki wept with her. The gods sat bowed and weeping. They covered their mouths.

For six days and six nights blew the wind, the deluge and the tempest overwhelmed the land. When the seventh day drew nigh, the tempest spent itself in the battle, which it had fought like an army. Then rested the sea, the storm fell asleep, the flood ceased. I looked upon the sea. There was silence come, and all mankind was turned to clay. Like a roof, the surface lay level. I opened the window, and the light fell upon my face. I bowed, I sat down, I wept, and over my face ran my tears. I looked in all directions. Terrible was the sea. After twelve days an island arose. To the land of Nisir the ship made its way. The mount of Nisir held it fast, so that it moved not. One day, a second day did the mount of Nisir hold it, and it moved not. A third day, a fourth day did the mount of Nisir hold it, so that it moved not. A fifth day, a sixth day did the mount of Nisir hold it, so that it moved not.

When the seventh day approached, I sent forth a dove and let her go. The dove flew away and came back, because there was no resting place, and she returned. I sent forth a swallow and let her go. The swallow flew away and came back, because there was no resting place, and she returned. I sent forth a raven and let her go. The raven flew away. She saw the abatement of the waters. She drew near, she croaked and came not back. Then I sent everything forth to the four quarters of heaven, I offered sacrifice, I made a libation upon the mountain's peak. By sevens I set out the sacrificial vessels. Beneath them I heaped up reed and cedar wood and myrtle. The gods smelled the savor, the gods smelled the sweet savor, the gods gathered like flies over the sacrificer.

When at last the Lady of the gods drew near, she raised the great jewel of her necklace, which Anu had once made according to her wish. "Oh ye gods here, even as I shall not forget the jewels of my neck, upon these days shall I think, I shall never forget them. Let the gods come to the offering, but let Enlil not come to the offering, because he took not counsel and sent the deluge, and my people he gave to destruction." When at last Enlil drew near, he saw the ship; then was Enlil wroth. He was filled with anger against the gods: "Who then has escaped with life? No man must live in the destruction!" Then Ninurta opened his mouth and spake, he said to the warrior Enlil, "Who but Ea can plan anything? And Ea knoweth every matter." Ea opened his mouth and spake, he spake to the warrior Enlil, "Thou wise among the gods, warrior

Enlil, why couldst thou, without thought, send a flood? On the sinner lay his sin, on the slanderer lay his slander. Forbear; let not all be destroyed, have mercy, so that men be not destroyed. Instead of thy sending a deluge, would that a lion had come and mankind lessened! Instead of thy sending a deluge, would that a wolf had come and mankind lessened! Instead of thy sending a deluge, would that a famine had come and the land .... Instead of thy sending a deluge, would that a plague had come and mankind slain! I have not divulged the decision of the great gods. I made Utnapishtim see a dream, and so he discovered the secret of the gods. Now take counsel for him."

Ea went up into the ship. He took my hand and brought me forth. He brought forth my wife and made her kneel at my side. He turned us toward each other. He stood between us, he blessed us: "Formerly Utnapishtim was only a man, but now let Utnapishtim and his wife be like the gods, even us. Let Utnapishtim dwell afar off at the mouth of the rivers." They took me, and afar off at the mouth of the rivers they placed me to dwell.

E. The End of the Poem

After hearing the story of the flood, but failing to obtain immortality for himself, Gilgamesh prepares to depart from Dilmun with Urshanabi. But as they are ready to sail off, Utnapishtim offers Gilgamesh a consolation prize in place of his failed attempt to gain everlasting life. It is in the form of a mysterious plant that will rejuvenate Gilgamesh. It grows at the bottom of the sea. So, after they have set out, Gilgamesh ties heavy stones to his feet, jumps overboard, descends to the bottom of the sea, finds the plant, takes it in his hand, cuts the stones from his feet, and rises again to the surface with the plant. He plans on bringing it back to Uruk to feed to the old men, and he says that he will call this plant "old men become young again." But after Gilgamesh and Urshanabi reach land again and are traveling back to Uruk, Gilgamesh stops at a cool spring of water to bathe himself. Before doing so, he lays the plant on the ground; and while he is bathing, a snake smells the sweet fragrance of the plant and eats it, after which it sheds its skin and emerges rejuvenated and shiny. Thus, instead of mankind reaping the benefit of this wondrous plant, the blessing is conferred upon snakes.

The poem ends with Gilgamesh and Urshanabi returning to Uruk; and although Gilgamesh is saddened by the failure of his quest for immortality and by his loss of the wondrous plant, he urges Urshanabi to gaze upon the great wall surrounding Uruk, and Gilgamesh takes great pride in having been its builder. The final lines of the poem praise Gilgamesh for his wisdom, his mighty deeds, his wide travels, his discovery of the story of the great flood, and his recording in writing of all these things for posterity.

READING 3
GILGAMESH AND AGGA

The following text, consisting of only 115 lines of Sumerian cuneiform poetry, records a legendary conflict between two Sumerian city-states: Uruk (or Erech) ruled by Gilgamesh, and Kish ruled by Agga. The highly compressed language of the text makes its content somewhat difficult to follow, but the basic outline is this. The king of Kish sends envoys to Uruk with demands of surrender or to face war. Gilgamesh first consults an assembly of elders, and the latter reject Gilgamesh's desire not to submit to Kish. Instead, they advise submission. Displeased by this answer, Gilgamesh then consults a second assembly of men, who support Gilgamesh in not submitting to Kish. Uruk then finds itself besieged; and when Gilgamesh sends out Birhurturri, he is instantly seized and fails to overawe Agga with his praise of Gilgamesh. But when Gilgamesh mounts the city wall and addresses the besiegers, their resistance collapses, and they submit to Gilgamesh. This apparently marks the end of the hegemony of Kish and the beginning of that of Uruk.

One aspect of this text that has attracted much modern scholarly attention is Gilgamesh's initial consultation of two bodies at the very beginning of the story. It has led some scholars to speculate that in early Sumerian times there existed in the city-states two bodies: one of elders and another of citizen-warriors. If so, this three-part division of political authority (king, council of elders, and warrior assembly) would anticipate the basic organization of the ancient Greek city-state by two thousand years. This would really not be all that surprising, because the course of human history is full of instances in which similar conditions have given rise independently to the same human solution or pattern of life.

(Taken from pp. 10-13 of "Gilgamesh and Agga," by Samuel Noah Kramer and Thorkild Jacobsen, The American Journal of Archaeology 53 [1949], reprinted with the permission of the publisher)

The envoys of Agga, the son of Enmebaraggesi, proceeded from Kish to Gilgamesh in Erech. The lord Gilgamesh before the elders of his city put the matter, seeks out (their) word: "To complete the wells, to complete all the wells of the land, to complete the wells (and) the small bowls of the land, to dig the wells, to complete the fastening ropes, let us not submit to the house of Kish, let us smite it with weapons." The convened assembly of the elders of his city answer Gilgamesh: "To complete the wells, to complete all the wells of the land, to complete the wells (and) the small bowls of the land, to dig the wells, to complete the fastening ropes, let us submit to the house of Kish, let us not smite it with weapons." Gilgamesh, the lord of Kullab, who performs heroic deeds for manna, took not the word of the elders of his city to heart. A second time Gilgamesh, the lord of Kullab, before the men of his city put the matter, seeks out their word: "To complete all the wells, to complete all the wells of the land, to complete the wells (and) the small bowls of the land, to dig the wells, to complete the fastening ropes, do not submit to the house of Kish, let us smite it with weapons." The convened assembly of the men of his city answer Gilgamesh: "O ye who stand, O ye who sit, O ye who are raised with the sons of the king, O ye who press the donkey's thigh, whoever holds its life, do not submit to the house of Kish, let us smite it with weapons. Erech, the handiwork of the gods, Eanna, the house descending from heaven, it is the great gods who have fashioned its parts, its great wall touching the clouds, its lofty dwelling place established by Anu, thou hast cared for, thou who art king (and) hero. O thou ... -headed, thou prince beloved of Anu, how hast thou feared his coming! Its army is small. It is scattered behind it. Its men do not hold high (their) face." Then Gilgamesh, the lord of Kullab, at the wo[rd] of the men of his city his heart rejoiced, his spirit brightened; he says to his servant Enkidu: "Therefore let the nukara-implement be put aside for the violence of battle. Let the weapons of battle return to your side. Let them produce fear (and) terror. As for him, when he comes, verily my great fear will fall upon him. Verily his judgment will be confounded. Verily his counsel will be dissipated."

The days were not five. The days were not ten. Agga, the son of En-mebaraggesi, besieged Erech; Erech—its judgment was confounded. Gil-gamesh, the lord of Kullab, says to its heroes: "My heroes frown. Who has heart, let him stand up. To Agga I would have him go." Birhurturri, his head ... man, utters praises to his king: "I would go to Agga. Verily his judgment will be confounded. Verily his counsel will be dissipated." Birhurturri went out through the city-gate. As Birhurturri went out through the city-gate, they seized him at the entrance of the city-gate. Birhurturri, they crush his flesh. He was brought before Agga. He speaks to Agga. He had not finished his word (when) Zabar ... ga ascends toward the wall; he peered over the wall. He saw Agga. Birhurturri says to him: "O servant of the stout man, thy king the stout man is he not (also) my king? Verily the stout man is my king. Verily it is his ... forehead, verily it is his .... face, verily it is his beard of lapis-lazuli, verily it is his gracious finger."

The multitude did not cast itself down. The multitude did not rise. The multitude did not cover itself with dust. (The people) of all the foreign lands were not overwhelmed. On the mouths of (the people) of the lands dust was not heaped. The prow of the magurru-boat was not cut down. Agga, the king of Kish, restrained not his soldierly heart. They keep on striking him. They keep on beating him. Birhurturri they crushed his flesh.

After Zabar ... ga, Gilgamesh ascends toward the wall. Terror fell upon the old and young of Kullab. The men of Erech held their battle weapons at their sides. The door of the city-gate they stationed themselves in its ap-proaches. Enkidu went out toward the city-gate. Gilgamesh peered over the wall. He saw Agga: "O servant of the stout man, thy king the stout man is my king." As he spoke, the multitude cast itself down. The multitude arose. The multitude covered itself with dust. (The people) of all the foreign lands were overwhelmed. On the mouths of (the people) of the lands dust was heaped. The prow of the magurru-boat was cut down. Agga, the king of Kish, re-strained his soldierly heart.

Gilgamesh, the lord of Kullab, Says to Agga: "O Agga, my overseer, O Agga, my steward, O Agga, my army leader, O Agga, the fleeing bird thou hast sated with grain. O Agga, thou hast given me breath; thou hast given me life. O Agga, thou bringest the fleeing man to rest." Erech, the handiwork of the gods, the great wall touching the sky, the lofty dwelling place established by

Anu, thou hast cared for, thou who art king (and) hero. O thou ... -headed, thou prince beloved of Anu, Agga has set thee free for Kish. Before Utu he has returned to thee the power of former days; O Gilgamesh, lord of Kullab, thy praise is good.

Reading 4
War Between Lagash and Umma

Although archaeological excavations have turned up thousands and thousands of clay cuneiform tablets from sites in Mesopotamia, only a small fraction of these texts is historical in their content. Almost all are simple records of sales, loans, payments, legal documents, legal decisions, and word lists made to teach and learn how to write. This situation is particularly true for the Sumerian period of Mesopotamia. In fact, about the only real "historical" texts from this period date to its end and concern a decades-long border war fought between Lagash and Umma over a piece of land called Guedinna. French archaeologists of the late nineteenth century unearthed in the territory of ancient Lagash a series of inscribed clay objects that give us some idea of the long history of this border war, fought during the twenty-fifth and twenty-fourth centuries B.C.

The following translated text comes from an inscribed clay cone that was dedicated to the chief guardian divinities of Lagash, the god Ningirsu and the goddess Nanshe. The text was composed during the reign of Entemena, the fifth in a dynasty of eight rulers of Lagash; and fortunately for us, despite the religious nature of this text, it provides us with some basic historical information about the on-going conflict between the two city-states. According to this text, the boundary dispute was first arbitrated by Mesilim, the king of Kish, who erected an upright inscribed stone slab (stele) to record his decision and to mark the border between the two states. Mesilim's arbitration is seen as simply carrying out the will of Enlil, the chief god of the Sumerians, who settled this dispute between Ningirsu and Shara, the chief gods of the two warring states. But the ruler of Umma eventually violated the settlement, removed the stele, and went to war with Lagash. Eventually, Lagash prevailed under its ruler Eannatum, the third member of the dynasty and uncle of Entemena. As we learn from another text, Eannatum proved to be the most successful of his dynasty in establishing the power of Lagash throughout Sumer; and he commemorated his victory over umma by erecting the famous Vulture Stele, which is our most important portrait of Sumerian warfare. It depicts a phalanx of soldiers armed with helmets, shields, spears, and axes; and Eannatum is shown as being transported in a four-wheeled cart drawn by asses (horses did not enter Mesopotamia until, during, or after the Sargonid period). Vultures are also shown preying upon the bodies of the dead. Eannatum reestablished the former border between the two states and marked the border with a ditch and series of inscribed stelae. In addition, he allowed the people of Umma to farm the disputed territory as long as they gave Lagash a fixed portion of the produce. But eventually Umma violated this settlement, and this led to further war, which eventually came to an end with the victory of Entemena and his reestablishment of the old border. The text ends with a curse placed upon anyone who violates this settlement.

> (Taken from pp. 313-315 of The Sumerians: Their History, Culture, and Character, by Samuel Noah Kramer, U. of Chicago Press, copyright 1963, reprinted with the permission of the publisher)

Enlil, the king of all the lands, the father of all the gods, marked off the boundary for Ningirsu (and) Shara by his steadfast word; (and) Mesilim, the king of Kish, measured it off in accordance with the word of Sataran (and) erected a stele there. (But) Ush, the ensi of Umma, violated (both) the decree (of the gods) (and) the word (given by man to man), ripped out its (the boundary's) stele, and entered the plain of Lagash.

(Then) did Ningirsu, Enlil's foremost warrior, do battle with (the men of) Umma in accordance with his (Enlil's) straightforward word; by the word of Enlil he hurled the great net upon them (and) heaped up their skeleton(?) piles in the plain in their (various) places. (As a result), Eannatum, the ensi of Lagash, the uncle of Entemena, the ensi of Lagash, marked off the boundary with Enakalle, the ensi of Umma. He made its (the boundary's) ditch reach from the Idnun (canal) to the Guedinna and inscribed (several) stelae along that ditch. He restored Mesilim's stele to its (former) place; (but) he did not enter the plain of Umma. He (then) built there the Imdubba of Ningirsu, the Namnunda-kigarra, (as well as) the shrine of Enlil, the shrine of Ninhursag, the shrine of Ningirsu, (and) the shrine of Utu.

(Moreover, following the boundary settlement), the Ummaites could eat the barley of (the goddess) Nanshe (and) the barley of Ningirsu to the amount of one karu (for each Ummaite and only) for interest; (also), he (Eannatum) levied a tax on them (and thus) brought in for himself (as revenue) 144,000 "large" karu. Because this barley remained unpaid, (besides), Ur-Lumma, the ensi of Umma, deprived of water the boundary ditch of Ningirsu (and) the boundary ditch of Nanshe; ripped out its (the boundary ditch's) steles (and) put them to fire; destroyed the dedicated(?) shrines of the gods which had been built in the Namnunda-kigarra; obtained (the help of) the foreign lands; and (finally) crossed the boundary ditch of Ningirsu. Enannatum fought with him in the Gana-ugigga, (where) the fields and farms of Ningirsu (are), (and) Entemena, Enannatum's beloved son, defeated him. Ur-Lumma (then) fled, (while) he (Entemena) slew (the Ummaite forces) up into Umma (itself); (moreover), his (Ur-Lumma's) elite force (consisting of) sixty soldiers he wiped out(?) on the bank of the Lummagirnunta canal. (As for) its (Umma's fighting) men, he (Entemena) left their bodies in the plain (for the birds and beasts to devour) (and then) heaped up their skeleton(?) piles in five (separate) places. At that time, (however), Il, the temple-head of Zabalam, ravaged(?) (the land) from Girsu to Umma. Il took to himself the ensi-ship of Umma; he deprived of water the boundary ditch of Ningirsu, the boundary ditch of Nanshe, the Imdubba of Ningirsu, that tract (of arable land) of the Girsu tracts which lies toward the Tigris, (and) the Namnunda-kigarra of Ninhursag; (and) he paid (no more than) 3,600 karu of the barley (due) Lagash. (And) when Entemena, the ensi of Lagash, repeatedly sent (his) men to Il because of that (boundary) ditch, Il, the ensi of Umma, the plunderer of fields and farms, the speaker of evil, said: "The boundary ditch of Ningirsu (and) the boundary ditch of Nanshe are mine;" (indeed), he (even) said: "I shall exercise control from the Antasurra to the Dimgal-Abzu temple." (However), Enlil (and) Ninhursag did not grant this to him. Entemena, the ensi of Lagash, whose name Ningirsu had pronounced, made this (boundary) ditch from the Tigris to the Idnun in accordance with the straightforward word of Enlil, in accordance with the straightforward word of Ningirsu, (and) with the straightforward word of Nanshe; (and) he restored it for his beloved king Ningirsu and for his beloved queen Nanshe (after) he had constructed of bricks the foundation of the Namnunda-kigarra. May Shulutula, the god of Entemena, the ensi of Lagash, whom Enlil gave the scepter, whom Enki gave understanding, whom Nanshe chose in (her) heart, the great ensi of Ningirsu, the man who had received the words of the gods, stand forever (literally, "unto distant days") before Ningirsu and Nanshe (and plead) for the life of Entemena. The Ummaite who (at any future time) will cross the boundary ditch of Ningirsu (and) the boundary ditch of Nanshe in order to take to himself fields and farms by force, whether he be (really) an Ummaite or a foreigner, may Enlil destroy him; may Ningirsu, after hurling his great net on him, bring down on him his lofty hand (and) his lofty foot; may the people of his city, having risen in rebellion, strike him down in the midst of his city.

READING 5
THE LEGEND OF SARGON

Sargon was one of the earliest great conquerors in history. He was the first one who succeeded in uniting the separate city-states of early Mesopotamia into a single kingdom, and he founded a dynasty of rulers that lasted for about a century and a half, after which his united kingdom fell apart. As the result of his achievements, Sargon soon became a great figure of legend; and his greatness as a conqueror and ruler was embodied in a mythical story of his unusual birth, rescue from death while still a helpless infant, and his survival to realize his divinely ordained destiny as a great conqueror and ruler. Variations of this story were later associated with other great figures of the ancient world, who were the founders of nations or empires, such as Cyrus the Great of Persia, Moses in the Hebrew tradition, different heroes of ancient Greece, and Romulus and Remus, the twin founders of ancient Rome.

(Taken from pp. 87-93 of Chronicles Concerning Early Babylonian Kings, by Leonard William King, published by Luzac and Co., London 1907, revised by Gary Forsythe)

Sargon, the mighty king, the king of Agade, am I. My mother was lowly [or a high priestess], my father I knew not, and the brothers of my father dwelleth in the mountains. My city is Azupiranu, which lieth on the bank of the Euphrates. My lowly mother [or the high priestess] conceived me, in secret she brought me forth. She set me in a basket of rushes; with bitumen she closed my door [i.e., lid]. She cast me into the river, which rose not over me. The river bore me up; unto Akki, the irrigator, it carried me. Akki, the irrigator, with his dipper lifted me out. Akki, the irrigator, reared me as his own son; Akki, the irrigator, appointed me as his gardener. While I was a gardener, the goddess Ishtar loved me, and for [...]-four years I ruled the kingdom. The black-headed peoples [i.e., the Sumerians] I ruled, I governed; mighty mountains with axes of bronze did I destroy. I bolted fast the upper mountains; I burst through the lower mountains. The Country of the Sea three times did I besiege; Dilmun did ... Unto the great ... I went up; I altered .... Whatsoever king shall be exalted after me, let him rule, let him govern the black-headed peoples; mighty mountains with axes of bronze let him destroy. Let him bolt fast the upper mountains; let him burst through the lower mountains. The Country of the Sea let him three times besiege. [The remainder is fragmentary.]

READING 6
THE END OF THE SARGONID DYNASTY

Sargon established a dynasty that endured about a century and a half. His grandson, Naram-Sin, was the fourth ruler of this dynasty; and during his reign he was faced with major rebellions; and after quelling them, he adopted the novel title of "king of the four corners of the universe;" and to our knowledge, he was also the first Mesopotamian king to be acknowledged by his subjects as a living god. Nevertheless, toward the end of his reign the Sargonid Empire of Mesopotamia began to be assaulted by the Gutians, fierce tribesmen from the Zagros Mountains that bordered Sumer to the northeast. The following text offers us a very interesting interpretation of why the Sargonid dynasty with its flourishing capital of Agade came to an end. Its author declares that its ruin was caused by the Sumerian god Enlil, whose most holy shrine, the Ekur (Mountain House) in the Sumerian city of Nippur, was desacrated by Naram-Sin; and the Gutian invaders from the Zagros Mountains were simply the instruments of Enlil's wrath. This idea that the gods used the historical process to punish or reward humankind was a standard view throughout the ancient Near Eastern civilizations, and it was adopted by the Hebrews and thus survives today in the writings of The Old Testament.

> (Translated by Samuel Noah Kramer, and taken from pp. 647-651 of Ancient Near Eastern Texts Relating to The Old Testament, edited by James B. Pritchard, Third Edition, Princeton U. Press, copyright 1969, reprinted with the permission of the publisher)

After the frowning forehead of Enlil had killed (the people of) Kish like the "Bull of Heaven," after he had ground the house of Erech into dust, like a giant bull, after in due time, to Sargon the king of Agade, from below to above, Enlil had given him lordship and kingship, then did holy Inanna, the shrine of Agade, erect as her noble chamber. In Ulmash did she set up a throne.

Like a "little fellow" building (his) house anew, like a young son erecting the (wife's) chamber that everything be collected (safely) in the storehouses, that their city be a firmly established dwelling place, that its people eat "dependable" food, that its people drink "dependable" water, that the bathed "heads" make the courtyards joyous, That the people beautify the places of festivity, that the men of the city "eat" in harmony, that the outsiders scurry about like "unknown" birds, that Marhashi be turned to clay," that in future days the giant elephant, (and) the abzaza," the beasts of distant lands, roam about all together in the midst of (its) boulevards, (also) the "princely" dogs, the Elamite dogs, the "asses" of the mountain, long-haired alum-sheep, Inanna allowed herself no sleep. In those days the dwellings of Agade were filled with gold, its bright-shining houses were filled with silver. Into its granaries were brought copper, lead, (and) slabs of lapis lazuli. Its silos bulged at the sides, its old women were endowed with counsel, its old men were endowed with eloquence, its young men with endowed with the "strength of weapons, its little children were endowed with joyous hearts, the nurse-raised children of the governors played on the algarsur-instruments. Inside, the city (was full of) tigi-music. Outside, it (was full of) reed-pipe (and) zamzam-music. Its quay where the boats docked were all abustle. All lands lived in security. Their people witnessed (nothing but) happiness. Their king Naram-Sin, the shepherd, stepped forth like the sun on the holy dais of Agade. Its walls reached skyward like a mountain, the gates-like the Tigris emptying its water into the sea, holy Inanna opened its gates. The Sumerians eagerly sailed (their) goods-(laden) boats to it (Agade). The Martu, (the people of) the lord who knows not grain, brought her perfect oxen, perfect sheep. The Meluhhaites, the people of the black land, brought up to her the (exotic) wares of the foreign lands. The Elamites (and) Subaraeans carried for her (all sorts of) goods, like sack-carrying donkeys. Ensi's sanga's, the comptroller of the Guedinna, conduct their monthly and New Year gift (to Agade).

(But then) in the palace of Agade-what prostration! Holy Inanna accepted not its gifts. Like a princely son who ..., she shared not its wealth. The "word of the Ekur" was upon it like a (deathly) silence. Agade was all atremble. The Ulmash was in terror. She who had lived there left the city. Like a maiden forsaking her chamber, holy Inanna forsook the shrine Agade. Like a warrior hastening to (his) weapon, she went forth against the city in battle (and) combat. She attacked as if it were a foe.

In days not five, in days not ten, the fillet of lordship, the tiara of kingship, Mansium, the throne given over to kingship, Ninurta brought into his Eshumesha. Utu carried off the eloquence of the city. Enki poured out its wisdom. Its awesomeness that had reached towards heaven Anu brought up to the midst of heaven. Its boats that had been carefully caulked Enki [brought down] into the Abzu. Its weapons were .... The shrine Agade ... The city ..., Like a huge elephant .... Like a huge bull ..., Like a fierce ushumgal-dragon .... Its battles were [decreed] a bitter fate. The kingship of Agade was prostrated. Its future is extremely unhappy. At the "month house" the treasures lay scattered about.

(Then) Naram-Sin in a vision .... He kept it to himself, put it not in speech, spoke with nobody about it. Because of the Ekur, he dressed in sackcloth, covered his chariot with a boat-covering mat, loaded not his boat with ..., gave away everything desirable for kingship.

Seven years Naram-Sin remained firm. Who had ever seen that a king should "put hand on head for seven years!" (But then) seeking an oracle at the house, in the "built" house there was no oracle. Seeking an oracle a second time at the house, in the "built" house there was no oracle. (Whereupon) changing his line of action, he defied the word of Enlil, crushed those who had submitted to him, mobilized his troops. Like a mighty man accustomed to high-handed (action), he put a restraining hand on the Ekur. Like a runner contemptuous of (his body's) strength, he treated the giguna like thirty shekels. Like a bandit who plunders a city, he erected large ladders against the house to destroy the Ekur like a huge boat, to turn it into dust like a mountain mined for silver, to cut it to pieces like a mountain of lapis lazuli, to prostrate it like a city ravaged by Ishkur [a storm god]. Against the house that was not a mountain where cedar was felled, he forged great axes, sharpened double-edged "axes of destruction," fixed copper spikes at the bottom of it, levelled it down to the "foundation" of the land, fixed axes at the top of it. The house lay stretched "neck to ground," like a man who had been killed (in battle). He tore up its mes-trees. The raining dust rose sky high. He struck down its doorposts, cut off the vitality of the land. At the "Gate of no Grain Cutting," he cut grain. Grain was cut off from the "hand" of the land. Its "Gate of Peace" he broke down with the pickaxe. Peace was estranged from the lands. (And) from the "noble" fields (and) acres of the wide .... The Ekur-he forged its bronze spikes in (heaps of) firewood. The people (now) saw its cella, the house that knew not light. The Akkadian saw the holy vessels of the gods. Its great lahama of the dubla that stood at the house, (although) they were not among those who ate that which is tabu, Naram-Sin cast into the fire. Cedar, cypress, zabalum-tree, and boxtree, its giguna-trees he pulverized. Its gold he brought into ... -bags. Its silver he brought into ... leather sacks. Its copper he piled up on the quay like huge (heaps of) grain (ready to be) carried away. Its silver was worked over by the silversmith. Its precious stone was worked over by the jeweller. Its copper was hammered by the smith. (Although all these) were not the possessions of an attacking city, he docked large boats at the quay by the house, docked large boats at the quay by the house of Enlil, carried off the possessions from the city. (But with) the carrying off the possessions of the city, counsel departed from the city. As the boats took off from the quay, the good sense of Agade turned to folly. The ... storm that .... The rampant flood who knows no rival, Enlil, because his beloved Ekur had been attacked, what destruction he wrought! He lifted his eyes to the ... -mountain, mustered the "wide" mountain as one. The unsubmissive people, the land (whose people) is without number, Gutium, the land that brooks no control, whose understanding is human, (but) whose form (and) stuttering words are that of a dog, Enlil brought down from the mountain. In vast numbers, like locusts, they covered the earth. Their "arm" stretched out for him in the steppe like an animal-trap. Nothing escaped their "arm," no one eluded their "arm." The herald took not to the road. The (sea)-rider sailed not his boat along the river. The ... -goats of Enlil that broke out of their sheepfold -their shepherd made them follow him. The cows that broke out of their stalls, their cowherd made them follow him. On the trees of the (river)-banks watches were set up. Brigands dwelt on the road. In the gates of the land the doors stood (deep) in dust. All the lands raised a bitter cry on their city walls.

Furrows embedded the cities although (their) inside was not a steppe. (Their) outside was not wide (open land).

After the cities had been built, after they had been struck down, the large fields (and) acres produced no grain. The flooded acres produced no fish. The watered gardens produced no honey (and) wine. The heavy clouds brought not rain. There grew no mashgur-tree. Then did half a sila of oil equal one shekel, half a sila of grain-one shekel, half a mina of wool-one shekel, one ban of fish-one shekel. The commodities of their cities were bought up like good "words." Who slept on the roof died on the roof. Who slept inside the house was not brought to burial. The people droop helplessly because of their hunger. By the kiur, the "great place" of Enlil, the cedar-cutter held back (his) speech in (deathly) silence. In its midst men by two's were devoured. In its ... men by three's were devoured. Heads were crushed, heads were .... Mouths were crushed, "heads" were turned to seeds. The faithful "slaves" were changed into treacherous slaves. The valiant lay on top of the valiant. The blood of the treacherous flowed over the blood of the faithful.

Then did Enlil, out of his immense shrine, make a small reed-shrine. From sunrise to sunset its treasures decreased. The old women who were cut off from the day, the old men who were cut off from the day, the chief gala's who were cut off from the year, for seven days, seven nights, like "the seven lyres standing at the horizon," followed him (Enlil) about. Like Ishkur played for him the shem, mezi, and lilis. The old women ceased not (crying) "Oh, my city." The old men ceased not (crying) "Oh, its men." The gala's ceased not (crying) "Oh, the Ekur." Its maidens ceased not tearing (their) hair. Its youths ceased not (their) maceration. Their tears, the tears of the mothers and fathers of Enlil, they bring again and again in the awe-filled duku of holy Enlil. Because of all this, Enlil entered (his) holy cella, lay down on (his) katabba. Then did Sin, Enki, Inanna, Ninurta, Ishkur, (and) Utu, the great gods, a prayer to him: "Oh valiant Enlil, the city that has destroyed your city may it become like your city. (The city) that has demolished your giguna, may it become like Nippur. Of that city, may skulls fill its wells. May no sympathizing friends be found there. May brother not recognize his brother. May its maiden flagellate herself in her chamber. May its father utter bitter cries in the house of his dead wife. May he moan like a dove in its hole. May he thrash about like a swallow in its cranny. May he scurry about like a dove in terror."

A second time did Sin, Enki, Inanna, Ninurta, Ishkur, Utu, Nusku, (and) Nidaba, the great gods, direct their face to the city, curse Agade with a baleful curse: "City, you who dared assault the Ekur-it is Enlil (whom you assaulted). Agade, you who dared assault the Ekur-it is Enlil (whom you assaulted). At your holy wall, lofty as it is, may wailing resound. May your giguna be heaped up like dust. May your lahama that stand in the dubla, lie prostrate, like huge (fighting) men drunk with wine. May your clay return to its Abzu. May it be clay cursed by Enki. May your grain return to its furrows. May it be grain cursed by Ashnan. May your trees return to their forests. May they become trees cursed by Ninildu. May the oxen-slaughterer slaughter (his) wife (instead). May your sheep-butcher butcher his child (instead). May your poor hurl his precious children into the water. May the prostitute stretch herself out in the gate of her brother. May your hierodule mother, your courtesan mothers give back (their) children. May your gold be sold as silver. May your silver be sold as zaha-metal. May your copper be sold as lead. Agade, may your strong man be deprived of his strength. May he not be able to lift a leather bag .... May your wrestler rejoice not in his strength. may he lie in darkness. May famine kill (the people of) that city. May the princely children who ate (only) the very best bread lie about in the grass. May your man who used to carry off the first fruits eat the scraps of his tables, the leather thongs of the door of his father's house. May he munch these leather thongs with his teeth. May your palace built in joy fall to ruins in anguish. May the evil ones, the ghosts of "silent places," howl (there) evermore. OOver your usga-place" established for lustrations, May the fox of the ruined mounds glide (his) tail. In your great gates (firmly) established in the land, may the ukuku-birds of anguished heart set up (his) nest. In your city where you (no longer) sleep to (the sound of) tigi-music, where you (no longer) go to bed with a joyful heart, may the oxen of Nanna, that (used to) fill the stalls, moan evermore like ghosts who roam the silent places. May your canalboat towpaths grow (nothing but) tall grass. May your wagon-roads grow (nothing but) the wailing-plant'. Moreover, on your canalboat towpaths, the places where the channel is narrow, may no one walk among the wild goats, darting snakes of the mountain. May your steppe where grew the succulent plants, grow (nothing but) the reed of tears. Agade, (instead of) your sweet-flowing water, may salt water flow (there). May he who said 'I would sleep in that city,' not find a good dwelling there. May he who said 'I would sleep in Agade,' not find a good sleeping place there."

(And) lo, with Utu's bringing forth the day, so it came to pass! Its canalboat towpaths grew (nothing but) tall grass. Its wagon-roads grew (nothing but) the "wailing-plant." Moreover, on its canalboat towpaths, the places where the channel is narrow, no one walks among the wild goats and darting snakes of the mountain. Its steppe where grew the succulent plants, grew (nothing but) the "reed of tears." Agade, (instead of) its sweet-flowing water, salt water flowed (there). He who said, "I would dwell in that city," found not a good dwelling place there. He who said, "I would sleep in Agade," found not a good sleeping place there. Agade is destroyed! Praise Inanna.

READING 7
KING SHULGI OF UR

Out of the chaos of the Gutian destruction of the Sargonid Empire there emerged during the twenty-first century B.C. the Third Dynasty of Ur that established a century of peaceful and prosperous rule over the Sumerian city-states. The second ruler of this line of kings was Shulgi, who enjoyed a long reign of 48 years; and the following text boasts of his virtues as a ruler, his fostering of easy travel throughout his realm, and even his physical vigor and athleticism as a long-distance runner.

In this self-laudatory hymn to himself Shulgi claims to have run from Ur to Nippur and then back to Ur in a single day; but since these two cities were separated by a distance of one hundred miles, this claim can hardly be credited. Nevertheless, according to another surviving text, Shulgi performed this feat in the seventh year of his reign. In any case, it is interesting to note that this hymn contains the earliest reference in Mesopotamian writing to the horse, artistic representations of which date no earlier than this same period or slightly earlier. Shulgi likens himself to a horse swishing its tail on the highway. So, unless we dismiss Shulgi's exploit as nothing but royal hyperbole or propaganda, the question naturally arises. Did Shulgi accomplish his one-day 200-mile journey, either in whole or in part, on horseback or (more likely) by a horse-drawn conveyance?

(Translated by Samuel Noah Kramer, and taken from pp. 585-586 of Ancient Near Eastern Texts Relating to The Old Testament, edited by James B. Pritchard, Third Edition,

Princeton U. Press, copyright 1969, reprinted with the permission of the publisher)

I, the king, a hero from the (mother's) womb am I. I, Shulgi, a mighty man from (the day) I was born am I, a fierce-eyed lion, born of the ushumgal' am I. King of the four corners (of the universe) am I. Herdsman, shepherd of the blackheads' [name for the Sumerians] am I, The trustworthy, the god of all the lands am I. The son born of Ninsun am I. Called to the heart of holy Anu am I. He who was blessed by Enlil am I. Shulgi, the beloved of Ninlil am I. Faithfully nurtured by Nintu am I. Endowed with wisdom by Enki am I. The mighty king of Nanna am I. The open-jawed lion of Utu am I. Shulgi chosen for the vulva of Inanna am I. Princely donkey all set for the road am I. Horse that swings (his) tail on the highway am I. Noble donkey of Sumugan eager for the course am I. The wise scribe of Nidaba am I. Like my heroship, like my might, I am accomplished in wisdom (as well). I vie with its (wisdom's) true word. I love justice. I do not love evil. I hate the evil word. I, Shulgi, a mighty king, supreme, am I.

Because I am a powerful man rejoicing in his "loins," I enlarged the footpaths, straightened the highways of the land. I made secure travel, built there big houses, planted gardens alongside of them, established resting-places, settled there friendly folk, (so that) who comes from below, who come from above, might refresh themselves in its cool (shade), the wayfarer who travels the highway at night might find refuge there like in a well-built city.

That my name be established unto distant days, that it leave not the mouth (of men), that my praise be spread wide in the land, that I be eulogized in all the lands, I, the runner, rose in my strength, all set for the course; (And) from Nippur to Ur I resolved to traverse as if it were (but a distance) of one danna. Like a lion that wearies not of its virility, I arose, put a girdle about my loins. I swing (my) arms like a dove feverishly fleeing a snake. I spread wide the knees like the Indugud-bird that has lifted (its) eye toward the mountain. (The inhabitants of) the cities that I had established in the land, swarmed all about me. My blackheaded people, as numerous as ewes, marvelled at me, like a mountain-kid hurrying to its shelter. (As) Utu who sheds (his) broad light on (man's) habitations, I entered the Ekishnugal. I filled with abundance the great stall, the house of Sin. I slaughtered there oxen, multiplied (the slaughtering of) sheep, made resound there the drum and the timbrel, took charge there of the tigi-music, the sweet.

I, Shulgi, the all bountiful, brought there bread-offerings. I have inspired dread from (my) royal seat like a lion. In the lofty palace of Ninegal I rested (my) knees, bathed in fresh water, bent (my) knees, ate bread. Like an owl (and) a falcon I arose, returned to Nippur in my .... On that day, the storm howled, the tempest swirled, northwind (and) southwind roared eagerly, lightning devoured in heaven alongside the seven winds, the deafening storm made the earth tremble, Ishkur thundered throughout the heavenly expanse. The winds on high embraced the waters below. Its (the storm's) little stones, its big stones, lashed at my back. (But) I the king was unafraid, uncowed. Like a young lion (prepared to) spring, I shook myself loose. Like a donkey of the steppe, I covered up my ..., My heart full of happiness took delight in the course. Coursing like a noble donkey travelling all alone, like Utu eager (to come) home, I traversed the journey of 15 danna (in distance). My sagursag gazed at me (in wonder). As in one (and the same) day I celebrated the elef-feasts in (both) Ur (and) Nippur.

With valiant Utu my brother and friend, I drank strong drink in the palace founded by Anu. My minstrels sang for me the seven tigi-songs. By the side of my spouse, the maid Inanna, the queen, the "vulva" of heaven (and) earth, I sat at its (the palace's) banquet. She spoke not my judgment as a (final) judgment. Wheresoever I lift my eyes, thither I go. Wheresoever my heart moves me, thither I proceed.

Anu set the holy crown upon my head, made me take the scepter in the "lapis-lazuli" Ekur. On the radiant dais, he raised heaven high the firmly founded throne. He exalted there the power of (my) kingship. I bent low all the lands, made secure the people. The four-corners of the universe, the people in unison, call my name. They chant holy songs, pronounce my exaltation (saying): "He that is nurtured by the exalted power of kingship, presented by Sin, out of the Ekishnugal, with heroship, might, and a good life, endowed with lofty power by Nunamnir, Shulgi, the destroyer of all the foreign lands, who makes all the people secure, who in accordance with the me of the universe, Shulgi, cherished by the trusted son of Anu (Sin).

READING 8
THE LAW CODE OF HAMMURABI

Among many other aspects of social and political organization, the early Mesopotamians developed the earliest coherent body of written law. Although we possess portions of law codes earlier than that of Hammurabi, they were written on clay tablets and have thus survived in a fragmentary condition. Hammurabi's law code, on the other hand, was inscribed upon a seven-foot tall pillar of stone, so that its provisions have remained largely undamaged up to the modern day.

Hammurabi was king of the Old Babylonian Kingdom (which flourished from c.1900 to c.1600 B.C.) and reigned during the pinnacle of its power and influence. His reign of forty-two years is generally thought by modern scholars to have occurred during the years 1792-1750 B.C. In the prologue to the law code Hammurabi portrays himself as having been placed in power by the principal gods of the Babylonians, and in a relief carving on the pillar Hammurabi is shown as receiving a ring and staff from the Mesopotamian god Shamash, the god of the sun and of justice. Thus, as was the case with many other ancient peoples, Hammurabi viewed his law code as of divine origin and having the sanction of the gods.

The following extracts from the law code offer us important insights into the behavior, beliefs, customs, and social and economic conditions of the Old Babylonian Kingdom.

(Taken and adapted from The Code of Hammurabi, translated by Leonard William King, MacMillan, London 1920)

A. Administration of Justice

1. If anyone ensnare another, putting a death spell upon him, but he cannot prove it, then he that ensnared him shall be put to death.

2. If anyone bring an accusation against a man, and the accused go to the river and leap into the river, if he sink in the river, his accuser shall take possession of his house. But if the river prove that the accused is not guilty, and he escape unhurt, then he who had brought the accusation shall be put to death, while he who leaped into the river shall take possession of the house that had belonged to his accuser.

3. If anyone bring an accusation of any crime before the elders and does not prove what he has charged, he shall, if it be a capital offense charged, be put to death.

4. If he satisfy the elders to impose a fine of grain or money, he shall receive the fine that the action produces.

5. If a judge try a case, reach a decision, and present his judgment in writing; if later error shall appear in his decision, and it be through his own fault, then he shall pay twelve times the fine set by him in the case, and he shall be publicly removed from the judge's bench, and never again shall he sit there to render judgment.

6. If anyone steal the property of a temple or of the court, he shall be put to death, and also the one who receives the stolen thing from him shall be put to death.

8. If anyone steal cattle or sheep, or an ass, or a pig or a goat, if it belong to a god or to the court, the thief shall pay thirtyfold therefor; if they belonged to a commoner of the king, he shall pay tenfold; if the thief has nothing with which to pay, he shall be put to death.

10. If the purchaser does not bring the merchant and the witnesses before whom he bought the article, but its owner bring witnesses who identify it, then the buyer is the thief and shall be put to death, and the owner receives the lost article.

11. If the owner does not bring witnesses to identify the lost article, he is an evil-doer, he has traduced, and he shall be put to death.

12. If the witnesses be not at hand, then shall the judge set a limit, at the expiration of six months. If his witnesses have not appeared within the six months, he is an evil-doer and shall bear the fine of the pending case.

B. Damage to Crops

53. If anyone be too lazy to keep his dam in proper condition, and does not so keep it; if then the dam break and all the fields be flooded, then shall he in whose dam the break occurred be sold for money, and the money shall replace the grain which he has caused to be ruined.

54. If he be not able to replace the grain, then he and his possessions shall be divided among the farmers whose grain he has flooded.

55. If anyone open his ditches to water his crop, but is careless, and the water flood the field of his neighbor, then he shall pay his neighbor grain for his loss.

56. If a man let in the water, and the water overflow the plantation of his neighbor, he shall pay ten gur of grain for every ten gan of land.

C. Debt Servitude

117. If anyone fail to meet a claim for debt and sell himself, his wife, his son, and daughter for money or give them away to forced labor, they shall work for three years in the house of the man who bought them, or the proprietor; and in the fourth year they shall be set free.

118. If he give a male or female slave away for forced labor, and the merchant sublease them or sell them for money, no objection can be raised.

119. If anyone fail to meet a claim for debt, and he sell for money the maid-servant who has borne him children, the money which the merchant has paid shall be repaid to him by the owner of the slave, and she shall be freed.

D. Marriage, Divorce, and Adultery

127. If anyone "point the finger" (slander) at a sister of a god or the wife of anyone, and cannot prove it, this man shall be taken before the judges, and his brow shall be marked (by cutting the skin, or perhaps hair).

128. If a man take a woman to wife, but have no intercourse with her, this woman is no wife to him.

129. If a man's wife be surprised (in flagrante delicto) with another man, both shall be tied and thrown into the water, but the husband may pardon his wife and the king his slaves.

130. If a man violate the wife (betrothed or child-wife) of another man, who has never known a man, and still lives in her father's house, and sleep with her and be surprised, this man shall be put to death, but the wife is blameless.

131. If a man bring a charge against one's wife, but she is not surprised with another man, she must take an oath and then may return to her house.

132. If the "finger is pointed" at a man's wife about another man, but she is not caught sleeping with the other man, she shall jump into the river for her husband.

133. If a man is taken prisoner in war, and there is a sustenance in his house, but his wife leave house and court and go to another house: because this wife did not keep her court and went to another house, she shall be judicially condemned and thrown into the water.

134. If anyone be captured in war, and there is not sustenance in his house, if then his wife go to another house, this woman shall be held blameless.

135. If a man be taken prisoner in war, and there be no sustenance in his house, and his wife go to another house and bear children; and if later her husband return and come to his home: then this wife shall return to her husband, but the children follow their father.

136. If anyone leave his house, run away, and then his wife go to another house, if then he return and wishes to take his wife back: because he fled from his home and ran away, the wife of this runaway shall not return to her husband.

137. If a man wish to separate from a woman who has borne him children, or from his wife who has borne him children: then he shall give that wife her dowry and a part of the usufruct of field, garden, and property, so that she can rear her children. When she has brought up her children, a portion of all that is given to the children, equal as that of one son, shall be given to her. She may then marry the man of her heart.

138. If a man wishes to separate from his wife who has borne him no children, he shall give her the amount of her purchase money and the dowry which she brought from her father's house, and let her go.

139. If there was no purchase price, he shall give her one mina of gold as a gift of release.

140. If he be a commoner, he shall give her one-third of a mina of gold.

141. If a man's wife, who lives in his house, wishes to leave it, plunges into debt, tries to ruin her house, neglects her husband, and is judicially convicted: if her husband offer her release, she may go on her way, and he gives her nothing as a gift of release. If her husband does not wish to release her, and if he take another wife, she shall remain as servant in her husband's house.

142. If a woman quarrel with her husband and say: "You are not congenial to me," the reasons for her prejudice must be presented. If she is guiltless, and there is no fault on her part, but he leaves and neglects her, then no guilt attaches to this woman. She shall take her dowry and go back to her father's house.

143. If she is not innocent, but leaves her husband and ruins her house, neglecting her husband, this woman shall be cast into the water.

144. If a man take a wife, and this woman give her husband a maid-servant, and she bear him children, but this man wishes to take another wife, this shall not be permitted to him; he shall not take a second wife.

145. If a man take a wife, and she bear him no children, and he intend to take another wife: if he take this second wife and bring her into the house, this second wife shall not be allowed equality with his wife.

146. If a man take a wife, and she give this man a maid-servant as wife, and she bear him children, and then this maid assume equality with the wife: because she has borne him children, her master shall not sell her for money, but he may keep her as a slave, reckoning her among the maid-servants.

147. If she have not borne him children, then her mistress may sell her for money.

148. If a man take a wife, and she be seized by disease, if he then desire to take a second wife, he shall not put away his wife who has been attacked by disease, but he shall keep her in the house which he has built, and he shall support her so long as she lives.

149. If this woman does not wish to remain in her husband's house, then he shall compensate her for the dowry that she brought with her from her father's house, and she may go.

150. If a man give his wife a field, garden, and house and a deed therefor, if then after the death of her husband the sons raise no claim, then

the mother may bequeath all to one of her sons whom she prefers, and she need leave nothing to his brothers.

151. If a woman who lived in a man's house made an agreement with her husband that no creditor can arrest her, and he has given a document therefor: if that man, before he married that woman, had a debt, the creditor cannot hold the woman for it. But if the woman, before she entered the man's house, had contracted a debt, her creditor cannot arrest her husband therefor.

152. If after the woman had entered the man's house, both contracted a debt, both must pay the merchant.

153. If the wife of one man on account of another man has their mates (her husband and the other man's wife) murdered, both of them shall be impaled.

154. If a man be guilty of incest with his daughter, he shall be driven from the place (exiled).

155. If a man betroth a girl to his son, and his son have intercourse with her, but he (the father) afterward defile her and be surprised, then he shall be bound and cast into the water (drowned).

156. If a man betroth a girl to his son, but his son has not known her, and if then he defile her, he shall pay her half a gold mina and compensate her for all that she brought out of her father's house. She may marry the man of her heart.

157. If anyone be guilty of incest with his mother after his father, both shall be burned.

158. If anyone be surprised after his father with his chief wife who has borne children, he shall be driven out of his father's house.

E. Disowning and Acknowledging Children

168. If a man wish to put his son out of his house and declare before the judge: "I want to put my son out," then the judge shall examine into his reasons. If the son be guilty of no great fault for which he can be rightfully put out, the father shall not put him out.

169. If he be guilty of a grave fault which should rightfully deprive him of the filial relationship, the father shall forgive him the first time; but if he be guilty of a grave fault a second time, the father may deprive his son of all filial relation.

170. If his wife bear sons to a man, or if his maid-servant have borne sons, and the father while still living says to the children whom his maid-servant has borne: "My sons," and he count them with the sons of his wife; if then the father die, then the sons of the wife and of the maid-servant shall divide the paternal property in common. The son of the wife is to partition and choose.

171. If, however, the father while still living did not say to the sons of the maid-servant: "My sons," and then the father dies, then the sons of the maid-servant shall not share with the sons of the wife, but the freedom of the maid and her sons shall be granted. The sons of the wife shall have no right to enslave the sons of the maid; the wife shall take her dowry (from her father), and the gift that her husband gave her and deeded to her (separate from dowry, or the purchase-money paid her father), and live in the home of her husband: so long as she lives, she shall use it. It shall not be sold for money. Whatever she leaves shall belong to her children.

185. If a man adopt a child in his name as son and rear him, this grown son cannot be demanded back again.

188. If an artisan has undertaken to rear a child and teaches him his craft, he cannot be demanded back.

189. If he has not taught him his craft, this adopted son may return to his father's house.

190. If a man does not maintain a child whom he has adopted as a son and reared with his other children, then his adopted son may return to his father's house.

192. If a son of a paramour or a prostitute say to his adoptive father or mother: "You are not my father, or my mother," his tongue shall be cut off.

195. If a son strike his father, his hands shall be hewn off.

F. Personal Injury

196. If a man put out the eye of another man, his eye shall be put out.

197. If he break another man's bone, his bone shall be broken.

198. If he put out the eye of a commoner or break the bone of a commoner, he shall pay one gold mina.

199. If he put out the eye of a man's slave or break the bone of a man's slave, he shall pay one-half of its value.

200. If a man knock out the teeth of his equal, his teeth shall be knocked out.

201. If he knock out the teeth of a commoner, he shall pay one-third of a gold mina.

202. If anyone strike the body of a man higher in rank than he, he shall receive sixty blows with an ox-whip in public.

203. If a free-born man strike the body of another free-born man of equal rank, he shall pay one gold mina.

204. If a commoner strike the body of another commoner, he shall pay ten shekels in money.

205. If the slave of a commoner strike the body of a commoner, his ear shall be cut off.

206. If during a quarrel one man strike another and wound him, then he shall swear, "I did not injure him wittingly," and pay the physicians.

207. If the man die of his wound, he shall swear similarly, and if he (the deceased) was a free-born man, he shall pay half a mina in money.

208. If he was a commoner, he shall pay one-third of a mina.

209. If a man strike a free-born woman so that she lose her unborn child, he shall pay ten shekels for her loss.

210. If the woman die, his daughter shall be put to death.

211. If a woman of the common class lose her child by a blow, he shall pay five shekels in money.

212. If this woman die, he shall pay half a mina.

213. If he strike the maid-servant of a man, and she lose her child, he shall pay two shekels in money.

214. If this maid-servant die, he shall pay one-third of a mina.

215. If a physician make a large incision with an operating knife and cure it, or if he open a tumor (over the eye) with an operating knife and saves the eye, he shall receive ten shekels in money.

216. If the patient be a commoner, he receives five shekels.

217. If he be the slave of someone, his owner shall give the physician two shekels.

218. If a physician make a large incision with the operating knife and kill him, or if he open a tumor with the operating knife and cut out the eye, his hands shall be cut off.

219. If a physician make a large incision in the slave of a commoner and kill him, he shall replace the slave with another slave.

220. If he had opened a tumor with the operating knife and put out his eye, he shall pay half his value.

221. If a physician heal the broken bone or diseased soft part of a man, the patient shall pay the physician five shekels in money.

222. If he were a commoner, he shall pay three shekels.

223. If he were a slave, his owner shall pay the physician two shekels.

G. Damage to Property

224. If a veterinary surgeon perform a serious operation on an ass or an ox and cure it, the owner shall pay the surgeon one-sixth of a shekel as a fee.

225. If he perform a serious operation on an ass or ox and kill it, he shall pay the owner one-fourth of its value.

226. If a barber, without the knowledge of his master, cut the sign of a slave on a slave not to be sold, the hands of this barber shall be cut off.

227. If anyone deceive a barber and have him mark a slave not for sale with the sign of a slave, he shall be put to death and buried in his house. The barber shall swear: "I did not mark him wittingly," and shall be guiltless.

228. If a builder build a house for someone and complete it, he shall give him a fee of two shekels in money for each sar of surface.

229. If a builder build a house for someone and does not construct it properly, and if the house which he built fall in and kill its owner, then that builder shall be put to death.

230. If it kill the son of the owner, the son of that builder shall be put to death.

231. If it kill a slave of the owner, then he shall pay slave for slave to the owner of the house.

232. If it ruin goods, he shall make compensation for all that has been ruined, and inasmuch as he did not construct properly this house

which he built, and it fell, he shall re-erect the house from his own means.

233. If a builder build a house for someone, even though he has not yet completed it; if then the walls seem toppling, the builder must make the walls solid from his own means.

234. If a shipbuilder build a boat of sixty gur for a man, he shall pay him a fee of two shekels in money.

235. If a shipbuilder build a boat for someone and do not make it tight, if during that same year that boat is sent away and suffers injury, the shipbuilder shall take the boat apart and put it together tight at his own expense. The tight boat he shall give to the boat owner.

236. If a man rent his boat to a sailor, and if the sailor is careless, and the boat is wrecked or goes aground, the sailor shall give the owner of the boat another boat as compensation.

237. If a man hire a sailor and his boat and provide it with grain, clothing, oil, dates, and other things of the kind needed for fitting it: if the sailor is careless, the boat is wrecked, and its contents ruined, then the sailor shall compensate for the boat which was wrecked and all in it that he ruined.

238. If a sailor wreck anyone's ship, but saves it, he shall pay the half of its value in money.

239. If a man hire a sailor, he shall pay him six gur of grain per year.

244. If anyone hire an ox or an ass, and if a lion kill it in the field, the loss is upon its owner.

245. If anyone hire oxen and kill them by bad treatment or blows, he shall compensate the owner, oxen for oxen.

246. If a man hire an ox, and he break its leg or cut the ligament of its neck, he shall compensate the owner with ox for ox.

247. If anyone hire an ox and put out its eye, he shall pay the owner one-half of its value.

248. If anyone hire an ox and break off a horn or cut off its tail or hurt its muzzle, he shall pay one-fourth of its value in money.

249. If anyone hire an ox, and God strike it that it die, the man who hired it shall swear by God and be considered guiltless.

250. If while an ox is passing on the street, someone push it and kill it, the owner can set up no claim in the suit (against the hirer).

251. If an ox be a goring ox, and it is shown that he is a gorer, and if he do not bind his horns or fasten the ox up, and if the ox gore a free-born man and kill him, the owner shall pay one-half a mina in money.

252. If he kill a man's slave, he shall pay one-third of a mina.

265. If a herdsman, to whose care cattle or sheep have been entrusted, be guilty of fraud and make false returns of the natural increase or sell them for money, then shall he be convicted and pay the owner ten times the loss.

266. If the animal be killed in the stable by God (an accident), or if a lion kill it, the herdsman shall declare his innocence before God, and the owner bears the accident in the stable.

267. If the herdsman overlook something, and if an accident happen in the stable, then the herdsman is at fault for the accident which he has caused in the stable, and he must compensate the owner for the cattle or sheep.

READING 9
EGYPTIAN BOOK OF THE DEAD

The famous pyramids of Egypt's Old Kingdom were the everlasting tombs of the kings, whom the Egyptians regarded as incarnate gods on earth during their lifetime and as merging into the sun-god Re after their death to travel across the sky each day in his sacred boat. Over the course of time the Egyptians developed a very complex system of beliefs and ceremonies surrounding the mummification and burial of the dead to ensure their resurrection and enjoyment of a happy afterlife. Our earliest body of written incantations and spells date to the reign of the last king of the fifth dynasty, Unas (mid-twenty-fourth century B.C.); and since these texts were written on the walls of his pyramid, they are known today as "The Pyramid Texts." Not long thereafter similar texts began to be written inside the wooden coffins of Egyptian nobles, and these are termed "The Coffin Texts." Even later the Egyptians began to compose collections of these incantations and spells on rolls of papyrus and buried them with the dead to serve as a kind of book of instructions to guarantee that the deceased properly did everything necessary to receive a favorable judgment of his life by Osiris, the god of the Egyptian afterlife. Several copies of these papyri have survived and are termed "Books of the Dead."

According to Egyptian belief, the deceased came before a panel of gods, headed by Osiris, ; and these gods judged the life of the deceased and thus decided his fate for eternity. One aspect of the judgment was the weighing of the deceased person's heart in a set of balance scales against the weight of a feather, representing justice (what the Egyptians termed Maat). If the person had lived a decent life, the heart would not weigh more than the feather; but if the person had engaged in wrong-doing, his heart would outweigh the feather, and the heart was then fed to a demon, who devoured it and thus annihilated the person forever. If the person received a favorable judgment on his life, he was allowed to enter the Egyptian afterlife, where he enjoyed an eternal existence similar to what he had experienced during his lifetime.

The following passage comes from a papyrus scroll that was placed in the tomb of an Egyptian official of the thirteenth century B.C. the long series of denials contained in this text gives us an interesting glimpse into ancient Egyptian views of conventional morality.

(Taken and adapted from pp. 194-205 of The Egyptian Book of the Dead, by E. A. Wallis Budge, published by the trustees of the British Museum, London 1895)

Great god, lord of Maat, I have come to thee, my lord. I have been brought that I may see thy beauty. I know thee, I know the names of the gods who exist with thee in this hall of Maat, who live as the punishers of sinners, who live upon their blood on that day of computing dispositions before Maat. Lord of justice is thy name. Verily, I have come to thee, I have brought justice to thee. I have driven away for thee wickedness, I have not done iniquity to mankind. I have not done harm unto animals. I have not done wickedness in the place of Maat. I have not known evil. I have not acted wickedly. Each day and at every work I have not done above what I should do. My name hath not come forth to the boat of the Prince. I have not despised any god. I have not caused misery. I have not caused affliction. I have not done what is abominable to the gods. I have not caused harm to be done to the servant by his chief. I have not caused pain. I have not caused anyone to weep. I have not killed. I have not given the order for killing on my behalf. I have not done harm to mankind. I have not taken any of the offerings in the temples. I have not purloined the cakes of the gods. I have not carried off offerings of the blessed dead. I have not fornicated. I have not defiled myself. I have not added to, I have not diminished the offerings. I have not stolen from the orchard. I have not trampled down the fields. I have not added to the weight of the balance. I have not diminished from the weight of the balance. I have not carried off the milk from the mouth of the babe. I have not driven away the cattle which were upon their pastures. I have not captured the birds of the preserves of the gods. I have not taken fishes out of the marshes. I have not turned back water at its season. I have not cut a cutting in water running. I have not extinguished a fire at its proper hour. I have not violated the times for the chosen offerings. I have not driven away the cattle of gods' property. I have not blocked a god in procession. I, even I, am pure. Times four! ... Let not evil be done to me in this land, in this hall of Double Maat, because I, I know the names of these gods who are in it, the followers of the great god.

> [At this point the deceased reformulates his denials of wrong-
> ful acts by addressing them to specific divinities with their
> ceremonial names.]

Hail, Strider, coming forth from Annu, I have not done wrong. Hail, Em-braced with flame, coming forth from Kher-dba, I have not despoiled. Hail, Fentiu, coming forth from Khemennu, I have not robbed. Hail, Eater of shades, coming forth from Qernet, I have not slain men twice. Hail, Nehaa-hra coming forth from Re-stau, I have not defrauded the offerings. Hail, Dou-ble Lion-god, coming forth from heaven, I have not diminished offerings. Hail, whose two eyes are of fire, coming forth from Saut, I have not despoiled the things of the god. Hail, Flame, coming forth in going back, I have not spo-ken lies. Hail, Breaker of bones, coming forth from Suten-henen, I have not carried off food. Hail, Shooter forth of flame, coming forth from Memphis, I have not afflicted any. Hail, Qererti, coming forth from Amentet, I have not committed fornication. Hail, whose face is behind him, coming forth from his cavern, I have not caused anyone to weep. Hail, Bast, coming forth from the secret place, I have not eaten my heart. Hail, Blazing legs, coming forth from the darkness, I have not transgressed. Hail, Eater of blood, coming forth from the block, I have not acted deceitfully. Hail, Eater of intestines, coming forth from Maat, I have not desolated ploughed lands. Hail, Lord of Maat, coming forth from Maat, I have not been an eavesdropper. Hail, Strider backwards, coming forth from Bast, I have not set my mouth in motion against any man. Hail, Sertiu, coming forth from Annu, I have not raged except with a cause. Hail, Doubly wicked, coming forth from Ati, I have not defiled the wife of a man. Hail, Double Serpent, coming forth from the torture chamber, I have not defiled the wife of a man. Hail, Looker at what is brought to him, coming forth from Per-Amsu, I have not polluted myself. Hail, Chief of the mighty, coming forth from Amemt, I have not caused terror. Hail, Ikkhemiu, coming forth from Kesiu, I have not committed offence. Hail, Disposer of speech, coming forth from Urit, I have not inflamed myself with rage. Hail, Babe, coming forth from Uab, I have not made myself deaf to the words of right and truth. Hail, Kennememti, coming forth from Kennemmet, I have not caused grief. Hail, Bringer of his offering, coming forth from Sais, I have not acted insolently. Hail, Disposer of speech, coming forth from Unset, I have not stirred up strife. Hail, Lord of faces, coming forth from Netchefet, I have not judged hastily. Hail, Sekheriu, coming forth from Uten, I have not been an eavesdropper. Hail, Lord of two horns, coming forth from Sais, I have not multiplied my words upon words. Hail, Nefer-Tmu, coming forth from Memphis, I have not harmed, I have not done evil. Hail, Tmu in his seasons, coming forth from Tattu, I have not made curses on the king. Hail, Working in his heart, coming forth from Tebu, I have not fouled water. Hail, Sistrum bearer, coming forth from Nu, I have not made my voice haughty. Hail, Provider of mankind, coming forth from Sais, I have not cursed a god. Hail, Neheb-ka, coming forth from his cavern, I have not committed theft. Hail, Neheb-nefert, coming forth from his cavern, I have not defrauded the offerings of the gods. Hail, Arranger of his head, coming forth from his shrine, I have not carried away offerings from the beatified ones. Hail, Bringer of his arm, coming forth from the double, I have not carried off the food of the infant, I have not sinned against the god of the town. Hail, White-teeth, coming forth from Ta-she, I have not slaughtered the cattle divine.

Homage to you, o gods, I, even I know you. I know your names. Do not cast me down to your slaughtering knives, do not bring forward my wickedness before this god whom ye follow. Declare ye right and truth for me before the hand of Neb-er-tcher, because to you, o gods, I have done right and truth. I have not cursed god. My moment hath not come. Homage to you, o gods, who live in your hall of Maat at right and truth, without evil in their bodies, who live in right and truth in Annu, who consume their entrails in the presence of Horus in his disk; deliver ye me from Baabi, who liveth upon the intestines of princes, on that day of the great judgment by you.

I have come to you. I have not committed faults, I have not sinned, I have not done evil, I have not borne false witness. Therefore, let not anything be done to me. I live by right and truth, I feed upon right and truth in my heart. I have done that which men commanded, and with which the gods are satisfied. I have appeased god by doing his will. I have given bread to the hungry, water to the thirsty, clothes to the naked, and a boat to the shipwrecked. I have made offerings to the gods and sacrificial meals to the shining ones. Deliver ye me then; protect ye me then; do ye, not make accusation against me before the great god. I am pure of mouth, pure of hands....

READING 10
AN EGYPTIAN TALE OF MAGIC

Egypt was famous throughout the rest of the ancient world (as well as today) as the source of the most powerful magic. The following story not only represents Egypt's tradition of magic, but it is also a good example of popular Egyptian storytelling. It was recorded on a papyrus during the Second Intermediate Period, but its historical setting is the Old Kingdom. The tale is portrayed as having been told to King Khufu, the pharaoh of Egypt's largest pyramid, concerning his father King Snefru. Furthermore, it is noteworthy that the magician in this story is not only a chief priest (i.e., one who possesses a wealth of expert religious knowledge), but one who is termed "the scribe of the book," that is, a man highly skilled in writing hieroglyphics: for in the realm of magic, writing is viewed as an important source of magical power. It is also noteworthy that this tale involves the use of magical power to part the waters of a lake, thereby resembling the story of how God parted the sea for the Hebrews fleeing from the land of Egypt. See Exodus 7:9-13 for a contest involving Gods magic overcoming that of the Egyptian pharaoh's best magicians.

(Taken from pp. 38-40 of The Literature of the Ancient Egyptians: Poems, Narratives, and Manuals of Instruction from the Third and Second Millennia B.C., by Adolf Erman, translated by A. M. Blackman, published by Methuen and Co., London 1927)

Then Prince Daufre stood up to speak and said: I relate to thy majesty a wonder that came to pass in the time of thy father Snefru, one of the deeds of the cheif kerheb [learned priest], Zazamonkh. One day King Snefru was sad. So, he assembled the officers of the palace in order to seek for him a diversion, but he found none. Then said he, "Go, bring me the chief kerheb, the scribe of the book, Zazamonkh." And he was brought unto him straightway, and his majesty said unto him, "I had assembled the officers of the palace together in order to seek for me a diversion, but I could find none." And Zazamonkh said unto him, "If thy majesty would but betake thee to the Lake of the Great House [i.e., the palace], man thee a boat with all fair damsels from the inner apartments of thy palace. Then will the heart of thy majesty be diverted when thou shalt see how they row to and fro. Then, as thou viewest the pleasant nesting places of thy lake and viewest its fields and its pleasant banks, thine heart will be diverted thereby." His majesty said unto him, "I will do this. Get thee back to thine house, but I will go boating. Have brought to me twenty paddles of ebony inwrought with gold, the handles thereof being of sekeb wood inwrought with fine gold. Have brought to me twenty women of those with the fairest limbs and with beautious breasts and braided tresses, such as have not yet given birth. And moreover, have brought to me twenty nets, and give these nets to these women instead of their clothes."

And it was done according to all that his majesty commanded. And they rowed to and fro, and the heart of his majesty was glad when he beheld how they rowed. Then a leader became entangled with her braided tresses, and a fish pendant of new malachite fell into the water; and she became silent [i.e., stopped singing in time] and ceased rowing. And her side [of the boat] became silent and ceased rowing. Then said his majesty, "Is it that you will not row then?" And they said, "Our leader is silent and roweth not." And his majesty said unto her, "Wherefore rowest thou not?" And she said, "It is the fish pendant of new malachite that hath fallen into the water."

He had another brought to her and said, "I give thee this instead." And she said, "I want my pot down to its bottom" [= I want my very own thing]. Then said his majesty, "Go, bring me the chief kerheb Zazamonkh." And he was brought straightway. And his majesty said, "Zazamonkh, my brother, I have done as thou saidest, and the heart of my majesty was diverted when I beheld how they rowed. But a fish pendant of new malachite, belonging to a leader, fell into the water; and she was silent and rowed not; and so she spoiled her side. And I said unto her, 'Wherefor rowest thou not?' And she said unto me, 'It is a fish pendant of new malachite that hath fallen into the water.' And I said unto her, 'Row, and lo, I will replace it.' And she said unto me, 'I want my pot down to its bottom.'"

Then the cheif kerheb Zazamonkh said his say of magic. Then he placed one side of the water of the lake upon the other and found the fish pendant lying on a potsherd. And he brought it and gave it to its mistress. Now, as to the water, it was twelve cubits deep [eighteen feet] in the middle, and it reached twenty-four cubits after it was turned back. Then he said his say of magic, and he brought the waters of the lake back to their place. And his majesty spent the whole day in merriment with the entire palace, and he rewarded the cheif kerheb Zazamonkh with all good things.

Lo, it is a wonder that came to pass in the time of thy father Snefru, one of the deeds of the cheif kerheb, the scribe of the book, Zazamonkh.

PART II
THE LATE BRONZE AGE

READING 11
EGYPTIAN DEFEAT OF THE HYKSOS

During the Second Intermediate Period northern Egypt was occupied and ruled over by a band of foreigners whom the later Egyptians termed the Hyksos. They seem to have come from the area of Canaan, and they introduced into Egypt superior military technology, consisting of the horse-drawn chariot, the composite bow, and bronze weapons and armor. The Second Intermediate Period ended and the New Kingdom began (ca. 1550 B.C.) when the Egyptians, led by a new dynasty of rulers, the eighteenth dynasty from Thebes in the far south, attacked the Hyksos, captured their capital city of Avaris in the delta, and drove the Hyksos back into Canaan. Our knowledge of these events is very meager, but one important source of information is an inscription in the tomb of a man who had distinguished himself in the fighting against the Hyksos, as well as in campaigns waged in the far south of Upper Egypt. This man, named Ahmose (the same name as the pharaoh who founded the eighteenth dynasty and began the successful expulsion of the Hyksos from Egypt), served under the first four pharaohs of the eighteenth dynasty: Ahmose I, Amenhotep I, Thutmose I, and Thutmose II, who reigned during the second half of the sixteenth century B.C.

(Taken from pp. 6-12 of Ancient Records of Egypt, Volume II, by James Henry Breasted, U. of Chicago Press 1906)

Chief of the sailors, Ahmose, son of Ebana, triumphant, says: "I will tell you, o all ye people; I will cause you to know the honors which came to me. I was presented with gold seven times in the presence of the whole land; male and female slaves likewise. I was endowed with very many fields." The fame of one valiant in his achievements shall not perish in this land forever.

He speaks as follows: "I spent my youth in the city of Nekheb, my father being an officer of the king of Upper and Lower Egypt, Sekenenre, triumphant .... Then I served as an officer in his stead, in the ship, The Offering, in the time of the Lord of the Two Lands, Nebpehtire [Pharaoh Ahmose I], triumphant, while I was still young, not having taken a wife, and while I was still sleeping in the garment of boyhood. Then after I set up a household, I was transferred into the northern fleet because of my valor. I followed the king on foot when he rode abroad in his chariot. He besieged the city of Avaris; I showed valor on foot before his majesty; then I was appointed to the ship, Shining in Memphis. He fought on the water in the canal: Pezedku of Avaris. Then I fought hand to hand. I brought away a hand [as a trophy and as proof of having killed an enemy]. It was reported to the royal herald. The king gave to me the gold of valor. Then there was again fighting in this place. I again fought hand to hand there; I brought away a hand. He gave to me the gold of bravery in the second place. He fought in this Egypt, south of this city. Then I brought away a living captive, a man; I descended into the water; behold, he was brought as a seizure upon the road of this city, though I crossed with him over the water. It was announced to the royal herald. Then the king presented me with gold in double. He captured Avaris. I took captive there one man and three women, a total of four heads. His majesty gave them to me for slaves. He besieged Sharuhen [the final refuge of the Hyksos in Canaan] for six years, and his majesty took it. Then I took captive there two women and one hand. He gave me the gold of bravery, besides giving me the captives for slaves. Now, after his majesty had slain the Asiatics, he ascended the river to Khenthennofer to destroy the Nubian Troglodytes. His majesty made a great slaughter among them. Then I took captive there two living men and three hands. He presented me with gold in double measure, besides giving to me two female slaves. His majesty sailed downstream, his heart joyous with the might of victory: for he had seized Southerners and Northerners. There came an enemy of the South; his fate, his destruction approached; the gods of the South seized him, and his majesty found him in Tintto-emu. His majesty carried him off a living prisoner, and all his people were carried captive. I carried away two archers as a seizure in the ship of the enemy. The king gave to me five heads besides pieces of land amounting to five statd [about three and a half acres] in my city. It was done to all the sailors likewise. Then came that fallen one, whose name was Teti-en; he had gathered to himself rebels. His majesty slew him and his servants, annihilating them. There were given to me three heads and fields amounting to five state in my city."

Hereditary prince, count, wearer of the royal seal, chief treasurer, herald of his Lord, I, Ahmose, called Pen-Nekhbet, triumphant; he says: "I followed King Nebpehtire [Ahmose I], triumphant. I captured for him in Zahi [in Canaan] a living prisoner and a hand."

Ahmose, called Pen-Nekhbet; he says: "By the Sovereign, who lives forever! I was not separated from the king upon the battlefield, from the time of King Nebpehtire [Ahmose I], triumphant, to King Okhepernere [Thutmose II], triumphant; I was in the favor of the king's presence until King Menkhep-erre [Thutmose II], living forever.

King Zeserkere [Amenhotep I], triumphant, gave to me of gold: two bracelets, two necklaces, an armlet, a dagger, a headdress, a fan, and a mekhtebet.

King Okheperkere [Thutmose I], triumphant, gave to me of gold: two bracelets, four necklaces, one armlet, six flies, three lions, two golden axes.

King Okhepernere [Thutmose II], triumphant, gave to me of gold: three bracelets, six necklaces, three armlets, a mekhtebet, and a silver axe."

I, Ahmose, says: "I followed the Kings of Upper and Lower Egypt, the gods; I was with their majesties when they went to the South and North country, in every place where they went; from King Nebpehtire [Ahmose I], triumphant, King Zeserkere [Amenhotep I], triumphant, King Okheperkere [Thutmose I], triumphant, King Okhepernere [Thutmose II], triumphant, until this Good God, King Menkheperre [Thutmose III], who is given life forever. I have attained a good old age, having had a life of royal favor, having had honor under their majesties, and the love of me having been in the court."

READING 12
SUPPILULIUMAS AND THE EGYPTIAN
QUEEN

Following the Egyptian expulsion of the Hyksos from the Nile Delta, the pharaohs of the later sixteenth, fifteenth, and early fourteenth centuries B.C. carried out numerous military campaigns into the Levant and secured Egyptian control of the region, thus giving rise to the so-called Egyptian Empire. Egyptian affairs of the mid-fourteenth century were dominated by the religious revolution of Akhenaten, who attempted to establish the worship of the Aton as a kind of monotheism and also moved the Egyptian capital from Thebes to Amarna. The revolution failed; and after Akhenaten's death and reign of seventeen years Egypt soon reverted to its traditional polytheism with the country's capital moved back to Thebes; and the great eighteenth dynasty of pharaohs slowly sputtered to an end. Meanwhile, the Hittites under their ablest military king, Suppiluliumas (ruled ?1344-1322 B.C.), undermined the power of the Kingdom of Mitanni and extended Hittite control into northern Syria, thereby bringing the Hittites into direct competition with the Egyptians as the power in the region.

The following text records an interesting incident involving an Egyptian queen requesting King Suppiluliumas for one of his sons to be her husband. Given the uncertainties of the pharaonic succession during the last years of the eighteenth dynasty following the death of Akhenaten, there has been much modern speculation as to the identity of the Egyptian queen and of her deceased pharaonic husband. The most likely candidates seem to be Ankhesenamen, one of the daughters of Akhenaten, and the teen-age Pharaoh Tutankhamen. The Egyptian queen's appeal to Suppiluliumas apparently produced much turmoil at the Egyptian court. Suppiluliumas did eventually send one of his five sons (the fourth eldest named Zannanza) to Egypt; but when he was murdered by Egyptians who opposed the marriage, Ankhesenamen was obliged to marry a very elderly priest named Ay, who served as pharaoh for only a few years until his death; and his brief reign was followed by that of the general Horemheb, who was the last ruler of the eighteenth dynasty.

The first part of this reading comes from Suppiluliumas' annals compiled by his son Mursilis II (ruled ?1321-1295 B.C.). The later fragmentary portion of the reading comes from the text of a prayer of Mursilis II to halt a plague. After a plague raged among the Hittites for many years without abatement, King Mursilis II conducted numerous religious rites to appease the gods and even investigated past events to determine how the Hittites had incurred the displeasure of the gods. This part of the reading is part of a text recording this process that happens to relate to the incident described in the preceding portion of the reading.

> (Taken from pp. 94-98 and 107-108 of "The Deeds of Suppiluliuma as told by his Son, Mursili II," by Hans Gustav Guterbock, Journal of Cuneiform Studies 10 [1956], reprinted with the permission of the American Schools of Oriental Research, and available through JSTOR)

While my father was down in the country of Carchemish, he sent Lupakki and Tarbunta-zalma forth into the country of Amka. They went to attack Amka and brought deportees, cattle, and sheep back before my father. But when the people of Egypt heard of the attack on Amka, they were afraid. And since, in addition, their lord Nibbururiya had died, therefore the queen of Egypt, who was Dabamunzu, sent a messenger to my father and wrote to him thus: "My husband died. A son I have not. But to thee, they say, the sons are many. If thou wouldst give me one son of thine, he would become my husband. Never shall I pick out a servant of mine and make him my husband! I am afraid!"

When my father heard this, he called forth the Great Ones for council, saying: "Such a thing has never happened to me in my whole life!" So it happened that my father sent forth to Egypt Hattusaziti, the chamberlain, with this order: "Go, and bring thou back to me the true word! Maybe they deceive me! Maybe in fact they do have a son of their lord! Bring thou the true word back to me!"

In the meantime, until Hattusaziti came back from Egypt, my father finally conquered the city of Carchemish. He had besieged it for seven days; and on the eighth day he fought a battle against it for one day and took it in a terrific battle on the eighth day, in one day. And when he had conquered the city, since my father feared the gods on the upper citadel, he let no one into the presence of the deity Kubaba and of the deity Kai; and he did not rush close to any one of the temples. Nay, he even bowed to them and then gave .... But from the lower town he removed the inhabitants, silver, gold, and bronze utensils and carried them to Hattusa. And the deportees whom he brought to the palace were three thousand three hundred and thirty, whereas those whom the Hittites brought home were without number. Then he gave his son Sarri-Kusub the country of Carchemish and the city of Carchemish to govern, and he made him a king on his own. But when he had established Carchemish, he went back into the land of Hatti and spent the winter in the land of Hatti.

But when it became spring, Hattusaziti came back from Egypt; and the messenger of Egypt, Lord Hani, came with him. Now, since my father had, when he sent Hattusaziti to Egypt, given him orders as follows: "Maybe they have a son of their lord! Maybe they deceive me and do not want my son for the kingship!" therefore the queen of Egypt wrote back to my father in a letter thus: "Why didst thou say 'they deceive me' in that way? Had I a son, would I have written about my own and my country's shame to a foreign land? Thou didst not believe me and hast even spoken thus to me! He who was my husband has died. A son I have not! Never shall I take a servant of mine and make him my husband! I have written to no other country; only to thee have I written! They say that thy sons are many. So, give me one son of thine! To me he will be husband, but in Egypt he will be king." So, since my father was kindhearted, he complied with the word of the woman and concerned himself with the matter of a son.

[At this point there is a gap of several lines in the text; and when it resumes, Supiluliumas is addressing the Egyptian messenger Hani.]

"I myself was friendly, but you, you suddenly did me evil. You came and attacked the man of Kinza, whom I had taken away from the king of Hurri-land. When I heard this, I became angry, and I sent forth my own troops, chariots, and the lords. So, they came and attacked your territory, the country of Amka. And when they attacked Amka, which is your country, you probably were afraid; and therefore you keep asking me for a son of mine as if it were my duty. He will in some way become a hostage, but king you will not make him!"

Thus spoke Hani to my father: "Oh my Lord, this is our country's shame! If we had a son of the king at all, would we have come to a foreign country and kept asking for a lord for ourselves? Nibbururiya, who was our lord, died; a son he has not. Our lord's wife is solitary. We are seeking a son of our Lord for the kingship in Egypt; and for the woman, our lady, we seek him as her husband! Furthermore, we went to no other country; only here did we come! Now, oh our Lord, give us a son of thine!"

So then my father concerned himself on their behalf with the matter of a son. Then my father asked for the tablet of the treaty again, in which there was told how formerly the Storm God [chief god of the Hittites] took the people of Kurustama, sons of Hatti, and carried them to Egypt and made them Egyptians; and how the Storm God concluded a treaty between the countries of Egypt and Hatti, and how they were continuously friendly with each other. And when they had read aloud the tablet before them, my father then addressed them thus: "Of old, Hattusa and Egypt were friendly with each other; and now this, too, on our behalf, has taken place between them! Thus Hatti and Egypt will continuously be friendly with each other!"

... into the land of Hatti .... with each other ... And the land of Hatti and the country of Egypt with each other shall be! And to the country of Egypt to the end of days with each other ... was torn ... you will go into the country of Egypt ... shall be! And Egypt ... to the land of Hatti ... the king of Barga, Hu- ... the man of ... When they did not send ... then a tablet they ... and they one to another. When they brought this tablet, they spoke against my father thus: "The people of Egypt killed Zannanza;" and they brought word: Zannanza died. And when my father heard of the slaying of Zannanza, he began to lament for Zannanza, and to the gods he spoke thus: "Oh gods, I did no evil. Yet, the people of Egypt did this to me, and they also attacked the frontier of my country!"

... heard ... "... it in the country of Egypt I ...ed, but not a treaty, the man of the town of ... had concluded ... someone turned evil ... Gasgaeans [people to the north of Hattusas] not afraid ... they oppress ... before and the gods helped my father: the Sun Goddess of Arinna, the Storm God of Hatti, the Storm God of the Army, and Ishtar of the Battlefield, so that he defeated the enemy. He burned down the towns of ... And again he went to the town of Kammama and burned down the town of Kammama.

READING 13
THE BATTLE OF KADESH

The contest between the Hittites and the Egyptians for control of the Levant culminated in the battle of Kadesh, probably fought around the year 1275 B.C. Kadesh was a town located on the Orontes River that flowed through the valley between the Lebanon and Anti-Lebanon mountain ranges. This must have been the biggest battle of the Late Bronze Age and involved large numbers of chariots. Our knowledge of this engagement comes from several hieroglyphic texts and narrative scenes inscribed upon temples during the reign of Ramesses II, who portrayed himself as the all-powerful god-king pharaoh who defeated the Hittites single-handedly by killing thousands of them.

The following account blends both historical fact and typical pharaonic hyperbole. Many modern scholars have doubted that Ramesses emerged victorious from this battle. he seems to have stumbled into a well-laid ambush of the Hittites while leading one of his four divisions; and since the Hittites remained in control of this region, it hardly seems likely that the Egyptians defeated the Hittites. But of course, pharaonic ideology dictated that the pharaoh always be victorious, and that his enemies be thoroughly defeated and rendered wretchedly submissive. This text therefore illustrates how Egyptian texts always subordinated historical reality to pharaonic ideology, and how difficult it often is to extract historical facts from ancient Egyptian documents.

(Taken from pp. 261-270 of The Literature of the Ancient Egyptians: Poems, Narratives, and Manuals of Instruction from the Third and Second Millennia B.C., by Adolf Erman,

translated by A. M. Blackman, published by Methuen and
Co., London 1927)

Now his majesty had made ready his infantry and his chariotry, besides the
Shardana, whom his majesty had taken captive by the victories of his arm; and
he had given them the directions for the battle. His majesty proceeded north-
wards with his infantry and his chariotry, and he began the goodly march. In
the fifth year, on the ninth day of the second month of summer, his majesty
passed the fortress of Zaru. He was like Montu [an Egyptian war god] at his
appearing, and all foreign countries trembled before him. All (rebels?) came
bowing down for fear of the might of his majesty. His army marched along
the narrow defiles, and they were there as though upon the roadways of Egypt.

And many days after this his majesty was in Ramesses-Beloved-of-Amun,
the city which lieth in the land of the cedars. His majesty proceeded northward
and came to the mountain range of Kadesh. And his majesty went forward like
his father Montu, lord of Thebes, and crossed the ford of the Orontes with
the first army of Amun. His majesty came to the city of Kadesh.

And the wretched, vanquished chief of Hatti had come, after he had gathered to himself all lands as far as the ends of the sea; the whole land of Hatti
had come, and likewise Naharina, Aradus, Pedes, Irun, Kerkesh, Reke,
Kizwadna, Carchemish, Ekeret, Kedi, the whole land of Nushashi, Meshenet,
and Kadesh. He had left no land which he had not brought with him; all their
princes were with him, and everyone had his foot-soldiers with him and chariotry, a very great multitude without limit. They covered mountains and valleys
and were like grasshoppers in their multitude. He had left no silver in his land
and had stripped it of all its possessions; he had given them to all countries, in
order to lead them with him to the battle.

Now the wretched chief of Hatti, with the many nations which were
with him, stood hidden and ready for battle on the northwest of Kadesh.
His majesty was all alone (with) his body-guard. The army of Amun
marched behind him, the army of Re crossed over the ford in the region
south of the city of Shebten, the army of Ptah was south of the city of
Erenem, and the army of Sutekh was (yet) marching upon the road. His
majesty had made a vanguard of all the captains of his army; these were on
the coast in the land of Emor.

The wretched chief of Hatti stood in the midst of the army, which he had with him; and for fear of his majesty he came not forth to the battle. He had caused very many people and horses to come, multitudinous as the sand; they stood three men to a span and had joined themselves with warriors of every sort furnished with all the weapons of war, without number. They stood in battle array, concealed on the northwest of the city of Kadesh, and they came forth from the south side of Kadesh. They attacked the army of Re in its center, as it marched unheeding and unready for battle. The infantry and chariotry of his majesty fainted before them.

Now his majesty had halted north of Kadesh, on the west side of the Orontes; and one came and told it to his majesty. His majesty issued forth like his father Montu, after he had seized his panoply of war and had put on his corselet; he was like Baal in his hour. The great span, which bore his majesty, was called Victory-in-Thebes and was from the great stable of Ramesses. His majesty (rode) at a gallop and charged the hostile army of Hatti, being all alone and having none with him.

When his majesty looked behind him, he marked that two thousand five hundred chariots encircled him on his way out, with all the warriors of the wretched land of Hatti and of the many countries which were with him, from Aradus, Mese, Pedes, Keshkesh, Irun, Kizwadna, Khereb, Ekeret, Kadesh, and Reke. They stood three men to a span and had banded themselves together.

"No chief is with me, no charioteer, no officer of footsoldiery nor of chariotry. My foot-soldiery and my chariotry left me for a prey before them, and not one of them stood fast in order to fight with them."

And his majesty said: "What is it then, my father Amun? Hath a father indeed forgotten his son? Have I done ought without thee? Have I not gone or stood still because of thine utterance? And I never swerved from the counsels of thy mouth. How great is the great lord of Thebes, too great to suffer the foreign peoples to come nigh him! What are these Asiatics to thee, Amun? Wretches that know not God! Have I not fashioned for thee very many monuments and have filled thy temple with my captives? I have built for thee my temple of millions of years and have given thee my goods for a possession. I present unto thee all countries together, in order to furnish thine offering with victuals. I cause to be offered unto thee tens of thousands of oxen, together with all sweet-smelling plants. No good thing leave I undone in thy sanctuary.

I build for thee great pylons, and I myself set up their flag-staffs. I bring thee obelisks from Elephantine, and I it is who conveyeth stone. I cause galleys to voyage for thee upon the sea, in order to fetch for thee the tribute of the countries. Mischief shall befall him who thwarteth thy counsels, but well fareth he that understandeth(?) thee. One should work(?) for thee with loving heart. I call to thee, my father Amun. I am in the midst of foes whom I know not. All lands have joined themselves together against me, and I am all alone, and none other is with me. My soldiers have forsaken me, and not one among my chariotry hath looked around for me. If I cry to them, not one of them hearkeneth. But I call, and I find that Amun is worth more to me than millions of foot-soldiers, and hundreds of thousands of chariots, than ten thousand men in brethren and children, who with one mind hold together. The work of many men is nothing; Amun is worth more than they. I have come hither by reason of the counsels of thy mouth, O Amun, and from thy counsels have I not swerved. I pray at the limits of the lands, and yet my voice reacheth unto Hermonthis [a town south of Thebes]; Amun hearkeneth unto me and cometh, when I cry to him. He stretcheth out his hand to me, and I rejoice; he calleth out behind me: 'Forward, forward! I am with thee, I thy father. Mine hand is with thee, and I am of more avail than an hundred thousand men, I, the lord of victory, that loveth strength!'

I have found my courage again, mine heart swelleth for joy, all that I was fain to do cometh to pass. I am like Montu; I shoot on the right hand and fight on the left. I am as Baal in his time before them. I find that the two thousand five hundred chariots, in whose midst I was, lie hewn in pieces before my steeds. Not one of them hath found his hand to fight. Their hearts are become faint in their bodies for fear, their arms are all become powerless. They are unable to shoot and have not the heart to take their lances. I cause them to plunge into the water, as plunge the crocodiles. They stumble one over the other, and I slay of them whom I will. Not one of them looketh back, and there is none that turneth him about. Whosoever of them falleth lifteth not up himself again."

Now the wretched Prince of Hatti stood in the midst of his army and watched the fight, which his majesty fought all alone without foot-soldiery or chariotry. He stood with face averted and irresolute. He caused many chieftains to come; all of them had horse-chariots, and they were equipped with all their weapons of war: namely, the prince of Aradus, of Mese, of Irun, of Reke, and of Derdeni; the prince of Carchemish, of Kerkesh, and of Khereb, and the brethren of the princes of Hatti—all these together were two thousand horse-chariots, who came straight ahead on to the fire.

"I made for them. I was like Montu. I caused them to taste my hand in a single moment. I slaughtered them, slaying them where they stood; and one cried out to the other, saying: 'This is no man who is among us. He is Sutekh, great of strength; Baal is in his limbs. They are not the deeds of a man that he doeth. (Never yet) hath one man alone, without foot-soldiers and chariotry, overcome hundreds of thousands. Come quickly, that we may flee from before him, that we may seek for ourselves life and yet draw breath. Lo, as for anyone that ventureth to approach him, his hand is paralyzed and every limb. None can grasp bow or lance, when it is seen how he cometh, having run the course.'"

His majesty was behind them, as it were a gryphon. "I slew among them, and none escaped me. I shouted out to my army: 'Steady, steady your hearts, my soldiers. Ye behold my victory, I being alone. But Amun is my protector, and his hand is with me. How faint-hearted ye are, my chariotry; and it is useless to trust in you. There is not one among you to whom I had not done good in my land. Stood I not as lord there, while ye were in poverty? Yet, I caused you to become notables, and daily ye partook of my sustenance. I set the son over the possessions of his father. All that was evil in this land is abolished. I remitted to you your dues and gave to you other things that had been taken away from you. Whosoever came with a petition, to him I said at all times: 'Yea, I will do it.' Never has a lord done for his soldiers what I have done according to your desire: (for) I made you dwell in your houses and your cities, albeit ye did no soldier's service. My chariotry likewise, to them gave I the road to many cities; and I thought to experience today a like thing in you in this hour of entering into battle. But behold, ye all with one consent do a coward's deed; not one of you standeth firm in order to reach me his hand, while I am fighting. As the ka of my father, Amun, endureth, would that I were in Egypt like my fathers, who saw not the Syrians, and not one of you had come in order to tell his news in the land of Egypt. What a goodly existence he hath, who conveyeth many monuments to Thebes, the city of Amun!'

The crime which my foot-soldiery and chariotry have committed is greater than can be told. But, behold, Amun gave me his victory, although no foot-soldiery and no chariotry were with me. I let every far-off land see my victory and my might, while I was all alone, without a great one to follow me, and without a charioteer, without an officer of the foot-soldiery or of the chariotry. The foreign countries who see me shall speak of my name as far as the farthest lands which are unknown. Whosoever of them escapeth from mine hand, he standeth turned about and seeth what I do. When I attack millions of them, their feet stand not firm, but they flee away. All who shoot at me, their arrows are dispersed when they reach me.

But when Menna, my charioteer, saw that a great multitude of chariots compassed me round about, he became faint, and his heart failed him, and very great fear entered into his limbs. Then said he unto his majesty: 'My good lord, valiant prince, great protector of Egypt in the day of battle, we stand alone in the midst of the foe. Behold, the foot-soldiery and chariotry have abandoned us. Wherefore wilt thou stay until they bereave (us of breath)? Let us remain unscathed; save us, Ramesses.'"

Then said his majesty unto his charioteer: "Steady, steady thine heart, my charioteer. I shall enter in among them even as a hawk striketh; I slay, hew in pieces, and I cast to the ground. What mean these cowards to thee? My face groweth not pale for a million of them."

His majesty hastened forwards; he charged the foe and charged them until the sixth time. "I am behind them as Baal in the hour of his might. I make slaughter of them and am not slothful.

Now when my foot-soldiers and chariotry saw that I was like Montu in might and strength, and that Amun, my father, was joined with me and made every land straw before me, they approached one by one in order to (creep?) at eventide into the camp, and they found that all peoples, among whom I had forced my way, were lying slaughtered in heaps in their blood, even all the best warriors of Hatti, and the children and brethren of their prince. I had caused the field of Kadesh to become white, and one knew not where to tread because of their multitude. And my soldiers came to reverence my name, when they saw what I had done; my notables came to extol my might, and my chariotry likewise, who glorified my name: 'Ah, thou goodly warrior, who maketh steady the heart, thou rescuest thy foot-soldiery and thy chariotry. O son of Amun, deft of hands, thou destroyest the land of Hatti with thy mighty arms. Thou art a goodly warrior without thy like, a king that fighteth for his soldiers on the day of battle. Thou art stout of heart and art foremost when the fight is joined. All lands, united in one, have not withstood(?) thee; thou wast victorious in the presence of the host, in the sight of the whole earth—that is no boast. Thou art the protector of Egypt, the subduer of the foreign countries; thou hast broken the back of Hatti for ever.'"

And his majesty said unto his foot-soldiers, his chief captains, and his chariotry: "What a crime ye have committed(?), my chief captains, my foot-soldiery, and my chariotry—ye who have not fought! Hath not one boasted in his city that he would do a deed of valor for his good lord? Have I not done good to one of you? Your leaving me alone in the midst of the enemy, how excellent that is in you, your breathing the air while I am alone! Could ye then not say in your hearts that I am your wall of iron? It will be heard said that ye left me alone, without another, and no chief captain, no officer either of chariotry or of foot-soldiery came to hold out his hand to me. I fought and overcame millions of lands, all alone. I was with Victory-in-Thebes and Mut-is-Content, my great steeds; in them (alone) found I succor, when I was all alone in the midst of many countries. Furthermore, I myself will cause them to eat their provender in my presence every day, when I shall be once more in my palace: for it was in them that I found succor, and also in Menna, my charioteer, and in the butlers of the palace, who were beside me. These were present at the battle. Lo, I found that they came to my majesty in valor and victory, after I had overthrown with my mighty arm hundreds of thousands united together."

The Second Day of Battle and the Overthrow of the Enemy
"When the day dawned, I began(?) the fighting in the battle. I was ready for the fray like a bull on the alert; I shone forth against them like Montu, furnished with fighters and with mighty men. I forced my way into the melee and fought even as a hawk striketh. The royal snake upon my brow, it overthrew mine enemies; it spat forth fire into the face of the foe. I was like Re when he ascendeth in the morning, and my rays burned the limbs of the enemy. One cried out to the other: 'Look to yourselves! Protect yourselves! Lo, the mighty Sekhmet [lion-headed Egyptian goddess of battle] is with him; she is by him on his horses, and her hand is with him. If any draweth nigh unto him, the blast of fire cometh and burneth his limbs.'

Then they began to kiss the ground before me. My majesty was mighty behind them. I made slaughter among them and was not slack(?). They were cut to pieces before my steeds. They lay together stretched out in their blood.

Then the wretched fallen prince of Hatti sent and revered the great name of his majesty: "Thou are Re-Harakhti, thou art Sutekh, great in strength, son of Nut; Baal is in thy limbs, and terror of thee is in the land of Hatti. Thou hast broken for ever the back of the prince of Hatti." He sent his envoy with a letter, which was addressed to the great name of my majesty and apprised the Majesty of the Palace of Horus, Strong Bull, Beloved of Truth, as followeth: 'O King, who protecteth his soldiers, valiant in his might, a wall for his troops in the day of battle, king of Upper and Lower Egypt, UsimareChosen-of-Re, son of Re, Ramesses-Beloved-of-Amun! The servant there saith and would have thee know that thou art the son of Re, who issued from his limbs; and he hath given thee all lands united in one. The land of Egypt and the land of Hatti, they are thy servants, and they lie at thy feet. Thine august father, Re, hath given them unto thee. Be not violent with us! Behold, thy prowess is great, and thy might is heavy upon the land of Hatti. Is it good that thou shouldest slay thy servants? Yesterday thou didst slay hundreds of thousands, and today thou comest and leavest (us) no heirs surviving. Be not severe in thine utterance, O mighty king; peaceableness is better than strife of battle. Give us breath!'

My majesty allowed myself repose, full of life and good fortune; and I was as Montu in his time, when his victory hath been achieved. My majesty caused to be brought all the generals of the foot-soldiers, of the chariotry, and all other troops, altogether, in order to inform them of what the great prince of Hatti had written unto Pharaoh. They answered and said unto his majesty: 'Mercy is good exceedingly, our lord O king; in peaceableness is there nought to harm(?). Who will revere thee on the day wherein thou art wroth?'"

Then his majesty commanded his words to be heard, and he extended his hand in peace upon the march southwards. And when his majesty drew near in peace to Egypt with his chief captains, his foot-soldiers, and his chariotry, life, stability, and happiness were with him, and gods and goddesses and all lands praised his fair countenance. He arrived safely at House-of-Ramesses-Great-of-Victories and rested in his palace, full of life like Re upon his throne; and the gods greeted his ka, saying unto him: "Welcome, our beloved son,

Ramesses-Beloved-of-Amun!" They gave him millions of jubilees and eternity upon the throne of his father(?) Atum, while all lands and all foreign countries lie under his feet.

READING 14
TREATY BETWEEN THE EGYPTIANS
AND THE HITTITES

Sixteen years after the battle of Kadesh the kings of Egypt and Hatti concluded a treaty, texts of which have been found both in the Hittite capital of Hattusas and in Egypt, carved in Hieroglyphics on the walls of the temple of Amun at Thebes. The treaty is an excellent example of the international diplomatic system that prevailed among the various civilized peoples of the eastern Mediterranean during the Late Bronze Age.

> (Taken from "The Treaty of Alliance Between Hattusilis, King of the Hittites, and the Pharaoh Ramesses II of Egypt," by S. Langdon and A. H. Gardiner, Journal of Egyptian Archaeology 6 [1920] pp. 185-194, reprinted with the permission of the publisher)

Heading to the Egyptian Translation of the Treaty
Copy of the tablet of silver which the great chief of Hatti, Hattusilis, caused to be brought to Pharaoh by the hand of his messenger Tartesub and his messenger Ramose, in order to beg peace from the Majesty of Usimaresetpenre, son of Re, Ramesse-mi-Amun, bull of rulers, who makes his boundary where he will in every land.

And so be it. Riamasesa-mai-Amana, king of Egypt, the strong, with Hattusilis, the great king, king of the land Hatti, his brother, in order to give good peace, good brotherhood and to obtain a mighty kingdom(?) between them as long as we live (and) forever a treaty has made.

The treaty which the great prince of Hatti, Hattusilis, the strong, the son of Mursilis, the great chief of Hatti, the strong, the son of the son of Suppiluli-umas, the great chief of Hatti, the strong, made up a tablet of silver for Usi-mar-setpenre, the great ruler of Egypt, the strong, the son of Menmare, the great ruler of Egypt, the Strong, the son of the son of Menpehtire, the great ruler of Egypt, the strong; the good treaty of peace and brotherhood, giving peace [and brotherhood(?) ... between us by means of a treaty(?) of Hatti with Egypt] forever.

Now aforetime, since eternity, as regards the policy of the great ruler of Egypt and the great chief of Hatti—the god did not permit hostility to be made between them by means of a treaty. But in the time of Muwattallis, the great chief of Hatti, my brother, he fought with Ramesse-mi-Amun, the great ruler of Egypt [at the battle of Kadesh]. But hereafter, beginning from this day, be-hold Hattusilis, the great chief of Hatti, is [in?] a treaty for making permanent the policy which Pre made and Setekh made for the land of Egypt with the land of Hatti, so as not to permit hostilities to be made between them forever.

Behold, Hattusilis, the great chief of Hatti, has made himself in a treaty with Usimare-setpenre, the great ruler of Egypt, beginning with this day, to cause to be made good peace and good brotherhood between us forever; and he is in brotherhood with me and at peace with me, and I am in brotherhood with him and at peace with him forever. And since Muwattallis, the great chief of Hatti, my brother, hastened after his fate, and Hattusilis took his seat as great chief of Hatti on the throne of his father; behold, I have become with Ramesse-mi-Amun, the great ruler of Egypt, we(?) being [together in?] our peace and our brotherhood; and it is better than the peace and the brotherhood of formerly, which was in the land. Behold, I, being the great chief of Hatti, am with Ramesse-mi-Amun, the great ruler of Egypt, in good peace and good brotherhood. And the children of the children of the great chief of Hatti shall be(?) in brotherhood and at peace with the children of the children of Ramesse-mi-Amun, the great ruler of Egypt; they being in our policy of broth-erhood and our policy of peace. [And the land of Egypt?] with the land of Hatti [shall be?] at peace and in brotherhood like us forever; and hostilities shall not be made between them forever.

And the great chief of Hatti shall not trespass into the land of Egypt forever to take aught from it; and Usimare-setpenre, the great ruler of Egypt, shall not trespass into the land of Hatti to take (aught) from it forever.

As to the regular treaty which there was in the time of Suppiluliumas, the great chief of Hatti, and likewise the regular treaty which was in the time of Muwattallis, the great chief of Hatti, my father, I take hold of it. Behold, Ramesse-mi-Amun, the great ruler of Egypt, takes hold of the peace(?) which it(?) makes together with us from this day; and we will act according to this regular policy.

And if another enemy come to the lands of Usimare-setpenre, the great ruler of Egypt, and he send to the great chief of Hatti saying, "Come with me as help against him," the great chief of Hatti shall come to him, the great chief of Hatti shall slay his enemy. But if it be not the desire of the great chief of Hatti to come, he shall send his troops and his chariotry and shall slay his enemy.

Or if Ramesse-mi-Amun, the great ruler of Egypt, become incensed against servants of his, and they do another offense against him, and he go to slay his enemy: the great chief of Hatti shall act with him to destroy everyone against whom they shall be incensed.

But if another enemy come against the great chief of Hatti, then shall Usimare-setpenre, [the great ruler of Egypt], come to him as help to slay his enemy. (But) if it be (not) the desire of Ramesse-mi-Amun, the great ruler of Egypt, to come, he ... Hatti, and he shall send his troops and his chariotry, besides returning answer to the land of Hatti.

But if servants of the great chief of Hatti trespass against him, and Ramesse-mi-Amun, the great ruler of Egypt,...

If any great man flee from the land of Egypt, and he come to the lands of(?) the great chief of Hatti; or a town (or district ...) belonging to the lands of Ramesse-mi-Amun, the great ruler of Egypt, and they come to the great chief of Hatti: the great chief of Hatti shall not receive them. The great chief of Hatti shall cause them to be brought to Usimare-setpenre, the great ruler of Egypt, their lord, on account of it.

Or if one man or two men who are unknown flee .... and they come to the land of Hatti to be servants of another, they shall not be left in the land of Hatti. They shall be brought to Ramesse-mi-Amun, the great ruler of Egypt.

Or if a great man flee from the land of Hatti, and he come to the lands of(?) Usimare-setpenre, the great ruler of Egypt; or a town or a district or ... belonging to the land of Hatti, and they come to Ramesse-mi-Amun, the great ruler of Egypt: Usimare-setpenre, the great ruler of Egypt, shall not receive them. Ramesse-mi-Amun, the great ruler of Egypt, shall cause them to be brought to the chief ... They shall not be left.

Likewise, if one man or two men who are not known flee to the land of Egypt to be subjects of others, Usimare-setpenre, the great ruler of Egypt, shall not leave them; he shall cause them to be brought to the great chief of Hatti.

Divine Witnesses to the Treaty

As for these words of the treaty [made by(?)] the great chief of Hatti with Ramesse-mi-Amun, the great ruler of Egypt, in writing upon this tablet of silver; as for these words, a thousand gods, male gods and female gods of those of the land of Hatti, together with a thousand gods, male gods and female gods of those of the land of Egypt—they are with me as witnesses [hearing(?)] these words.

[A long list of divinities follows]

As to these words which are upon this tablet of silver of the land of Hatti and of the land of Egypt, as to him who shall not keep them, a thousand gods of the land of Hatti and a thousand gods of the land of Egypt shall destroy his house, his land, and his servants. But he who shall keep these words which are on this tablet of silver, be they Hatti, or be they Egyptians, and who do not neglect them(?), a thousand gods of the land of Hatti and a thousand gods of the land of Egypt will cause him to be healthy and to live together with his houses, his (land), and his servants.

If one man flee from the land of Egypt, or two, or three, and they come to the great chief of Hatti, the great chief of Hatti shall seize them and shall cause them to be brought back to Usimare-setpenre, the great ruler of Egypt. But as for the man who shall be brought to Ramesse-mi-Amun, the great ruler of Egypt, let not his crime be charged against him. Let not his house, his wives, or his children be destroyed. Let him not be killed. Let no injury be done to his eyes, to his ears, to his mouth or to his legs. Let not any crime be charged against him.

Likewise, if a man flee from the land of Hatti, be he one, be he two, or be he three, and they come to Usimare-setpenre, the great ruler of Egypt, let Ramesse-mi-Amun, the great ruler of Egypt, cause them to be brought to the great chief of Hatti; and the great chief of Hatti shall not charge their crime against them, and they shall not destroy his house, his wives, or his children; and they shall not kill him; and they shall not do injury to his eyes, to his mouth, or to his legs; and they shall not charge any crime against him.

Description of the Silver Tablet

What is in the middle of the tablet of silver? On its front side: a relief(?) consisting of an image of Setekh embracing an image of the great prince of Hatti, surrounded by a legend(?) saying: the seal of Setekh, the ruler of the sky, the seal of the treaty made by Hattusilis, the great chief of Hatti, the strong, the son of Mursilis, the great chief of Hatti, the strong. What is within the surrounding (frame) of the relief: the seal of Setekh, the ruler of the sky. What is on its other side: a relief(?) consisting of a female image of the goddess of Hatti embracing a female image of the chieftainess of Hatti, surrounded by a legend saying: the seal of Pre of the town of Arinna, the lord of the land, the seal of Puduhepa, the chieftainess of the land of Hatti, the daughter of the land of Kizuwadna, the [princess?] of [the town(?) of] Arinna, the lady of the land, the servant of the goddess. What is within the surrounding (female) of the relief: the seal of Pre of Arinna, the lord of every land.

READING 15
AHHIYAWA IN THE HITTITE TEXTS

A number of Hittite texts refer to a land called Ahhiyawa and to its king. Over the course of the twentieth century scholars debated whether Ahhiyawa should be equated with Achaea and thus identified with the Mycenaean world. In recent years a growing consensus has emerged that accepts the equation between Ahhiyawa and Achaea; and given the fact that the Hittite texts show Ahhiyawan attacks upon the coast of Anatolia, the content of the Hittite texts have rendered plausible the notion that a Mycenaean attack upon the Troad later became the kernel about which grew the later Greek myth of the Trojan War.

A. The Indictment of Madduwatta

The events mentioned in the following text occurred during the first half of the fourteenth century B.C. in western Anatolia during the reigns of the Hittite kings Tudhaliya and his son and successor Arnuwanda. The latter is the one who addresses Madduwatta throughout. Apart from being of interest due to its likely connection with the Mycenaean world, the text also exhibits the nature of Hittite domination throughout Anatolia by establishing local rulers as loyal vassals; but as the events here described demonstrate, the system did not always work very well, because the Hittite vassals were often ready to act independently, and the Hittite king could not always count upon the other vassals to do his bidding in forcing disloyal vassals back into line.

It should be further noted that Attarsiya of Ahhiyawa, who figures in this text, is never given any title, but at least at one point he was able to command somewhere in Anatolia a military force that included 100 chariots; and at the close of the text he is described as having attacked the island of Cyprus (Alasiya).

Note that the term 'Sun' is regularly used as an honorific title of the Hittite king, synonymous with 'Majesty'. Thus, throughout the following text King Arnuwanda refers to himself as 'My Sun' and to his father Tudhaliya as 'father of My Sun'.

(Taken from pp. 33-38 of Historical and Social Documents of the Hittite World, by Trevor R. Bryce, U. of Queensland Press, copyright 1982, reprinted with the permission of the publisher)

Madduwatta is given refuge by Tudhaliya

1. Attarsiya, the man of Ahhiya [an alternative spelling of Ahhiyawa], expelled you from your land, Madduwatta. Thereupon he pursued you and hunted you and sought to kill you, and he would have killed you. But you, Madduwatta, fled to the father of My Sun, and the father of My Sun rescued you from death, and he defended you against Attarsiya. Otherwise, Attarsiya would not have let up on you and would have killed you.

2. When the father of My Sun had defended you against Attarsiya, he took you, Madduwatta, together with your wives, your children, your troops, and your chariots; and he gave you wagons, grain, seeds in abundance; and he he also gave you beer and wine, malt and malt bread, rennet and cheese in abundance. And the father of My Sun preserved your life, Madduwatta, and that of your wives, your children, and your troops when you were hungry.

3. And the father of My Sun rescued you from the sword of Attarsiya; he saved you, Madduwatta, together with your wives, your children, your servants, together with your troops and chariots. Otherwise, the dogs would have devoured you out of hunger. If you had escaped from Attarsiya with your life, you would have died of hunger.

Tudhaliya appoints Madduwatta as a vassal ruler

4. Thereupon the father of My Sun placed you, Madduwatta, under oath as follows: "Behold! I, the father of My Sun, have protected you, Madduwatta, from the sword of Attarsiya. Thus you must be loyal to the father of My Sun and to the Land of Hatti. And behold! I have given you the mountain land Zippasla to rule, and you, Madduwatta, together with your people, are to inhabit the mountain land Zippasla."

The father of My Sun also spoke to you as follows, Madduwatta: "Go! Dwell in the mountain land Hariyati. Thus you are also near the Land of Hatti." Madduwatta declined to dwell in the mountain land Hariyati. And the father of My Sun came and spoke further to Madduwatta as follows: "Behold! I gave you the mountain land Zippasla; so dwell there. But further, you are to occupy no other subject land in addition, and no other land of your own accord. The mountain land Zippasla is to be your boundary. Thus be my servant; also, your troops are to be my troops."

5. Madduwatta spoke thus to the father of My Sun: "You have given me, My Lord, the mountain land Zippasla to dwell in. So I am in these lands as outpost and guard. And whoever speaks a word of enmity before me, and from whichever land I hear a word of enmity, I will not conceal from you, the father of My Sun, this man and this land; rather, I will write to you. But whichever land begins hostilities with you, so long as My Sun's [troops stand in the field(?)], so far as I am in the vicinity, I will attack it at once and bathe my hands in its blood." And you swore this thing under divine oath.

6. The father of My Sun also imposed upon him the following oath: "Whoever is an enemy to the father of My Sun and to the Land of Hatti is also to be an enemy to you, Madduwatta. And as I, the father of My Sun, will fight resolutely against him, you must also fight him resolutely, Madduwatta, and your troops likewise. And as Kupanta-Inara is an enemy of the father of My Sun, he must likewise be your enemy, Madduwatta. And as I, the father of My Sun, will fight resolutely against him, you too, Madduwatta, must likewise fight resolutely against him. And whoever comes to you as a fugitive from the

Land of Hatti do not conceal him or let him go to another land, but seize him and send him back to the father of My Sun.

7. And whoever speaks an evil word before you, whether it be that one speaks a word of enmity before you, or that one abuses the King and the King's son—that person you must not conceal. Send word to My Sun and seize the man, and send him to the father of My Sun. Also, you must have no communication with Attarsiya; if Attarsiya sends a communication to you, you must seize the messenger and send him to the father of My Sun; and the word he writes, that you must not conceal. Write it fully to the father of My Sun, but send back nothing of your own accord to Attarsiya."

Madduwatta's campaign against Arzawa

8. You, Madduwatta, violated the oath with the father of My Sun.
The father of My Sun had given you the mountain land Zippasla to dwell in, and he had put you under divine oath as follows: "Behold! I gave you the mountain land Zippasla. Now you must dwell here. Further, you must occupy no other land and no other subject land." And Madduwatta took the whole land, and together with his own troops raised forces in large numbers and marched against Kupanta-Inara to do battle. But when Kupanta-Inara heard of this, he marched forth with the troops of the Land of Arzawa. And the troops of the Land of Arzawa attacked Madduwatta and destroyed his troops entirely. Madduwatta fled alone. And the few of his army who escaped, they (the enemy) destroyed them all.

9. The wives, children, prisoners, and personal slaves of Madduwatta had taken to the hills. Kupanta-Inara came after them(??) and captured his wives, his children, his prisoners, his personal slaves all together. And Madduwatta again escaped, naked; and only a handful of people escaped, but these they (the enemy) destroyed [all together].

10. But when the father of My Sun heard of this, he sent Piseniya the [...], troops, and chariots to Madduwatta's assistance; and they marched forth(??). When they came down to him, they found the wives, the children, the prisoners, and property of Madduwatta in Sallawassa; and they gave them back to Madduwatta. They found also the wives,

the children, the prisoners, and property of Kupanta-Inara in Sallawassa; and they gave these also to Madduwatta. And Kupanta-Inara's luck turned sour, and he fled... And they placed Madduwatta again in his subject land.

[We omitt here Attarsiya's expedition against Madduwatta]

12. Subsequently, Attarsiya, the man of Ahhiya, came and sought to kill you, Madduwatta. But when the father of My Sun heard of this, he despatched Kisnapili, troops, and chariots to do battle against Attarsiya. And you, Madduwatta, offered no resistance to Attarsiya, and you fled before him. Kisnapili marched in battle against Attarsiya. And on Attarsiya's side, 100 chariots and [... infantry took the field]. They engaged each other in battle, and they (my forces) killed a nobleman of Attarsiya, and on our side they (the enemy) killed a nobleman, Zidanza. And Attarsiya abandoned (his attack on) (??) Madduwatta and went back to his own land. And they restored Madduwatta to his vassal status.

The affair of Dalawa and Hinduwa

13. But Dalawa began hostilities, and Madduwatta wrote as follows to Kisnapili: "I will go forth to attack Dalawa, but you go to Hinduwa. I will attack Dalawa, and therefore the troops of Dalawa will not come to the assistance of Hinduwa; so shall Hinduwa be destroyed." And Kisnapili led troops out to do battle with Hinduwa.

14. Thereupon Madduwatta marched to Dalawa, but in no way for battle. Rather, he wrote to the people of Dalawa: "Behold! Hatti troops have marched forth to Hinduwa to do battle. Block their way and attack them." And they led forth troops from Dalawa along the road, and they came and blocked our troops' way. Then they attacked Kisnapili and Partahulla. But it was Madduwatta who had incited them.

15. Thereupon Madduwatta detached the people of Dalawa from the Land of Hatti. And on the resolution of the elders, the men of Dalawa were prepared to march with this man. He took them into allegiance, and they were prepared to bring him tribute in the future.

Madduwatta's marriage alliance with Kupanta-Inara

16. But Kupanta-Inara was hostile to the father of My Sun; and you, Madduwatta, concluded a peace with him and gave him your daughter as wife. But you wrote to My Sun thus: "Behold! [I will deceive] Kupanta-Inara, and I will write thus to him: 'Listen to me. I will give you my daughter as wife.' But if he comes to me, I will seize him and kill him." This was the manner in which Madduwatta wrote to me. 17-19. are fragmentary

[Reverse of Tablet]

20. fragmentary. Madduwatta establishes control over Hittite subject territories.

21. And although the father of My Sun had given you the Land of the River Siyanta as a dwelling place, you took another land. But you, Madduwatta, were outpost and guard(?) against the enemy lands. But when the father of My Sun gave to you the Land of the River Siyanta as a dwelling place, he placed you under the following divine oath: "Behold! The father of My Sun gave you the Land of the River Siyanta. So, to the lands of the father of My Sun you are outpost and guard. Preserve these lands against the enemy. And if anyone speaks to you a word of hostility, you are to conceal nothing from the father of My Sun; write everything to me. If a land begins hostilities, attack it at once, and at once bathe your hands in its blood.

22. But further, you are not of your own accord to occupy any other land or any other subject land beyond the Land of the River Siyanta." And Madduwatta violated the oath to the father of My Sun and took the whole land of Arzawa and occupied it. But regarding the Land of Hapalla, Madduwatta had sworn an oath as follows: "I will either conquer the Land of Hapalla, or I will take (from it) prisoners, cattle, and sheep, and I will hand it over to My Sun." But thereupon you did not conquer the Land of Hapalla; you did not capture it, nor did you give it to My Sun.

23. To the Chief of the Cup-Bearers, however, he wrote thus: "I will act in concert with you against the Land of Hapalla. Come forth to me,

and conquer the Land of Hapalla, or carry it off." But when the Chief of the Cup-Bearers came forth to him, he (Madduwatta) would have blocked his way and would have fallen upon him from the rear. And on this occasion Antahitta, the Chief and Mazlawa of Kuwaliya, showed themselves loyal subjects.

24. Subsequently, he (Madduwatta) captured the lands belonging to My Sun: the Land of Zumanti, the Land of Wallarimma, the Land of Iyalanti, the Land of Zumarri, the Land of Mutamutassa, the Land of Attarimma, the Land of Suruta, and the Land of Hursunassa. And he no longer allowed envoys from these lands to come before My Sun, and he no longer allowed troops from these lands to come before My Sun; and he no longer allowed tribute to be brought before My Sun, (an obligation) which had been imposed on everyone. He took it (for himself). And he yoked the horses of My Sun, which were there, to the plough(??).

25. You occupied the town of Upnihuwala (or Pinihuwala) of your own accord. Further, you received, Madduwatta, from the Land of Hatti fugitives who came to you. The father of My Sun and My Sun subsequently wrote to you, but you did not hand them over.

26. I, My Sun, carried off troops and chariots from the Land of Salpa and [from the Land of ...]. But Madduwatta, in opposition to My Sun, placed the princes of the Land of Pitassa and the elders of Pitassa under oath and seduced them: "Be mine! Then occupy the lands of My Sun, and invade the Land of Hatti!" And they came and occupied the lands of My Sun and burned the fortified towns.

[27-28 are here omitted]

Arnuwanda demands back the territories taken over by Madduwatta

29. But subsequently I, My Sun, came and sent Mulliyara, the Scepter-Man, to Madduwatta as an envoy and commissioned(??) him (to speak) as follows to Madduwatta: "The Land of Hapalla which belongs to My Sun, why have you taken it? Give it back to me!" And Madduwatta spoke thus to Mulliyara: "The Land of Hapalla is a [royal](?) domain, and it belongs to My Sun. But the Land of Ialanti,

the Land of Zumarri, and the Land of Wallarimma I have conquered by the sword; they are mine!"

Arnuwanda demands the return of Hittite refugees

30. Niwalla, the huntsman of My Sun, fled and sought refuge with Madduwatta; and Madduwatta received him. And I, My Sun, wrote to him a first time: "Niwalla, the huntsman of My Sun, fled, and he came to you. Arrest him, and deliver him up to me!" And Madduwatta exclaimed "No one came to me."

31. Mulliyara now came and found the fugitive in his house. And he spoke to Madduwatta as follows: "The situation concerning fugitives under the divine oath is as follows: 'Whatever fugitive from the Land of Hatti seeks refuge with you, send him back to My Sun.' Already Niwalla, the huntsman of My Sun, has fled and come to you. My Sun has written several times to you; and you hide and conceal him (Niwalla). Arrest him!"

32. And Madduwatta replied to Mulliyara as follows: "The huntsman ..., and he belongs to the house of Piseni. The house of Piseni, my son, has nothing to do with me."

[33-35 are fragmentary]

The dispute over Alasiya

36. My Sun spoke as follows: "The Land of Alasiya which is a land of My Sun and brings him tribute, why have you taken it?" But Madduwatta replied as follows: "The Land of Alasiya .... Attarsiya and the Man of Piggaya have ravaged it. But the father of My Sun did not write to me afterwards; the father of My Sun never signified to me. 'The Land of Alasiya is mine; leave it so!' And now if My Sun also claims back prisoners from Alasiya, I will give them back to him."

[37 is fragmentary]

B. The Tawagalawa Letter
The following text records a letter sent by the Hittite king around 1250 B.C.

to the king of Ahhiyawa, whom the Hittite king addresses as 'my Brother', thereby acknowledging him as his royal equal. The letter is primarily concerned with the plundering activity of a man named Piyamaradu, who has been carrying off as captives people from areas subject to the Hittite king; and Piyamaradu has been finding safe refuge in the land of Ahhiyawa. The Hittite king therefore appeals to the king of Ahhiyawa to somehow restrain Piyamaradu. The text also mentions various events that occurred at this time in southern and western Anatolia, including the Hittite king advancing upon Millawanda, which is generally thought to be the Hittite name for Miletus. Lukka, which also figures in this text, was probably Lycia in southern Anatolia; and toward the end of the letter the Hittite king alludes to an earlier disagreement with the king of Ahhiyawa over Wilusa, which is now generally regarded as the Hittite rendering of the later Greek toponym Ilios, another name for Troy.

(Taken from pp. 57-60 of Historical and Social Documents of the Hittite World, by Trevor R. Bryce, U. of Queensland Press, copyright 1982, reprinted with the permission of the publisher)

Expedition against insurrectionists in Lukka

1. [Then] as went forth and destroyed the city Attarimma and burned it up, even to the wall of the king's palace. And just as the Lukka-men had approached(?), Tawagalawa and he had come to these lands, so that they approached(?) me also; and I came down to these lands. Now when I came to Sallapa, he sent a man to meet me, (saying): "Take me into vassalage, and send me the 'tuhkantis'; and he will conduct me to My Sun!" And I sent him the tartenu, (saying): "Go, set him beside you on the chariot, and bring him here!" But he snubbed the tartenu and said "no." But is not a tartenu the proper representative(?) of the king? He had my hand. But he answered(?) him "no" and humiliated him before the lands; and moreover, he said this: "Give me a kingdom here on the spot! If not, I will not come."

2. But when I reached Waliwanda, I wrote to him: "If you desire my overlordship, see now, when I come to Iyalanda, let me not find any of your men in Iyalanda; and you shall not let anyone go back there,

99

and you shall not trespass in my domain. I will see to my own subjects myself(?)." But when I [came] to Iyalanda, the enemy attacked me in three places. Now [in those parts] it is difficult ground. So, I went up on foot [and] smote the enemy [there?], and the population thence; But Lahurzi his brother promptly [departed before] me. Only enquire, my Brother, if it is not so! Lahurzi was not present at the battle, and in the territory of Iyalanda I did not find him. [He had gone from] that [place] in accordance with his declaration about Iyalanda: "I will not [again] enter Iyalanda."

3. These matters which I have written to you, how they [occurred], I, the Great King, have taken my oath; [let] the Storm-god hear, [and] let [the other gods] hear, how these things [took place].

4. Now when I had destroyed the land of Iyalanda, though I destroyed the whole land, in loyalty to [Millawanda] Atriya as the one remaining fortress I left, and back to Iyalanda I came up. So long as I was up in Iyalanda and was annihilating the whole land, I [did not go after the] prisoners. When there was no water, [I would have gone after them,] but my forces were too small, and I did not go after the prisoners, but I came up [to rest in Aba.] If Piyamaradu had [not taken them (i.e., the prisoners), I would have had] nothing against him. Now, while I was up in Aba, I wrote to Piyamaradu at Millawanda: "Come here to me!" And to my Brother [the king of Ahhiyawa] also, before (I crossed) the frontier, I wrote thus and charged him in this matter: "The fact that Piyamaradu is making repeated attacks on this land, does my Brother know this, or does he not know it?"

Request for the Surrender of Piyamaradu

5. But when [my Brother's messenger] arrived at my quarters, he brought me no greeting, and he brought me no present, but he spoke as follows: "He has written to Atpa (saying), 'Put Piyamaradu at the disposal of the king of Hatti.'" So I went into Millawanda. But I went firm also in this resolution: "The words which I shall speak to Piyamaradu, the subjects of my Brother also shall hear them." But Piyamaradu escaped by ship. Awayana and Atpa heard the charges that I had against him. Now since he is their father-in-law, why are they

concealing the matter? I obtained an oath from them, so that they ought to report the matter truthfully to you.... I went forth; and when I had alighted, I said to Atpa: "Since my Brother has written to you: 'Go, bring him (Piyamaradu) to the king of Hatti,' so conduct him here! But if he says 'I am afraid,' see now, I will send a dignitary, or I will send a brother, and he will take his (Piyamaradu's) place."...

Text omitted here.

See now, I have sent Dabala-Tarhunda the groom. Now Dabala-Tarhunda is not some man of low rank; from my youth up he used to ride with me as groom on the chariot. Also with your brother and with Tawagalawa he used to ride on the chariot. To Piyamaradu I have already given the guarantee. Now in the land of Hatti the guarantee is as follows: if one has given any man bread and salt, then he plans no evil against him. But over and above the guarantee I sent this (message): "Come, make an appeal to me, and I will set you on the road to promotion; and how I will set you on that road, that I will write to my Brother. If you are satisfied, let it be so; but if you are not satisfied, then one of my men will bring you back, just as you came, into the land of Ahhiyawa." Otherwise, this groom shall stay in his place until he comes (and) until he returns thither again. And who is this groom? Since he has (a wife) of the family of the Queen—in the land of Hatti the family of the Queen is highly respected—is he not actually a brother-in-law of mine? And he shall stay in his place until he comes (and) until he returns. Greet him kindly, my Brother. And let one of your [men] bring him (i.e., Piyamaradu); and, my Brother, convey to him (my) guarantee in the following form: "Do not offend against me, the Sun, any more; and I will let you go back into your land."

Request for the Return of Hittite Prisoners

9. Prisoners in large numbers have departed across the borders of my land, and my Brother has taken(?) 7,000 prisoners from me. Now one of my people will come; and you, my Brother, should examine the leaders. Because he (Piyamaradu) has taken some of them across the borders by force, (a man) whom my Brother sends (as representative)

and one of my own people are to be appointed. [If one of the leaders(?) now] claims: ["I crossed the borders as a fugitive]," he may remain there. [But if he claims:] "He (Piyamaradu) compelled me," t[hat man is to return (to me?)].

[10 is omitted here]

Request to keep Piyamaradu in check

11. Further, behold, it is [reported that] he (Piyamaradu) is accustomed to say: "I will go over into the land of Masa (or) the land of Karkiya, but the captives, my wife, children, and household I will leave here." Now according to this rumor, during the time when he leaves behind his wife, children, and household in my Brother's land, your land is affording him protection. But he is continually raiding my land; but whenever I have prevented him in that, he comes back into your territory. Are you now, my Brother, favorably disposed to this conduct?

12. (If not), now, my Brother, write him at least this: "Rise up, go forth into the land of Hatti. Your lord has settled his account. You, otherwise, come into the land of Ahhiyawa; and in whatever place I settle you', [you must remain there]. Rise up with your captives, your wives, and children; and settle down in another place!(........ So) long as you are at enmity with the king of Hatti, exercise your hostility from (some) other country! From my country you shall not conduct hostilities. If your heart is in the land of Karkiya (or) the land of Masa, then go there! The king of Hatti and I—in that matter of Wilusa over which we were at enmity, he has converted me, and we have made friends;.... a war would not be right for us." [Write?] that to him! But even if he leaves Millawanda, subjects of mine will always willingly(?) flee there after him. And because of this, my Brother, I have sent my troops into the Land of Millawanda, [but only with peaceful intent(?).

The Hittite king's conciliatory overtures

13. Now as we have reached agreement on the matter of Wilusa over which we went to war, what more (is there to do)? If anyone admits an offense before another, the (latter) will not reject him who admits

the offense before another. My offense, which I have admitted before my Brother, he (my Brother) has forgiven; and I will not offend again against my Brother.

But my Brother once wrote to me [as follows:] "You have acted aggressively towards me." [But at that time, my Brother] I was young; if at that time I wrote [anything insulting], it was not [done deliberately.] Such a remark may very well fall from the lips [of a leader of troops, and such a man may very well] chide his men [if in a battle anyone is idle or] cowardly. Let such words be judged before the Sun-god of heaven, whether those words should be laid to my charge, and whether I have acted aggressively towards you. But now from my Brother's mouth evil words have gone forth; and to the Great King, the king of the Land of Hatti, they have come. Let us then try this case. Send, my Brother, one of your subjects; and the man who brought that message to you, him I will here put on trial, and that man shall be beheaded. And if your man has distorted the message, then that man shall be beheaded. And when that blood has flowed, then the words which your subject spoke, those words did not proceed from your mouth, but a subject distorted them afterwards, (and) he (i.e., the god) will not have laid them to your charge.

READING 16
THE LAST DAYS OF UGARIT

Modern excavations at the site of Ugarit have revealed that around 1200 B.C.
it was destroyed violently by human agents. Since no traces of metal have been
found except for buried hoards that were not reclaimed by their owners (probably because the latter had been killed, taken prisoner, or otherwise driven
off), it is generally assumed that the buildings were systematically stripped
clean by the people who captured the city. The destruction layer contains
abundant evidence of fire, as well as numerous arrowheads. Fortunately, in addition to the archaeological data, there have also been discovered three clay
tablets bearing the texts of letters between the ruler of Cyprus (Alashiya) and
the king of Ugarit, Hammurapi. These letters report news of sea raiders, probably the ones who captured and destroyed Ugarit. At first it was thought that
the last of these three letters was never sent, because it was believed to have
still been in the kiln, about to be baked when the city was attacked, sacked,
and burned. Subsequent research, however, has suggested that this third letter
had rather fallen down from a shelf into the kiln, where it was found by archaeologists. In any case, the site was not reoccupied.

(Taken from "New Evidence on the Last Days of Ugarit," by
Michael C. Astour, American Journal of Archaeology 69 [1965]
pp. 253-258, reprinted with the permission of the publisher)

1. [The King of Alashiya to the King of Ugarit]: Greetings to yourself
and to your country. As to those matters concerning the enemy, it was

indeed men of your country and your boats that did it. Your people were indeed responsible for that offense, but do not complain to me. The twenty boats that the enemy left previously in the mountainous parts did not stay there, but they went off suddenly, and now we do not know where to look for them. I write to inform you and to put you on your guard.

2. From the King of Alashiya to Hammurapi: Thus says the King to Hammurapi, King of Ugarit. Greetings, may the gods keep you in good health. What you have written to me, enemy shipping has been sighted at sea. Well now, even if it is true that enemy ships have been sighted, be firm. Indeed then, what of your troops, your chariots, where are they stationed? Are they stationed close at hand, or are they not? Who presses you behind the enemy? Fortify your towns, bring the troops and the chariots into them, and wait for the enemy with feet firm.

3. To the King of Alashiya, my father: Thus says the King of Ugarit, his son. I fall at my father's feet. Greetings to my father, to your house, your wives, your troops, to all that belongs to the King of Alashiya. Many many greetings! My father, the enemy ships are already here. They have set fire to my towns and have done very great damage in the country. My father, did you not know that all my troops were stationed in the Hittite country, and that all my ships are still stationed in Lycia and have not yet returned, so that the country is abandoned to itself? Consider this, my father. There are seven enemy ships that have come and done very great damage. Now if there are more enemy ships, let me know about them, so that I can decide what to do [or know the worst'].

READING 17
RAMESSES III AND THE SEA PEOPLES

During the first half of the twelfth century B.C. the Bronze-Age civilizations of the eastern Mediterranean came to an abrupt end. This rather sudden upheaval seems to have been brought about by the violent actions of various groups of people, whom contemporary Egyptian texts term the Sea Peoples. Apart from archaeological evidence of destruction of major sites (e.g., Hattusas in Anatolia, Ugarit on the Syrian coast, and Tiryns, Pylos, and Mycenae in mainland Greece), our only contemporary written information about this phenomenon comes from Egyptian royal inscriptions carved on the funerary temple of Ramesses III at Medinet Habu west of Thebes in Upper Egypt. They accompany and explain scenes of the fighting between the Egyptians and the Sea Peoples both on land somewhere in Palestine and on sea near the Nile delta. Both the inscriptions and reliefs portray the pharaoh as a godlike figure who destroys all before him.

> (Taken and adapted from pp. 37-39 of Ancient Records of Egypt, Volume IV, by James Henry Breasted, U. of Chicago Press 1906)

Year 8 [1179 B.C.], under the majesty of Horus: mighty Bull, valiant Lion, strong-armed, lord of might.... The countries being taken away in the fray, the Northerners at one time in their isles were disturbed. Not one stood before their hands. They were wasted. They set up from Hatti, Kode, Carchemish, Arvad, Alashiya, a camp in one place in Amuru [Syria]. They desolated his

107

people and his land like that which is not. They came forward to Egypt with fire prepared before them. Their main support were the Peleset, Tjeker, Shekelesh, Denyen, and Weshesh. (These) lands were united, and they laid their hands upon the land as far as the Circle of the Earth. Their hearts were confident, full of their plans.

Now, it happened through this god, the lord of gods [Pharaoh Ramesses III], that I was prepared and armed to trap them like wild fowl. He furnished my strength and caused my plans to prosper. I went forth, directing these marvelous things. I equipped my frontier in Zahi [the southern Levant], prepared before them. The chiefs, the captains of infantry, the nobles I caused to equip the harbor-mouths, like a strong wall, with warships, galleys, and barges. They were manned completely from bow to stern with valiant warriors bearing their arms, soldiers of all the choicest of Egypt, being like lions roaring upon the mountain-tops. The charioteers were warriors, and all good officers, ready of hand. Their horses were quivering in their very limbs, ready to crush the countries under their feet. I was the valiant Montu, stationed before them, that they might behold the hand-to-hand fighting of my arms. I, King Ramesses III, was made a far-striding hero, conscious of his might, valiant to lead his army in the day of battle.

Those who reached my boundary, their seed is not; their heart and their soul are finished for ever and ever. As for those who had assembled before them on the sea, the full flame was in their front, before the harbor-mouths; and a wall of metal upon the shore surrounded them. They were dragged, overturned, laid low upon the beach, slain, and made (into) heaps from stern to bow of their galleys, while all their things were cast upon the water. (Thus) I turned back the waters to remember Egypt. When they mention my name in their land, may it consume them, while I sit upon the throne of Harakhte, and the serpent-diadem is fixed upon my head, like Re. I permit not the countries to see the boundaries of Egypt among them. As for the Nine Bows [traditional enemies of Egypt], I have taken away their land and their boundaries; they are added to mine. Their chiefs and their people (come) to me with praise. I carried out the plans of the All-Lord, the august, divine father, lord of the gods.

PART III
THE GREAT EMPIRES AND THE HEBREWS

READING 18
THE VEILING OF WOMEN
IN ANCIENT ASSYRIA

We possess portions of a law code of Assyria dating to the reign of Tiglath-Pileser I (ruled 1114-1076 B.C.). One of its characteristic features is the imposition of very harsh punishments for violating many of its provisions. These punishments usually take the form of bodily mutilation, such as the cutting off of one's ears, nose, or lips, the gouging out of one's eyes, or a flogging consisting of a specified number of blows. This early Assyrian law code therefore differs from Hammurabi's in having been far harsher, and this harshness could be viewed as anticipating the severity of the Assyrian Empire. One provision of this law code concerns the requirement that all respectable women be veiled when in public, whereas all prostitutes had to go unveiled so as to distinguish themselves from non-prostitutes. As can be seen, it even held the male relatives of the women responsible for their non-compliance. These legal provisions are the earliest evidence for the Near Eastern custom of women being veiled. It eventually became well established throughout the Near East and was eventually integrated by Muhammad into Islamic culture.

(Taken from pp. 407-411 of The Assyrian Laws, edited with Translation and Commentary by G. R. Driver and John C. Miles, Oxford U. Press, copyright 1935, reprinted by permission of Oxford University Press)

Women, whether married or widows or Assyrians who go out into the public street, must not have their heads uncovered. Ladies by birth ... whether it is a veil(?) or robe or mantle(?), must be veiled; they must not have their heads uncovered. Whether ... or ... or ... shall not be veiled; but when they go in the public street alone, they shall surely be veiled. A concubine(?), who goes with her mistress in the public streets, must be veiled. A hierodule [i.e., a temple slave], whom a husband has married, must be veiled in the public streets; but one, whom a husband has not married, must have her head uncovered in a public street; she shall not be veiled. A harlot shall not be veiled; her head must be uncovered. He who sees a veiled harlot shall arrest(?) her; he shall produce free men as witnesses and bring her to the entrance of the residency. Her jewellery shall not be taken from her, but the man who has arrested her shall take her clothing; she shall be beaten fifty stripes with rods, and pitch shall be poured on her head. Or, if a man has seen a veiled harlot and has let her go and has not brought her to the entrance of the residency, that man shall be beaten fifty stripes with rods; the informer(?) against him shall take his clothing; his ears shall be pierced, and a cord shall be passed through them and be tied behind him; he shall do labor for the king for a full month. Slave-girls shall not be veiled, and he who sees a veiled slave-girl shall arrest her and bring her to the entrance of the residency; her ears shall be cut off, and the man who has arrested her shall take her clothes. If a man has seen a veiled slave-girl and has let her go and has not arrested her and brought her to the entrance of the residency, and charge and proof have been brought against him, he shall be beaten fifty stripes with rods; his ears shall be pierced, and a cord shall be passed through them and be tied behind him; the informer(?) against him shall take his clothes; he shall do labor for the king for a full month.

If a man will veil his concubine(?), he shall summon five or six of his neighbors to be present and veil her before them and shall speak, saying: "She is my wife." She thus becomes his wife. A concubine(?) who has not been veiled before the men and whose husband has not spoken, saying: "She is my wife," is not a wife, but still a concubine(?). If a man has died, and his veiled wife has no sons, the sons of concubines(?) become his sons; they shall take a share of his property.

READING 19
THE ROYAL ANNALS OF ASHURNASIRPAL

The kings of the Assyrian Empire have left behind detailed accounts of their military conquests, testifying to the brutality and predatory nature of their reigns. One of the first great Assyrian conquering kings was Ashurnasirpal, who ruled from 883 to 859 B.C.; and the following are extracts taken from a very long inscription that he erected to record his exploits for posterity.

(Taken from Babylonian and Assyrian Literature, translated by the Reverend J. M. Rodwell, published by P. F. Collier and Son, New York 1901)

In my first campaign, when the Sun-god [Ashur], guider of the lands, threw over me his beneficent protection on the throne of my dominion, I firmly seated myself; a scepter, the dread of man, into my hands I took; my chariots (and) armies I collected; rugged paths, difficult mountains, which for the passage of chariots and armies was not suited, I passed; and to the land of Nairi I went. Libie, their capital city, the cities Zurra and Abuqu, Arura, Arubie, situated within the limits of the land of Aruni and Etini, fortified cities, I took; their fighting-men in numbers I slew; their spoil, their wealth, their cattle I spoiled; their soldiers were discouraged; they took possession of a difficult mountain, a mountain exceedingly difficult; after them I did not proceed: for it was a mountain ascending up like lofty points of iron, and the beautiful birds of heaven had not reached up into it: like nests of the young birds in the midst of the mountain, their defense they placed, into which none of the kings, my fathers, had ever penetrated. In three days successfully on one large mountain his courage vanquished opposition. Along the feet of that mountain I crept and hid; their nests, their tents I broke up; 200 of their warriors with weapons I destroyed; their spoil in abundance, like the young of sheep, I carried off; their corpses like rubbish on the mountains I heaped up; their relics in tangled hollows of the mountains I consumed; their cities I overthrew, I demolished, in fire I burned.

From the land of Nummi to the land of Kirruri I came down; the tribute of Kirruri of the territory of Zimizi, Zimira, Ulmanya, Adavas, Kargai, Harmasai—horses, fish?, oxen, horned sheep in numbers, copper—as their tribute I received. An officer to guard boundaries over them I placed. While in the land of Kirruri, they detained me. The fear of Ashur, my Lord, overwhelmed the lands of Gilzanai and Khubuskai; horses, silver, gold, tin, copper, kams of copper as their tribute they brought to me. From the land of Kirruri I withdrew; to a territory close by the town Khulun in Gilhi Bitani I passed. The cities of Khatu, Khalaru, Nistun, Irbidi, Mitkie, Arzanie, Zila, Khalue, cities of Gilhi situated in the environs of Uzie and Arue and Mardi—powerful lands—I occupied. Their soldiers in numbers I slew; their spoil, their riches I carried off; their soldiers were discouraged. The summits projecting over against the city of Nistun, which were menacing like the storms of heaven, I captured; into which no one among the princes, my sires, had ever penetrated. My soldiers, like birds (of prey), rushed upon them; 260 of their warriors by the sword I smote down; their heads cut off in heaps I arranged; the rest of them, like birds in a nest, in the rocks of the mountains nestled; their spoil, their riches from the midst of the mountains I brought down; cities, which were in the midst of vast forests situated, I overthrew, destroyed, burned in fire; the rebellious soldiers fled from before my arms; they came down; my yoke they received; impost tribute and a Viceroy I set over them. Bubu, son of Bubua, son of the Prefect of Nistun, in the city of Arbela I flayed; his skin I stretched in contempt upon the wall. At that time an image of my person I made; a history of my supremacy upon it I wrote, and (on) a mountain of the land of Ikin(?) in the city of Ashurnasirpal at the foot I erected (it).

In my own eponym [yearly office] in the month of —- and the 24th day (probably B.C. 882) in honor of Ashur and Ishtar, the great gods, my Lords, I quitted the city of Nineveh. To cities situated below Nipur and Pazate, powerful countries, I proceeded; Atkun, Nithu, Pilazi, and 20 other cities in their environs I captured; many of their soldiers I slew; their spoil, their riches I carried off; the cities I burned with fire; the rebel soldiers fled from before my arms, submitted, and took my yoke; I left them in possession of their land.

From the cities below Nipur and Pazate I withdrew; the Tigris I passed; to the land of Commagene I approached; the tribute of Commagene and of the Moschi in kams of copper, sheep, and goats I received; while in Commagene I was stationed, they brought me intelligence that the city Suri in Bit-Khalupe had revolted. The people of Hamath had slain their governor. Ahiyababa, the son of Lamamana they brought from Bit-Adini and made him their King. By help of Ashur and Yav, the great gods who aggrandize my royalty, chariots (and) an army I collected: the banks of the Chaboras I occupied; in my passage tribute in abundance from Salman-haman-ilin of the city of Sadikannai and of Il-yav of the city of Sunai—silver, gold, tin, kams of copper, vestments of wool, vestments of linen—I received.

To Suri, which is in Bit-Halupe, I drew near; the fear of the approach of Ashur, my Lord, overwhelmed them; the great men and the multitudes of the city, for the saving of their lives, coming up after me, submitted to my yoke; some slain, some living, some tongueless I made: Ahiyababa, son of Lamamana, whom from Bit-Adini they had fetched, I captured; in the valor of my heart and the steadfastness of my soldiers I besieged the city; the soldiers, rebels all, were taken prisoners; the nobles to the principal palace of his land I caused to send; his silver, his gold, his treasure, his riches, copper(?), tin, kams, tabhani, hariati of copper, choice copper in abundance, alabaster and iron-stone of large size, the treasures of his harem, his daughters and the wives of the rebels with their treasures, the gods with their treasures, precious stones of the land of ..., his swift chariot, his horses, the harness, his chariot-yoke, trappings for horses, coverings for men, vestments of wool, vestments of linen, handsome altars of cedar, handsome ..., bowls of cedar-wood, beautiful black coverings, beautiful purple coverings, carpets, his oxen, his sheep, his abundant spoil, which like the stars of heaven could not be reckoned, I carried off; Aziel as my lieutenant over them I placed; a trophy along the length of the great gate I erected. The rebellious nobles who had revolted against me and whose skins I had stripped off, I made into a trophy: some in the middle of the pile I left to decay; some on the top of the pile on stakes I impaled; some by the side of the pile I placed in order on stakes; many within view of my land I flayed;

their skins on the walls I arranged; of the officers of the king's officer, rebels, the limbs I cut off; I brought Ahiyababa to Nineveh; I flayed him and fastened his skin to the wall.... In honor of Ashur, the Sun-god, and Yav, the gods in whom I trust, my chariots and army I collected at the head of the river Zupnat, the place of an image which Tiglath-Pileser and Tiglath-Adar, Kings of Assyria, my fathers, had raised; an image of My Majesty I constructed and put up with theirs. In those days I renewed the tribute of the land of Izala: oxen, sheep, goats. To the land of Kasyari I proceeded; and to Kinabu, the fortified city of the province of Hulai, I drew near; with the impetuosity of my formidable attack I besieged and took the town; 600 of their fighting men with (my) arms I destroyed; 3,000 of their captives I consigned to the flames; as hostages I left not one of them alive; Hulai, the governor of their town, I captured by (my) hand alive; their corpses into piles I built; their boys and maidens I dishonored; Hulai, the governor of their city, I flayed: his skin on the walls of Damdamusa I placed in contempt; the city I overthrew, demolished, burned with fire; the city of Mariru within their territory I took; 50 warrior fighting men by (my) weapons I destroyed; 200 of their captives in the flame I burned....

To Tila I drew near—a strong city with three forts facing each other. The soldiers to their strong forts and numerous army trusted and would not submit; my yoke they would not accept; (then) with onset and attack I besieged the city; their fighting men with my weapons I destroyed; of their spoil, their riches, oxen and sheep I made plunder; much booty I burned with fire; many soldiers I captured alive; of some I chopped off the hands and feet; of others the noses and ears I cut off; of many soldiers I destroyed the eyes; one pile of bodies while yet alive, and one of heads I reared up on the heights within their town; their heads in the midst I hoisted; their boys and their maidens I dishonored; the city I overthrew, razed, and burned with fire....

From Bit-Adini I withdrew; the Euphrates, in a difficult part of it, I crossed in ships of hardened skins. I approached the land of Carchemish. the tribute of Sangara, king of Syria—twenty talents of silver, sahri gold, bracelets of gold, scabbards of gold, 100 talents of copper, 250 talents of annui kami, hariate, nirmakate kibil of copper, the extensive furniture of his palace of incomprehensible perfection, different kinds of woods, ka and sara, 200 female slaves, vestments of wool and linen, beautiful black coverings, beautiful purple coverings, precious stones, horns of buffaloes, white chariots, images of gold, their coverings, the treasures of his Royalty—I received of him; the chariots and warlike engines of the general of Carchemish I laid up in my magazines; the kings of all those lands who had come out against me received my yoke; their hostages I received; they did homage in my presence.

To the land of Lebanon I proceeded. From Carchemish I withdrew and marched to the territory of Munzigani and Harmurga. The land of Ahanu I reduced; to Gaza, the town of Lubarna of the Khatti, I advanced; gold and vestments of linen I received. Crossing the river Abrie, I halted; and then leaving that river, I approached the town of Kanulua, a royal city belonging to Lubarna of the Khatti. From before my mighty arms and my formidable onset he fled in fear, and for the saving of his life he submitted to my yoke; twenty talents of silver, one talent of gold, 100 talents in tin, 100 talents in annui, 1,000 oxen, 10,000 sheep, 1,000 vestments of wool and linen, nimati and ki woods, coverings, ahusate thrones, kui wood, wood for seats, their coverings, sarai, zueri-wood, horns of kui in abundance, the numerous utensils of his palace, whose beauty could not be comprehended: ... pagatu(?) from the wealth of great lords as his tribute I imposed upon him. The chariots and warlike engines of the land of the Khatti-I laid up in my magazines; their hostages I took.

In those days (I received) the tribute of Guzi of the land of Yahanai: silver, gold, tin.... Oxen, sheep, vestments of wool and linen I received. From Kunalua, the capital of Lubarna, I withdrew....

In those days I occupied the environs of Lebanon. To the Great Sea of Phoenicia I went up. Up to the Great Sea my arms I carried. To the gods I sacrificed; I took tribute of the princes of the environs of the sea-coast: of the lands of Tyre, Sidon, Gebal, Maacah, Maizai, Kaizai, of Phoenicia and Arvad on the sea-coast—silver, gold, tin, copper, kam of copper, vestments of wool and linen, pagutu great and small, strong timber, wood of ki, teeth of dolphins, the produce of the sea—I received as their tribute. My yoke they accepted; the mountains of Amanus I ascended; wood for bridges, pines, box, cypress, li-wood I cut down; I offered sacrifices for my gods; a trophy of victory I made, and in a central place I erected it.

READING 20
SENNACHERIB'S SIEGE
OF JERUSALEM

In 721 B.C. the Assyrians captured Samaria, the capital of the northern kingdom of Israel; and in their typical manner of treating people who had resisted the Assyrian army, they carried off movable items of value and deported large numbers of farm animals and people from ten of the twelve tribes of the Hebrews, and they resettled the depopulated land with other non-Hebrew people so as to reduce the threat of the area rising up in rebellion. The Assyrian army returned twenty years later under its King Sennacherib and laid siege to the heavily fortified city of Jerusalem, the capital of the much smaller and poorer southern kingdom of Judah, which was ruled at the time by King Hezekiah. Although the Assyrians failed to capture Jerusalem itself, they did capture many outlying smaller towns, from which they deported thousands of animals and people and forced the two tribes of the Hebrews to be vassals of the Assyrian Empire until the latter finally succumbed to the Medes and Babylonians toward the end of the seventh century B.C. The earliest writings in The Old Testament were composed during this traumatic period of Hebrew history that therefore formed the historical background to these writings; and since we happen to possess both Biblical and Assyrian accounts of Sennacherib's expedition of 701 B.C., comparing the two can offer interesting insights into the differing perspectives of the Biblical and Assyrian narratives.

A. The Assyrian Royal Annals of King Sennacherib

(Taken from pp. 120-121 of Volume II of Ancient Records of Assyria and Babylonia, by Daniel David Luckenbill, U. of Chicago Press, copyright 1927, reprinted by courtesy of the Oriental Institute of the University of Chicago)

As for Hezekiah, the Jew, who did not submit to my yoke, 46 of his strong, walled cities, as well as the small cities in their neighborhood, which were without number, by escalade' and by bringing up siege engines(?), by attacking and storming on foot, by mines, tunnels and breaches(?), I besieged and took those cities. 200,150 people, great and small, male and female, horses, mules, asses, camels, cattle and sheep, without number, I brought away from them and counted as spoil. Himself, like a caged bird, I shut up in Jerusalem, his royal city. Earthworks I threw up against him; the one coming out of his city gate I turned back to his misery. The cities of his, which I had despoiled, I cut off from his land and to Mitinti, king of Ashdod, Padi, king of Ekron, and Sillibel, king of Gaza, I gave them. And thus I diminished his land. I added to the former tribute and laid upon him as their yearly payment a tax in the form of gifts for my majesty. As for Hezekiah, the terrifying splendor of my majesty overcame him, and the Arabs and his mercenary(?) troops which he had brought in to strengthen Jerusalem, his royal city, deserted him. In addition to 30 talents of gold and 800 talents of silver, there were gems, antimony, jewels(?), large sandustones, couches of ivory, house chairs of ivory, elephant's hide, ivory (lit., elephant's "teeth"), maple(?), boxwood, all kinds of valuable heavy treasures, as well as his daughters, his harem, his male and female musicians, which he had them bring after me to Nineveh, my royal city. To pay tribute and to accept servitude, he dispatched his messengers.

B. The Biblical Account

(Taken from The Old Testament, II Kings 18:13-19:37 in the King James Version)

Chapter 18: 13 Now in the fourteenth year of king Hezekiah did Sennacherib king of Assyria come up against all the fenced cities of Judah, and took them. 14 And Hezekiah king of Judah sent to the king of Assyria to Lachish [a town of southern Judah, which Sennacherib was besieging and eventually captured and destroyed], saying, I have offended; return from me: that which thou puttest on me will I bear. And the king of Assyria appointed unto Hezekiah king of Judah three hundred talents of silver and thirty talents of gold. 15 And Hezekiah gave him all the silver that was found in the house of the LORD, and in the treasures of the king's house. 16 At that time did Hezekiah cut off the gold from the doors of the temple of the LORD, and from the pillars which Hezekiah king of Judah had overlaid, and gave it to the king of Assyria. 17 And the king of Assyria sent Tartan and Rabsaris and Rabshakeh from Lachish to king Hezekiah with a great host against Jerusalem. And they went up and came to Jerusalem. And when they were come up, they came and stood by the conduit of the upper pool, which is in the highway of the fuller's field. 18 And when they had called to the king, there came out to them Eliakim the son of Hilkiah, which was over the household, and Shebna the scribe, and Joah the son of Asaph the recorder. 19 And Rabshakeh said unto them, Speak ye now to Hezekiah. Thus saith the great king, the king of Assyria. What confidence is this wherein thou trustest? 20 Thou sayest, (but they are but vain words). I have counsel and strength for the war. Now on whom dost thou trust, that thou rebellest against me? 21 Now, behold, thou trustest upon the staff of this bruised reed, even upon Egypt, on which if a man lean, it will go into his hand, and pierce it: so is Pharaoh king of Egypt unto all that trust on him. 22 But if ye say unto me, We trust in the LORD our God: is not that he, whose high places and whose altars Hezekiah hath taken away, and hath said to Judah and Jerusalem, Ye shall worship before this altar in Jerusalem? 23 Now therefore, I pray thee, give pledges to my lord the king of Assyria, and I will deliver thee two thousand horses, if thou be able on thy part to set riders upon them. 24 How then wilt thou turn away the face of one captain of the least of my master's servants, and put thy trust on Egypt for chariots and for horsemen? 25 Am I now come up without the LORD against this place to destroy it? The LORD said to me, Go up against this land, and destroy it. 26 Then said Eliakim the son of Hilkiah, and Shebna, and Joah, unto Rabshakeh, Speak, I pray thee, to thy servants in the Syrian language; for we understand it: and talk not with us in the Jews' language in the ears of the people that are on the wall. 27 But Rabshakeh said unto them, Hath my master sent me to thy master, and to thee, to speak these words? Hath he not sent me to the men which sit on the wall, that they may eat their own dung, and drink their own piss with you? 28 Then Rabshakeh stood and cried with a loud voice in the Jews' language, and spake, saying, Hear the word of the great king, the king of Assyria: 29 Thus saith the king, Let not Hezekiah deceive you: for he shall not be able to deliver you out of his hand: 30 Neither let Hezekiah make you trust in the LORD, saying, The LORD will surely deliver us, and this city shall not be delivered into the hand of the king of Assyria. 31 Hearken not to Hezekiah: for thus saith the king of Assyria, Make an agreement with me by a present, and come out to me, and then eat ye every man of his own vine, and every one of his fig tree, and drink ye every one the waters of his cistern: 32 Until I come and take you away to a land like your own land, a land of corn and wine, a land of bread and vineyards, a land of oil olive and of honey, that ye may live, and not die: and hearken not unto Hezekiah, when he persuadeth you, saying, The LORD will deliver us. 33 Hath any of the gods of the nations delivered at all his land out of the hand of the king of Assyria? 34 Where are the gods of Hamath, and of Arpad? where are the gods of Sepharvaim, Hena, and Ivah? have they delivered Samaria out of mine hand? 35 Who are they among all the gods of the countries, that have delivered their country out of mine hand, that the LORD should deliver Jerusalem out of mine hand? 36 But the people held their peace, and answered him not a word: for the king's commandment was, saying, Answer him not. 37 Then came Eliakim the son of Hilkiah, which was over the household, and Shebna the scribe, and Joah the son of Asaph the recorder, to Hezekiah with their clothes rent, and told him the words of Rabshakeh.

Chapter 19: 1 And it came to pass, when king Hezekiah heard it, that he rent his clothes, and covered himself with sackcloth, and went into the house of the LORD. 2 And he sent Eliakim, which was over the household, and Shebna the scribe, and the elders of the priests, covered with sackcloth, to Isaiah the prophet the son of Amoz. 3 And they said unto him, Thus saith Hezekiah, This day is a day of trouble, and of rebuke, and blasphemy; for the children are come to the birth, and there is not strength to bring forth. 4 It may be the LORD thy God will hear all the words of Rabshakeh, whom the king of Assyria his master hath sent to reproach the living God; and will reprove the words which the LORD thy God hath heard: wherefore lift up thy prayer for the remnant that are left. 5 So the servants of king Hezekiah came to Isaiah. 6 And Isaiah said unto them, Thus shall ye say to your master, Thus saith the LORD, Be not afraid of the words which thou hast heard, with which the servants of the king of Assyria have blasphemed me. 7 Behold, I will send a blast upon him, and he shall hear a rumor, and shall return to his own land; and I will cause him to fall by the sword in his own land. 8 So Rabshakeh returned, and found the king of Assyria warring against Libnah: for he had heard that he was departed from Lachish. 9 And when he heard say of Tirhakah king of Ethiopia, Behold, he is come out to fight against thee: he sent messengers again unto Hezekiah, saying, 10 Thus shall ye speak to Hezekiah king of Judah, saying, Let not thy God in whom thou trustest deceive thee, saying, Jerusalem shall not be delivered into the hand of the king of Assyria. 11 Behold, thou hast heard what the kings of Assyria have done to all lands, by destroying them utterly: and shalt thou be delivered? 12 Have the gods of the nations delivered them which my fathers have destroyed; as Gozan, and Haran, and Rezeph, and the children of Eden which were in Thelasar? 13 Where is the king of Hamath, and the king of Arpad, and the king of the city of Sepharvaim, of Hena, and Ivah? 14 And Hezekiah received the letter of the hand of the messengers, and read it: and Hezekiah went up into the house of the LORD, and spread it before the LORD. 15 And Hezekiah prayed before the LORD, and said, O LORD God of Israel, which dwellest between the cherubims, thou art the God, even thou alone, of all the kingdoms of the earth; thou hast made heaven and earth. 16 LORD, bow down thine ear, and hear: open, LORD, thine eyes, and see: and hear the words of Sennacherib, which hath sent him to reproach the living God. 17 Of a truth, LORD, the kings of Assyria have destroyed the nations and their lands, 18 And have cast their gods into the fire: for they were no gods, but the work of men's hands, wood and stone: therefore they have destroyed them. 19 Now therefore, O LORD our God, I beseech thee, save thou us out of his hand, that all the kingdoms of the earth may know that thou art the LORD God, even thou only. 20 Then Isaiah the son of Amoz sent to Hezekiah, saying, Thus saith the LORD God of Israel, That which thou hast prayed to me against Sennacherib king of Assyria I have heard. 21 This is the word that the LORD hath spoken concerning him; The virgin the daughter of Zion hath despised thee, and laughed thee to scorn; the daughter of Jerusalem hath shaken her head at thee. 22 Whom hast thou reproached and blasphemed? and against whom hast thou exalted thy voice, and lifted up thine eyes on high? even against the Holy One of Israel. 23 By thy messengers thou hast reproached the LORD, and hast said, With the multitude of my chariots I am come up to the height of the mountains, to the sides of Lebanon, and will cut down the tall cedar trees thereof, and the choice fir trees thereof: and I will enter into the lodgings of his borders, and into the forest of his Carmel. 24 I have digged and drunk strange waters, and with the sole of my feet have I dried up all the rivers of besieged places. 25 Hast thou not heard long ago how I have done it, and of ancient times that I have formed it? now have I brought it to pass, that thou shouldest be to lay waste fenced cities into ruinous heaps. 26 Therefore their inhabitants were of small power, they were dismayed and confounded; they were as the grass of the field, and as the green herb, as the grass on the house tops, and as corn blasted before it be grown up. 27 But I know thy abode, and thy going out, and thy coming in, and thy rage against me. 28 Because thy rage against me and thy tumult is come up into mine ears, therefore I will put my hook in thy nose, and my bridle in thy lips, and I will turn thee back by the way by which thou camest. 29 And this shall be a sign unto thee, Ye shall eat this year such things as grow of themselves, and in the second year that which springeth of the same; and in the third year sow ye, and reap, and plant vineyards, and eat the fruits thereof. 30 And the remnant that is escaped of the house of Judah shall yet again take root downward, and bear fruit upward. 31 For out of Jerusalem shall go forth a remnant, and they that escape out of mount Zion: the zeal of the LORD of hosts shall do this. 32 Therefore thus saith the LORD concerning the king of Assyria, He shall not come into this city, nor shoot an arrow there, nor come before it with shield, nor cast a bank against it. 33 By the way that he came, by the same shall he return, and shall not come into this city, saith the LORD. 34 For I will defend this city, to save it, for mine own sake, and for my servant David's sake. 35 And it came to pass that night, that the angel of the LORD went out, and smote in the camp of the Assyrians an hundred fourscore and five thousand: and when they arose early in the morning, behold, they were all dead corpses. 36 So Sennacherib king of Assyria departed, and went and returned, and dwelt at Nineveh. 37 And it came to pass, as he was worshipping in the house of Nisroch his god, that Adrammelech and Sharezer his sons smote him with the sword: and they escaped into the land of Armenia. And Esarhaddon his son reigned in his stead.

READING 21
THE OLD TESTAMENT

The Hebrew Bible or Old Testament has been one of the most important texts in shaping the religious thought and morality of the Western tradition. It forms the basis of Judaism, and out of it later arose Christianity and The New Testament. Both The Old Testament and The New Testament are not unitary literary works, but they are collections of many separate writings by different people at different times to record the events of different periods or to address a wide range of different issues. The various writings of The Old Testament were composed over a period of about 600 years, c.750 B.C. to c.150 B.C. with many of the works having been written during the period of the three great empires of the ancient Near East.

The twelve tribes of the Hebrews do not appear to us with any degree of historical clarity until c.1100 B.C., shortly after the destruction of the Bronze-Age civilizations of the eastern Mediterranean. By that time the Fertile Crescent had been inhabited by different civilizations for more than 2,000 years; and these different civilizations had already developed the general pattern of life in this region of the world and had also produced law codes, myths, popular stories, and the practice of recording basic historical events. The authors of the various books of The Old Testament drew upon this rich and varied literary tradition of the ancient Near East and through a complex process of adoption and adaptation fashioned their own versions of myths, popular stories, legal practices, and religious traditions. The single most distinctive element of Hebrew culture was its strict monotheism, the belief in the existence of one and only one god who had created the universe, and who adopted the Hebrews as his chosen people.

(Taken from the King James Version)

A. The Two Accounts of Creation (Genesis)

By careful analysis of language and content Biblical scholars of the nineteenth century established beyond reasonable doubt that the Hebrew text of the first several books of The Old Testament is the result of the complex weaving together of material from four major distinct sources, each written at a different time by a different author. People who are unacquainted with modern Biblical scholarship, and who read The Bible only in English translation are likely to be unaware of the multiple authorship of the first five books, known as The Torah (Hebrew for Instruction) or Pentateuch (Greek meaning 'Five Scrolls'), traditionally attributed to Moses himself. The first two chapters of Genesis constitute an excellent illustration of this multiple authorship: for 1:1-2:3 sets forth one version of creation, whereas 2:4-25 presents a different account.

Chapter 1: 1 In the beginning God created the heaven and the earth. 2 And the earth was without form, and void; and darkness was upon the face of the deep. And the Spirit of God moved upon the face of the waters. 3 And God said, Let there be light: and there was light. 4 And God saw the light, that it was good: and God divided the light from the darkness. 5 And God called the light Day, and the darkness he called Night. And the evening and the morning were the first day. 6 And God said, Let there be a firmament in the midst of the waters, and let it divide the waters from the waters. 7 And God made the firmament, and divided the waters which were under the firmament from the waters which were above the firmament: and it was so. 8 And God called the firmament Heaven. And the evening and the morning were the second day. 9 And God said, Let the waters under the heaven be gathered together unto one place, and let the dry land appear: and it was so. 10 And God called the dry land Earth; and the gathering together of the waters called he Seas: and God saw that it was good. 11 And God said, Let the earth bring forth grass, the herb yielding seed, and the fruit tree yielding fruit after his kind, whose seed is in itself, upon the earth: and it was so. 12 And the earth brought forth grass, and herb yielding seed after his kind, and the tree yielding fruit, whose seed was in itself, after his kind: and God saw that it was good. 13 And the evening and the morning were the third day. 14 And God said, Let there be lights in the firmament of the heaven to divide the day from the night;

and let them be for signs, and for seasons, and for days, and years: 15 And let them be for lights in the firmament of the heaven to give light upon the earth: and it was so. 16 And God made two great lights; the greater light to rule the day, and the lesser light to rule the night: he made the stars also. 17 And God set them in the firmament of the heaven to give light upon the earth, 18 And to rule over the day and over the night, and to divide the light from the darkness: and God saw that it was good. 19 And the evening and the morning were the fourth day. 20 And God said, Let the waters bring forth abundantly the moving creature that hath life, and fowl that may fly above the earth in the open firmament of heaven. 21 And God created great whales, and every living creature that moveth, which the waters brought forth abundantly, after their kind, and every winged fowl after his kind: and God saw that it was good. 22 And God blessed them, saying, Be fruitful, and multiply, and fill the waters in the seas, and let fowl multiply in the earth. 23 And the evening and the morning were the fifth day. 24 And God said, Let the earth bring forth the living creature after his kind, cattle, and creeping thing, and beast of the earth after his kind: and it was so. 25 And God made the beast of the earth after his kind, and cattle after their kind, and every thing that creepeth upon the earth after his kind: and God saw that it was good. 26 And God said, Let us make man in our image, after our likeness: and let them have dominion over the fish of the sea, and over the fowl of the air, and over the cattle, and over all the earth, and over every creeping thing that creepeth upon the earth. 27 So God created man in his own image, in the image of God created he him; male and female created he them. 28 And God blessed them, and God said unto them, Be fruitful, and multiply, and replenish the earth, and subdue it: and have dominion over the fish of the sea, and over the fowl of the air, and over every living thing that moveth upon the earth. 29 And God said, Behold, I have given you every herb bearing seed, which is upon the face of all the earth, and every tree, in the which is the fruit of a tree yielding seed; to you it shall be for meat. 30 And to every beast of the earth, and to every fowl of the air, and to every thing that creepeth upon the earth, wherein there is life, I have given every green herb for meat: and it was so. 31 And God saw every thing that he had made, and, behold, it was very good. And the evening and the morning were the sixth day.

Chapter 2: 1 Thus the heavens and the earth were finished, and all the host of them. 2 And on the seventh day God ended his work which he had made; and he rested on the seventh day from all his work which he had made. 3 And God blessed the seventh day, and sanctified it: because that in it he had rested from all his work which God created and made. 4 These are the generations of the heavens and of the earth when they were created, in the day that the LORD God made the earth and the heavens, 5 And every plant of the field before it was in the earth, and every herb of the field before it grew: for the LORD God had not caused it to rain upon the earth, and there was not a man to till the ground. 6 But there went up a mist from the earth, and watered the whole face of the ground. 7 And the LORD God formed man of the dust of the ground, and breathed into his nostrils the breath of life; and man became a living soul. 8 And the LORD God planted a garden eastward in Eden; and there he put the man whom he had formed. 9 And out of the ground made the LORD God to grow every tree that is pleasant to the sight, and good for food; the tree of life also in the midst of the garden, and the tree of knowledge of good and evil. 10 And a river went out of Eden to water the garden; and from thence it was parted, and became into four heads. 11 The name of the first is Pison: that is it which compasseth the whole land of Havilah, where there is gold; 12 And the gold of that land is good: there is bdellium and the onyx stone. 13 And the name of the second river is Gihon: the same is it that compasseth the whole land of Ethiopia. 14 And the name of the third river is Hiddekel: that is it which goeth toward the east of Assyria. And the fourth river is Euphrates. 15 And the LORD God took the man, and put him into the garden of Eden to dress it and to keep it. 16 And the LORD God commanded the man, saying, Of every tree of the garden thou mayest freely eat: 17 But of the tree of the knowledge of good and evil, thou shalt not eat of it: for in the day that thou eatest thereof thou shalt surely die. 18 And the LORD God said, It is not good that the man should be alone; I will make him an help meet for him. 19 And out of the ground the LORD God formed every beast of the field, and every fowl of the air; and brought them unto Adam to see what he would call them: and whatsoever Adam called every living creature, that was the name thereof. 20 And Adam gave names to all cattle, and to the fowl of the air, and to every beast of the field; but for Adam there was not found an help meet for him. 21 And the LORD God caused a deep sleep to fall upon Adam, and he slept: and he took one of his ribs, and closed up the flesh instead thereof; 22 And the rib, which the LORD God had taken from man, made he a woman, and brought her unto the man. 23 And Adam said, This is now bone of my bones, and flesh of my flesh: she shall be called Woman, because she was taken out of Man. 24 Therefore shall a man leave his father and his mother, and shall cleave unto his wife: and they shall be one flesh. 25 And they were both naked, the man and his wife, and were not ashamed.

B. The Garden of Eden (Genesis)

Chapter 3: 1 Now the serpent was more subtil than any beast of the field which the LORD God had made. And he said unto the woman, "Yea, hath God said, Ye shall not eat of every tree of the garden?" 2 And the woman said unto the serpent, We may eat of the fruit of the trees of the garden: 3 But of the fruit of the tree which is in the midst of the garden, God hath said, Ye shall not eat of it, neither shall ye touch it, lest ye die.'" 4 And the serpent said unto the woman, "Ye shall not surely die: 5 For God doth know that in the day ye eat thereof, then your eyes shall be opened, and ye shall be as gods, knowing good and evil." 6 And when the woman saw that the tree was good for food, and that it was pleasant to the eyes, and a tree to be desired to make one wise, she took of the fruit thereof, and did eat, and gave also unto her husband with her; and he did eat. 7 And the eyes of them both were opened, and they knew that they were naked; and they sewed fig leaves together, and made themselves aprons. 8 And they heard the voice of the LORD God walking in the garden in the cool of the day: and Adam and his wife hid themselves from the presence of the LORD God among the trees of the garden. 9 And the LORD God called unto Adam, and said unto him, "Where art thou?" 10 And he said, "I heard thy voice in the garden, and I was afraid, because I was naked; and I hid myself." 11 And he said, Who told thee that thou wast naked? Hast thou eaten of the tree, whereof I commanded thee that thou shouldest not eat?" 12 And the man said, The woman whom thou gayest to be with me, she gave me of the tree, and I did eat." 13 And the LORD God said unto the woman, "What is this that thou hast done?" And the woman said, The serpent beguiled me, and I did eat." 14 And the LORD God said unto the serpent, "Because thou hast done this, thou art cursed above all cattle, and above every beast of the field; upon thy belly shalt thou go, and dust shalt thou eat all the days of thy life: 15 And I will put enmity between thee and the woman, and between thy seed and her seed; it shall bruise thy head, and thou shalt bruise his heel." 16 Unto the woman he said, "I will greatly multiply thy sorrow and thy conception; in sorrow thou shalt bring forth children; and thy desire shall be to thy husband, and he shall rule over thee." 17 And unto Adam he said, "Because thou hast hearkened unto the voice of thy wife, and hast eaten of the tree, of which I commanded thee, saying, Thou shalt not eat of it: cursed is the ground for thy sake; in sorrow shalt thou eat of it all the days of thy life; 18 Thorns also and thistles shall it bring forth to thee; and thou shalt eat the herb of the field; 19 In the sweat of thy face shalt thou eat bread, till thou return unto the ground; for out of it wast thou taken: for dust thou art, and unto dust shalt thou return." 20 And Adam called his wife's name Eve; because she was the mother of all living. 21 Unto Adam also and to his wife did the LORD God make coats of skins, and clothed them. 22 And the LORD God said, "Behold, the man is become as one of us, to know good and evil: and now, lest he put forth his hand, and take also of the tree of life, and eat, and live for ever:" 23 Therefore the LORD God sent him forth from the garden of Eden, to till the ground from whence he was taken. 24 So he drove out the man; and he placed at the east of the garden of Eden Cherubims, and a flaming sword which turned every way, to keep the way of the tree of life.

C. The Biblical Flood Story (Genesis)

Chapter 5: 1 This is the book of the generations of Adam. In the day that God created man, in the likeness of God made he him; 2 Male and female created he them; and blessed them, and called their name Adam, in the day when they were created. 3 And Adam lived an hundred and thirty years, and begat a son in his own likeness, and after his image; and called his name Seth: 4 And the days of Adam after he had begotten Seth were eight hundred years: and he begat sons and daughters: 5 And all the days that Adam lived were nine hundred and thirty years: and he died. 6 And Seth lived an hundred and five years, and begat Enos: 7 And Seth lived after he begat Enos eight hundred and seven years, and begat sons and daughters: 8 And all the days of Seth were nine hundred and twelve years: and he died. 9 And Enos lived ninety years, and begat Cainan: 10 And Enos lived after he begat Cainan eight hundred and fifteen years, and begat sons and daughters: 11 And all the days of Enos were nine hundred and five years: and he died. 12 And Cainan lived seventy years and begat Mahalaleel: 13 And Cainan lived after he begat Mahalaleel eight hundred and forty years, and begat sons and daughters: 14 And all the days of Cainan were nine hundred and ten years: and he died. 15 And Mahalaleel lived sixty and five years, and begat Jared: 16 And Mahalaleel lived after he begat Jared eight hundred and thirty years, and begat sons and daughters: 17 And all the days of Mahalaleel were eight hundred ninety and five years: and he died. 18 And Jared lived an hundred sixty and two years, and he begat Enoch: 19 And Jared lived after he begat Enoch eight hundred years, and begat sons and daughters: 20 And all the days of Jared were nine hundred sixty and two years: and he died. 21 And Enoch lived sixty and five years, and begat Methuselah: 22 And Enoch walked with God after he begat Methuselah three hundred years, and begat sons and daughters: 23 And all the days of Enoch were three hundred sixty and five years: 24 And Enoch walked with God: and he was not; for God took him. 25 And Methuselah lived an hundred eighty and seven years, and begat Lamech. 26 And Methuselah lived after he begat Lamech seven hundred eighty and two years, and begat sons and daughters: 27 And all the days of Methuselah were nine hundred sixty and nine years: and he died. 28 And Lamech lived an hundred eighty and two years, and begat a son: 29 And he called his name Noah, saying, This same shall comfort us concerning our work and toil of our hands, because of the ground which the LORD hath cursed." 30 And Lamech lived after he begat Noah five hundred ninety and five years, and begat sons and daughters: 31 And all the days of Lamech were seven hundred seventy and seven years: and he died. 32 And Noah was five hundred years old: and Noah begat Shem, Ham, and Japheth.

Chapter 6: 1 And it came to pass, when men began to multiply on the face of the earth, and daughters were born unto them, 2 That the sons of God saw the daughters of men that they were fair; and they took them wives of all which they chose. 3 And the LORD said, "My spirit shall not always strive with man: for that he also is flesh: yet, his days shall be an hundred and twenty years." 4 There were giants in the earth in those days; and also after that, when the sons of God came in unto the daughters of men, and they bare children to them, the same became mighty men which were of old, men of renown. 5 And God saw that the wickedness of man was great in the earth, and that every imagination of the thoughts of his heart was only evil continually. 6 And it repented the LORD that he had made man on the earth, and it grieved him at his heart.

7 And the LORD said, "I will destroy man whom I have created from the face of the earth; both man, and beast, and the creeping thing, and the fowls of the air; for it repenteth me that I have made them." 8 But Noah found grace in the eyes of the LORD. 9 These are the generations of Noah: Noah was a just man and perfect in his generations, and Noah walked with God. 10 And Noah begat three sons, Shem, Ham, and Japheth. 11 The earth also was corrupt before God, and the earth was filled with violence. 12 And God looked upon the earth, and, behold, it was corrupt; for all flesh had corrupted his way upon the earth. 13 And God said unto Noah, The end of all flesh is come before me; for the earth is filled with violence through them; and, behold, I will destroy them with the earth. 14 Make thee an ark of gopher wood; rooms shalt thou make in the ark, and shalt pitch it within and without with pitch. 15 And this is the fashion which thou shalt make it of: The length of the ark shall be three hundred cubits, the breadth of it fifty cubits, and the height of it thirty cubits. 16 A window shalt thou make to the ark, and in a cubit shalt thou finish it above; and the door of the ark shalt thou set in the side thereof; with lower, second, and third stories shalt thou make it. 17 And, behold, I, even I, do bring a flood of waters upon the earth, to destroy all flesh, wherein is the breath of life, from under heaven; and every thing that is in the earth shall die. 18 But with thee will I establish my covenant; and thou shalt come into the ark, thou, and thy sons, and thy wife, and thy sons' wives with thee. 19 And of every living thing of all flesh, two of every sort shalt thou bring into the ark, to keep them alive with thee; they shall be male and female. 20 Of fowls after their kind, and of cattle after their kind, of every creeping thing of the earth after his kind, two of every sort shall come unto thee, to keep them alive. 21 And take thou unto thee of all food that is eaten, and thou shalt gather it to thee; and it shall be for food for thee, and for them." 22 Thus did Noah; according to all that God commanded him, so did he.

Chapter 7: 1 And the LORD said unto Noah, "Come thou and all thy house into the ark; for thee have I seen righteous before me in this generation. 2 Of every clean beast thou shalt take to thee by sevens, the male and his female: and of beasts that are not clean by two, the male and his female. 3 Of fowls also of the air by sevens, the male and the female; to keep seed alive upon the face of all the earth. 4 For yet seven days, and I will cause it to rain upon the earth forty days and forty nights; and every living substance that I have made will I destroy from off the face of the earth." 5 And Noah did according unto all that the LORD commanded him. 6 And Noah was six hundred years old when the flood of waters was upon the earth. 7 And Noah went in, and his sons, and his wife, and his sons' wives with him, into the ark, because of the waters of the flood. 8 Of clean beasts, and of beasts that are not clean, and of fowls, and of every thing that creepeth upon the earth, 9 There went in two and two unto Noah into the ark, the male and the female, as God had commanded Noah. 10 And it came to pass after seven days, that the waters of the flood were upon the earth. 11 In the six hundredth year of Noah's life, in the second month, the seventeenth day of the month, the same day were all the fountains of the great deep broken up, and the windows of heaven were opened. 12 And the rain was upon the earth forty days and forty nights. 13 In the selfsame day entered Noah, and Shem, and Ham, and Japheth, the sons of Noah, and Noah's wife, and the three wives of his sons with them, into the ark; 14 They, and every beast after his kind, and all the cattle after their kind, and every creeping thing that creepeth upon the earth after his kind, and every fowl after his kind, every bird of every sort. 15 And they went in unto Noah into the ark, two and two of all flesh, wherein is the breath of life. 16 And they that went in, went in male and female of all flesh, as God had commanded him: and the LORD shut him in. 17 And the flood was forty days upon the earth; and the waters increased, and bare up the ark, and it was lift up above the earth. 18 And the waters prevailed, and were increased greatly upon the earth; and the ark went upon the face of the waters. 19 And the waters prevailed exceedingly upon the earth; and all the high hills, that were under the whole heaven, were covered. 20 Fifteen cubits upward did the waters prevail; and the mountains were covered. 21 And all flesh died that moved upon the earth, both of fowl, and of cattle, and of beast, and of every creeping thing that creepeth upon the earth, and every man: 22 All in whose nostrils was the breath of life, of all that was in the dry land, died. 23 And every living substance was destroyed which was upon the face of the ground, both man, and cattle, and the creeping things, and the fowl of the heaven; and they were destroyed from the earth: and Noah only remained alive, and they that were with him in the ark. 24 And the waters prevailed upon the earth an hundred and fifty days.

Chapter 8: 1 And God remembered Noah, and every living thing, and all the cattle that was with him in the ark: and God made a wind to pass over the earth, and the waters asswaged; 2 The fountains also of the deep and the windows of heaven were stopped, and the rain from heaven was restrained; 3 And the waters returned from off the earth continually: and after the end of the hundred and fifty days the waters were abated. 4 And the ark rested in the seventh month, on the seventeenth day of the month, upon the mountains of Ararat. 5 And the waters decreased continually until the tenth month: in the tenth month, on the first day of the month, were the tops of the mountains seen. 6 And it came to pass at the end of forty days, that Noah opened the window of the ark which he had made: 7 And he sent forth a raven, which went forth to and fro, until the waters were dried up from off the earth. 8 Also he sent forth a dove from him, to see if the waters were abated from off the face of the ground; 9 But the dove found no rest for the sole of her foot, and she returned unto him into the ark: for the waters were on the face of the whole earth: then he put forth his hand, and took her, and pulled her in unto him into the ark. 10 And he stayed yet other seven days; and again he sent forth the dove out of the ark; 11 And the dove came in to him in the evening; and, lo, in her mouth was an olive leaf pluckt off: so Noah knew that the waters were abated from off the earth. 12 And he stayed yet other seven days; and sent forth the dove; which returned not again unto him any more. 13 And it came to pass in the six hundredth and first year, in the first month, the first day of the month, the waters were dried up from off the earth: and Noah removed the covering of the ark, and looked, and, behold, the face of the ground was dry. 14 And in the second month, on the seven and twentieth day of the month, was the earth dried. 15 And God spake unto Noah, saying, 16 "Go forth of the ark, thou, and thy wife, and thy sons, and thy sons' wives with thee. 17 Bring forth with thee every living thing that is with thee, of all flesh, both of fowl, and of cattle, and of every creeping thing that creepeth upon the earth; that they may breed abundantly in the earth, and be fruitful, and multiply upon the earth." 18 And Noah went forth, and his sons, and his wife, and his sons' wives with him: 19 Every beast, every creeping thing, and every fowl, and whatsoever creepeth upon the earth, after their kinds, went forth out of the ark. 20 And Noah builded an altar unto the LORD; and took of every clean beast, and of every clean fowl, and offered burnt offerings on the altar. 21 And the LORD smelled a sweet savor; and the LORD said in his heart, "I will not again curse the ground any more for mans sake; for the imagination of mans heart is evil from his youth; neither will I again smite any more every thing living, as I have done. 22 While the earth remaineth, seedtime and harvest, and cold and heat, and summer and winter, and day and night shall not cease."

Chapter 9: 1 And God blessed Noah and his sons, and said unto them, "Be fruitful, and multiply, and replenish the earth. 2 And the fear of you and the dread of you shall be upon every beast of the earth, and upon every fowl of the air, upon all that moveth upon the earth, and upon all the fishes of the sea; into your hand are they delivered. 3 Every moving thing that liveth shall be meat for you; even as the green herb have I given you all things. 4 But flesh with the life thereof, which is the blood thereof, shall ye not eat. 5 And surely your blood of your lives will I require; at the hand of every beast will I require it, and at the hand of man; at the hand of every mans brother will I require the life of man. 6 Whoso sheddeth man's blood, by man shall his blood be shed: for in the image of God made he man. 7 And you, be ye fruitful, and multiply; bring forth abundantly in the earth, and multiply therein." 8 And God spake unto Noah, and to his sons with him, saying, 9 And I, behold, I establish my covenant with you, and with your seed after you; 10 And with every living creature that is with you, of the fowl, of the cattle, and of every beast of the earth with you; from all that go out of the ark, to every beast of the earth. 11 And I will establish my covenant with you, neither shall all flesh be cut off any more by the waters of a flood; neither shall there any more be a flood to destroy the earth." 12 And God said, This is the token of the covenant which I make between me and you and every living creature that is with you, for perpetual generations: 13 I do set my bow in the cloud, and it shall be for a token of a covenant between me and the earth. 14 And it shall come to pass, when I bring a cloud over the earth, that the bow shall be seen in the cloud: 15 And I will remember my covenant, which is between me and you and every living creature of all flesh; and the waters shall no more become a flood to destroy all flesh. 16 And the bow shall be in the cloud; and I will look upon it, that I may remember the everlasting covenant between God and every living creature of all flesh that is upon the earth." 17 And God said unto Noah, This is the token of the covenant, which I have established between me and all flesh that is upon the earth."

D. The Exposure of Moses (Exodus)

Chapter 1: 7 And the children of Israel were fruitful, and increased abundantly, and multiplied, and waxed exceeding mighty; and the land was filled with them. 8 Now there arose up a new king over Egypt, which knew not Joseph. 9 And he said unto his people, "Behold, the people of the children of Israel are more and mightier than we: 10 Come on, let us deal wisely with them; lest they multiply, and it come to pass, that, when there falleth out any war, they join also unto our enemies, and fight against us, and so get them up out of the land." 11 Therefore they did set over them taskmasters to afflict them with their burdens. And they built for Pharaoh treasure cities, Pithom and Ramses. 12 But the more they afflicted them, the more they multiplied and grew. And they were grieved because of the children of Israel. 13 And the Egyptians made the children of Israel to serve with rigour: 14 And they made their lives bitter with hard bondage, in morter, and in brick, and in all manner of service in the field: all their service, wherein they made them serve, was with rigour. 15 And the king of Egypt spake to the Hebrew midwives, of which the name of the one was Shiphrah, and the name of the other Puah: 16 And he said, When ye do the office of a midwife to the Hebrew women, and see them upon the stools; if it be a son, then ye shall kill him: but if it be a daughter, then she shall live." 17 But the midwives feared God, and did not as the king of Egypt commanded them, but saved the men children alive. 18 And the king of Egypt called for the midwives, and said unto them, "Why have ye done this thing, and have saved the men children alive?" 19 And the midwives said unto Pharaoh, "Because the Hebrew women are not as the Egyptian women; for they are lively, and are delivered ere the midwives come in unto them." 20 Therefore God dealt well with the midwives: and the people multiplied, and waxed very mighty. 21 And it came to pass, because the midwives feared God, that he made them houses. 22 And Pharaoh charged all his people, saying, "Every son that is born ye shall cast into the river, and every daughter ye shall save alive."

Chapter 2: 1 And there went a man of the house of Levi, and took to wife a daughter of Levi. 2 And the woman conceived, and bare a son: and when she saw him that he was a goodly child, she hid him three months. 3 And when she could not longer hide him, she took for him an ark of bulrushes, and daubed it with slime and with pitch, and put the child therein; and she laid it in the flags by the river's brink. 4 And his sister stood afar off, to wit what would be done to him. 5 And the daughter of Pharaoh came down to wash herself at the river; and her maidens walked along by the river's side; and when she saw the ark among the flags, she sent her maid to fetch it. 6 And when she had opened it, she saw the child: and, behold, the babe wept. And she had compassion on him, and said, This is one of the Hebrews' children." 7 Then said his sister to Pharaoh's daughter, "Shall I go and call to thee a nurse of the Hebrew women, that she may nurse the child for thee?" 8 And Pharaoh's daughter said to her, "Go." And the maid went and called the child's mother. 9 And Pharaoh's daughter said unto her, "Take this child away, and nurse it for me, and I will give thee thy wages." And the women took the child, and nursed it. 10 And the child grew, and she brought him unto Pharaoh's daughter, and he became her son. And she called his name Moses: and she said, "Because I drew him out of the water."

E. The Miracle of the Burning Bush (Exodus)

Chapter 3: 1 Now Moses kept the flock of Jethro his father in law, the priest of Midian: and he led the flock to the backside of the desert, and came to the mountain of God, even to Horeb. 2 And the angel of the LORD appeared unto him in a flame of fire out of the midst of a bush: and he looked, and, behold, the bush burned with fire, and the bush was not consumed. 3 And Moses said, "I will now turn aside, and see this great sight, why the bush is not burnt." 4 And when the LORD saw that he turned aside to see, God called unto him out of the midst of the bush, and said, "Moses, Moses." And he said, "Here am I." 5 And he said, "Draw not nigh hither: put off thy shoes from off thy feet: for the place whereon thou standest is holy ground." 6 Moreover, he said, "I am the God of thy father, the God of Abraham, the God of Isaac, and the God of Jacob." And Moses hid his face; for he was afraid to look upon God. 7 And the LORD said, "I have surely seen the affliction of my people which are in Egypt, and have heard their cry by reason of their taskmasters; for I know their sorrows; 8 And I am come down to deliver them out of the hand of the Egyptians, and to bring them up out of that land unto a good land and a large, unto a land flowing with milk and honey; unto the place of the Canaanites, and the Hittites, and the Amorites, and the Perizzites, and the Hivites, and the Jebusites. 9 Now therefore, behold, the cry of the children of Israel is come unto me: and I have also seen the oppression wherewith the Egyptians oppress them. 10 Come now therefore, and I will send thee unto Pharaoh, that thou mayest bring forth my people the children of Israel out of Egypt...."

F. The Ten Commandments (Exodus)

Chapter 19: 16 And it came to pass on the third day in the morning, that there were thunders and lightnings, and a thick cloud upon the mount, and the voice of the trumpet exceeding loud; so that all the people that was in the camp trembled. 17 And Moses brought forth the people out of the camp to meet with God; and they stood at the nether part of the mount. 18 And mount Sinai was altogether on a smoke, because the LORD descended upon it in fire: and the smoke thereof ascended as the smoke of a furnace, and the whole mount quaked greatly. 19 And when the voice of the trumpet sounded long, and waxed louder and louder, Moses spake, and God answered him by a voice. 20 And the LORD came down upon mount Sinai, on the top of the mount: and the LORD called Moses up to the top of the mount; and Moses went up. 21 And the LORD said unto Moses, "Go down, charge the people, lest they break through unto the LORD to gaze, and many of them perish. 22 And let the priests also, which come near to the LORD, sanctify themselves, lest the LORD break forth upon them." 23 And Moses said unto the LORD, The people cannot come up to mount Sinai: for thou chargedst us, saying, 'Set bounds about the mount, and sanctify it.'" 24 And the LORD said unto him, "Away, get thee down, and thou shalt come up, thou, and Aaron with thee: but let not the priests and the people break through to come up unto the LORD, lest he break forth upon them." 25 So Moses went down unto the people, and spake unto them.

Chapter 20: 1 And God spake all these words, saying, 2 "I am the LORD thy God, which have brought thee out of the land of Egypt, out of the house of bondage. 3 Thou shalt have no other gods before me. 4 Thou shalt not make unto thee any graven image, or any likeness of any thing that is in heaven above, or that is in the earth beneath, or that is in the water under the earth. 5 Thou shalt not bow down thyself to them, nor serve them: for I the LORD thy God am a jealous God, visiting the iniquity of the fathers upon the children unto the third and fourth generation of them that hate me; 6 And showing mercy unto thousands of them that love me, and keep my commandments. 7 Thou shalt not take the name of the LORD thy God in vain; for the LORD will not hold him guiltless that taketh his name in vain. 8 Remember the sabbath day, to keep it holy. 9 Six days shalt thou labor, and do all thy work: 10 But the seventh day is the sabbath of the LORD thy God: in it thou shalt not do any work, thou, nor thy son, nor thy daughter, thy manservant, nor thy maidservant, nor thy cattle, nor thy stranger that is within thy gates: 11 For in six days the LORD made heaven and earth, the sea, and all that in them is, and rested the seventh day: wherefore the LORD blessed the sabbath day, and hallowed it. 12 Honor thy father and thy mother: that thy days may be long upon the land which the LORD thy God giveth thee. 13 Thou shalt not kill. 14 Thou shalt not commit adultery. 15 Thou shalt not steal. 16 Thou shalt not bear false witness against thy neighbor. 17 Thou shalt not covet thy neighbor's house, thou shalt not covet thy neighbor's wife, nor his manservant, nor his maidservant, nor his ox, nor his ass, nor any thing that is thy neighbor's." 18 And all the people saw the thunderings, and the lightnings, and the noise of the trumpet, and the mountain smoking: and when the people saw it, they removed, and stood afar off. 19 And they said unto Moses, "Speak thou with us, and we will hear: but let not God speak with us, lest we die." 20 And Moses said unto the people, "Fear not: for God is come to prove you, and that his fear may be before your faces, that ye sin not." 21 And the people stood afar off, and Moses drew near unto the thick darkness where God was. 22 And the LORD said unto Moses, "Thus thou shalt say unto the children of Israel, Ye have seen that I have talked with you from heaven. 23 Ye shall not make with me gods of silver, neither shall ye make unto you gods of gold. 24 An altar of earth thou shalt make unto me, and shalt sacrifice thereon thy burnt offerings, and thy peace offerings, thy sheep, and thine oxen: in all places where I record my name I will come unto thee, and I will bless thee. 25 And if thou wilt make me an altar of stone, thou shalt not build it of hewn stone: for if thou lift up thy tool upon it, thou hast polluted it. 26 Neither shalt thou go up by steps unto mine altar, that thy nakedness be not discovered thereon.'"

Chapter 21: 1 Now these are the judgments which thou shalt set before them. 2 If thou buy an Hebrew servant, six years he shall serve: and in the seventh he shall go out free for nothing. 3 If he came in by himself, he shall go out by himself: if he were married, then his wife shall go out with him. 4 If his master have given him a wife, and she have born him sons or daughters; the wife and her children shall be her master's, and he shall go out by himself. 5

And if the servant shall plainly say, I love my master, my wife, and my children; I will not go out free: 6 Then his master shall bring him unto the judges; he shall also bring him to the door, or unto the door post; and his master shall bore his ear through with an aul; and he shall serve him for ever. 7 And if a man sell his daughter to be a maidservant, she shall not go out as the menservants do. 8 If she please not her master, who hath betrothed her to himself, then shall he let her be redeemed: to sell her unto a strange nation he shall have no power, seeing he hath dealt deceitfully with her. 9 And if he have betrothed her unto his son, he shall deal with her after the manner of daughters. 10 If he take him another wife; her food, her raiment, and her duty of marriage, shall he not diminish. 11 And if he do not these three unto her, then shall she go out free without money. 12 He that smiteth a man, so that he die, shall be surely put to death. 13 And if a man lie not in wait, but God deliver him into his hand; then I will appoint thee a place whither he shall flee. 14 But if a man come presumptuously upon his neighbor, to slay him with guile; thou shalt take him from mine altar, that he may die. 15 And he that smiteth his father, or his mother, shall be surely put to death. 16 And he that stealeth a man, and selleth him, or if he be found in his hand, he shall surely be put to death. 17 And he that curseth his father, or his mother, shall surely be put to death. 18 And if men strive together, and one smite another with a stone, or with his fist, and he die not, but keepeth his bed: 19 If he rise again, and walk abroad upon his staff, then shall he that smote him be quit: only he shall pay for the loss of his time, and shall cause him to be thoroughly healed. 20 And if a man smite his servant, or his maid, with a rod, and he die under his hand; he shall be surely punished. 21 Notwithstanding, if he continue a day or two, he shall not be punished: for he is his money. 22 If men strive, and hurt a woman with child, so that her fruit depart from her, and yet no mischief follow: he shall be surely punished, according as the woman's husband will lay upon him; and he shall pay as the judges determine. 23 And if any mischief follow, then thou shalt give life for life, 24 Eye for eye, tooth for tooth, hand for hand, foot for foot, 25 Burning for burning, wound for wound, stripe for stripe. 26 And if a man smite the eye of his servant, or the eye of his maid, that it perish; he shall let him go free for his eye's sake. 27 And if he smite out his manservant's tooth, or his maidservant's tooth; he shall let him go free for his tooth's sake. 28 If an ox gore a man or a woman, that they die: then the ox shall be surely stoned, and his flesh shall not be eaten; but the owner of the ox shall be quit. 29 But if the ox were wont to push with his horn in time past, and it hath been testified to his owner, and he hath not kept him in, but that he hath killed a man or a woman; the ox shall be stoned, and his owner also shall be put to death...."

READING 22
CYRUS THE GREAT

By the time that Cyrus the Great united the Persian tribes and led them to victory over the various peoples of western Asia in creating the Persian Empire, the Fertile Crescent and Anatolia had long enjoyed centuries of civilized life, and the inhabitants had developed specific traditions and ideologies with which they enveloped their rulers. It is therefore not surprising to find the ancient Near Eastern peoples attaching these ideas to Cyrus, the newest world ruler of the region.

A. The Babylonian View

The following passage is a translation of a cuneiform text inscribed upon a clay cylinder, known as the Cyrus Cylinder. The object measures about nine inches high and about 3.5-4.0 inches in diameter. It was discovered in 1879 in the ruins of Marduk's famous temple, the Esagila, during the earliest modern excavations conducted at the site of Babylon; and since then it has been among the prized possessions of the British Museum in London. This text was apparently composed at the time that Cyrus the Great captured Babylon in 539 B.C. In this text the Babylonians cast Cyrus into the familiar mold of a king divinely appointed to rule by Marduk, the chief god of Babylon. The text begins with complaints about the preceding king, Nabonidus, the last ruler of the Neo-Babylonian Kingdom, because he neglected to worship and honor Marduk as he deserved. Consequently, Marduk withdrew his support from Nabonidus and, after casting about, chose Cyrus to be the next legitimate ruler of Babylon.

The first four lines of the inscription are broken beyond legibility; and portions of the last eleven lines (as well as others throughout the text) are lost.

(Taken from pp. 315-316 of Ancient Near Eastern Texts Relating to The Old Testament, edited by James B. Pritchard, Third Edition, Princeton U. Press, copyright 1969, reprinted with the permission of the publisher)

[The beginning of the text is damaged and is unreadable] A weakling has been installed as the end of his country; [the correct images of the gods he removed from their thrones; imitations he ordered to place upon them. A replica of the temple Esagila he has ... for Ur and the other sacred cities inappropriate rituals ... daily he did blabber [incorrect prayers]. He (furthermore) interrupted in a fiendish way the regular offerings; he did ... he established within the sacred cities. The worship of Marduk, the king of the gods, he [chang]ed into abomination; daily he used to do evil against his (i.e., Marduk's) city.... He [tormented] its [inhabitant]s with corvee-work (lit.: a yoke) without relief; he ruined them all. Upon their complaints the lord of the gods became terribly angry and [departed from] their region; (also), the (other) gods living among them left their mansions, wroth that he had brought (them) into Babylon. (But) Marduk, [who does care for] ... on account of (the fact that) the sanctuaries of all their settlements were in ruins, and the inhabitants of Sumer and Akkad had become like (living) dead, turned back (his countenance); [his] an[ger] [abated], and he had mercy (upon them). He scanned and looked (through) all the countries, searching for a righteous ruler willing to lead him (i.e., Marduk) (in the annual procession). (Then) he pronounced the name of Cyrus, king of Anshan, declared him (lit.: pronounced his name) to be(come) the ruler of all the world. He made the Guti country and all the Manda-hordes bow in submission to his (i.e., Cyrus') feet. And he (Cyrus) did always endeavor to treat according to justice the blackheaded [i.e., the Sumerians] whom he (Marduk) has made him conquer. Marduk, the great lord, a protector of his people/worshipers, beheld with pleasure his (i.e., Cyrus') good deeds and his upright mind (lit.: heart) (and therefore) ordered him to march against his city Babylon. He made him set out on the road to Babylon, going at his side like a real friend. His widespread troops—their number, like that of the water of a river, could not be established-strolled along, their weapons packed away. Without any battle he made him enter his town Babylon, sparing Babylon any calamity. He delivered into his (i.e., Cyrus') hands Nabonidus, the king who did not worship him (i.e., Marduk). All the inhabitants of Babylon, as well as of the entire country of Sumer and Akkad, princes and governors (included), bowed to him (Cyrus) and kissed his feet, jubilant that he (had received) the kingship, and with shining faces. Happily they greeted him as a master through whose help they had come (again) to life from death (and) had all been spared damage and disaster, and they worshiped his (very) name.

I am Cyrus, king of the world, great king, legitimate king, king of Babylon, king of Sumer and Akkad, king of the four rims (of the earth), son of Cambyses, great king, king of Anshan, grandson of Cyrus, great king, king of Anshan, descendant of Teispes, great king, king of Anshan, of a family (which) always (exercised) kingship; whose rule Bel and Nebo love, whom they want as king to please their hearts.

When I entered Babylon as a friend, and (when) I established the seat of the government in the palace of the ruler under jubilation and rejoicing, Marduk, the great lord, [induced] the magnanimous inhabitants of Babylon [to love me], and I was daily endeavoring to worship him. My numerous troops walked around in Babylon in peace; I did not allow anybody to terrorize (any place) of the [country of Sumer] and Akkad. I strove for peace in Babylon and in all his (other) sacred cities. As to the inhabitants of Babylon, [who] against the will of the gods [had / were .... I abolished] the corvee which was against their (social) standing. I brought relief to their dilapidated housing, putting (thus) an end to their (main) complaints. Marduk, the great lord, was well pleased with my deeds and sent friendly blessings to myself, Cyrus, the king who worships him, to Cambyses, my son, the offspring of [my] loins, as well as to all my troops; and we all [praised] his great [godhead] joyously, standing before him in peace.

All the kings of the entire world from the Upper to the Lower Sea, those who are seated in throne rooms, (those who) live in other [types of buildings, as well as] all the kings of the West land living in tents, brought their heavy tributes and kissed my feet in Babylon. (As to the region) from ... as far as Ashur and Susa, Agade, Eshnunna, the towns Zamban, Me-Turnu, Der, as well as the region of the Gutians, I returned to (these) sacred cities on the other side of the Tigris, to the sanctuaries which have been ruins for a long time, the images which (used) to live therein; and I established for them permanent sanctuaries. I (also) gathered all their (former) inhabitants and returned (to them) their habitations. Furthermore, I resettled upon the command of Marduk, the great lord, all the gods of Sumer and Akkad whom Nabonidus has brought into Babylon to the anger of the lord of the gods, unharmed, in their (former) chapels, the places which make them happy.

May all the gods whom I have resettled in their sacred cities ask daily Bel and Nebo for a long life for me; and may they recommend me (to him), to Marduk, my lord. They may say this: "Cyrus, the king who worships you, and Cambyses, his son .... all of them I settled in a peaceful place ... ducks and doves, ... endeavored to fortify/repair their dwelling places.... (six lines destroyed)

> [A fragment of this text was later identified in 1970 and shows that after the ending of the preceding text Cyrus describes how he presided over the rebuilding and repair of Babylon's canal system.]

B. The Biblical View
In the first chapter of Ezra in The Old Testament Cyrus is portrayed as having been chosen by the monotheistic Hebrew god Yahweh to rule over the nations and to restore Yahweh's temple in Jerusalem along with releasing the Hebrews from their captivity in Babylon.

(Taken from the King James Version of The Bible)

Chapter 1: 1 Now in the first year of Cyrus king of Persia, that the word of the LORD by the mouth of Jeremiah might be fulfilled, the LORD stirred up the spirit of Cyrus king of Persia, that he made a proclamation throughout all his kingdom, and put it also in writing, saying, 2 Thus saith Cyrus king of Persia, The LORD God of heaven hath given me all the kingdoms of the earth; and he hath charged me to build him an house at Jerusalem, which is in Judah. 3 Who is there among you of all his people? his God be with him, and let him go up to Jerusalem, which is in Judah, and build the house of the LORD God of Israel, (he is the God,) which is in Jerusalem. 4 And whosoever remaineth in any place where he sojourneth, let the men of his place help him with silver, and with gold, and with goods, and with beasts, beside the freewill offering for the house of God that is in Jerusalem. 5 Then rose up the chief of the fathers of Judah and Benjamin, and the priests, and the Levites, with all them whose spirit God had raised, to go up to build the house of the LORD which is in Jerusalem. 6 And all they that were about them strengthened their hands with vessels of silver, with gold, with goods, and with beasts, and with precious things, beside all that was willingly offered. 7 Also Cyrus the king brought forth the vessels of the house of the LORD, which Nebuchadnezzar had brought forth out of Jerusalem, and had put them in the house of his gods; 8 Even those did Cyrus king of Persia bring forth by the hand of Mithredath the treasurer, and numbered them unto Sheshbazzar, the prince of Judah. 9 And this is the number of them: thirty chargers of gold, a thousand chargers of silver, nine and twenty knives, 10 Thirty basons of gold, silver basons of a second sort four hundred and ten, and other vessels a thousand. 11 All the vessels of gold and of silver were five thousand and four hundred. All these did Sheshbazzar bring up with them of the captivity that were brought up from Babylon unto Jerusalem.

C. The Account of Herodotus (Book I)

(Taken from History of Herodotus, translated by George Rawlinson, published by Murray of London, 1875, revised by Gary Forsythe)

107. Astyages, the son of Cyaxares, succeeded to the throne [of the Medes]. He had a daughter who was named Mandane, concerning whom he had a wonderful dream. He dreamt that from her such a stream of water flowed forth as not only to fill his capital, but to flood the whole of Asia. This vision he laid before such of the Magi as had the gift of interpreting dreams, who expounded its meaning to him in full, whereat he was greatly terrified. On this account, when his daughter was now of ripe age, he would not give her in marriage to any of the Medes who were of suitable rank, lest the dream should be

accomplished; but he married her to a Persian of good family indeed, but of a quiet temper, whom he looked on as much inferior to a Mede of even middle condition.

108. Thus Cambyses (for so was the Persian called) wedded Mandane and took her to his home, after which, in the very first year, Astyages saw another vision. He fancied that a vine grew from the womb of his daughter and overshadowed the whole of Asia. After this dream, which he submitted also to the interpreters, he sent to Persia and fetched away Mandane, who was now with child and was not far from her time. On her arrival he set a watch over her, intending to destroy the child to which she should give birth; for the Magian interpreters had expounded the vision to foreshow that the offspring of his daughter would reign over Asia in his stead. To guard against this, Astyages, as soon as Cyrus was born, sent for Harpagus, a man of his own house and the most faithful of the Medes, to whom he was wont to entrust all his affairs, and addressed him thus: "Harpagus, I beseech thee neglect not the business with which I am about to charge thee; neither betray thou the interests of thy lord for others' sake, lest thou bring destruction on thine own head at some future time. Take the child born of Mandane my daughter; carry him with thee to thy home, and slay him there. Then bury him as thou wilt." "Oh! king," replied the other, "never in time past did Harpagus disoblige thee in anything, and be sure that through all future time he will be careful in nothing to offend. If therefore it be thy will that this thing be done, it is for me to serve thee with all diligence."

109. When Harpagus had thus answered, the child was given into his hands, clothed in the garb of death, and he hastened weeping to his home. There on his arrival he found his wife, to whom he told all that Astyages had said. "What then," said she, "is it now in thy heart to do?" "Not what Astyages requires," he answered; "no, he may be madder and more frantic still than he is now, but I will not be the man to work his will, or lend a helping hand to such a murder as this. Many things forbid my slaying him. In the first place, the boy is my own kith and kin; and next, Astyages is old and has no son. If then, when he dies, the crown should go to his daughter, that daughter whose

child he now wishes to slay by my hand, what remains for me but danger of the fearfullest kind? For my own safety, indeed, the child must die; but someone belonging to Astyages must take his life, not I or mine."

110. So saying, he sent off a messenger to fetch a certain Mitradates, one of the herdsmen of Astyages, whose pasturages he knew to be the fittest for his purpose, lying as they did among mountains infested with wild beasts. This man was married to one of the king's female slaves, whose Median name was Spaco, which is in Greek Cyno [dog], since in the Median tongue the word "Spaca" means a bitch. The mountains, on the skirts of which his cattle grazed, lie to the north of Agbatana, towards the Euxine. That part of Media which borders on the Saspirians is an elevated tract, very mountainous, and covered with forests, while the rest of the Median territory is entirely level ground. On the arrival of the herdsman, who came at the hasty summons, Harpagus said to him: "Astyages requires thee to take this child and lay him in the wildest part of the hills, where he will be sure to die speedily. And he bade me tell thee, that if thou dost not kill the boy, but anyhow allowest him to escape, he will put thee to the most painful of deaths. I myself am appointed to see the child exposed."

111. The herdsman on hearing this took the child in his arms and went back the way that he had come till he reached the folds. There, providentially, his wife, who had been expecting daily to be put to bed, had just, during the absence of her husband, been delivered of a child. Both the herdsman and his wife were uneasy on each other's account, the former fearful because his wife was so near her time, the woman alarmed because it was a new thing for her husband to be sent for by Harpagus. When therefore he came into the house upon his return, his wife, seeing him arrive so unexpectedly, was the first to speak and begged to know why Harpagus had sent for him in such a hurry. "Wife," said he, "when I got to the town, I saw and heard such things as I would to heaven that I had never seen such things as I would to heaven had never happened to our masters. Everyone was weeping in Harpagus' house. It quite frightened me, but I went in. The moment I stepped inside, what should I see but a baby lying on the floor, panting

and whimpering, and all covered with gold, and wrapped in clothes of such beautiful colors. Harpagus saw me and directly ordered me to take the child in my arms and to carry him off. And what was I to do with him, think you? Why, to lay him in the mountains, where the wild beasts are most plentiful. And he told me that it was the king himself who ordered it to be done; and he threatened me with such dreadful things if I failed. So, I took the child up in my arms and carried him along. I thought that it might be the son of one of the household slaves. I did wonder certainly to see the gold and the beautiful baby-clothes, and I could not think why there was such a weeping in Harpagus' house. Well, very soon, as I came along, I got at the truth. They sent a servant with me to show me the way out of the town and to leave the baby in my hands; and he told me that the child's mother is the king's daughter Mandane, and his father Cambyses, the son of Cyrus; and that the king orders him to be killed; and look, here the child is."

112. With this the herdsman uncovered the infant and showed him to his wife, who, when she saw him and observed how fine a child and how beautiful he was, burst into tears, and clinging to the knees of her husband, besought him on no account to expose the babe; to which he answered that it was not possible for him to do otherwise, as Harpagus would be sure to send persons to see and report to him, and he was to suffer a most cruel death if he disobeyed. Failing thus in her first attempt to persuade her husband, the woman spoke a second time, saying, "If then there is no persuading thee, and a child must needs be seen exposed upon the mountains, at least do thus. The child of which I have just been delivered is stillborn; take it, and lay it on the hills; and let us bring up as our own the child of the daughter of Astyages. So shalt thou not be charged with unfaithfulness to thy lord, nor shall we have managed badly for ourselves. Our dead babe will have a royal funeral, and this living child will not be deprived of life."

113. It seemed to the herdsman that this advice was the best under the circumstances. He therefore followed it without loss of time. The child which he had intended to put to death he gave over to his wife, and his own dead child he put in the cradle wherein he had carried

the other, clothing it first in all the other's costly attire; and taking it in his arms, he laid it in the wildest place of all the mountain-range. When the child had been three days exposed, leaving one of his helpers to watch the body, he started off for the city; and going straight to Harpagus' house, he declared himself ready to show the corpse of the boy. Harpagus sent certain of his bodyguard, on whom he had the firmest reliance, to view the body for him; and satisfied with their seeing it, he gave orders for the funeral. Thus was the herdsman's child buried; and the other child, who was afterwards known by the name of Cyrus, was taken by the herdsman's wife and brought up under a different name.

114. When the boy was in his tenth year, an accident, which I will now relate, caused it to be discovered who he was. He was at play one day in the village where the folds of the cattle were, along with the boys of his own age, in the street. The other boys who were playing with him chose the cowherd's son, as he was called, to be their king. He then proceeded to order them about. Some he set to build him houses, others he made his guards, one of them was to be the king's eye [the king's traveling inspector], another had the office of carrying his messages; all had some task or other. Among the boys there was one, the son of Artembares, a Mede of distinction, who refused to do what Cyrus had set him. Cyrus told the other boys to take him into custody; and when his orders were obeyed, he chastised him most severely with the whip. The son of Artembares, as soon as he was let go, full of rage at treatment so little befitting his rank, hastened to the city and complained bitterly to his father of what had been done to him by Cyrus. He did not, of course, say "Cyrus," by which name the boy was not yet known, but called him the son of the king's cowherd. Artembares, in the heat of his passion, went to Astyages, accompanied by his son, and made complaint of the gross injury that had been done him. Pointing to the boy's shoulders, he exclaimed, "Thus, oh! king, has thy slave, the son of a cowherd, heaped insult upon us."

115. At this sight and these words Astyages, wishing to avenge the son of Artembares for his father's sake, sent for the cowherd and his boy. When they came together into his presence, fixing his eyes on Cyrus,

Astyages said, "Hast thou then, the son of so mean a fellow as that, dared to behave thus rudely to the son of yonder noble, one of the first in my court?" "My lord," replied the boy, "I only treated him as he deserved. I was chosen king in play by the boys of our village, because they thought me the best for it. He himself was one of the boys who chose me. All the others did according to my orders; but he refused and made light of them, until at last he got his due reward. If for this I deserve to suffer punishment, here I am ready to submit to it."

116. While the boy was yet speaking, Astyages was struck with a suspicion who he was. He thought that he saw something in the character of his face like his own; and there was a nobleness about the answer that he had made; besides which, his age seemed to tally with the time when his grandchild was exposed. Astonished at all this, Astyages could not speak for a while. At last, recovering himself with difficulty, and wishing to be quit of Artembares, so that he might examine the herdsman alone, he said to the former, "I promise thee, Artembares, so to settle this business that neither thou nor thy son shall have any cause to complain." Artembares retired from his presence; and the attendants, at the bidding of the king, led Cyrus into an inner apartment. Astyages then, being left alone with the herdsman, inquired of him where he had got the boy, and who had given him to him; to which he made answer that the lad was his own child, begotten by himself, and that the mother who bore him was still alive with him in his house. Astyages remarked that he was very ill-advised to bring himself into such great trouble, and at the same time he signed to his bodyguard to lay hold of him. Then the herdsman, as they were dragging him to the rack, began at the beginning and told the whole story exactly as it happened, without concealing anything, ending with entreaties and prayers to the king to grant him forgiveness.

117. Astyages, having got the truth of the matter from the herdsman, was very little further concerned about him, but with Harpagus he was exceedingly enraged. The guards were bidden to summon him into the presence; and on his appearance Astyages asked him, "By what death was it, Harpagus, that thou slewest the child of my daughter

whom I gave into thy hands?" Harpagus, seeing the cowherd in the room, did not betake himself to lies, lest he should be confuted and proved false, but he replied as follows: "Sire, when thou gavest the child into my hands, I instantly considered with myself how I could contrive to execute thy wishes, and yet, while guiltless of any unfaithfulness towards thee, avoid imbruing my hands in blood which was in truth thy daughter's and thine own. And this was how I contrived it. I sent for this cowherd and gave the child over to him, telling him that by the king's orders it was to be put to death. And in this I told no lie: for thou hadst so commanded. Moreover, when I gave him the child, I enjoined him to lay it somewhere in the wilds of the mountains and to stay near and to watch till it was dead; and I threatened him with all manner of punishment if he failed. Afterwards, when he had done according to all that I commanded him, and the child had died, I sent some of the most trustworthy of my eunuchs, who viewed the body for me, and then I had the child buried. This, sire, is the simple truth, and this is the death by which the child died."

118. Thus Harpagus related the whole story in a plain, straightforward way; upon which Astyages, letting no sign escape him of the anger that he felt, began by repeating to him all that he had just heard from the cowherd; and then he concluded with saying, "So the boy is alive, and it is best as it is: for the child's fate was a great sorrow to me, and the reproaches of my daughter went to my heart. Truly fortune has played us a good turn in this. Go thou home then, and send thy son to be with the new comer; and tonight, as I mean to sacrifice thank-offerings for the child's safety to the gods to whom such honor is due, I look to have thee a guest at the banquet."

119. Harpagus, on hearing this, made obeisance and went home, rejoicing to find that his disobedience had turned out so fortunately, and that instead of being punished, he was invited to a banquet given in honor of the happy occasion. The moment he reached home, he called for his son, a youth of about thirteen, the only child of his parents; and he bade him go to the palace and to do whatever Astyages should direct. Then, in the gladness of his heart, he went to his wife and told her all that had happened. Astyages, meanwhile, took the son of

Harpagus and slew him, after which he cut him in pieces and roasted some portions before the fire, and boiled others; and when all were duly prepared, he kept them ready for use. The hour for the banquet came, and Harpagus appeared, and with him the other guests; and all sat down to the feast. Astyages and the rest of the guests had joints of meat served up to them; but on the table of Harpagus nothing was placed except the flesh of his own son. This was all put before him, except the hands, feet, and head, which were laid by themselves in a covered basket. When Harpagus seemed to have eaten his fill, Astyages called out to him to know how he had enjoyed the repast. On his reply that he had enjoyed it excessively, they whose business it was brought him the basket, in which were the hands, feet, and head of his son; and they bade him open it and take out what he pleased. Harpagus accordingly uncovered the basket and saw within it the remains of his son. The sight, however, did not scare him or rob him of his self-possession. Being asked by Astyages if he knew what beast's flesh it was that he had been eating, he answered that he knew very well, and that whatever the king did was agreeable. After this reply, he took with him such morsels of the flesh as were uneaten, and he went home, intending, as I conceive, to collect the remains and bury them.

120. Such was the mode in which Astyages punished Harpagus. Afterwards, proceeding to consider what he should do with Cyrus, his grandchild, he sent for the Magi, who formerly interpreted his dream in the way which alarmed him so much; and he asked them how they had expounded it. They answered, without varying from what they had said before, that "the boy must needs be a king if he grew up and did not die too soon." Then Astyages addressed them thus: "The boy has escaped and lives; he has been brought up in the country, and the lads of the village where he lives have made him their king. All that kings commonly do he has done. He has had his guards, his door-keepers, his messengers, and all the other usual officers. Tell me, then, to what, think you, does all this tend?" The Magi answered, "If the boy survives and has ruled as a king without any craft or contrivance, in that case we bid thee cheer up and feel no more alarm

on his account. He will not reign a second time: for we have found even oracles sometimes fulfilled in an unimportant way; and dreams, still oftener, have wondrously mean accomplishments." "It is what I myself most incline to think," Astyages rejoined; "the boy having been already king, the dream is out, and I have nothing more to fear from him. Nevertheless, take good heed, and counsel me the best you can for the safety of my house and your own interests." "Truly," said the Magi in reply, "it very much concerns our interests that thy kingdom be firmly established; for if it went to this boy, it would pass into foreign hands, since he is a Persian: and then we Medes should lose our freedom and be quite despised by the Persians as being foreigners. But so long as thou, our fellow countryman, art on the throne, all manner of honors are ours, and we are even not without some share in the government. Much reason therefore have we to forecast well for thee and for thy sovereignty. If then we saw any cause for present fear, be sure that we would not keep it back from thee. But truly we are persuaded that the dream has had its accomplishment in this harmless way; and so our own fears being at rest, we recommend thee to banish thine. As for the boy, our advice is that thou send him away to Persia, to his father and mother."

121. Astyages heard their answer with pleasure; and calling Cyrus into his presence, he said to him, "My child, I was led to do thee a wrong by a dream that has come to nothing. From that wrong thou wert saved by thy own good fortune. Go now with a light heart to Persia; I will provide thy escort. Go; and when thou gettest to thy journey's end, thou wilt behold thy father and thy mother, quite other people from Mitradates the cowherd and his wife."

122. With these words Astyages dismissed his grandchild. On his arrival at the house of Cambyses, he was received by his parents, who, when they learned who he was, embraced him heartily, having always been convinced that he died almost as soon as he was born. So, they asked him by what means he had chanced to escape; and he told them how that till lately he had known nothing at all about the matter, but had been mistaken—oh! so widely!—and how he had learned his history by the way, as he came from Media. He had been quite sure that he

was the son of the king's cowherd, but on the road the king's escort had told him all the truth; and then he spoke of the cowherd's wife who had brought him up, and he filled his whole talk with her praises; in all that he had to tell them about himself, it was always Cyno— Cyno was everything. So it happened that his parents, catching the name at his mouth, and wishing to persuade the Persians that there was a special providence in his preservation, spread the report that Cyrus, when he was exposed, was suckled by a bitch. This was the sole origin of the rumor.

123. Afterwards, when Cyrus grew to manhood and became known as the bravest and most popular of all his compeers, Harpagus, who was bent on revenging himself upon Astyages, began to pay him court by gifts and messages. His own rank was too humble for him to hope to obtain vengeance without some foreign help. When therefore he saw Cyrus, whose wrongs were so similar to his own, growing up expressly (as it were) to be the avenger whom he needed, he set to work to procure his support and aid in the matter. He had already paved the way for his designs by persuading, severally, the great Median nobles, whom the harsh rule of their monarch had offended, that the best plan would be to put Cyrus at their head and dethrone Astyages. These preparations made, Harpagus, being now ready for revolt, was anxious to make known his wishes to Cyrus, who still lived in Persia; but as the roads between Media and Persia were guarded, he had to contrive a means of sending word secretly, which he did in the following way. He took a hare; and cutting open its belly without hurting the fur, he slipped in a letter containing what he wanted to say; and then carefully sewing up the paunch, he gave the hare to one of his most faithful slaves, disguising him as a hunter with nets; and he sent him off to Persia to take the game as a present to Cyrus, bidding him tell Cyrus, by word of mouth, to paunch the animal himself and to let no one be present at the time.

124. All was done as he wished; and Cyrus, on cutting the hare open, found the letter inside and read as follows: "Son of Cambyses, the gods assuredly watch over thee, or never wouldst thou have passed through thy many wonderful adventures. Now is the time when thou

mayst avenge thyself upon Astyages, thy murderer. He willed thy death, remember; to the gods and to me thou owest that thou art still alive. I think that thou art not ignorant of what he did to thee, nor of what I suffered at his hands, because I committed thee to the cowherd and did not put thee to death. Listen now to me, and obey my words; and all the empire of Astyages shall be thine. Raise the standard of revolt in Persia, and then march straight on Media. Whether Astyages appoint me to command his forces against thee, or whether he appoint any other of the princes of the Medes, all will go as thou couldst wish. They will be the first to fall away from him; and joining thy side, they will exert themselves to overturn his power. Be sure that on our part all is ready; wherefore do thou thy part, and that speedily."

125. Cyrus, on receiving the tidings contained in this letter, set himself to consider how he might best persuade the Persians to revolt. After much thought, he hit on the following as the most expedient course: he wrote what he thought proper upon a roll; and then calling an assembly of the Persians, he unfolded the roll and read out of it that Astyages appointed him their general. "And now," said he, "since it is so, I command you to go and bring each man his reaping-hook." With these words he dismissed the assembly. Now the Persian nation is made up of many tribes. Those which Cyrus assembled and persuaded to revolt from the Medes were the principal ones on which all the others are dependent. These are the Pasargadae, the Maraphians, and the Maspians, of whom the Pasargadae are the noblest. The Achaemenidae, from which spring all the Perseid kings, is one of their clans. The rest of the Persian tribes are the following: the Panthialaeans, the Derusiaeans, the Germanians, who are engaged in husbandry; the Daans, the Mardians, the Dropicans, and the Sagartians, who are nomads.

126. When, in obedience to the orders which they had received, the Persians came with their reaping-hooks, Cyrus led them to a tract of ground, about eighteen or twenty furlongs each way, covered with thorns; and he ordered them to clear it before the day was out. They accomplished their task; upon which he issued a second order to them: to take the bath the day following, and again to come to him. Meanwhile,

he collected together all his father's flocks, both sheep and goats, and all his oxen; and he slaughtered them and made ready to give an entertainment to the entire Persian army. Wine, too, and bread of the choicest kinds were prepared for the occasion. When the morrow came, and the Persians appeared, he bade them recline upon the grass and to enjoy themselves. After the feast was over, he requested them to tell him "which they liked best, today's work, or yesterday's?" They answered that "the contrast was indeed strong: yesterday brought them nothing but what was bad, today everything that was good." Cyrus instantly seized on their reply and laid bare his purpose in these words: "Ye men of Persia, thus do matters stand with you. If you choose to hearken to my words, you may enjoy these and ten thousand similar delights and never condescend to any slavish toil; but if you will not hearken, prepare yourselves for unnumbered toils as hard as yesterday's. Now therefore follow my bidding, and be free. For myself I feel that I am destined by Providence to undertake your liberation; and you, I am sure, are no whit inferior to the Medes in anything, least of all in bravery. Revolt, therefore, from Astyages without a moment's delay."

127. The Persians, who had long been impatient of the Median dominion, now that they had found a leader, were delighted to shake off the yoke. Meanwhile, Astyages, informed of the doings of Cyrus, sent a messenger to summon him to his presence. Cyrus replied, "Tell Astyages that I shall appear in his presence sooner than he will like." Astyages, when he received this message, instantly armed all his subjects; and as if God had deprived him of his senses, he appointed Harpagus to be their general, forgetting how greatly he had injured him. So, when the two armies met and engaged, only a few of the Medes, who were not in the secret, fought; others deserted openly to the Persians, while the greater number counterfeited fear and fled.

128. Astyages, on learning the shameful flight and dispersion of his army, broke out into threats against Cyrus, saying, "Cyrus shall nevertheless have no reason to rejoice;" and directly he seized the Magian interpreters who had persuaded him to allow Cyrus to escape; and he impaled them; after which, he armed all the Medes who had remained

in the city, both young and old; and leading them against the Persians, he fought a battle, in which he was utterly defeated, his army being destroyed, and he himself falling into the enemy's hands.

READING 23
PERSIAN RELIGIOUS TOLERATION

Despite the fact that the Persians, more or less, employed the same ruthless techniques of conquest and exploitation as did their imperial predecessors, the Assyrians and Babylonians, they tended to be more tolerant of the cultural and religious traditions of their diverse subjects. Indeed, one of Cyrus' first acts after taking control of Babylon in 539 B.C. was to allow the Jews in captivity there since Nebuchadnezzar's destruction of Jerusalem in 586 B.C. to return home; and the Jews henceforth were allowed to develop and follow the evolving precepts of Judaism peacefully during the two centuries of the Persian Empire's existence. The following two inscriptions testify to this general Persian policy of religious toleration toward their subjects.

A. The Egyptian Goddess Neith
The following is a translation of an Egyptian hieroglyphic inscription carved on the base of a statue to honor Udjahorresne, who served as a naval officer during the last years of Egypt's 26th dynasty of Sais and continued to serve the Persian King Cambyses after his conquest of Egypt in 525 B.C.

(Taken from pp. 37-38 of Volume III of Ancient Egyptian Literature, The Late Period, by Miriam Lichtheim, U. of California Press, Berkeley, copyright 1980, reprinted with the permission of the publisher)

The one honored by Neith-the-Great, the mother of god, and by the gods of Sais, the prince, count, royal seal-bearer, sole companion, true beloved King's friend, the scribe, inspector of council scribes, chief scribe of the great outer hall, administrator of the palace, commander of the royal navy under the King of Upper and Lower Egypt, ... Udjahorresne; engendered by the administrator of the castles of the red crown [of Lower Egypt], ... priest of the Horus Eye, prophet of Neith who presides over the nome of Sais; he says: "The Great Chief of all foreign lands, Cambyses came to Egypt, and the foreign peoples of every foreign land were with him. When he had conquered this land in its entirety, they established themselves in it, and he was Great Ruler of Egypt and Great Chief of all foreign lands." His majesty assigned to me the office of chief physician. He made me live at his side as companion and administrator of the palace. I let his majesty know the greatness of Sais, that it is the seat of Neith-the-Great, the mother who bore Re and inaugurated birth when birth had not yet been; and the nature of the greatness of the temple of Neith, that it is heaven in its every aspect; and the nature of the greatness of the castles of Neith, and of all the gods and goddesses who are there; and the nature of the greatness of the Palace, that it is the seat of the Sovereign, the Lord of Heaven; and the nature of the greatness of the Resenet and Mehenet sanctuaries; and of the House of Re and the House of Atum, the mystery of all the gods.

The one honored by his city-god and all the gods, the prince, count, royal seal-bearer, sole companion, true beloved King's friend, the chief physician, Udjahorresne, born of Atemirdis, he says: "I made a petition to the majesty of the King of Upper and Lower Egypt, Cambyses, about all the foreigners who dwelled in the temple of Neith, in order to have them expelled from it, so as to let the temple of Neith be in all its splendor, as it had been before. His majesty commanded to expel all the foreigners who dwelled in the temple of Neith, to demolish all their houses and all their unclean things that were in this temple. When they had carried all their personal belongings outside the wall of the temple, his majesty commanded to cleanse the temple of Neith and to return all its personnel to it and the hour-priests of the temple. His majesty commanded to give divine offerings to Neith-the-Great, the mother of god, and to the great gods of Sais, as it had been before. His majesty commanded to perform all their festivals and all their processions, as had been done before.

His majesty did this because I had let his majesty know the greatness of Sais, that it is the city of all the gods, who dwell there on their seats forever."

The one honored by the gods of Sais, the chief physician, Udjahorresne, he says: "The King of Upper and Lower Egypt, Cambyses, came to Sais. His majesty went in person to the temple of Neith. He made a great prostration before her majesty, as every king has done. He made a great offering of every good thing to Neith-the-Great, the mother of god, and to the great gods who are in Sais, as every beneficent king has done. His majesty did this because I had let his majesty know the greatness of her majesty Neith, that she is the mother of Re himself."

B. The Cult of Apollo at Magnesia

The following is a translation of a Greek inscription from the Greek city of Magnesia located on the Meander River in western Anatolia. This Greek text was in turn a Greek translation of an order issued by Darius I the Great (ruled 521-486 B.C.) to his governor of the district concerning the tax-exempt status of a local temple of Apollo.

> (Taken from p. 67 of Greek Historical Documents, The Fifth Century B.C., by Naphtali Lewis, published by A. M. Hakkert, Toronto, copyright 1971, reprinted with the permission of the publisher)

The king of kings, Darius, son of Hystaspes, to his slave Gadatas speaks thus: I hear that you are not carrying out my instructions in all respects: that you are cultivating my land by planting fruits from the other side of the Euphrates in the region of Lower Asia. This decision of yours I praise, and for this reason great favor will continue to exist for you in the house of the king. But that you are ignoring my instruction about the gods I shall give you, if you do not change, proof of my annoyance, because you have demanded a tax from the sacred gardeners of Apollo and ordered them to cultivate unconsecrated land, misunderstanding the intention of my ancestors towards the god, who announced the precise truth.

READING 24
DARIUS' BUILDING
OF THE PALACE AT SUSA

The following text, translated from Old Persian, describes how King Darius I the Great (ruled 521-486 B.C.) recorded the construction of the royal palace at Susa that henceforth served as the winter residence of the Persian kings. The great variety of rare materials used in the building and the diverse peoples employed as workers on the project clearly testify to the vast resources available to the Persian king for creating a royal palace of magnificent splendor; and it illustrates indirectly the way in which the three great empires of the ancient Near East (Assyrian, Babylonian, and Persian) succeeded in exploiting the human and material resources available throughout their domains.

> (Taken from p. 144 of Old Persian: Grammar, Texts, Lexicon, by R. G. Kent, published by the Yale U. Press on behalf of the American Schools of Oriental Research, copyright 1953, reprinted with the permission of the American Schools of Oriental Research, and available through Jstor)

This palace, which I built at Susa, from afar its ornamentation was brought. Downward the earth was dug, until I reached rock in the earth. When the excavation had been made, then rubble was packed down, some 40 cubits in depth, another (part) 20 cubits in depth. On that rubble the palace was constructed.

That earth was dug downward, and that the rubble was packed down, and that the sun-dried brick was moulded, the Babylonian people—it did (these tasks).

The cedar timber, this—a mountain by name Lebanon—from there was brought. The Assyrian people, it brought it to Babylon; from Babylon the Carians and the Ionians brought it to Susa. The yakatimber (type of wood) was brought from Gandara (Kabul region) and from Carmania (Kirman). The gold was brought from Sardis and from Bactria, which here was worked. The precious stone lapis-lazuli and carnelian which was worked here, this was brought from Sogdiana (Uzbekistan/Tadjlklstan). The precious stone turquoise, this was brought from Chorasmia (lower Oxus), which was worked here.

The silver and the ebony were brought from Egypt. The ornamentation with which the wall was adorned, that from Ionia was brought. The ivory which was worked here, was brought from Kush (Nubia), and from India and from Arachosia (Kandahar region).

The stone columns which were worked here, a village by name Abiradu, in Elam—from there were brought. The stone-cutters who worked the stone, those were Ionians and Sardians.

The goldsmiths who worked the gold, those were Medes and Egyptians. The men who worked the wood, those were Sardians and Egyptians. The men who worked the baked brick, those were Babylonians. The men who adorned the wall, those were Medes and Egyptians.

Says Darius the King: At Susa a very excellent (work) was ordered, a very excellent (work) was (brought to completion). Me may Ahuramazda protect, and Hystaspes my father, and my country.

PART IV
THE GREEK ARCHAIC PERIOD

READING 25
HOMERIC SOCIETY

Not long after the Greeks of the early Archaic Period relearned the art of writing from the Phoenicians and adapted their consonantal script into the Greek alphabet, the rich oral tradition of storytelling that had flourished during the Greek Dark age found expression in writing in the form of the majestic epics of The Iliad and The Odyssey. Besides being magnificent works of literature, these poems serve as important sources of information about the basic characteristics of Greek society at the dawn of the Archaic Period. The following two excerpts from The Iliad portray the Greek army before Troy as an embryonic Greek city-state with its typical three-fold form of government: elected officials serving as an executive authority, a group of nobles serving as an important deliberative body, and the adult male citizenry organized into a general assembly. In The Iliad Agamemnon, the king of Mycenae, is the chief executive, who surrounds himself with the kings of the other Greek kingdoms; and these kings serve as his advisory council; and the ordinary Greek warriors form a primitive assembly that expresses its will by shouting assent or disapproval. Moreover, Odysseus' polite treatment of his royal peers vs. his harsh punishment of the ordinary soldier Thersites exhibit the hierarchical nature of early Greek society.

A. The Quarrel Between Agamemnon and Achilles

(Taken from Book I of The Iliad of Homer, translated by Samuel Butler, published by Longman, Green, London and New York 1898, revised by Gary Forsythe)

Sing, O goddess, the anger of Achilles son of Peleus, that brought countless ills upon the Achaeans. Many a brave soul did it send hurrying down to Hades, and many a hero did it yield a prey to dogs and vultures: for so were the counsels of Zeus fulfilled from the day on which the son of Atreus, king of men, and great Achilles first fell out with one another.

And which of the gods was it that set them on to quarrel? It was the son of Zeus and Leto; for he was angry with the king and sent a pestilence upon the host to plague the people, because the son of Atreus had dishonored Chryses his priest. Now Chryses had come to the ships of the Achaeans to free his daughter and had brought with him a great ransom: moreover, he bore in his hand the scepter of Apollo wreathed with a suppliant's wreath, and he besought the Achaeans, but most of all the two sons of Atreus [Agamemnon and Menelaus], who were their chiefs.

"Sons of Atreus," he cried, "and all other Achaeans, may the gods who dwell in Olympus grant you to sack the city of Priam and to reach your homes in safety; but free my daughter, and accept a ransom for her in reverence to Apollo, son of Zeus."

On this the rest of the Achaeans with one voice were for respecting the priest and taking the ransom that he offered; but not so Agamemnon, who spoke fiercely to him and sent him roughly away. "Old man," said he, "let me not find you tarrying about our ships, nor yet coming hereafter. Your scepter of the god and your wreath shall profit you nothing. I will not free her. She shall grow old in my house at Argos far from her own home, busying herself with her loom and visiting my couch; so go, and do not provoke me, or it shall be the worse for you."

The old man feared him and obeyed. Not a word he spoke, but went by the shore of the sounding sea and prayed apart to King Apollo whom lovely Leto had borne. "Hear me," he cried, "O god of the silver bow, that protectest Chryse and holy Cilla and rulest Tenedos with thy might; hear me, oh thou of Sminthe. If I have ever decked your temple with garlands or burned your thigh bones in fat of bulls or goats, grant my prayer, and let your arrows avenge these my tears upon the Danaans."

Thus did he pray, and Apollo heard his prayer. He came down furious from the summits of Olympus with his bow and his quiver upon his shoulder, and the arrows rattled on his back with the rage that trembled within him. He sat himself down away from the ships with a face as dark as night, and his silver bow rang death as he shot his arrow in the midst of them. First he smote their mules and their hounds, but presently he aimed his shafts at the people themselves; and all day long the pyres of the dead were burning.

For nine whole days he shot his arrows among the people, but upon the tenth day Achilles called them in assembly, moved thereto by Hera, who saw the Achaeans in their death throes and had compassion upon them. Then, when they were got together, he arose and spoke among them.

"Son of Atreus," said he, "I deem that we should now turn roving home if we would escape destruction: for we are being cut down by war and pestilence at once. Let us ask some priest or prophet, or some reader of dreams (for dreams, too, are of Zeus) who can tell us why Phoebus Apollo is so angry, and say whether it is for some vow that we have broken, or hecatomb that we have not offered, and whether he will accept the savor of lambs and goats without blemish, so as to take away the plague from us."

With these words he sat down; and Calchas son of Thestor, wisest of augurs, who knew things past, present, and to come, arose to speak. He it was who had guided the Achaeans with their fleet to Ilios through the prophesyings with which Phoebus Apollo had inspired him. With all sincerity and goodwill he addressed them thus:

"Achilles, loved of heaven, you bid me tell you about the anger of King Apollo. I will therefore do so; but consider first, and swear that you will stand by me heartily in word and deed: for I know that I shall offend one who rules the Argives with might, to whom all the Achaeans are in subjection. A plain man cannot stand against the anger of a king, who if he swallow his displeasure now, will yet nurse revenge till he has wreaked it. Consider, therefore, whether or no you will protect me."

And Achilles answered, "Fear not, but speak as it is borne in upon you from heaven: for by Apollo, Calchas, to whom you pray, and whose oracles you reveal to us, not a Danaan at our ships shall lay his hand upon you, while I yet live to look upon the face of the earth. No, not though you name Agamemnon himself, who is by far the foremost of the Achaeans."

Thereon the seer spoke boldly. "The god," he said, "is angry neither about vow nor hecatomb, but for his priest's sake, whom Agamemnon has dishonored in that he would not free his daughter nor take a ransom for her; therefore has he sent these evils upon us and will yet send others. He will not deliver the Danaans from this pestilence till Agamemnon has restored the girl without fee or ransom to her father and has sent a holy hecatomb to Chryse. Thus we may perhaps appease him."

With these words he sat down, and Agamemnon arose in anger. His heart was black with rage, and his eyes flashed fire as he scowled on Calchas and said, "Seer of evil, you never yet prophesied smooth things concerning me, but have ever loved to foretell that which was evil. You have brought me neither comfort nor performance; and now you come seeing among Danaans, and saying that Apollo has plagued us, because I would not take a ransom for this girl, the daughter of Chryses. I have set my heart on keeping her in my own house: for I love her better even than my own wife Clytemnestra, whose peer she is alike in form and feature, in understanding and accomplishments. Still, I will give her up if I must: for I would have the people live, not die; but you must find me a prize instead, or I alone among the Argives shall be without one. This is not well; for you behold, all of you, that my prize is to go elsewhither."

And Achilles answered, "Most noble son of Atreus, covetous beyond all mankind, how shall the Achaeans find you another prize? We have no common store from which to take one. Those whom we took from the cities have been awarded; we cannot disallow the awards that have been made already. Give this girl, therefore, to the god; and if ever Zeus grants us to sack the city of Troy, we will requite you three and fourfold."

Then Agamemnon said, "Achilles, valiant though you be, you shall not thus outwit me. You shall not overreach, and you shall not persuade me. Are you to keep your own prize, while I sit tamely under my loss and give up the girl at your bidding? Let the Achaeans find me a prize in fair exchange to my liking, or I will come and take your own, or that of Ajax or of Odysseus; and he to whomsoever I may come shall rue my coming. But of this we will take thought hereafter; for the present, let us draw a ship into the sea and find a crew for her expressly; let us put a hecatomb on board, and let us send Chryseis also; further, let some chief man among us be in command: either Ajax, or Idomeneus, or yourself, son of Peleus, mighty warrior that you are, that we may offer sacrifice and appease the anger of the god."

Achilles scowled at him and answered, "You are steeped in insolence and lust of gain. With what heart can any of the Achaeans do your bidding, either on foray or in open fighting? I came not warring here for any ill that the Trojans had done me. I have no quarrel with them. They have not raided my cattle nor my horses, nor cut down my harvests on the rich plains of Phthia; for between me and them there is a great space, both mountain and sounding sea. We have followed you, Sir Insolence, for your pleasure, not ours, to gain satisfaction from the Trojans for your shameless self and for Menelaus. You forget this and threaten to rob me of the prize for which I have toiled, and which the sons of the Achaeans have given me. Never when the Achaeans sack any rich city of the Trojans do I receive so good a prize as you do, though it is my hands that do the better part of the fighting. When the sharing comes, your share is far the largest; and I, forsooth, must go back to my ships, take what I can get, and be thankful, when my labor of fighting is done. Now, therefore, I shall go back to Phthia; it will be much better for me to return home with my ships: for I will not stay here dishonored to gather gold and substance for you."

And Agamemnon answered, "Fly if you will. I shall make you no prayers to stay you. I have others here who will do me honor, and above all Zeus, the lord of counsel. There is no king here so hateful to me as you are: for you are ever quarrelsome and ill affected. What though you be brave? Was it not heaven that made you so? Go home, then, with your ships and comrades to lord it over the Myrmidons. I care neither for you nor for your anger; and thus will I do: since Phoebus Apollo is taking Chryseis from me, I shall send her with my ship and my followers, but I shall come to your tent and take your own prize Briseis, that you may learn how much stronger I am than you are, and that another may fear to set himself up as equal or comparable with me."

The son of Peleus was furious, and his heart within his shaggy breast was divided whether to draw his sword, push the others aside, and kill the son of Atreus, or to restrain himself and check his anger. While he was thus in two minds and was drawing his mighty sword from its scabbard, Athena came down from heaven (for Hera had sent her in the love that she bore to them both) and seized the son of Peleus by his yellow hair, visible to him alone: for of the others no man could see her. Achilles turned in amaze, and by the fire that flashed from her eyes at once he knew that she was Athena. "Why are you here," said he, "daughter of aegis-bearing Zeus? To see the pride of Agamemnon, son of Atreus? Let me tell you, and it shall surely be. He shall pay for this insolence with his life."

And Athena said, "I come from heaven, if you will hear me, to bid you to stay your anger. Hera has sent me, who cares for both of you alike. Cease, then, this brawling, and do not draw your sword; rail at him if you will, and your railing will not be vain: for I tell you, and it shall surely be that you shall hereafter receive gifts three times as splendid by reason of this present insult. Hold, therefore, and obey."

"Goddess," answered Achilles, "however angry a man may be, he must do as you two command him. This will be best: for the gods ever hear the prayers of him who has obeyed them."

He stayed his hand on the silver hilt of his sword and thrust it back into the scabbard as Athena bade him. Then she went back to Olympus among the other gods and to the house of aegis-bearing Zeus.

But the son of Peleus again began railing at the son of Atreus: for he was still in a rage. "Wine bibber," he cried, "with the face of a dog and the heart of a hind, you never dare to go out with the host in fight, nor yet with our chosen men in ambuscade. You shun this as you do death itself. You had rather go around and rob his prizes from any man who contradicts you. You devour your people: for you are king over a feeble folk; otherwise, son of Atreus, henceforward you would insult no man. Therefore I say and swear it with a great oath, nay, by this my scepter which shalt sprout neither leaf nor shoot, nor bud anew from the day on which it left its parent stem upon the mountains, because the axe stripped it of leaf and bark, and now the sons of the Achaeans bear it as judges and guardians of the decrees of heaven, so surely and solemnly do I swear that hereafter they shall look fondly for Achilles and shall not find him. In the day of your distress, when your men fall dying by the murderous hand of Hector, you shall not know how to help them and shall rend your heart with rage for the hour when you offered insult to the bravest of the Achaeans."

With this the son of Peleus dashed his gold-bestudded scepter on the ground and took his seat, while the son of Atreus was beginning fiercely from his place upon the other side. Then uprose smooth-tongued Nestor, the facile speaker of the Pylians, and the words fell from his lips sweeter than honey. Two generations of men born and bred in Pylos had passed away under his rule, and he was now reigning over the third. With all sincerity and goodwill, therefore, he addressed them thus:

"Of a truth," he said, "a great sorrow has befallen the Achaean land. Surely Priam with his sons would rejoice, and the Trojans be glad at heart if they could hear this quarrel between you two, who are so excellent in fight and counsel. I am older than either of you; therefore be guided by me. Moreover, I have been the familiar friend of men even greater than you are, and they did not disregard my counsels. Never again can I behold such men as Pirithous and Dryas shepherd of his people, or as Caeneus, Exadius, godlike Polyphemus, and Theseus son of Aegeus, peer of the immortals. These were the mightiest men ever born upon this earth: mightiest were they; and when they fought the fiercest tribes of mountain savages, they utterly overthrew them. I came from distant Pylos and went about among them: for they would have me come, and I fought as it was in me to do. Not a man now living could withstand them, but they heard my words and were persuaded by them. So be it also with yourselves: for this is the more excellent way. Therefore, Agamemnon, though you be strong, take not this girl away: for the sons of the Achaeans have already given her to Achilles; and you, Achilles, strive not further with the king: for no man who by the grace of Zeus wields a scepter has like honor with Agamemnon. You are strong and have a goddess for your mother; but Agamemnon is stronger than you: for he has more people under him. Son of Atreus, check your anger, I implore you; end this quarrel with Achilles, who in the day of battle is a tower of strength to the Achaeans."

And Agamemnon answered, "Sir, all that you have said is true, but this fellow must needs become our lord and master: he must be lord of all, king of all, and captain of all; and this shall hardly be. Granted that the gods have made him a great warrior, have they also given him the right to speak with railing?"

Achilles interrupted him. "I should be a mean coward," he cried, "were I to give in to you in all things. Order other people about, not me: for I shall obey no longer. Furthermore, I say, and lay my saying to your heart. I shall fight neither you nor any man about this girl: for those who take were those also that gave. But of all else that is at my ship you shall carry away nothing by force. Try, that others may see; if you do, my spear shall be reddened with your blood."

When they had quarrelled thus angrily, they arose and broke up the assembly at the ships of the Achaeans. The son of Peleus went back to his tents and ships with the son of Menoetius [Patroclus, Achilles' best friend] and his company, while Agamemnon drew a vessel into the water and chose a crew of twenty oarsmen. He escorted Chryseis on board and sent, moreover, a hecatomb for the god. And Odysseus went as captain.

B. Odysseus and Thersites

Following the quarrel between Achilles and Agamemnon, the former prays to his goddess-mother, the sea nymph Thetis; and when she comes to him, Achilles begs her to go to Olympus to ask Zeus to somehow intervene in the war so as to make the Greeks (and especially Agamemnon) to realize that they must have Achilles' involvement in the war in order to achieve victory, and that in order to persuade Achilles to reenter the war, Agamemnon must admit his error and repay Achilles with many gigts. Unknown to Achilles, however, Zeus' plan to force Agamemnon to do honor to Achilles eventually brings about the death of Achilles' dearest friend Patroclus. The following passage describes the very first step that Zeus takes in carrying out his complex plan.

(Taken from Book II of The Iliad of Homer, translated by Samuel Butler, published by Longman, Green, London and New York 1898, revised by Gary Forsythe)

Now the other gods and the armed warriors on the plain slept soundly, but Zeus was wakeful: for he was thinking how to do honor to Achilles and to destroy much people at the ships of the Achaeans. In the end he deemed that it would be best to send a lying dream to King Agamemnon. So, he called one to him and said to it, "Lying Dream, go to the ships of the Achaeans, into the tent of Agamemnon; and say to him word to word as I now bid you. Tell him to get the Achaeans instantly under arms: for he shall take Troy. There are no longer divided counsels among the gods; Hera has brought them to her own mind, and woe betides the Trojans."

The dream went when it had heard its message, and it soon reached the ships of the Achaeans. It sought Agamemnon son of Atreus and found him in his tent, wrapped in a profound slumber. It hovered over his head in the likeness of Nestor, son of Neleus, whom Agamemnon honored above all his councillors; and it said:

"You are sleeping, son of Atreus; one who has the welfare of his host and so much other care upon his shoulders should dock his sleep. Hear me at once: for I come as a messenger from Zeus, who, though he be not near, yet takes thought for you and pities you. He bids you get the Achaeans instantly under arms: for you shall take Troy. There are no longer divided counsels among the gods; Hera has brought them over to her own mind, and woe betides the Trojans at the hands of Zeus. Remember this; and when you wake, see that it does not escape you."

The dream then left him; and he thought of things that were surely not to be accomplished. He thought that on that same day he was to take the city of Priam, but he little knew what was in the mind of Zeus, who had many another hard fought fight in store alike for Danaans and Trojans. Then presently he awoke with the divine message still ringing in his ears; so, he sat upright and put on his soft shirt so fair and new, and over this his heavy cloak. He bound his sandals on to his comely feet and slung his silver-studded sword about his shoulders; then he took the imperishable staff of his father and sallied forth to the ships of the Achaeans.

The goddess Dawn now wended her way to vast Olympus that she might herald day to Zeus and to the other immortals, and Agamemnon sent the criers around to call the people in assembly; so they called them, and the people gathered thereon. But first, he summoned a meeting of the elders at the ship of Nestor, king of Pylos; and when they were assembled, he laid a cunning counsel before them.

"My friends," said he, "I have had a dream from heaven in the dead of night, and its face and figure resembled none but Nestor's. It hovered over my head and said, 'You are sleeping, son of Atreus; one who has the welfare of his host and so much other care upon his shoulders should dock his sleep. Hear me at once: for I am a messenger from Zeus, who, though he be not near, yet takes thought for you and pities you. He bids you get the Achaeans instantly under arms: for you shall take Troy. There are no longer divided counsels among the gods; Hera has brought them over to her own mind, and woe betides the Trojans at the hands of Zeus. Remember this'. The dream then vanished, and I awoke. Let us now, therefore, arm the sons of the Achaeans. But it will be well that I should first sound them, and to this end I will tell them to fly with their ships; but do you others go about among the host and prevent their doing so."

He then sat down, and Nestor the prince of Pylos with all sincerity and goodwill addressed them thus: "My friends," said he, "princes and councillors of the Argives, if any other man of the Achaeans had told us of this dream, we should have declared it false and would have had nothing to do with it. But he who has seen it is the foremost man among us; we must therefore set about getting the people under arms."

With this he led the way from the assembly, and the other sceptered kings arose with him in obedience to the word of Agamemnon; but the people pressed forward to hear. They swarmed like bees that sally from some hollow cave and flit in countless throng among the spring flowers, bunched in knots and clusters; even so did the mighty multitude pour from ships and tents to the assembly and range themselves upon the wide-watered shore, while among them ran Wildfire Rumor, messenger of Zeus, urging them ever to the fore. Thus they gathered in a pell-mell of mad confusion, and the earth groaned under the tramp of men as the people sought their places. Nine heralds went crying about among them to stay their tumult and bid them listen to the kings, till at last they were got into their several places and ceased their clamor. Then King Agamemnon arose, holding his scepter. This was the work of Hephaestus, who gave it to Zeus the son of Kronos. Zeus gave it to Hermes, slayer of Argus, guide and guardian. King Hermes gave it to Pelops, the mighty charioteer, and Pelops to Atreus, shepherd of his people. Atreus, when he died, left it to Thyestes, rich in flocks; and Thyestes in his turn left it to be borne by Agamemnon, that he might be lord of all Argos and of the isles. Leaning, then, on his scepter, he addressed the Argives.

"My friends," he said, "heroes, servants of Ares, the hand of heaven has been laid heavily upon me. Cruel Zeus gave me his solemn promise that I should sack the city of Priam before returning, but he has played me false and is now bidding me go ingloriously back to Argos with the loss of much people. Such is the will of Zeus, who has laid many a proud city in the dust, as he will yet lay others: for his power is above all. It will be a sorry tale hereafter that an Achaean host, at once so great and valiant, battled in vain against men fewer in number than themselves; but as yet the end is not in sight. Think that the Achaeans and Trojans have sworn to a solemn covenant, and that they have each been numbered: the Trojans by the roll of their householders, and we by companies of ten; think further that each of our companies desired to have a

Trojan householder to pour out their wine; we are so greatly more in number that full many a company would have to go without its cup bearer. But they have in the town allies from other places, and it is these that hinder me from being able to sack the rich city of Ilios. Nine of Zeus' years are gone; the timbers of our ships have rotted; their tackling is sound no longer. Our wives and little ones at home look anxiously for our coming, but the work that we came hither to do has not been done. Now, therefore, let us all do as I say: let us sail back to our own land: for we shall not take Troy."

With these words he moved the hearts of the multitude, so many of them as knew not the cunning counsel of Agamemnon. They surged to and fro like the waves of the Icarian Sea, when the east and south winds break from heaven's clouds to lash them; or as when the west wind sweeps over a field of grain, and the ears bow beneath the blast. Even so were they swayed as they flew with loud cries towards the ships, and the dust from under their feet rose heavenward. They cheered each other on to draw the ships into the sea; they cleared the channels in front of them; they began taking away the stays from underneath them, and the sky rang with their glad cries, so eager were they to return.

Then surely the Argives would have returned after a fashion that was not fated. But Hera said to Athena, "Alas, daughter of aegis-bearing Zeus, unweariable, shall the Argives fly home to their own land over the broad sea and leave Priam and the Trojans the glory of still keeping Helen, for whose sake so many of the Achaeans have died at Troy, far from their homes? Go about at once among the host, and speak fairly to them, man by man, that they draw not their ships into the sea."

Athena was not slack to do her bidding. Down she darted from the topmost summits of Olympus, and in a moment she was at the ships of the Achaeans. There she found Odysseus, peer of Zeus in counsel, standing alone. He had not as yet laid a hand upon his ship: for he was grieved and sorry; so she went close up to him and said, "Odysseus, noble son of Laertes, are you going to fling yourselves into your ships and be off home to your own land in this way? Will you leave Priam and the Trojans the glory of still keeping Helen, for whose sake so many of the Achaeans have died at Troy, far from their homes? Go about at once among the host, and speak fairly to them, man by man, that they draw not their ships into the sea."

Odysseus knew the voice as that of the goddess: he flung his cloak from him and set off to run. His servant Eurybates, a man of Ithaca, who waited on him, took charge of the cloak, whereon Odysseus went straight up to Agamemnon and received from him his ancestral, imperishable staff. With this he went about among the ships of the Achaeans.

Whenever he met a king or chieftain, he stood by him and spoke to him fairly. "Sir," said he, "this flight is cowardly and unworthy. Stand to your post, and bid your people also to keep their places. You do not yet know the full mind of Agamemnon; he was sounding us and ere long will visit the Achaeans with his displeasure. We were not all of us at the council to hear what he then said; see to it lest he be angry and do us a mischief; for the pride of kings is great, and the hand of Zeus is with them."

But when he came across any common man who was making a noise, he struck him with his staff and rebuked him, saying, "Sirrah, hold your peace, and listen to better men than yourself. You are a coward and no soldier; you are nobody either in fight or council; we cannot all be kings; it is not well that there should be many masters; one man must be supreme, one king to whom the son of scheming Kronos has given the scepter of sovereignty over you all."

Thus masterfully did he go about among the host, and the people hurried back to the council from their tents and ships with a sound as the thunder of surf when it comes crashing down upon the shore, and all the sea is in an uproar.

The rest now took their seats and kept to their own several places, but Thersites still went on wagging his unbridled tongue, a man of many words, and those unseemly; a monger of sedition, a railer against all who were in authority, who cared not what he said, so that he might set the Achaeans in a laugh. He was the ugliest man of all those who came before Troy, bandy legged, lame of one foot, with his two shoulders rounded and hunched over his chest. His head ran up to a point, but there was little hair on the top of it. Achilles and Odysseus hated him worst of all: for it was with them that he was most wont to wrangle; now, however, with a shrill squeaky voice he began heaping his abuse on Agamemnon. The Achaeans were angry and disgusted. Yet, nonetheless, he kept on brawling and bawling at the son of Atreus.

"Agamemnon," he cried, "what ails you now, and what more do you want? Your tents are filled with bronze and with fair women: for whenever we take a town, we give you the pick of them. Would you have yet more gold, which some Trojan is to give you as a ransom for his son, when I or another Achaean has taken him prisoner? Or is it some young girl to hide and lie with? It is not well that you, the ruler of the Achaeans, should bring them into such misery. Weakling cowards, women rather than men, let us sail home and leave this fellow here at Troy to stew in his own meeds of honor and to discover whether we were of any service to him or no. Achilles is a much better man than he is, and see how he has treated him, robbing him of his prize and keeping it himself. Achilles takes it meekly and shows no fight; if he did, son of Atreus, you would never again insult him."

Thus railed Thersites, but Odysseus at once went up to him and rebuked him sternly. "Check your glib tongue, Thersites," said he, "and babble not a word further. Chide not with princes when you have none to back you. There is no viler creature who has come before Troy with the sons of Atreus. Drop this chatter about kings, and neither revile them nor keep harping about going home. We do not yet know how things are going to be, nor whether the Achaeans are to return with good success or evil. How dare you gibe at Agamemnon, because the Danaans have awarded him so many prizes? I tell you, therefore, and it shall surely be: that if I again catch you talking such nonsense, I will either forfeit my own head and be no more called father of Telemachus, or I will take you, strip you stark naked, and whip you out of the assembly till you go blubbering back to the ships."

On this he beat him with his staff about the back and shoulders till he dropped and fell a weeping. The golden scepter raised a bloody weal on his back. So, he sat down frightened and in pain, looking foolish as he wiped the tears from his eyes. The people were sorry for him. Yet, they laughed heartily, and one would turn to his neighbor saying, "Odysseus has done many a good thing ere now in fight and council, but he never did the Argives a better turn than when he stopped this fellow's mouth from prating further. He will give the kings no more of his insolence."

Thus said the people. Then Odysseus arose, scepter in hand; and Athena in the likeness of a herald bade the people be still that those who were far off might hear him and consider his council. He therefore with all sincerity and goodwill addressed them thus:

"King Agamemnon, the Achaeans are for making you a by-word among all mankind. They forget the promise that they made you when they set out from Argos, that you should not return till you had sacked the town of Troy; and, like children or widowed women, they murmur and would set off homeward. True it is that they have had toil enough to be disheartened. A man chafes at having to stay away from his wife even for a single month, when he is on shipboard at the mercy of wind and sea, but it is now nine long years that we have been kept here; I cannot, therefore, blame the Achaeans if they turn restive; still, we shall be shamed if we go home empty after so long a stay. therefore, my friends, be patient yet a little longer that we may learn whether the prophesyings of Calchas were false or true. All who have not since perished must remember as though it were yesterday or the day before, how the ships of the Achaeans were detained in Aulis when we were on our way hither to make war on Priam and the Trojans. We were ranged round about a fountain, offering hecatombs to the gods upon their holy altars; and there was a fine plane tree from beneath which there welled a stream of pure water. Then we saw a prodigy; for Zeus sent a fearful serpent out of the ground with blood red stains upon its back, and it darted from under the altar onto the plane tree. Now there was a brood of young sparrows, quite small, upon the topmost bough, peeping out from under the leaves, eight in all; and their mother that hatched them made nine. The serpent ate the poor cheeping things, while the old bird flew about lamenting her little ones; but the serpent threw his coils about her and caught her by the wing as she was screaming. Then, when he had eaten both the sparrow and her young, the god who had sent him made him become a sign; for the son of scheming Kronos turned him into stone; and we stood there wondering at that which had come to pass. Seeing, then, that such a fearful portent had broken in upon our hecatombs, Calchas forthwith declared to us the oracles of heaven. 'Why, Achaeans,' said he, 'are you thus speechless? Zeus has sent us this sign, long in coming, and long ere it be fulfilled, though its fame shall last for ever. As the serpent ate the eight fledglings and the sparrow that hatched them, which makes nine, so shall we fight nine years at Troy, but in the tenth we shall take the town'. This was what he said, and now it is all coming true. Stay here, therefore, all of you, till we take the city of Priam."

On this the Argives raised a shout till the ships rang again with the uproar. Nestor, knight of Gerene, then addressed them. "Shame on you," he cried, "to stay talking here like children, when you should fight like men. Where are our covenants now, and where the oaths that we have taken? Shall our counsels be flung into the fire with our drink offerings and the right hands of fellowship wherein we have put our trust? We waste our time in words, and for all our talking here we shall be no further forward. Stand, therefore, son of Atreus, by your own steadfast purpose; lead the Argives on to battle; and leave this handful of men to rot, who scheme and scheme in vain, to get back to Argos ere they have learned whether Zeus be true or a liar: for the mighty son of Kronos surely promised that we should succeed, when we Argives set sail to bring death and destruction upon the Trojans. He showed us favorable signs by flashing his lightning on our right hands; therefore, let none make haste to go till he has first lain with the wife of some Trojan and has avenged the toil and sorrow that he has suffered for the sake of Helen. Nevertheless, if any man is in such haste to be at home again, let him lay his hand to his ship that he may meet his doom in the sight of all...."

READING 26
GREEK COLONIZATION

One of the most important phenomena of the Greek Archaic Period was Greek colonization. It seems to have begun around 750 B.C. and had largely come to an end by 500 B.C., although Greek colonies continued to be founded occasionally during the Classical Period. Modern scholars have long debated whether this colonizing activity was principally motivated by a desire to promote trade or by the need for cultivable land. It seems apparent that both reasons were at work. In some instances a site was chosen in order to provide large numbers of people from the founding community with land to cultivate for agriculture, but commercial considerations seem to explain why other sites were chosen for settlement; and it is likely that Greek colonists were always sensitive to both considerations. When Greek colonization began around 750 B.C., some Greek communities, especially Chalcis and Eretria on the island of Euboea, were beginning to engage in trade with the more highly civilized peoples of the Near East; and their foundation of colonies assisted in their manufacturing and exportation of goods. On the other hand, it seems likely that many colonies were sent out in order to relieve communities of the Greek mainland, Aegean islands, and the western coast of Anatolia of portions of their population that could not be supported by their farmland.

Greek colonization became so well established among the Greeks that the latter developed a standard procedure for founding a colony. Once a community reached the decision to send out a colony, it consulted an oracle (often Delphi) in order to receive divine approval for the enterprise. Then a prominent citizen was given the task of organizing and leading the venture. This man was termed the oikistes, meaning 'the one who sets up house'; and when he died, his body was buried in a prominent place in the town center of the colony, and his spirit received quasi-divine (i.e., heroic) honors. Once a site for the colony was chosen and secured against the native inhabitants, an area was marked out to serve as the town center, and land was divided into allotments for the colonists. From what we can tell, colonies began as small settlements, but once they were firmly established, they received more people from their mother-city and soon became flourishing self-governing city-states in their own right with strong ties to their mother-city.

The effects of Greek colonization were quite profound. The Greeks thereby expanded outside the Aegean area to dominate the coastal area of the Black Sea, the southern coast of italy, eastern Sicily, and even the southern coast of France. Colonies spread the Greek language, the Greek alphabet, Greek artistic traditions, and the distinctive Greek pattern of political organization (the polis), so that by the beginning of the Classical Period Greek culture was becoming the prestige culture of much of the Mediterranean. Colonization also enabled the Greeks to take advantage of the mineral resources of areas outside of their Aegean homeland, and this fostered a thriving well-integrated economic system.

A. Greek Colonization of Sicily

In the early months of 415 B.C. the Athenians launched a large fleet against the island of Sicily with the goal of conquering the entire island and adding it to their Aegean empire. This ambitious expedition ultimately failed and marked an important turning point in the Peloponnesian War between Athens and Sparta (see below Reading 35F-G). In narrating this episode in the war Thucydides prefaces his account of the Athenian expedition against Sicily with a brief account of the Greek colonization of the island in order to show how populous the island was at the time; and this passage is one of our most important sources of information for the foundations of these colonies.

(Taken from Book VI of The History of Thucydides, translated by Richard Crawley, Oxford 1866, revised by Gary Forsythe)

1. During the same winter the Athenians resolved to sail again to Sicily with a greater armament than that under Laches and Eurymedon and, if possible, to conquer the island; most of them being ignorant of its size and of the number of its inhabitants, Hellenic and barbarian, and of the fact that they were undertaking a war not much inferior to that against the Peloponnesians: for the voyage around Sicily in a merchantman is not far short of eight days; and yet, large as the island is, there are only two miles of sea to prevent its being mainland [i.e., joined to the toe of Italy]....

3. These were the barbarians in Sicily, settled as I have said. Of the Hellenes, the first to arrive were Chalcidians from Euboea with Thucles, their founder. They founded Naxos [734 B.C.] and built the altar to Apollo Archegetes, which now stands outside the town, and upon which the deputies for the games sacrifice before sailing from Sicily. Syracuse was founded the year afterwards [733 B.C.] by Archias, one of the Heraclids from Corinth, who began by driving out the Sicels from the island upon which the inner city now stands, though it is no longer surrounded by water: in process of time the outer town also was taken within the walls and became populous. Meanwhile, Thucles and the Chalcidians set out from Naxos in the fifth year after the foundation of Syracuse [729 B.C.], drove out the Sicels by arms, and founded Leontini and afterwards Catana [728 B.C.], the Catanians themselves choosing Evarchus as their founder.

4. About the same time [728 B.C.] Lamis arrived in Sicily with a colony from Megara; and after founding a place called Trotilus beyond the river Pantacyas, and afterwards leaving it and for a short while joining the Chalcidians at Leontini, he was driven out by them and founded Thapsus. After his death his companions were driven out of Thapsus and founded a place called the Hyblaean Megara: Hyblon, a Sicel king, having given up the place and inviting them thither. Here they lived two hundred and forty-five years, after which they were expelled from the city and the country by the Syracusan tyrant Gelon. Before their expulsion, however, a hundred years after they had settled there, they sent out Pamillus and founded Selinus [628 B.C.]; he had come from their mother country Megara to join them in its foundation.

Gela was founded by Antiphemus from Rhodes and Entimus from Crete, who joined in leading a colony thither, in the forty-fifth year after the foundation of Syracuse [688 B.C.]. The town took its name from the river Gelas: the place where the citadel now stands, and which was first fortified, being called Lindii. The institutions that they adopted were Dorian. Nearly one hundred and eight years after the foundation of Gela [580 B.C.] the Geloans founded Acragas [Agrigentum], so called from the river of that name; and they made Aristonous and Pystilus their founders, giving their own institutions to the colony. Zancle was originally founded by pirates from Cumae, the Chalcidian town in the country of the Opicans [near the Bay of Naples in Italy]. Afterwards, however, large numbers came from Chalcis and the rest of Euboea and helped to people the place, the founders being Perieres and Crataemenes from Cumae and Chalcis respectively. It first had the name of Zancle given it by the Sicels, because the place is shaped like a sickle, which the Sicels call zanclon; but upon the original settlers being afterwards expelled by some Samians and other Ionians who landed in Sicily flying from the Medes, and the Samians in their turn not long afterwards by Anaxilas, tyrant of Rhegium, the town was by him colonized with a mixed population, and its name was changed to Messana, after his old country.

5 Himera was founded from Zancle by Euclides, Simus, and Sacon [648 B.C.], most of those who went to the colony being Chalcidians, although they were joined by some exiles from Syracuse, who had been defeated in a civil war and were called the Myletidae. The language was a mixture of Chalcidian and Doric, but the institutions that prevailed were the Chalcidian. Acrae and Casmenae were founded by the Syracusans: Acrae seventy years after Syracuse [663 B.C.], Casmenae nearly twenty after Acrae [643 B.C.]. Camarina was first founded by the Syracusans, close upon a hundred and thirty-five years after the building of Syracuse [598 B.C.], its founders being Daxon and Menecolus. But the Camarinaeans, being expelled in arms by the Syracusans for having revolted, Hippocrates, tyrant of Gela, some time later receiving their land in ransom for some Syracusan prisoners, resettled Camarina with himself acting as its founder. Lastly, it

was again depopulated by Gelon and settled once more for the third time by the Geloans.

B. The Foundation of Cyrene

The following passage from Herodotus (484-425 B.C.) gives us a relatively detailed account of the colonization of Cyrene in Libya by the people of Thera, an island of the Aegean. The colony was established around 630 B.C., and Herodotus' account, written nearly 200 years later, is based upon oral tradition handed down by the Theraeans and Cyrenaeans whom he interviewed. By the time that he recorded the story, the foundation account had taken on folkloristic elements involving the oracle of Apollo at Delphi, but many details in the story are very revealing about the phenomenon of Greek colonization: a local crisis (a prolonged drought) forcing the community to rid itself of surplus population, appointment of a leader (Battus as oikistes), the use of the lot in choosing those who were to be sent out, the initial small size of the expedition to serve as scouts (two fifty-oared ships), cautious settlement of a small offshore island followed by a later move to the mainland, initial good relations with the natives followed by hostility as the colony grew and expanded at their expense. By the middle of the sixth century B.C. Cyrene had emerged as a large and flourishing Greek city-state, rich in flocks of sheep and especially from its trade of a local plant called silphium, which was widely used throughout the Mediterranean as a medicinal drug.

(Taken from Book IV of History of Herodotus, translated by George Rawlinson, published by Murray of London, 1875, revised by Gary Forsythe)

150. Thus far the history is delivered without variation both by the Theraeans and the Lacedaemonians; but from this point we have only the Theraean narrative. Grinus (they say), the son of Aesanius, a descendant of Theras, and king of the island of Thera, went to Delphi to offer a hecatomb on behalf of his native city. He was accompanied by a large number of the citizens, and among the rest by Battus, the son of Polymnestus, who belonged to the Minyan family of the Euphemidae. On Grinus consulting the oracle about sundry matters, the

Pythoness gave him for answer "that he should found a city in Libya." Grinus replied to this: "I, O king, am too far advanced in years and too inactive for such a work. Bid one of these youngsters to undertake it." As he spoke, he pointed towards Battus; and thus the matter rested for that time. When the embassy returned to Thera, small account was taken of the oracle by the Theraeans, as they were quite ignorant where Libya was, and they were not so venturesome as to send out a colony in the dark.

151. Seven years passed from the utterance of the oracle, and not a drop of rain fell in Thera. All the trees in the island, except one, were killed with the drought. The Theraeans upon this sent to Delphi and were reminded reproachfully that they had never colonized Libya. So, as there was no help for it, they sent messengers to Crete to inquire whether any of the Cretans or of the strangers sojourning among them had ever travelled as far as Libya. And these messengers of theirs in their wanderings about the island, among other places, visited Itanus, where they fell in with a man whose name was Corobius, a dealer in purple. In answer to their inquiries he told them that contrary winds had once carried him to Libya, where he had gone ashore on a certain island that was named Platea. So, they hired this man's services and took him back with them to Thera. A few persons then sailed from Thera to reconnoiter. Guided by Corobius to the island of Platea, they left him there with provisions for a certain number of months and returned home with all speed to give their countrymen an account of the island.

152. During their absence, which was prolonged beyond the time that had been agreed upon, Corobius' provisions failed him. He was relieved, however, after a while by a Samian vessel under the command of a man named Colaeus, which, on its way to Egypt, was forced to put in at Platea. The crew, informed by Corobius of all the circumstances, left him sufficient food for a year. They themselves quitted the island; and anxious to reach Egypt, they made sail in that direction, but were carried out of their course by a gale of wind from the east. The storm not abating, they were driven past the Pillars of Herakles [the Strait of Gibraltar]; and at last, by some special guiding providence, they

reached Tartessus. This trading town was in those days a virgin port, unfrequented by the merchants. The Samians in consequence made by the return voyage a profit greater than any Greeks before their day, excepting Sostratus, son of Laodamas, an Aeginetan, with whom no one else can compare. From the tenth part of their gains, amounting to six talents, the Samians made a brazen vessel, in shape like an Argive wine-bowl, adorned with the heads of griffins standing out in high relief. This bowl, supported by three kneeling colossal figures in bronze, of the height of seven cubits, was placed as an offering in the temple of Hera at Samos. The aid given to Corobius was the original cause of that close friendship which afterwards united the Cyrenaeans and Theraeans with the Samians.

153. The Theraeans who had left Corobius at Platea, when they reached Thera, told their countrymen that they had colonized an island on the coast of Libya. They of Thera, upon this, resolved that men should be sent to join the colony from each of their seven districts, and that the brothers in every family should draw lots to determine who were to go. Battus was chosen to be king and leader of the colony. So, these men departed for Platea on board of two pentecounters [fifty-oared ships].

154. Such is the account which the Theraeans give. In the sequel of the history their accounts tally with those of the people of Cyrene; but in what they relate of Battus these two nations differ most widely....

155. At Thera Polymnestus, one of the chief citizens of the place, took Phronima to be his concubine. The fruit of this union was a son, who stammered and had a lisp in his speech. According to the Cyrenaeans and Theraeans the name given to the boy was Battus [meaning 'stammerer']. In my opinion, however, he was called at the first something else and only got the name of Battus after his arrival in Libya, assuming it either in consequence of the words addressed to him by the Delphian oracle, or on account of the office which he held: for in the Libyan tongue the word "Battus" means "a king." And this, I think, was the reason why the Pythoness addressed him as she did: she knew that he was to be a king in Libya, and so she used the Libyan word in speaking to him: for after he had grown to man's estate, he made a

journey to Delphi to consult the oracle about his voice; when, upon his putting his question, the Pythoness thus replied to him: "Battus, thou camest to ask of thy voice; but Phoebus Apollo bids thee establish a city in Libya, abounding in fleeces," which was as if she had said in her own tongue, "King, thou camest to ask of thy voice." Then he replied, "Mighty lord, I did indeed come hither to consult thee about my voice, but thou speakest to me of quite other matters, bidding me colonize Libya, an impossible thing! What power have I? What followers?" Thus he spake, but he did not persuade the Pythoness to give him any other response; so, when he found that she persisted in her former answer, he left her speaking and set out on his return to Thera.

156. After a while everything began to go wrong both with Battus and with the rest of the Theraeans, whereupon these last, ignorant of the cause of their sufferings, sent to Delphi to inquire for what reason they were afflicted. The Pythoness in reply told them "that if they and Battus would make a settlement at Cyrene in Libya, things would go better with them." Upon this the Theraeans sent out Battus with two penteconters, and with these he proceeded to Libya, but within a little time, not knowing what else to do, the men returned and arrived off Thera. The Theraeans, when they saw the vessels approaching, received them with showers of missiles, would not allow them to come near the shore, and ordered the men to sail back whence they came. Thus compelled to return, they settled on an island near the Libyan coast, which (as I have already said) was called Platea. In size it is reported to have been about equal to the city of Cyrene, as it now stands.

157. In this place they continued two years, but at the end of that time, as their ill luck still followed them, they left the island to the care of one of their number and went in a body to Delphi, where they made complaint at the shrine to the effect that, notwithstanding they had colonized Libya, they prospered as poorly as before. Hereon the Pythoness made them the following answer: "Knowest thou better than I fair Libya abounding in fleeces? Better the stranger than he who has trod it? Oh! clever Theraeans!" Battus and his friends, when

they heard this, sailed back to Platea: it was plain that the god would not hold them acquitted of the colony till they were absolutely in Libya [i.e., on the mainland]. So, taking with them the man whom they had left upon the island, they made a settlement on the mainland directly opposite Platea, fixing themselves at a place called Aziris, which is closed in on both sides by the most beautiful hills and on one side is washed by a river.

158. Here they remained six years, at the end of which time the Libyans induced them to move, promising that they would lead them to a better situation. So, the Greeks left Aziris and were conducted by the Libyans towards the west, their journey being so arranged by the calculation of their guides that they passed in the night the most beautiful district of that whole country, which is the region called Irasa. The Libyans brought them to a spring, which goes by the name of Apollo's Fountain; and they told them, "Here, Grecians, is the proper place for you to settle; for here the sky leaks."

159. During the lifetime of Battus, the founder of the colony, who reigned forty years, and during that of his son Arcesilaus, who reigned sixteen, the Cyrenaeans continued at the same level, neither more nor fewer in number than they were at the first. But in the reign of the third king, Battus, surnamed the Happy, the advice of the Pythoness brought Greeks from every quarter into Libya to join the settlement. The Cyrenaeans had offered to all comers a share in their lands; and the oracle had spoken as follows: "He that is backward to share in the pleasant Libyan acres, sooner or later, I warn him, will feel regret at his folly."

160. Thus a great multitude was collected together to Cyrene, and the Libyans of the neighborhood found themselves stripped of large portions of their lands. So, they and their king Adicran, being robbed and insulted by the Cyrenaeans, sent messengers to Egypt and put themselves under the rule of Apries, the Egyptian monarch, who, upon this, levied a vast army of Egyptians and sent them against Cyrene. The inhabitants of that place left their walls and marched out in force to the district of Irasa, where near the spring called Theste they engaged the Egyptian host and defeated it. The

Egyptians, who had never before made trial of the prowess of the Greeks and so thought but meanly of them, were routed with such slaughter that but a very few of them ever got back home. For this reason the subjects of Apries, who laid the blame of the defeat on him, revolted from his authority.

READING 27
THE GREEK TYRANTS

Beginning around 650 B.C. several Greek city-states came under the rule of a single aristocrat through his illegal seizure of power. Unfortunately, given the poor state of our surviving evidence for this early period of Greek history, we often lack very precise and detailed knowledge of how and why tyrants came to power; and this circumstance has led to much speculation among modern scholars. Since the phenomenon of Greek tyranny coincided with the spread of hoplite warfare among the Greeks, some scholars have argued that tyrants came to power with the support of their fellow hoplite citizens in order to replace the oppressive rule of an aristocratic oligarchy. But since tyrants seem to have always disarmed their fellow citizens, this hoplite thesis seems unlikely. On the other hand, the widespread availability of hoplites in the Greek world allowed would-be tyrants to hire non-citizens as mercenaries, with whom they were able to overcome the resistance of their fellow citizens. One common characteristic of Greek tyranny during the Archaic Period was that these men were all aristocrats, who were extremely ambitious and able individuals. Moreover, in many (if not in all) instances they succeeded in exploiting some source of discontent within their communities, so that they could gain some degree of support by playing one group off against the other.

A. Aristotle on Tyranny
The Greeks of the Classical Period regarded tyranny as the worst form of government. It was a perversion of monarchy or kingship, which was the rule by one man for the benefit of the entire community, whereas tyranny was one man

ruling a community in his own interest. Aristotle's Politics is a masterful treatment of Greek political thought, whose concepts, principles, and conclusions
are amply supported by a wealth of empirical data drawn from the histories of
numerous city-states. Aristotle discusses tyranny sporadically throughout this
long work. The following brief passage is one of his few passages devoted to
tyranny that combine both historical facts and generalizations.

(Taken from Book V of The Politics of Aristotle, translated
by Benjamin Jowett, Oxford 1885, revised by Gary Forsythe)

5.   ...Of old, the demagogue was also a general, and then democracies
changed into tyrannies. Most of the ancient tyrants were originally demagogues. They are not so now, but they were then; and the reason is that
they were generals and not orators: for oratory had not yet come into
fashion. Whereas in our day, when the art of rhetoric has made such
progress, the orators lead the people, but their ignorance of military
matters prevents them from usurping power; at any rate, instances to
the contrary are few and slight. Tyrannies were more common formerly
than now for this reason also: that great power was placed in the hands
of individuals; thus, a tyranny arose at Miletus out of the office of the
Prytanis, who had supreme authority in many important matters. Moreover, in those days, when cities were not large, the people dwelt in the
fields, busy at their work; and their chiefs, if they possessed any military
talent, seized the opportunity; and winning the confidence of the masses
by professing their hatred of the wealthy, they succeeded in obtaining
the tyranny. Thus, at Athens Peisistratus led a faction against the men
of the plain, and Theagenes at Megara slaughtered the cattle of the
wealthy, which he found by the river-side, where they had put them to
graze in land not their own. Dionysius, again, was thought worthy of
the tyranny [in Syracuse] because he denounced Daphnaeus and the rich;
his enmity to the notables won for him the confidence of the people.

B. How to Become a Tyrant

The following passage comes from the historical account of Herodotus, whose
vast and complex narrative, replete with numerous digressions into past events,

provides us with much of our information about the Greek Archaic Period. In the following passage Herodotus attempts to explain the origin of the royal line of kings among the Medes, who preceded the Persians as the dominant people in western Iran. Herodotus' explanation fits with how the Greeks of his day conceived of how a man could make himself tyrant over his fellow citizens. The one exceptional aspect of this story is that Deioces made himself popular with his people by exercising justice rather than by seizing power. He therefore became a legitimate monarch (i.e., a king) rather than an illegitimate monarch (i.e., a tyrant).

(Taken from Book I of History of Herodotus, translated by George Rawlinson, published by Murray of London, 1875, revised by Gary Forsythe)

96. Thus the nations over that whole extent of country obtained the blessing of self-government, but they fell again under the sway of kings in the manner which I will now relate. There was a certain Mede named Deioces, son of Phraortes, a man of much wisdom, who had conceived the desire of obtaining to himself the sovereign power. In furtherance of his ambition, therefore, he formed and carried into execution the following scheme. As the Medes at that time dwelt in scattered villages without any central authority, and lawlessness in consequence prevailed throughout the land, Deioces, who was already a man of mark in his own village, applied himself with greater zeal and earnestness than ever before to the practice of justice among his fellows. It was his conviction that justice and injustice are engaged in perpetual war with one another. He therefore began his course of conduct; and presently the men of his village, observing his integrity, chose him to be the arbiter of all their disputes. Bent on obtaining the sovereign power, he showed himself an honest and an upright judge, and by these means he gained such credit with his fellow citizens as to attract the attention of those who lived in the surrounding villages. They had long been suffering from unjust and oppressive judgments, so that, when they heard of the singular uprightness of Deioces and of the equity of his decisions, they joyfully had recourse to him in

the various quarrels and suits that arose, until at last they came to put confidence in no one else.

97. The number of complaints brought before him continually increasing, as people learned more and more the fairness of his judgments, Deioces, feeling himself now all important, announced that he did not intend any longer to hear causes, and he appeared no more in the seat in which he had been accustomed to sit and administer justice. "It did not square with his interests," he said, "to spend the whole day in regulating other men's affairs to the neglect of his own." Hereupon robbery and lawlessness broke out afresh and prevailed through the country even more than heretofore; wherefore, the Medes assembled from all quarters and held a consultation on the state of affairs. The speakers, as I think, were chiefly friends of Deioces. "We cannot possibly," they said, "go on living in this country if things continue as they now are; let us therefore set a king over us, that the land may thus be well governed, and we ourselves may be able to attend to our own affairs and not be forced to quit our country on account of anarchy." The assembly was persuaded by these arguments and resolved to appoint a king.

98. It followed to determine who should be chosen to the office. When this debate began, the claims of Deioces and his praises were at once in every mouth, so that presently all agreed that he should be king. Upon this he required a palace to be built for him suitable to his rank, and a guard to be given him for his person. The Medes complied and built him a strong and large palace on a spot that he himself pointed out, and they likewise gave him liberty to choose himself a bodyguard from the whole nation. Thus settled upon the throne, he further required them to build a single great city; and disregarding the petty towns in which they had formerly dwelt, he make the new capital the object of their chief attention. The Medes were again obedient and built the city now called Agbatana, the walls of which are of great size and strength, rising in circles one within the other....

99. All these fortifications Deioces caused to be raised for himself and his own palace. The people were required to build their dwellings outside the circuit of the walls. When the town was finished, he proceeded to

arrange the ceremonial. He allowed no one to have direct access to the person of the king, but made all communication pass through the hands of messengers, and he forbade the king to be seen by his subjects. He also made it an offense for anyone whatsoever to laugh or spit in the royal presence. This ceremonial, of which he was the first inventor, Deioces established for his own security, fearing that his compeers, who were brought up together with him and were of as good family as he and no whit inferior to him in manly qualities, if they saw him frequently, would be pained at the sight and would therefore be likely to conspire against him; whereas if they did not see him, they would think him quite a different sort of being from themselves.

100. After completing these arrangements and firmly settling himself upon the throne, Deioces continued to administer justice with the same strictness as before. Causes were stated in writing and sent in to the king, who passed his judgment upon the contents and transmitted his decisions to the parties concerned: besides which, he had spies and eaves-droppers in all parts of his dominions; and if he heard of any act of oppression, he sent for the guilty party and awarded him the punishment meet for his offense.

101. Thus, Deioces collected the Medes into a nation and ruled over them alone.

C. Cylon of Athens

In the year 632 B.C. the Athenian Cylon attempted but failed to make himself tyrant of Athens. Cylon must have been fairly well known and perhaps even popular among his fellow Athenians as the result of his success at the Olympic Games. The following passage illustrates the role of personal ambition, a would-be tyrant's mobilization of outside assistance (from Cylon's father-in-law, Theagenes, the tyrant of the neighboring state of Megara), and the need for the tyrant to be able to play upon discontent within his community: for Cylon's failure to bring off the latter allowed Athenian officials to mobilize enough support to crush his attempt to seize power.

(Taken from Book I of The History of Thucydides, translated by Richard Crawley, Oxford 1866, revised by Gary Forsythe)

126. ... In former generations there was an Athenian of the name of Cylon, a victor at the Olympic Games, of good birth and powerful position, who had married a daughter of Theagenes, a Megarian, at that time tyrant of Megara. Now this Cylon was inquiring at Delphi, when he was told by the god to seize the Acropolis of Athens on the grand festival of Zeus. Accordingly, procuring a force from Theagenes and persuading his friends to join him, when the Olympic festival in Peloponnese came, he seized the Acropolis with the intention of making himself tyrant, thinking that this was the grand festival of Zeus, and also an occasion appropriate for a victor at the Olympic Games. Whether the grand festival that was meant was in Attica or elsewhere was a question which he never thought of, and which the oracle did not offer to solve: for the Athenians also have a festival which is called the grand festival of Zeus Meilichios or Gracious, viz., the Diasia. It is celebrated outside the city, and the whole people sacrifice not real victims but a number of bloodless offerings peculiar to the country. However, fancying that he had chosen the right time, he made the attempt. As soon as the Athenians perceived it, they flocked in, one and all, from the country; and they sat down and laid siege to the citadel. But as time went on, weary of the labor of blockade, most of them departed, the responsibility of keeping guard being left to the nine archons with plenary powers to arrange everything according to their good judgment. It must be known that at that time most political functions were discharged by the nine archons. Meanwhile, Cylon and his besieged companions were distressed for want of food and water. Accordingly, Cylon and his brother made their escape; but the rest, being hard pressed and some even dying of famine, seated themselves as suppliants at the altar in the Acropolis. The Athenians who were charged with the duty of keeping guard, when they saw them at the point of death in the temple, raised them up on the understanding that no harm should be done to them, led them out, and slew them. Some, who, as they passed by, took refuge at the altars of the awful goddesses, were dispatched on the spot.

D. Cypselus and Periander of Corinth

The following passage concerns the Cypselid tyranny that ended the rule of the aristocratic clan of the Bacchiads in Corinth and held sway in the city from the mid-seventh century to the early sixth. The passage comes from Herodotus' narration of how the Spartans attempted to intervene into the affairs of Athens around 510 B.C. and to install a tyrant favorable to Sparta by reinstating the deposed tyrant Hippias, but the plan met with the fierce opposition of Corinth, Sparta's most important ally. The following speech, delivered by the Corinthian spokesman on this occasion, offers us a brief outline of the Cypselid tyranny told from a hostile perspective.

(Taken from Book V of History of Herodotus, translated by George Rawlinson, published by Murray of London, 1875, revised by Gary Forsythe)

92. Such was the address of the Spartans. The greater number of the allies listened without being persuaded. None, however, broke silence but Sosicles the Corinthian, who exclaimed, "Surely the heaven will soon be below, and the earth above, and men will henceforth live in the sea, and fish take their place upon the dry land, since you, Lacedaemonians, propose to put down free governments in the cities of Greece and to set up tyrannies in their room. There is nothing in the whole world so unjust, nothing so bloody, as a tyranny. If, however, it seems to you a desirable thing to have the cities under despotic rule, begin by putting a tyrant over yourselves, and then establish despots in the other states. While you continue yourselves, as you have always been, unacquainted with tyranny and take such excellent care that Sparta may not suffer from it, to act as you are now doing is to treat your allies unworthily. If you knew what tyranny was as well as ourselves, you would be better advised than you now are in regard to it.

The government at Corinth was once an oligarchy, a single race called Bacchiadae, who intermarried only among themselves and held the management of affairs. Now it happened that Amphion, one of these, had a daughter named Labda, who was lame, and whom therefore none of the Bacchiadae would consent to marry; so, she was taken to wife by Aetion, son of Echecrates, a man of the township of Petra, who was, however, by descent of the race of the Lapithae and of the house of Caeneus. Aetion, as he had no child, either by this wife or by any other, went to Delphi to consult the oracle concerning the matter. Scarcely had he entered the temple when the Pythoness greeted him in these words: "No one honors thee now, Aetion, worthy of honor. Labda shall soon be a mother, her offspring a rock [petra] that will one day fall on the kingly race and right the city of Corinth."

By some chance this address of the oracle to Aetion came to the ears of the Bacchiadae, who till then had been unable to perceive the meaning of another earlier prophecy that likewise bore upon Corinth and pointed to the same event as Aetion's prediction. It was the following: "When amid the rocks an eagle shall bear a carnivorous lion, mighty and fierce, he shall loosen the limbs of many beneath them. Brood ye well upon this, all ye Corinthian people, ye who dwell by fair Peirene and beetling Corinth." The Bacchiadae had possessed this oracle for some time; but they were quite at a loss to know what it meant until they heard the response given to Aetion; then, however, they at once perceived its meaning, since the two agreed so well together. Nevertheless, though the bearing of the first prophecy was now clear to them, they remained quiet, being minded to put to death the child which Aetion was expecting.

As soon, therefore, as his wife was delivered, they sent ten of their number to the township where Aetion lived, with orders to make away with the baby. So, the men came to Petra, went into Aetion's house, and there asked if they might see the child; and Labda, who knew nothing of their purpose, but thought that their inquiries arose from a kindly feeling towards her husband, brought the child and laid him in the arms of one of them. Now they had agreed by the way that whoever first got hold of the child should dash it against the ground. It happened, however, by a providential chance that the babe, just as Labda put him into the man's arms, smiled in his face. The man saw the smile and was touched with pity, so that he could not kill it; he therefore passed it on to his next neighbor, who gave it to a third; and so it went through all the ten without anyone choosing to be the murderer. The mother received her child back; and the men went out of the house, stood near the door, and there blamed and reproached one another; chiefly, however, accusing the man who had first had the child in his arms, because he had not done as had been agreed upon. At last, after much time had been thus spent, they resolved to go into the house again and all take part in the murder. But it was fated that evil should come upon Corinth from the progeny of Aetion; and so it chanced that Labda, as she stood near the door, heard all that the men said to one another; and fearful of their changing their mind and returning to destroy her baby, she carried him off and hid him in what seemed to her the most unlikely place to be suspected, viz., a 'cypsel' or grain-bin. She knew that if they came back to look for the child, they would search all her house; and so indeed they did, but not finding the child after looking everywhere, they thought it best to go away and declare to those by whom they had been sent that they had done their bidding. And thus they reported on their return home.

Aetion's son grew up; and in remembrance of the danger from which he had escaped, he was named Cypselus after the grain-bin. When he reached to man's estate, he went to Delphi; and on consulting the oracle, he received a response which was two-sided. It was the following: "See there comes to my dwelling a man much favor'd of fortune, Cypselus, son of Aetion, and king of the glorious Corinth: he and his children too, but not his children's children." Such was the oracle; and Cypselus put so much faith in it that he forthwith made his attempt and thereby became master of Corinth.

Having thus got the tyranny, he showed himself a harsh ruler. Many of the Corinthians he drove into banishment, many he deprived of their fortunes, and a still greater number of their lives. His reign lasted thirty years and was prosperous to its close, insomuch that he left the government to Periander, his son. This prince at the beginning of his reign was of a milder temper than his father; but after he corresponded by means of messengers with Thrasybulus, tyrant of Miletus, he became even more sanguinary. On one occasion he sent a herald to ask Thrasybulus what mode of government it was safest to set up in order to rule with honor. Thrasybulus led the messenger without the city and took him into a field of grain, through which he began to walk, while he asked him again and again concerning his coming from Corinth, ever as he went breaking off and throwing away all such ears of grain as over-topped the rest. In this way he went through the whole field and destroyed all the best and richest part of the crop; then, without a word he sent the messenger back. On the return of the man to Corinth, Periander was eager to know what Thrasybulus had counselled, but the messenger reported that he had said nothing; and he wondered that Periander had sent him to so strange a man, who seemed to have lost his senses, since he did nothing but destroy his own property. And upon this he told how Thrasybulus had behaved at the interview. Periander, perceiving what the action meant, and knowing that Thrasybulus advised the destruction of all the leading citizens, treated his subjects from this time forward with the very greatest cruelty. Where Cypselus had spared any and had neither put them to death nor banished them, Periander completed what his father had left unfinished. One day he stripped all the women of Corinth stark naked for the sake of his own wife Melissa. He had sent messengers into Thesprotia to consult the oracle of the dead upon the Acheron concerning a pledge that had been given into his charge by a stranger; and Melissa appeared, but refused to speak or tell where the pledge was. 'She was chill,' she said, 'having no clothes; the garments buried with her were of no manner of use, since they had not been burned. And this should be her token to Periander that what she said was true: the oven was cold when he baked his loaves in it.' When this message was brought him, Periander knew the token; wherefore he straightway made proclamation that all the wives of the Corinthians should go forth to the temple of Hera. So, the women apparelled themselves in their finest and went forth, as if to a festival. Then, with the help of his guards, whom he had placed for the purpose, he stripped them one and all, making no difference between the free women and the slaves; and taking their clothes to a pit, he called on the name of Melissa and burned the whole heap. This done, he sent a second time to the oracle; and Melissa's ghost told him where he would find the stranger's pledge.

Such, O Lacedaemonians, is tyranny, and such are the deeds that spring from it. We Corinthians marvelled greatly when we first knew of your having sent for Hippias; and now it surprises us still more to hear you speak as you do. We adjure you by the common gods of Greece: plant not despots in her cities. If, however, you are determined, if you persist against all justice in seeking to restore Hippias, know, at least, that the Corinthians will not approve your conduct."

E. Cleisthenes of Sicyon

In this passage Herodotus tells us how the famous aristocratic family of the Alcmaeonidae of Athens formed an important marriage alliance with Cleisthenes, the tyrant of Sicyon (ca. 600-570 B.C.). The picturesque story reveals the aristocratic origin of these tyrants and how they cultivated ties with other fellow aristocrats in other city-states.

(Taken from Book VI of History of Herodotus, translated by George Rawlinson, published by Murray of London, 1875, revised by Gary Forsythe)

126. Afterwards, in the generation which followed, Cleisthenes, king of Sicyon, raised the family to still greater eminence among the Greeks than even that to which it had attained before: for this Cleisthenes, who was the son of Aristonymus, the grandson of Myron, and the great-grandson of Andreas, had a daughter, called Agarista, whom he wished to marry to the best husband whom he could find in the whole of Greece. At the Olympic Games, therefore, having gained the prize in the chariot race, he caused public proclamation to be made to the following effect: "Whoever among the Greeks deems himself worthy to become the son-in-law of Cleisthenes, let him come sixty days hence, or, if he will, sooner, to Sicyon; for within a year's time, counting from the end of the sixty days, Cleisthenes will decide on the man to whom he shall contract his daughter." So, all the Greeks who were proud of their own merit or of their country flocked to Sicyon as suitors; and Cleisthenes had a foot-course and a wrestling-ground made ready to try their powers.

127. From Italy there came Smindyrides, the son of Hippocrates, a native of Sybaris, which city about that time was at the very height of its prosperity. He was a man who in luxuriousness of living exceeded all other persons. Likewise, there came Damasus, the son of Amyris, surnamed the Wise, a native of Siris. These two were the only suitors from Italy. From the Ionian Gulf appeared Amphimnestus, the son of Epistrophus, an Epidamnian; from Aetolia, Males, the brother of that Titormus who excelled all the Greeks in strength, and who, wishing to avoid his fellow men, withdrew himself into the remotest parts of the Aetolian territory. From the Peloponnese came several: Leocedes, son of that Pheidon, king of the Argives, who established weights and

measures throughout the Peloponnese and was the most insolent of all the Grecians, the same who drove out the Elean directors of the Games, and he himself presided over the contests at Olympia. Leocedes, I say, appeared, this Pheidon's son; and likewise, Amiantus, son of Lycurgus, an Arcadian of the city of Trapezus; Laphanes, an Azenian of Paeus, whose father, Euphorion, as the story goes in Arcadia, entertained the Dioscuri at his residence and thenceforth kept open house for all comers; and lastly, Onomastus, the son of Agaeus, a native of Elis. These four came from the Peloponnese. From Athens there arrived Megacles, the son of that Alcmaeon who visited Croesus; and Tisander's son, Hippoclides, the wealthiest and handsomest of the Athenians. There was likewise one Euboean, Lysanias, who came from Eretria, then a flourishing city. From Thessaly came Diactorides, a Cranonian, of the race of the Scopadae; and Alcon arrived from the Molossians. This was the list of the suitors.

128. Now when they were all come, and the day appointed had arrived, Cleisthenes first of all inquired of each concerning his country and his family; after which he kept them with him a year and made trial of their manly bearing, their temper, their accomplishments, and their disposition, sometimes drawing them apart for converse, sometimes bringing them all together. Such as were still youths he took with him from time to time to the gymnasia; but the greatest trial of all was at the banquet-table. During the whole period of their stay he lived with them, as I have said; and, further, from first to last he entertained them sumptuously. Somehow or other the suitors who came from Athens pleased him the best of all; and of these Hippoclides, Tisander's son, was specially in favor, partly on account of his manly bearing, and partly also because his ancestors were of kin to the Corinthian Cypselids.

129. When at length the day arrived which had been fixed for the espousals, and Cleisthenes had to speak out and declare his choice, he first of all made a sacrifice of a hundred oxen and held a banquet, whereat he entertained all the suitors and the whole people of Sicyon. After the feast was ended, the suitors vied with each other in music and in speaking on a given subject. Presently, as the drinking advanced, Hippoclides,

who quite dumbfoundered the rest, called aloud to the flute-player and bade him strike up a dance; which the man did; and Hippoclides danced to it. And he fancied that he was dancing excellently well; but Cleisthenes, who was observing him, began to misdoubt the whole business. Then Hippoclides, after a pause, told an attendant to bring in a table; and when it was brought, he mounted upon it and danced, first of all, some Laconian figures, then some Attic ones; after which he stood on his head upon the table and began to toss his legs about. Cleisthenes, notwithstanding that he now loathed Hippoclides for a son-in-law by reason of his dancing and his shamelessness, still, as he wished to avoid an outbreak, had restrained himself during the first and likewise during the second dance; when, however, he saw him tossing his legs in the air, he could no longer contain himself, but cried out, "Son of Tisander, thou hast danced thy wife away!" "What does Hippoclides care?" was the other's answer. And hence the proverb arose.

130. Then Cleisthenes commanded silence and spake thus before the assembled company: "Suitors of my daughter, well pleased am I with you all; and right willingly, if it were possible, would I content you all and not by making choice of one appear to put a slight upon the rest. But as it is out of my power, seeing that I have but one daughter to grant to all their wishes, I will present to each of you whom I must needs dismiss a talent of silver for the honor that you have done me in seeking to ally yourselves with my house, and for your long absence from your homes. But my daughter, Agarista, I betroth to Megacles, the son of Alcmaeon, to be his wife according to the usage and wont of Athens." Then Megacles expressed his readiness; and Cleisthenes had the marriage solemnized.

131. Thus ended the affair of the suitors; and thus the Alcmaeonidae came to be famous throughout the whole of Greece. The issue of this marriage was the Cleisthenes, named after his grandfather the Sicyonian, who made the tribes at Athens and set up the popular government. Megacles had likewise another son, called Hippocrates, whose children were a Megacles and an Agarista, the latter named after Agarista the daughter of Cleisthenes. She married Xanthippus, the son of

Ariphron; and when she was with child by him, she had a dream, wherein she fancied that she was delivered of a lion; after which, within a few days she bore Xanthippus a son, to wit, Pericles.

READING 28
CONTRASTING VIEWS OF
THE SPARTAN STATE

During the Archaic Period Sparta underwent social and political changes that resulted in a state that differed in many ways from other Greek states. Although it developed a typical three-part constitution consisting of magistrates (the two kings and the five annually elected ephors), a deliberative body (the gerousia of 28 elders plus the two kings), and a citizen assembly (consisting of a hoplite class of the Spartiate warriors), Sparta's conquest of Messenia and its subjugation of the population to serfdom led to the evolution of a highly militarized society, in which Spartan males were not farmers and artisans, but were trained as warriors in order to guard against uprisings by their serfs (known as Helots). In addition, Sparta's social institutions (e.g., marriage, child-rearing, land tenure, and public messes) were designed to instil complete obedience and subordination to the state. Although this complex system developed in stages over several generations, the later Greeks believed that it had been the product of a single lawgiver named Lycurgus. Hence, the Spartan system is often termed the Lycurgan system.

A. Xenophon
Xenophon (431-354 B.C.) was an Athenian who well represents the Greek aristocratic adoration of the order and military discipline and efficiency of the Spartan way of life. While serving as a mercenary under Spartan commanders during the 390s B.C., Xenophon became a close friend of King Agesilaus of

Sparta, one of the dominant figures of the early fourth century B.C. The following passage, taken from Xenophon's brief treatise entitled The Constitution of the Lacedaemonians, was composed when Sparta was enjoying political and military supremacy throughout the Aegean area.

(From Xenophon's Constitution of the Lacedaemonians, taken from The Works of Xenophon, Volume II, translated by Henry Graham Dakyns, MacMillan, London 1892, revised by Gary Forsythe)

1. I recall the astonishment with which I first noted the unique position of Sparta among the states of Hellas, the relatively sparse population, and at the same time the extraordinary power and prestige of the community. I was puzzled to account for the fact. It was only when I came to consider the peculiar institutions of the Spartans that my wonderment ceased. Or rather, it is transferred to the legislator who gave them those laws, obedience to which has been the secret of their prosperity. This legislator, Lycurgus, I must needs admire and hold him to have been one of the wisest of mankind. Certainly he was no servile imitator of other states. It was by a stroke of invention rather, and on a pattern much in opposition to the commonly-accepted one, that he brought his fatherland to this pinnacle of prosperity. Take, for example,—and it is well to begin at the beginning—the whole topic of the begetting and rearing of children. Throughout the rest of the world the young girl, who will one day become a mother (and I speak of those who may be held to be well brought up), is nurtured on the plainest food attainable with the scantiest addition of meat or other condiments, while as to wine, they train them either to total abstinence or to take it highly diluted with water. And in imitation, as it were, of the handicraft type, since the majority of artificers are sedentary, we, the rest of the Hellenes, are content that our girls should sit quietly and work wools. That is all that we demand of them. But how are we to expect that women nurtured in this fashion should produce a splendid offspring? Lycurgus pursued a different path. Clothes were things, he held, the furnishing of which might well enough be left to

female slaves. And believing that the highest function of a free woman was the bearing of children, in the first place he insisted on the training of the body as incumbent no less on the female than the male; and in pursuit of the same idea he instituted rival contests in running and feats of strength for women as for men. His belief was that where both parents were strong, their progeny would be found to be more vigorous.... To meet the case which might occur of an old man wedded to a young wife: considering the jealous watch which such husbands are apt to keep over their wives, he introduced a directly opposite custom; that is to say, he made it incumbent on the aged husband to introduce someone whose qualities, physical and moral, he admired, to play the husband's part and to beget him children. Or again, in the case of a man who might not desire to live with a wife permanently, but yet might still be anxious to have children of his own worthy name, the lawgiver laid down a law in his behalf. Such a one might select some woman, the wife of some man, well born herself and blest with fair offspring, and, the sanction and consent of her husband first obtained, raise up children for himself through her....

2. ... I wish now to explain the systems of education in fashion here and elsewhere. Throughout the rest of Hellas the custom on the part of those who claim to educate their sons in the best way is as follows. As soon as the children are of an age to understand what is said to them, they are immediately placed under the charge of Paidagogoi (or tutors), who are also attendants, and they are sent off to the school of some teacher to be taught "grammar, "music," and the concerns of the palestra [wrestling ground]. Besides this, they are given shoes to wear that tend to make their feet tender; and their bodies are enervated by various changes of clothing. And as for food, the only measure recognized is that which is fixed by appetite. But when we turn to Lycurgus, instead of leaving it to each member of the state privately to appoint a slave to be his son's tutor, he set over the young Spartans a public guardian, the Paidonomos or "pastor," to give them his proper title, with complete authority over them. This guardian was selected from those who filled the highest magistracies. He had authority to hold musters of the boys, and as their overseer, in case of

any misbehavior, to chastise severely. The legislator further provided his pastor with a body of youths in the prime of life and bearing whips to inflict punishment when necessary, with this happy result that in Sparta modesty and obedience ever go hand in hand, nor is there lack of either. Instead of softening their feet with shoe or sandal, his rule was to make them hardy through going barefoot. This habit, if practised, would, as he believed, enable them to scale heights more easily and clamber down precipices with less danger. In fact, with his feet so trained the young Spartan would leap and spring and run faster unshod than another shod in the ordinary way. Instead of making them effeminate with a variety of clothes, his rule was to habituate them to a single garment the whole year through, thinking that so they would be better prepared to withstand the variations of heat and cold. Again, as regards food, according to his regulation the Eiren, or head of the flock, must see that his messmates gathered to the club meal with such moderate food as to avoid that heaviness which is engendered by repletion, and yet not to remain altogether unacquainted with the pains of penurious living. His belief was that by such training in boyhood they would be better able, when occasion demanded, to continue toiling on an empty stomach. They would be all the fitter, if the word of command were given, to remain on the stretch for a long time without extra dieting.... He did give them permission to steal this thing or that in the effort to alleviate their hunger. It was not, of course, from any real difficulty how else to supply them with nutriment that he left it to them to provide themselves by this crafty method. Nor can I conceive that anyone will so misinterpret the custom. Clearly, its explanation lies in the fact that he who would live the life of a robber must forgo sleep by night, and in the daytime he must employ shifts and lie in ambuscade; he must prepare and make ready his scouts, and so forth, if he is to succeed in capturing the quarry. It is obvious, I say, that the whole of this education tended and was intended to make the boys craftier and more inventive in getting in supplies, while at the same time it cultivated their warlike instincts. An objector may retort: "But if he thought it so fine a feat to steal, why did he inflict all those blows on the unfortunate who was caught?" My answer is: for the self-same reason which induces people, in other matters which are taught, to punish the mal-performance of a service. So they, the Lacedaemonians, visit penalties on the boy who is detected thieving as being but a sorry bungler in the art....

5.   ... When Lycurgus first came to deal with the question [of meals], the Spartans, like the rest of the Hellenes, used to mess privately at home. Tracing more than half the current misdemeanors to this custom, he was determined to drag his people out of holes and corners into the broad daylight, and so he invented the public mess-rooms. Whereby he expected at any rate to minimize the transgression of orders. As to food, his ordinance allowed them so much as, while not inducing repletion, should guard them from actual want. And, in fact, there are many exceptional dishes in the shape of game supplied from the hunting field. Or, as a substitute for these, rich men will occasionally garnish the feast with wheaten loaves, so that from beginning to end, till the mess breaks up, the common board is never stinted for viands, nor yet extravagantly furnished....

7.   ... We all know that in the generality of states everyone devotes his full energy to the business of making money: one man as a tiller of the soil, another as a mariner, a third as a merchant, while others depend on various arts to earn a living. But at Sparta Lycurgus forbade his freeborn citizens to have anything whatsoever to do with the concerns of money-making. As freemen, he enjoined upon them to regard as their concern exclusively those activities upon which the foundations of civic liberty are based....

8.   .. The ephors are competent to punish whomsoever they choose; they have power to exact fines on the spur of the moment; they have power to depose magistrates in mid career—nay, actually to imprison them and bring them to trial on the capital charge. Entrusted with these vast powers, they do not, as do the rest of states, allow the magistrates elected to exercise authority as they like, right through the year of office; but in the style rather of despotic monarchs or presidents of the games, at the first symptom of an offense against the law they inflict chastizement without warning and without hesitation....

10. That too was a happy enactment, in my opinion, by which Lycurgus provided for the continual cultivation of virtue, even to old age. By fixing the election to the council of elders [gerousia] as a last ordeal at the goal of life, he made it impossible for a high standard of virtuous living to be disregarded even in old age. So, too, it is worthy of admiration in him that he lent his helping hand to virtuous old age. Thus, by making the elders sole arbiters in the trial for life he contrived to charge old age with a greater weight of honor than that which is accorded to the strength of mature manhood....

15. I wish to explain with sufficient detail the nature of the covenant between king and state as instituted by Lycurgus.... Lycurgus laid it down as law that the king shall offer in behalf of the state all public sacrifices, as being himself of divine descent; and whithersoever the state shall despatch her armies, the king shall take the lead.... Moreover, all rise from their seats to give place to the king, save only that the ephors rise not from their thrones of office. Monthly they exchange oaths: the ephors in behalf of the state, the king himself in his own behalf. And this is the oath on the king's part: "I will exercise my kingship in accordance with the established laws of the state." And on the part of the state the oath runs: "So long as he (who exercises kingship) shall abide by his oaths, we will not suffer his kingship to be shaken."...

B. Aristotle

In the second book of his Politics Aristotle critically analyzed ideal states, such as the one proposed by Plato in his Republic, along with three actual constitutions that Aristotle regarded as most closely approaching the ideal. The latter were the political systems of Sparta, Crete, and the non-Greek state of Carthage, the last being the only non-Greek state treated by Aristotle in the treatise. Although Greek writers of the fifth and early fourth centuries B.C. had singled out Sparta as possessing the best form of government among the Greeks, Aristotle wrote his analysis of the Spartan constitution after the battle of Leuctra (371 B.C.), which resulted in the end of Sparta's hegemony in the Aegean world, the disintegration of its Peloponnesian League, and its loss of Messenia with its large Helot population. Consequently, Aristotle's evaluation of the Spartan social and political system had the advantage of hindsight and differed sharply from Xenophon's glowing appraisal as set forth in the previous passage.

(Taken from Book II, Chapter 9 of The Politics of Aristotle, translated by Benjamin Jowett, Oxford 1885, revised by Gary Forsythe)

In the governments of Lacedaemon and Crete, and indeed in all governments, two points have to be considered: first, whether any particular law is good or bad, when compared with the perfect state; secondly, whether it is or is not consistent with the idea and character which the lawgiver has set before his citizens. That in a well-ordered state the citizens should have leisure and not have to provide for their daily wants is generally acknowledged, but there is a difficulty in seeing how this leisure is to be attained. The Thessalian Penestae [serfs] have often risen against their masters, and the Helots in like manner against the Lacedaemonians, for whose misfortunes they are always lying in wait. Nothing, however, of this kind has as yet happened to the Cretans; the reason probably is that the neighboring cities, even when at war with one another, never form an alliance with rebellious serfs, rebellions not being for their interest, since they themselves have a dependent population. Whereas all the neighbors of the Lacedaemonians, whether Argives, Messenians, or Arcadians, were their enemies. In Thessaly, again, the original revolt of the slaves occurred, because the Thessalians were still at war with the neighboring Achaeans, Perrhaebians, and Magnesians. Besides, if there were no other difficulty, the treatment or management of slaves is a troublesome affair; for, if not kept in hand, they are insolent and think that they are as good as their masters; and if harshly treated, they hate and conspire against them. Now it is clear that when these are the results, the citizens of a state have not found out the secret of managing their subject population.

Again, the license of the Lacedaemonian women defeats the intention of the Spartan constitution and is adverse to the happiness of the state: for, a husband and wife being each a part of every family, the state may be considered as about equally divided into men and women; and, therefore, in those states in which the condition of the women is bad, half the city may be regarded as having no laws. And this is what has actually happened at Sparta; the legislator wanted to make the whole state hardy and temperate, and he has carried out his intention in the case of the men, but he has neglected the women, who live in every sort of intemperance and luxury. The consequence is that in such a state wealth is too highly valued, especially if the citizen fall under the dominion of their wives, after the manner of most warlike races, except the Celts and a few others who openly approve of male loves. The old mythologer [i.e., Homer] would seem to have been right in uniting Ares and Aphrodite: for all warlike races are prone to the love either of men or of women. This was exemplified among the Spartans in the days of their greatness; many things were managed by their women. But what difference does it make whether women rule, or the rulers are ruled by women? The result is the same. Even in regard to courage, which is of no use in daily life and is needed only in war, the influence of the Lacedaemonian women has been most mischievous. The evil showed itself in the Theban invasion [369 B.C.], when, unlike the women of other cities, they were utterly useless and caused more confusion than the enemy.

This license of the Lacedaemonian women existed from the earliest times and was only what might be expected: for during the wars of the Lacedaemonians, first against the Argives, and afterwards against the Arcadians and Messenians, the men were long away from home; and, on the return of peace, they gave themselves into the legislator's hand, already prepared by the discipline of a soldier's life (in which there are many elements of virtue), to receive his enactments. But, when Lycurgus, as tradition says, wanted to bring the women under his laws, they resisted; and he gave up the attempt. These then are the causes of what then happened, and this defect in the constitution is clearly to be attributed to them.

We are not, however, considering what is or is not to be excused, but what is right or wrong; and the disorder of the women, as I have already said, not only gives an air of indecorum to the constitution considered in itself, but tends in a measure to foster avarice. The mention of avarice naturally suggests a criticism on the inequality of property. While some of the Spartan citizens have quite small properties, others have very large ones; hence, the land has passed into the hands of a few. And this is due also to faulty laws; for although the legislator rightly holds up to shame the sale or purchase of an inheritance, he allows anybody who likes to give or bequeath it. Yet, both practices lead to the same result. And nearly two fifths of the whole country are held by women; this is due to the number of heiresses and to the large dowries which are customary. It would surely have been better to have given no dowries at all, or, if any, but small or moderate ones. As the law now stands, a man may bestow his heiress on anyone whom he pleases; and if he die intestate, the privilege of giving her away descends to his heir. Hence, although the country is able to maintain 1500 cavalry and 30,000 hoplites, the whole number of Spartan citizens fell below 1000 [after the battle of Leuctra in 371 B.C.]. The result proves the faulty nature of their laws respecting property; for the city sank under a single defeat; the want of men was their ruin.

There is a tradition that in the days of their ancient kings they were in the habit of giving the rights of citizenship to strangers; and therefore, in spite of their long wars, no lack of population was experienced by them; indeed, at one time Sparta is said to have numbered not less than 10,000 citizens. Whether this statement is true or not, it would certainly have been better to have maintained their numbers by the equalization of property.

Again, the law that relates to the procreation of children is adverse to the correction of this inequality: for the legislator, wanting to have as many Spartans as he could, encouraged the citizens to have large families; and there is a law at Sparta that the father of three sons shall be exempt from military service, and he who has four from all the burdens of the state. Yet, it is obvious that if there were many children, the land being distributed as it is, many of them must necessarily fall into poverty.

The Lacedaemonian constitution is defective in another point: I mean the Ephoralty. This magistracy has authority in the highest matters, but the Ephors are chosen from the whole people, and so the office is apt to fall into the hands of very poor men, who, being badly off, are open to bribes. There have been many examples at Sparta of this evil in former times; and quite recently in the matter of the Andrians, certain of the Ephors who were bribed did their best to ruin the state. And so great and tyrannical is their power that even the kings have been compelled to court them, so that, in this way as well together with the royal office, the whole constitution has deteriorated, and from being an aristocracy has turned into a democracy. The Ephoralty certainly does keep the state together: for the people are contented when they have a share in the highest office; and the result, whether due to the legislator or to chance, has been advantageous: for if a constitution is to be permanent, all the parts of the state must wish that it should exist, and the same arrangements be maintained. This is the case at Sparta, where the kings desire its permanence, because they have due honor in their own persons; the nobles, because they are represented in the council of elders (for the office of elder is a reward of virtue); and the people, because all are eligible to the Ephoralty. The election of Ephors out of the whole people is perfectly right, but it ought not to be carried on in the present fashion, which is too childish [probably by the assembly shouting its approval rather than by voting]. Again, they have the decision of great causes, although they are quite ordinary men; and therefore they should not determine them merely on their own judgment, but according to written rules and to the laws. Their way of life, too, is not in accordance with the spirit of the constitution. They have a deal too much license; whereas, in the case of the other citizens, the excess of strictness is so intolerable that they run away from the law into the secret indulgence of sensual pleasures.

Again, the council of elders is not free from defects. It may be said that the elders are good men and well trained in manly virtue; and that, therefore, there is an advantage to the state in having them. But that judges of important causes should hold office for life is a disputable thing: for the mind grows old as well as the body; and when men have been educated in such a manner that even the legislator himself cannot trust them, there is real danger. Many of the elders are well known to have taken bribes and to have been guilty of partiality in public affairs. And therefore they ought not to be irresponsible; yet, at Sparta they are so. But it may be replied, "All magistracies are accountable to the Ephors." Yes, but this prerogative is too great for them, and we maintain that the control should be exercised in some other manner. Further, the mode in which the Spartans elect their elders is childish [probably by the assembly shouting its approval rather than by voting]; and it is improper that the person to be elected should canvass for the office; the worthiest should be appointed, whether he chooses or not. And here the legislator clearly indicates the same intention which appears in other parts of his constitution: he would have his citizens ambitious, and he has reckoned upon this quality in the election of the elders; for no one would ask to be elected if he were not. Yet, ambition and avarice, almost more than any other passions, are the motives of crime.

Whether kings are or are not an advantage to states, I will consider at another time; they should at any rate be chosen, not as they are now by heredeitary succession, but with regard to their personal life and conduct. The legislator himself obviously did not suppose that he could make them really good men; at least, he shows a great distrust of their virtue. For this reason the Spartans used to join enemies with them in the same embassy, and the quarrels between the kings were held to be conservative of the state.

Neither did the first introducer of the common meals, called phiditia, regulate them well. The entertainment ought to have been provided at the public cost, as in Crete; but among the Lacedaemonians everyone is expected to contribute, and some of them are too poor to afford the expense; thus the intention of the legislator is frustrated. The common meals were meant to be a popular institution, but the existing manner of regulating them is the reverse of popular: for the very poor can scarcely take part in them; and according to ancient custom, those who cannot contribute are not allowed to retain their rights of citizenship.

The law about the Spartan admirals has often been censured and with justice; it is a source of dissension: for the kings are perpetual generals, and this office of admiral is but the setting up of another king.

The charge which Plato brings in The Laws against the intention of the legislator is likewise justified. The whole constitution has regard to one part of virtue, only the virtue of the soldier, which gives victory in war. So long as they were at war, therefore, their power was preserved; but when they had attained empire, they fell: for of the arts of peace they knew nothing and had never engaged in any employment higher than war. There is another error, equally great, into which they have fallen. Although they truly think that the goods for which men contend are to be acquired by virtue rather than by vice, they err in supposing that these goods are to be preferred to the virtue which gains them.

Once more, the revenues of the state are ill managed. There is no money in the treasury, although they are obliged to carry on great wars; and they are unwilling to pay taxes. The greater part of the land being in the hands of the Spartans, they do not look closely into one another's contributions. The result which the legislator has produced is the reverse of beneficial: for he has made his city poor and his citizens greedy. Enough respecting the Spartan constitution, of which these are the principal defects.

READING 29
ARISTOTLE ON EARLY ATHENS

The following passage is taken from Aristotle's treatise, The Constitution of the Athenians. The first half of this work is a historical account of the political development of the Athenian state, followed in the second half by a detailed description of the workings of the various institutions of the Athenian democracy of Aristotle's day (the fourth century B.C.). The passage presented here describes Athenian political history from Solon's legislative activity in 594 to the end of the Peisistratid tyranny in 510 B.C, and it contains one of the fullest and most detailed accounts of a tyranny of the Greek Archaic Period.

(Taken from Aristotle on the Athenian Constitution, translated by Frederic G. Kenyon, published by G. Bell and Sons,
London 1891, revised by Gary Forsythe)

5. Since such, then, was the organization of the constitution, and the many were in slavery to the few, the people rose against the upper class. The strife was keen, and for a long time the two parties were ranged in hostile camps against one another, till at last, by common consent they appointed Solon to be mediator and Archon, and they committed the whole constitution to his hands. The immediate oc-casion of his appointment was his poem, which begins with the words:

I behold, and within my heart deep sadness has claimed its place, As I mark the oldest home of the ancient Ionian race Slain by the sword.

In this poem he fights and disputes on behalf of each party in turn against the other, and finally he advises them to come to terms and to put an end to the quarrel existing between them. By birth and reputation Solon was one of the foremost men of the day, but in wealth and position he was of the middle class, as is generally agreed, and is, indeed, established by his own evidence in these poems, where he exhorts the wealthy not to be grasping.

> But ye who have store of good, who are sated and overflow,
> Restrain your swelling soul, and still it and keep it low:
> Let the heart that is great within you be trained a lowlier way;
> Ye shall not have all at your will, and we will not for ever obey.

Indeed, he constantly fastens the blame of the conflict on the rich; and accordingly, at the beginning of the poem he says that he fears "the love of wealth and an overweening mind," evidently meaning that it was through these that the quarrel arose.

6. As soon as he was at the head of affairs, Solon liberated the people once and for all by prohibiting all loans on the security of the debtor's person. And in addition, he made laws by which he cancelled all debts, public and private. This measure is commonly called the Seisachtheia [removal of burdens], since thereby the people had their loads removed from them. In connection with it some persons try to traduce the character of Solon. It so happened that when he was about to enact the Seisachtheia, he communicated his intention to some members of the upper class. Whereupon, as the partisans of the popular party say, his friends stole a march on him, while those who wish to attack his character maintain that he too had a share in the fraud himself: for these persons borrowed money and bought up a large amount of land; and so, when a short time afterwards all debts were cancelled, they became wealthy; and this, they say, was the origin of the families who were afterwards looked on as having been wealthy from primeval times. However, the story of the popular party is by far the most probable: a man who was so moderate and public spirited in all his other actions, that when it was within his power to put his fellow citizens

beneath his feet and establish himself as tyrant, he preferred instead to incur the hostility of both parties by placing his honor and the general welfare above his personal aggrandisement, is not likely to have consented to defile his hands by such a petty and palpable fraud. That he had this absolute power is, in the first place, indicated by the desperate condition of the country; moreover, he mentions it himself repeatedly in his poems, and it is universally admitted. We are therefore bound to consider this accusation to be false.

7. Next, Solon drew up a constitution and enacted new laws; and the ordinances of Draco ceased to be used with the exception of those relating to murder. The laws were inscribed on the wooden stands and set up in the King's Porch, and all swore to obey them; and the nine Archons made oath upon the stone, declaring that they would dedicate a golden statue if they should transgress any of them. This is the origin of the oath to that effect which they take to the present day. Solon ratified his laws for a hundred years; and the following was the fashion in which he organized the constitution. He divided the population according to property into four classes, just as it had been divided before: namely, Pentacosiomedimni, Knights [hipeis], Zeugitae, and Thetes. The various magistracies—namely, the nine Archons, the Treasurers, the Commissioners for Public Contracts (Poletae), the Eleven, and Clerks (Colacretae)—he assigned to the Pentacosiomedimni, the Knights, and the Zeugitae, giving offices to each class in proportion to the value of their rateable property. To those who ranked among the Thetes he gave nothing but a place in the Assembly and in the juries. A man had to rank as a Pentacosiomedimnus if he made from his own land five hundred measures, whether liquid or solid. Those ranked as Knights who made three hundred measures, or, as some say, those who were able to maintain a horse. In support of the latter definition they adduce the name of the class, which may be supposed to be derived from this fact, and also some votive offerings of early times; for in the Acropolis there is a votive offering, a statue of Diphilus, bearing this inscription:

"The son of Diphilus, Athenion height,
Raised from the Thetes and become a knight,
Did to the gods this sculptured charger bring
For his promotion a thank offering."

And a horse stands in evidence beside the man, implying that this was what was meant by belonging to the rank of Knight. At the same time it seems reasonable to suppose that this class, like the Pentacosiomedimni, was defined by the possession of an income of a certain number of measures. Those ranked as Zeugitae were those who made two hundred measures, liquid or solid; and the rest were ranked as Thetes and were not eligible for any office. Hence, it is that even at the present day, when a candidate for any office is asked to what class he belongs, no one would think of saying that he belonged to the Thetes.

8. The elections to the various offices, Solon enacted, should be by lot out of candidates selected by each of the tribes. Each tribe selected ten candidates for the nine archonships, and among these the lot was cast. Hence, it is still the custom for each tribe to choose ten candidates by lot, and then the lot is again cast among these. A proof that Solon regulated the elections to office according to the property classes may be found in the law still in force with regard to the Treasurers, which enacts that they shall be chosen from the Pentacosiomedimni. Such was Solon's legislation with respect to the nine Archons; whereas in early times the Council of the Areopagus summoned suitable persons according to its own judgment and appointed them for the year to the several offices. There were four tribes, as before, and four tribe kings. Each tribe was divided into three Trittyes [Thirds] with twelve Naucraries in each; and the Naucraries had officers of their own, called Naucrari, whose duty it was to superintend the current receipts and expenditure. Hence, among the laws of Solon, now obsolete, it is repeatedly written that the Naucrari are to receive and to spend out of the Naucraric fund. Solon also appointed a Council of four hundred, a hundred from each tribe; but he assigned to the Council of the Areopagus the duty of superintending the laws, acting as before as the guardian of the constitution in general. It kept watch

over the affairs of the state in most of the more important matters and corrected offenders with full powers to inflict either fines or personal punishment. The money received in fines it brought up into the Acropolis without assigning the reason for the fine. It also tried those who conspired for the overthrow of the state, Solon having enacted a process of impeachment to deal with such offenders. Further, since he saw the state often engaged in internal disputes, while many of the citizens from sheer indifference accepted whatever might turn up, he made a law with express reference to such persons, enacting that any-one who in a time of civil factions did not take up arms with either party, should lose his rights as a citizen and cease to have any part in the state.

9. Such, then, was his legislation concerning the magistracies. There are three points in the constitution of Solon which appear to be its most democratic features: first and most important, the prohibition of loans on the security of the debtor's person; secondly, the right of every person who so willed to claim redress on behalf of anyone to whom wrong was being done; thirdly, the institution of the appeal to the jurycourts; and it is to this last, they say, that the masses have owed their strength most of all, since, when the democracy is master of the voting power, it is master of the constitution. Moreover, since the laws were not drawn up in simple and explicit terms (but like the one concerning inheritances and wards of state), disputes in-evitably occurred, and the courts had to decide in every matter, whether public or private. Some persons in fact believe that Solon deliberately made the laws indefinite in order that the final decision might be in the hands of the people. This, however, is not probable, and the reason no doubt was that it is impossible to attain ideal per-fection when framing a law in general terms; for we must judge of his intentions, not from the actual results in the present day, but from the general tenor of the rest of his legislation....

11. When he had completed his organization of the constitution in the manner that has been described, he found himself beset by people coming to him and harassing him concerning his laws, criticizing here and questioning there, till, as he wished neither to alter what he had

decided on nor yet to be an object of ill will to everyone by remaining in Athens, he set off on a journey to Egypt with the combined objects of trade and travel, giving out that he should not return for ten years. He considered that there was no call for him to expound the laws personally, but that everyone should obey them just as they were written. Moreover, his position at this time was unpleasant. Many members of the upper class had been estranged from him on account of his abolition of debts, and both parties were alienated through their disappointment at the condition of things that he had created. The mass of the people had expected him to make a complete redistribution of all property, and the upper class hoped that he would restore everything to its former position or, at any rate, make but a small change. Solon, however, had resisted both classes. He might have made himself a despot by attaching himself to whichever party he chose, but he preferred, though at the cost of incurring the enmity of both, to be the savior of his country and the ideal lawgiver.

12. The truth of this view of Solon's policy is established alike by common consent and by the mention that he has himself made of the matter in his poems. Thus:

I gave to the mass of the people such rank as befitted their need,
I took not away their honor, and I granted naught to their greed; While those who were rich in power, who in wealth were glorious and great,
I bethought me that naught should befall them unworthy their splendor and state;
So I stood with my shield outstretched, and both were sale in its sight,
And I would not that either should triumph, when the triumph was not with right.

Again, he declares how the mass of the people ought to be treated:

But thus will the people best the voice of their leaders obey,
When neither too slack is the rein, nor violence holdeth the sway;

> For indulgence breedeth a child, the presumption that
> spurns control,
> When riches too great are poured upon men of unbalanced soul.

And again, elsewhere he speaks about the persons who wished to redistribute the land:

> So they came in search of plunder, and their cravings knew
> no bound,
> Everyone among them deeming endless wealth would here
> be found.
> And that I with glozing smoothness hid a cruel mind within.
> Fondly then and vainly dreamt they; now they raise an angry din,
> And they glare askance in anger, and the light within their eyes
> Burns with hostile flames upon me. Yet, therein no justice lies.
> All I promised, fully wrought I with the gods at hand to cheer,
> Naught beyond in folly ventured. Never to my soul was dear
> With a tyrant's force to govern, nor to see the good and base
> Side by side in equal portion share the rich home of our race.

Once more, he speaks of the abolition of debts and of those who before were in servitude but were released due to the Seisachtheia:

Of all the aims for which I summoned forth The people, was there one I compassed not? Thou, when slow time brings justice in its train, O mighty mother of the Olympian gods, Dark Earth, thou best canst witness, from whose breast I swept the pillars broadcast planted there, And made thee free, who hadst been slave of yore. And many a man whom fraud or law had sold: for from his god-built land, an outcast slave, I brought again to Athens; yea, and some,

> Exiles from home through debt's oppressive load,
> Speaking no more the dear Athenian tongue,
> But wandering far and wide, I brought again;
> And those that here in vilest slavery
> Crouched 'neath a master's frown, I set them free.

Thus might and right were yoked in harmony,
Since by the force of law I won my ends
And kept my promise. Equal laws I gave
To evil and to good, with even hand
Drawing straight justice for the lot of each.
But had another held the goad as
One in whose heart was guile and greediness,
He had not kept the people back from strife: for had I
granted, now what pleased the one,
Then what their foes devised in counterpoise,
Of many a man this state had been bereft. Therefore I
showed my might on every side,
Turning at bay like wolf among the hounds.

And again, he reviles both parties for their grumblings in the times that followed:

Nay, if one must lay blame where blame is due,
Wer't not for me, the people ne'er had set
Their eyes upon these blessings e'en in dreams:
While greater men, the men of wealthier life,
Should praise me and should court me as their friend.

For had any other man, he says, received this exalted post,

He had not kept the people hack, nor ceased
Til he had robbed the richness of the milk.
But I stood forth a landmark in the midst,
And barred the foes from battle.

13. Such then were Solon's reasons for his departure from the country. After his retirement the city was still torn by divisions. For four years, indeed, they lived in peace; but in the fifth year after Solon's government they were unable to elect an Archon on account of their dissensions, and again four years later they elected no Archon for the same reason. Subsequently, after a similar period had elapsed, Damasias was

elected Archon; and he governed for two years and two months, until he was forcibly expelled from his office. After this, it was agreed, as a compromise, to elect ten Archons: five from the Eupatridae [well-fathered], three from the Agroikoi [countryfolk], and two from the Demiourgoi [artisans]; and they ruled for the year following Damasias. It is clear from this that the Archon was at the time the magistrate who possessed the greatest power, since it is always in connection with this office that conflicts are seen to arise. But altogether they were in a continual state of internal disorder. Some found the cause and justification of their discontent in the abolition of debts, because thereby they had been reduced to poverty; others were dissatisfied with the political constitution, because it had undergone a revolutionary change; while with others the motive was found in personal rivalries among themselves. The parties at this time were three in number. First, there was the party of the Shore, led by Megacles the son of Alcmeon, which was considered to aim at a moderate form of government; then, there were the men of the Plain, who desired an oligarchy and were led by Lycurgus; and thirdly, there were the men of the Highlands, at the head of whom was Peisistratus, who was looked on as an extreme democrat. This latter party was reinforced from motives of poverty by those who had been deprived of the debts due to them, and from motives of personal apprehension by those who were not of pure descent. A proof of this is seen in the fact that after the tyranny was overthrown, a revision was made of the citizen roll on the ground that many persons were partaking in the franchise without having a right to it. The names given to the respective parties were derived from the districts in which they held their lands.

14. Peisistratus had the reputation of being an extreme democrat, and he also had distinguished himself greatly in the war with Megara. Taking advantage of this, he wounded himself; and by representing that his injuries had been inflicted on him by his political rivals, he persuaded the people through a motion proposed by Aristion to grant him a bodyguard. After he had got these 'club bearers', as they were called, he made an attack with them on the people and seized the Acropolis.

This happened in the archonship of Comeas, thirty one years after the legislation of Solon [563 B.C.]. It is related that when Peisistratus asked for his bodyguard, Solon opposed the request and declared that in so doing he proved himself wiser than half the people and braver than the rest: wiser than those who did not see that Peisistratus designed to make himself tyrant, and braver than those who saw it and kept silence. But when all his words availed nothing, he carried forth his armor and set it up in front of his house, saying that he had helped his country so far as lay in his power (he was already a very old man), and that he called on all others to do the same. Solon's exhortations, however, proved fruitless, and Peisistratus assumed the sovereignty. His administration was more like a constitutional government than the rule of a tyrant; but before his power was firmly established, the adherents of Megacles and Lycurgus made a coalition and drove him out. This took place in the archonship of Hegesias, five years after the first establishment of his rule. Eleven years later Megacles, being in difficulties in a party struggle, again opened negotiations with Peisistratus, proposing that the latter should marry his daughter; and on these terms he brought him back to Athens by a very primitive and simple-minded device. He first spread abroad a rumor that Athena was bringing back Peisistratus; and then, having found a woman of great stature and beauty, named Phye (according to Herodotus, of the deme of Paeania, but as others say, a Thracian flower seller of the deme of Collytus), he dressed her in a garb resembling that of the goddess and brought her into the city with Peisistratus. The latter drove in on a chariot with the woman beside him; and the inhabitants of the city, struck with awe, received him with adoration.

15. In this manner did his first return take place. He did not, however, hold his power long: for about six years after his return he was again expelled. He refused to treat the daughter of Megacles as his wife; and being afraid, in consequence, of a combination of the two opposing parties, he retired from the country. First, he led a colony to a place called Rhaicelus in the region of the Thermaic Gulf; and thence he passed to the country in the neighborhood of Mt. Pangaeus. Here he acquired wealth and hired mercenaries; and not till ten years had

elapsed did he return to Eretria and make an attempt to recover the government by force. In this he had the assistance of many allies, notably the Thebans and Lygdamis of Naxos, and also the Knights who held the supreme power in the constitution of Eretria. After his victory in the battle at Pallene he captured Athens; and when he had disarmed the people, he at last had his tyranny securely established and was able to take Naxos and set up Lygdamis as ruler there. He effected the disarmament of the people in the following manner. He ordered a parade in full armor in the Theseum and began to make a speech to the people. He spoke for a short time, until the people called out that they could not hear him; whereupon he bade them come up to the entrance of the Acropolis in order that his voice might be better heard. Then, while he continued to speak to them at great length, men whom he had appointed for the purpose collected the arms and locked them up in the chambers of the Theseum hard by; and they came and made a signal to him that it was done. Peisistratus accordingly, when he had finished the rest of what he had to say, told the people also what had happened to their arms, adding that they were not to be surprised or alarmed, but they should go home and attend to their private affairs, while he would himself for the future manage all the business of the state.

16. Such was the origin and such the vicissitudes of the tyranny of Peisistratus. His administration was temperate, as has been said before, and more like constitutional government than a tyranny. Not only was he in every respect humane and mild and ready to forgive those who offended, but, in addition, he advanced money to the poorer people to help them in their labors, so that they might make their living by agriculture. In this he had two objects: first, that they might not spend their time in the city, but might be scattered over all the face of the country; and secondly, that, being moderately well off and occupied with their own business, they might have neither the wish nor the time to attend to public affairs. At the same time his revenues were increased by the thorough cultivation of the country, since he imposed a tax of one tenth on all the produce. For the same reasons he instituted the local justices and often made expeditions in person into the

country to inspect it and to settle disputes between individuals in order that they might not come into the city and neglect their farms. It was in one of these progresses that, as the story goes, Peisistratus had his adventure with the man of Hymettus, who was cultivating the spot afterwards known as "Tax-free Farm." He saw a man digging and working at a very stony piece of ground; and being surprised, he sent his attendant to ask what he got out of this plot of land. "Aches and pains," said the man; "and that's what Peisistratus ought to have his tenth of." The man spoke without knowing who his questioner was; but Peisistratus was so pleased with his frank speech and his industry that he granted him exemption from all taxes. And so in matters in general he burdened the people as little as possible with his government, but he always cultivated peace and kept them in all quietness. Hence, the tyranny of Peisistratus was often spoken of proverbially as "the age of gold;" for when his sons succeeded him, the government became much harsher. But most important of all in this respect was his popular and kindly disposition. In all things he was accustomed to observe the laws without giving himself any exceptional privileges. Once, he was summoned on a charge of homicide before the Areopagus, and he appeared in person to make his defense; but the prosecutor was afraid to present himself and abandoned the case. For these reasons he held power long; and whenever he was expelled, he regained his position easily. The majority alike of the upper class and of the people were in his favor; the former he won by his social intercourse with them, the latter by the assistance which he gave to their private purses, and his nature fitted him to win the hearts of both. Moreover, the laws in reference to tyrants at that time in force at Athens were very mild, especially the one which applies more particularly to the establishment of a tyranny. The law ran as follows: "These are the ancestral statutes of the Athenians: if any persons shall make an attempt to establish a tyranny, or if any person shall join in setting up a tyranny, he shall lose his civic rights, both himself and his whole house."

17. Thus did Peisistratus grow old in the possession of power, and he died a natural death in the archonship of Philoneos [527 B.C.], three and

thirty years from the time at which he first established himself as tyrant [560 B.C.], during nineteen of which he was in possession of power [546-527 B.C.]; the rest he spent in exile. It is evident from this that the story is mere gossip that states that Peisistratus was the youthful favorite of Solon and commanded in the war against Megara for the recovery of Salamis. It will not harmonize with their respective ages, as anyone may see who will reckon up the years of the life of each of them, and the dates at which they died. After the death of Peisistratus his sons took up the government and conducted it on the same system. He had two sons by his first and legitimate wife, Hippias and Hipparchus, and two by his Argive consort, Iophon and Hegesistratus, who was surnamed Thessalus: for Peisistratus took a wife from Argos, Timonassa, the daughter of a man of Argos, named Gorgilus; she had previously been the wife of Archinus of Ambracia, one of the descendants of Cypselus. This was the origin of his friendship with the Argives, on account of which a thousand of them were brought over by Hegesistratus and fought on his side in the battle at Pallene. Some authorities say that this marriage took place after his first expulsion from Athens, others while he was in possession of the government.

18. Hippias and Hipparchus assumed the control of affairs on grounds alike of standing and of age; but Hippias, as being also naturally of a statesmanlike and shrewd disposition, was really the head of the government. Hipparchus was youthful in disposition, amorous, and fond of literature (it was he who invited to Athens Anacreon, Simonides, and the other poets), while Thessalus was much junior in age and was violent and headstrong in his behavior. It was from his character that all the evils arose which befell the house. He became enamoured of Harmodius; and since he failed to win his affection, he lost all restraint upon his passion; and in addition to other exhibitions of rage, he finally prevented the sister of Harmodius from taking the part of a basket bearer in the Panathenaic procession, alleging as his reason that Harmodius was a person of loose life. Thereupon, in a frenzy of wrath Harmodius and Aristogeiton did their celebrated deed in conjunction with a number of confederates. But while they were lying in wait for

Hippias in the Acropolis at the time of the Panathenaea (Hippias, at this moment was awaiting the arrival of the procession, while Hipparchus was organizing its dispatch), they saw one of the persons privy to the plot talking familiarly with him. Thinking that he was betraying them, and desiring to do something before they were arrested, they rushed down and made their attempt without waiting for the rest of their confederates. They succeeded in killing Hipparchus near the Leocoreum while he was engaged in arranging the procession; but they ruined the design as a whole; of the two leaders, Harmodius was killed on the spot by the guards, while Aristogeiton was arrested and perished later after suffering long tortures. While under the torture, he accused many persons who belonged by birth to the most distinguished families and were also personal friends of the tyrants. At first the government could find no clue to the conspiracy; for the current story that Hippias made all who were taking part in the procession leave their arms, and then he detected those who were carrying secret daggers, cannot be true, since at that time they did not bear arms in the processions, this being a custom instituted at a later period by the democracy. According to the story of the popular party, Aristogeiton accused the friends of the tyrants with the deliberate intention that the latter might commit an impious act and at the same time weaken themselves by putting to death innocent men who were their own friends; others say that he told no falsehood, but was betraying the actual accomplices. At last, when for all his efforts he could not obtain release by death, he promised to give further information against a number of other persons; and having induced Hippias to give him his hand to confirm his word, as soon as he had hold of it, he reviled him for giving his hand to the murderer of his brother, till Hippias in a frenzy of rage lost control of himself, snatched out his dagger, and dispatched him.

19. After this event [514 B.C.] the tyranny became much harsher. In consequence of his vengeance for his brother and of the execution and banishment of a large number of persons, Hippias became a distrusted and an embittered man. About three years after the death of Hipparchus, finding his position in the city insecure, he set about fortifying

Munichia with the intention of establishing himself there. While he was still engaged on this work, however, he was expelled by Cleomenes, king of Lacedaemon, in consequence of the Spartans being continually incited by oracles to overthrow the tyranny. These oracles were obtained in the following way. The Athenian exiles, headed by the Alcmeonidae, could not by their own power effect their return, but failed continually in their attempts. Among their other failures they fortified a post in Attica, Lipsydrium, above Mt. Parnes, and were there joined by some partisans from the city; but they were besieged by the tyrants and reduced to surrender. After this disaster the following became a popular drinking song:

"Ah! Lipsydrium, faithless friend!
Lo, what heroes to death didst send,
Nobly born and great in deed!
Well did they prove themselves at need
Of noble sires a noble seed."

Having failed, then, in every other method they took the contract for rebuilding the temple at Delphi [which had been destroyed by a fire], thereby obtaining ample funds, which they employed to secure the help of the Lacedaemonians. All this time the Pythia kept continually enjoining on the Lacedaemonians who came to consult the oracle that they must free Athens, till finally she succeeded in impelling the Spartans to that step, although the house of Peisistratus was connected with them by ties of hospitality. The resolution of the Lacedaemonians was, however, at least equally due to the friendship which had been formed between the house of Peisistratus and Argos. Accordingly, they first sent Anchimolus by sea at the head of an army; but he was defeated and killed through the arrival of Cineas of Thessaly to support the sons of Peisistratus with a force of a thousand horsemen. Then, being roused to anger by this disaster, they sent their king, Cleomenes, by land at the head of a larger force; and he, after defeating the Thessalian cavalry when they attempted to intercept his march into Attica, shut up Hippias within what was known as the Pelargic Wall and blockaded him there with the assistance of the Athenians. While he was sitting down before the place, it so happened that the sons of the Peisistratidae were captured in an attempt to slip out; upon which the tyrants capitulated on condition of the safety of their children, and they surrendered the Acropolis to the Athenians, five days being first allowed them to remove their effects. This took place in the archonship of Harpactides, after they had held the tyranny for about seventeen years since their father's death [527-510 B.C.], or in all, including the period of their father's rule, for nine and forty years.

READING 30
EARLY GREEK LYRIC POETRY

The simplicity of the Greek alphabet enabled a sizable portion of the Greek population to become literate; and following the epic compositions of Homer and Hesiod during the early part of the Greek Archaic Period, there flourished numerous Greek poets from all walks of life who expressed their personal experiences, thoughts, and desires in a wide range of poetic meters. Consequently, the second half of the Greek Archaic Period is sometimes termed The Lyric Age of Greece. The following passages represent a very small sample of this rich and varied literature. Given the fact that our principal historical sources of information on Archaic Greece were written much later, these writings form one of our most important sources of contemporary evidence for Greek culture during the second half of the Archaic Period.

> (Taken from pp. 1-2, 14-16, 24-26, 38-40, and 54-56 of Greek Lyrics, translated by Richmond Lattimore, Second Edition, U. of Chicago Press, copyright 1949, reprinted with the permission of the publisher)

A. Archilochus
Archilochus seems to have lived during the middle part of the seventh century B.C. Although he was a man of aristocratic birth born on the Cycladic island of Paros, he joined a Greek expedition to colonize the northern Aegean island of Thasos. Since it was already inhabited by fierce Thracians, the Greeks had to engage in hard fighting in order to establish themselves on the island. As is

the case with so many of these early Greek poets, their writings have survived only in short fragmentary quotations found in later Greek works.

1. Some barbarian is waving my shield, since I was obliged to leave that perfectly good piece of equipment behind under a bush. But I got away. So what does it matter? Let the shield go; I can buy another one equally good....

2. In my spear-shaft is my kneaded barley meal. In my spear is my Ismaric wine. Leaning on my spear-shaft I drink.

3. I don't like the towering captain with the spraddly length of leg, one who swaggers in his lovelocks and cleanshaves beneath the chin. Give me a man short and squarely set upon his legs, a man full of heart, not to be shaken from the place he plants his feet....

4. I do not care for the goods of gold-rich Gyges. Envy has not gripped me, and I do not desire the works of gods. Nor do I lust for a great tyranny.

B. Tyrtaeus of Sparta

Tyrtaeus lived during the Second Messenian War (ca. 650-620 B.C.), and his poetry was written to stir the Spartans to feats of courage in fighting against the Messenians.

1. I would not say anything for a man nor take account of him for any speed of his feet or wrestling skill that he might have, not if he had the size of a Cyclops and strength to go with it, not if he could outrun Boreas, the North Wind of Thrace, not if he were more handsome and gracefully formed than Tithonos, or had more riches than Midas had, or Kinyras too, not if he were more of a king than Tantalid Pelops, or had the power of speech and persuasion Adrastos had, not if he had all splendors except for a fighting spirit: for no man ever proves himself a good man in war unless he can endure to face the blood and the slaughter, go close against the enemy and fight with his hands. Here is courage, mankind's finest possession, here is the noblest prize that a young man can endeavor to win, and it is a good thing that his city and all the people share with him when a man plants his feet and stands in

the foremost spears relentlessly, all thought of foul flight completely forgotten, and he has well trained his heart to be steadfast and to endure and with words encourages the man who is stationed beside him. Here is a man who proves himself to be valiant in war. With a sudden rush he turns to flight the rugged battalions of the enemy and sustains the beating waves of assault. And he who so falls among the champions and loses his sweet life, so blessing with honor his city, his father, and all his people, with wounds in his chest, where the spear that he was facing has transfixed that massive guard of his shield and gone through his breastplate as well, why, such a man is lamented alike by the young and the elders; and all his city goes into mourning and grieves for his loss. His tomb is pointed to with pride, and so are his children, and his children's children, and afterward all the race that is his. His shining glory is never forgotten, his name is remembered, and he becomes an immortal, though he lies under the ground, when one who was a brave man has been killed by the furious War God standing his ground and fighting hard for his children and land. But if he escapes the doom of death, the destroyer of bodies, and wins his battle and bright renown for the work of his spear, all men give place to him alike, the youth and the elders; and much joy comes his way before he goes down to the dead. Aging, he has reputation among his citizens. No one tries to interfere with his honors or all he deserves; all men withdraw before his presence and yield their seats to him, the youth, and the men his age, and even those older than he. Thus a man should endeavor to reach this high place of courage with all his heart, and, so trying, never be backward in war....

2. Now, since you are the seed of Herakles the invincible, courage! Zeus has not yet turned away from us. Do not fear the multitude of their men, nor run away from them. Each man should bear his shield straight at the foremost ranks and make his heart a thing full of hate, and hold the black flying spirits of death as dear as he holds the flash of the sun. You know what havoc is the work of the painful War God, you have learned well how things go in exhausting war: for you have been with those who ran and with the pursuers. O young men, you have had as much of both as you want. Those who, standing their

ground and closing their ranks together, endure the onset at close quarters and fight in the front, they lose fewer men. They also protect the army behind them. Once they flinch, the spirit of the whole army falls apart. And no man could count over and tell all the number of evils, all that can come to a man, once he gives way to disgrace: for once a man reverses and runs in the terror of battle, he offers his back, a tempting mark to spear from behind, and it is a shameful sight when a dead man lies in the dust there, driven through from behind by the stroke of an enemy spear.

3. No, no, let him take a wide stance and stand up strongly against them, digging both heels in the ground, biting his lip with his teeth, covering thighs and legs beneath, his chest and his shoulders under the hollowed-out protection of his broad shield, while in his right hand he brandishes the powerful war-spear and shakes terribly the crest high above his helm. Our man should be disciplined in the work of the heavy fighter and not stand out from the missiles when he carries a shield, but go right up and fight at close quarters and, with his long spear or short sword, thrust home and strike his enemy down. Let him fight toe to toe and shield against shield hard driven, crest against crest and helmet on helmet, chest against chest; let him close hard and fight it out with his opposite foeman, holding tight to the hilt of his sword, or to his long spear. And you, O light-armed fighters, from shield to shield of your fellows dodge for protection, and keep steadily throwing great stones, and keep on pelting the enemy with your javelins, only remember always to stand near your own heavy-armed men....

C. Sappho of Lesbos

Sappho was the most famous female poet of ancient Greece. She probably lived around 620-550 B.C. and seems to have been the leading member of a group of sophisticated aristocratic women on the island of Lesbos. Since her poetry is largely concerned with feelings of love between women, as well as between a man and a woman, our modern term 'Lesbian', referring to female homosexuality, derives from Sappho of Lesbos.

1. Throned in splendor, deathless, O Aphrodite, child of Zeus, charm-fashioner, I entreat you not with griefs and bitternesses to break my spirit; O goddess, standing by me rather, if once before now far away you heard, when I called upon you, left your father's dwelling place and descended, yoking the golden chariot to sparrows, who fairly drew you down in speed aslant the black world, the bright air trembling at the heart to the pulse of countless fluttering wingbeats. Swiftly then they came, and you, blessed lady, smiling on me out of immortal beauty, asked me what affliction was on me, why I called thus upon you, what beyond all else I would have befall my tortured heart: "Whom then would you have Persuasion force to serve desire in your heart? Who is it, Sappho, that hurt you? Though she now escape you, she soon will follow; though she take not gifts from you, she will give them; though she love not, yet she will surely love you even unwilling." In such guise come even again and set me free from doubt and sorrow; accomplish all those things my heart desires to be done; appear and stand at my shoulder.

2. Like the very gods in my sight is he who sits where he can look in your eyes, who listens close to you, to hear the soft voice, its sweetness murmur in love and laughter, all for him. But it breaks my spirit; underneath my breast all the heart is shaken. Let me only glance where you are, the voice dies, I can say nothing, but my lips are stricken to silence, underneath my skin the tenuous flame suffuses; nothing shows in front of my eyes, my ears are muted in thunder. And the sweat breaks running upon me, fever shakes my body, paler I turn than grass is; I can feel that I have been changed, I feel that death has come near me.

D. Semonides of Amorgos

An Essay on Women

In the beginning God made various kinds of women with various minds. He made one from the hairy sow, that one whose house is smeared with mud, and all within lies in dishevelment and rolls along the ground, while the pig-woman in unlaundered clothing sits unwashed herself among the dunghills and grows fat.

God made another woman from the mischievous vixen, whose mind gets into everything. No act of wickedness unknown to her; no act of good either, because the things she says are often bad but sometimes good. Her temper changes all the time.

One from a bitch, and good-for-nothing like her mother. She must be in on everything and hear it all. Out she goes ranging, poking her nose everywhere and barking, whether she sees anyone about or not. Her husband cannot make her stop by threats, neither when in a rage he knocks her teeth out with a stone, nor when he reasons with her in soft words, not even when there's company come, and she's with them. Day in, day out, she keeps that senseless yapping up.

The gods of Olympus made another one of mud and gave her lame to man. A woman such as this knows nothing good and nothing bad. Nothing at all. The only thing she understands is how to eat, and even if God makes the weather bad, she won't, though shivering, pull her chair up closer to the fire.

One from the sea. She has two different sorts of mood. One day she is all smiles and happiness. A man who comes to visit sees her in the house and says: "There is no better wife than this one anywhere in all mankind, nor prettier." Then, another day there'll be no living with her, you can't get within sight, or come near her, or she flies into a rage and holds you at a distance like a bitch with pups, cantankerous and cross with all the world. It makes no difference whether they are friends or enemies. The sea is like that also. Often it lies calm and innocent and still, the mariner's delight in summer weather. Then again it will go wild and turbulent with the thunder of big crashing waves. This woman's disposition is just like the sea's, since the sea's temper also changes all the time.

One was a donkey, dusty-gray and obstinate. It's hard to make her work. You have to curse and tug to make her do it, but in the end she gets it done quite well. Then she goes to her corner-crib and eats. She eats all day, she eats all night, and by the fire she eats. But when there's a chance to make love, she'll take the first one of her husband's friends who comes along.

One from a weasel—miserable, stinking thing. There's nothing pretty about her. She has no kind of charm, no kind of sweetness, and no sex appeal. She's always crazy to make love and go to bed, but makes her husband—if she has one—sick, when he comes near her. And she steals from neighbors. She's all bad. She robs the altar and eats up the sacrifice.

One was begotten from the maned, fastidious mare. She manages to avoid all housework and the chores of slaves. She wouldn't touch the mill, or lift a sieve, or sweep the dung from the house and throw it out of doors, or kneel by the fire. Afraid the soot will make her dirty. She makes her husband boon-companion to Hard Times. She washes the dirt off her body every day twice at least, three times some days, and anoints herself with perfume, and forever wears her long hair combed and shadowed deep with flowers. A woman such as this makes, to be sure, a lovely wife for someone else to look at, but her husband finds her an expense unless he is some baron or a sceptered king who can indulge his taste for luxuries like her.

One was a monkey; and this is the very worst, most exquisite disaster Zeus has wished on men. Hers is the ugliest face of all. When such a woman walks through the village, everybody turns to laugh. Her neck's so short that she can scarcely turn her head. Slab-sided, skinny-legged. Oh, unhappy man who has to take such a disaster in his arms! Yet, she has understanding of all tricks and turns, just like a monkey. If they laugh, she doesn't mind. Don't expect any good work done by her. She thinks of only one thing, plans for one thing, all day long: how she can do somebody else the biggest harm.

One from a bee. The man is lucky who gets her. She is the only one no blame can settle on. A man's life grows and blossoms underneath her touch. She loves her husband, he loves her, and they grow old together, while their glorious children rise to fame. Among the throngs of other women this one shines as an example. Heavenly grace surrounds her. She alone takes no delight in sitting with the rest when the conversation's about sex. It's wives like this who are God's gift of happiness to mortal men. These are the thoughtful wives, in every way the best.

But all those other breeds come to us too from God and by his will. And they stay with us. They won't go: for women are the biggest single bad thing Zeus has made for us. Even when a wife appears to help, her husband finds out in the end that after all she didn't. No one day goes by from end to end enjoyable, when you have spent it with your wife. She will not stir herself to push the hateful god Hard Times—that most unwelcome caller—out of doors. At home, when a man thinks that, by God's grace or by men's good will, there'll be peace for him and all go well, she finds some fault with him and starts a fight: for where there is a woman in the house, no one can ask a friend to come and stay with him, and still feel safe. Even the wife who appears to be the best-behaved turns out to be the one who lets herself go wrong. Her husband gawps and doesn't notice; neighbors do, and smile to see how still another man gets fooled. Each man will pick the faults in someone else's wife and boast of his own each time he speaks of her. And yet, the same thing happens to us all. But we don't see: for women are the biggest single bad thing Zeus has made for us; a ball-and-chain; we can't get loose since that time when the fight about a wife began the Great War, and they volunteered and went to hell.

E. Xenophanes of Colophon

After his native city of Colophon on the western coast of Anatolia was conquered by the Persians around 545 B.C., Xenophanes emigrated and settled down in Elea, a Greek colony on the western coast of Italy south of the Bay of Naples. There he lived out the rest of his life and founded in his new adopted community an important line of Greek philosophy known as the Eleatic school. He is therefore numbered among the early Greek philosophers; and since Greek prose writing did not come into existence until the very end of the Archaic Period, Xenophanes expressed his ideas in poetic verse.

1. Now, supposing a man were to win the prize for the foot race at Olympia, there where the precinct of Zeus stands beside the river at Pisa: or if he wins the pentathlon, or the wrestling, or if he endures the pain of boxing and wins, or that new and terrible game that they call the pankration, contest of all holds: why, such a man will obtain honor in the citizens' sight and be given a front seat [in the theater] and be on display at all civic occasions, and he would be given his meals all at the public expense, and be given a gift from the city to take and store for safekeeping. If he won with the chariot, too, all this would be granted to him; and yet, he would not deserve it, as I do. Better than brute strength of men, or horses either, is the wisdom that is mine. But custom is careless in all these matters, and there is no justice in putting strength on a level above wisdom that is sound: for if among the people there is one who is a good boxer, or one who excels in wrestling or in the pentathlon, or else for speed of his feet, and this is prized beyond other feats of strength that men display in athletic

games, the city will not on account of this man have better government. Small is the pleasure the city derives from one of its men if he
happens to come first in the games by the banks of Pisa. This does
not make rich the treasure house of the state....

2. But if oxen (and horses) and lions had hands or could draw with hands
   and create works of art like those made by men, horses would draw
   pictures of gods like horses, and oxen of gods like oxen, and they
   would make the bodies (of their gods) in accordance with the form
   that each species itself possesses.

PART V
THE CLASSICAL PERIOD
OF GREECE

READING 31
HERODOTUS AND XERXES'
INVASION OF GREECE

The first great work of historical writing in the Western tradition was an account of the wars fought between the Greeks and Persians written by Herodotus, who is often justifiably termed "the father of history." When completed, this lengthy narrative was copied onto nine ancient papyrus scrolls, which we now call Books. It described the long complex and often hostile relationship between the numerous self-governing Greek city-states and the great imperial power of Persia ruled by a single all-powerful king. The first six books of this historical account trace the rise of the Persian Empire under the rule of its first three kings (Cyrus, his son Cambyses, and Darius), their conquests, and the affairs of the various Greek city-states as they were affected by the Persians. The last three books form the culmination of the entire work by narrating the great Persian invasion of mainland Greece during the years 480-479 B.C. led by King Xerxes, who wished to follow in the footsteps of the three earlier Persian kings by being a great conqueror and by adding mainland Greece to the Persian Empire. Despite the vast numerical superiority of the Persian army and navy, the Greek city-states temporarily put aside their mutual quarrels and united under the joint leadership of Sparta and Athens to defeat this invasion.

Herodotus was born in 484 B.C. just a few years before this great invasion, but his birthplace was not in mainland Greece, but in the city-state of Halicarnassus located in the southwestern edge of Anatolia. As part of the Asian continent, Anatolia belonged at that time to the Persian Empire; and since the western coast of this region had long been inhabited by Greeks who had colonized the area from the Greek mainland, the Greek people of the Aegean area were divided into two groups: those who enjoyed freedom in their own self-governing city-states, and those who owed allegiance to Persia. Thus, the principal theme of Herodotus' historical account is the contrast between the Greek love of political freedom and self-determination and the despotic power that the Persian king exercised over his subjects, whom the Greeks regarded as little better than slaves.

(Taken from History of Herodotus, translated by George Rawlinson, published by Murray of London, 1875, revised by Gary Forsythe)

A. Preface to the History

These are the researches of Herodotus of Halicarnassus, which he publishes in the hope of thereby preserving from decay the remembrance of what men have done, and of preventing the great and wonderful actions of the Greeks and the Barbarians from losing their due meed of glory; and withal to put on record what were their grounds of feuds.

B. Debate of the Persian Nobles (Book III)

Cyrus the Great (king 559-530 B.C.) had founded the Persian Empire by bringing much of western Asia under Persian control by military conquest. He was succeeded on the royal throne by his son Cambyses (king 530-522 B.C.). But when the latter died under mysterious circumstances while leading the Persian conquest of Egypt, the throne in the Persian homeland was seized by a royal pretender. A group of seven Persian nobles formed a conspiracy that overthrew this pretender and resulted in Darius emerging as the new king. In his description of these events Herodotus portrays these Persian noble conspirators as conducting a debate as to which form of government is best (monarchy / tyranny, aristocracy / oligarchy, or democracy / mob rule). This is the earliest account that we possess of a Greek writer discussing the relative merits of what became for the Greeks the three basic forms of government: rule by one person, rule by the few, or rule by the many in both their ideal and perverted forms. It is virtually certain that following Cambyses' death, Persian nobles never did hold such a debate as described here that typify Greek (not Persian) political thought. In any case, the passage neatly encapsulates how the ancient Greeks assessed the strengths and weaknesses of these three forms of government.

80. And now when five days were gone, and the hubbub had settled down, the conspirators met together to consult about the situation of affairs. At this meeting speeches were made, to which many of the Greeks give no credence, but they were made nevertheless. Otanes recommended that the management of public affairs should be entrusted to the whole nation. "To me," he said, "it seems advisable that we should no longer have a single man to rule over us. The rule of one is neither good nor pleasant. Ye cannot have forgotten to what lengths Cambyses went in his haughty tyranny, and the haughtiness of the Magi ye have yourselves experienced. How indeed is it possible that monarchy should be a well-adjusted thing, when it allows a man to do as he likes without being answerable? Such license is enough to stir strange and unwonted thoughts in the heart of the worthiest of men. Give a person this power, and straightway his manifold good things puff him up with pride, while envy is so natural to human kind that it cannot but arise in him. But pride and envy together include all wickedness, both of them leading on to deeds of savage violence. True it is that kings, possessing as they do all that heart can desire, ought to be void of envy; but the contrary is seen in their conduct towards the citizens. They are jealous of the most virtuous among their subjects and wish their death, while they take delight in the meanest and basest, being ever ready to listen to the tales of slanderers. A king, besides, is beyond all other men inconsistent with himself. Pay him court in moderation, and he is angry because you do not show him more profound respect. Show him profound respect, and he is offended again, because (as he says) you fawn on him. But the worst of all is that he sets aside the laws of the land, puts men to death without trial, and subjects women to violence. The rule of the many, on the other hand, has, in the first place, the fairest of names, to wit, isonomy [i.e., democracy]; and further, it

is free from all those outrages which a king is wont to commit. There, places are given by lot, the magistrate is answerable for what he does, and measures rest with the commonalty. I vote, therefore, that we do away with monarchy and raise the people to power: for the people are all in all."

81. Such were the sentiments of Otanes. Megabyzus spoke next and advised the setting up of an oligarchy. "In all that Otanes has said to persuade you to put down monarchy," he observed, "I fully concur; but his recommendation that we should call the people to power seems to me not the best advice: for there is nothing so void of understanding, nothing so full of wantonness as the unwieldy rabble. It were folly not to be borne for men, while seeking to escape the wantonness of a tyrant, to give themselves up to the wantonness of a rude unbridled mob. The tyrant in all his doings at least knows what he is about, but a mob is altogether devoid of knowledge; for how should there be any knowledge in a rabble, untaught, and with no natural sense of what is right and fit? It rushes wildly into state affairs with all the fury of a stream swollen in the winter, and it confuses everything. Let the enemies of the Persians be ruled by democracies; but let us choose out from the citizens a certain number of the worthiest and put the government into their hands: for thus both we ourselves shall be among the governors; and power being entrusted to the best men, it is likely that the best counsels will prevail in the state."

82. This was the advice which Megabyzus gave, and after him Darius came forward and spoke as follows: "All that Megabyzus said against democracy was well said, I think; but about oligarchy he did not speak advisedly; for take these three forms of government: democracy, oligarchy, and monarchy; and let them each be at their best, I maintain that monarchy far surpasses the other two. What government can possibly be better than that of the very best man in the whole state? The counsels of such a man are like himself, and so he governs the mass of the people to their heart's content, while at the same time his measures against evil-doers are kept more secret than in other states. Contrariwise, in oligarchies, where men vie with each other in the service of the commonwealth, fierce enmities are apt to

arise between man and man, each wishing to be leader and to carry his own measures; whence violent quarrels come, which lead to open strife, often ending in bloodshed. Then monarchy is sure to follow; and this too shows how far that rule surpasses all others. Again, in a democracy it is impossible but that there will be malpractices: these malpractices, however, do not lead to enmities, but to close friendships, which are formed among those engaged in them, who must hold well together to carry on their villainies. And so things go on until a man stands forth as champion of the commonalty and puts down the evil-doers. Straightway the author of so great a service is admired by all; and from being admired he soon comes to be appointed king, so that here too it is plain that monarchy is the best government. Lastly, to sum up all in a word, whence, I ask, was it that we got the freedom which we enjoy? Did democracy give it us, or oligarchy, or a monarch? As a single man recovered our freedom for us, my sentence is that we keep to the rule of one. Even apart from this, we ought not to change the laws of our forefathers when they work fairly; for to do so is not well."

83. Such were the three opinions brought forward at this meeting. The four other Persians voted in favor of the last. Otanes, who wished to give his countrymen a democracy, when he found the decision against him, arose a second time and spoke thus before the assembly: "Brother conspirators, it is plain that the king who is to be chosen will be one of ourselves, whether we make the choice by casting lots for the prize or by letting the people decide which of us they will have to rule over them, in this or any other way. Now, as I have neither a mind to rule nor to be ruled, I shall not enter the lists with you in this matter. I withdraw, however, on one condition: none of you shall claim to exercise rule over me or my seed for ever." The six agreed to these terms, and Otanes withdrew and stood aloof from the contest. And still to this day the family of Otanes continues to be the only free family in Persia; those who belong to it submit to the rule of the king only so far as they themselves choose; they are bound, however, to observe the laws of the land like the other Persians.

C. Despotism of the Persian King (Book VII)

While narrating how Xerxes mobilized his vast army for his invasion of Greece, and how he proceeded on his march, Herodotus tells the following story that is intended to show how the Persian system of royal rule rendered all the inhabitants of the empire, no matter their wealth and status, vulnerable to the caprice of an absolute monarch.

27. Now there lived in this city a certain Pythius, the son of Atys, a Lydian. This man entertained Xerxes and his whole army in a most magnificent fashion, offering at the same time to give him a sum of money for the war. Xerxes, upon the mention of money, turned to the Persians who stood by, and he asked of them, "Who is this Pythius, and what wealth has he, that he should venture on such an offer as this?" They answered him, "this is the man, o king, who gave thy father Darius the golden plane-tree and likewise the golden vine; and he is still the wealthiest man whom we know of in all the world, excepting thee."

28. Xerxes marvelled at these last words; and now, addressing Pythius with his own lips, he asked him what the amount of his wealth really was. Pythius answered as follows: "O king, I will not hide this matter from thee, nor make pretence that I do not know how rich I am; but as I know perfectly, I will declare all fully before thee: for when thy journey was noised abroad, and I heard that thou wert coming down to the Grecian coast, straightway, as I wished to give thee a sum of money for the war, I made count of my stores and found them to be two thousand talents of silver, and of gold four millions of Daric staters, wanting seven thousand. All this I willingly make over to thee as a gift; and when it is gone, my slaves and my estates in land will be wealth enough for my wants."

29. This speech charmed Xerxes, and he replied, "Dear Lydian, since I left Persia, there is no man but thou who has either desired to entertain my army or has come forward of his own free will to offer me a sum of money for the war. Thou hast done both the one and the other: feasting my troops magnificently, and now making offer of a right noble sum. In return, this is what I will bestow on thee. Thou

shalt be my sworn friend from this day; and the seven thousand staters which are wanting to make up thy four millions I will supply, so that the full tale may be no longer lacking, and that thou mayest owe the completion of the round sum to me. Continue to enjoy all that thou hast acquired hitherto; and be sure to remain ever such as thou now art. If thou dost, thou wilt not repent of it so long as thy life endures."...

38. The army had begun its march, when Pythius the Lydian, affrighted at the heavenly portent, and emboldened by his gifts, came to Xerxes and said: "Grant me, o my lord, a favor which is to thee a light matter, but to me of vast account." Then Xerxes, who looked for nothing less than such a prayer as Pythius in fact preferred, engaged to grant him whatever he wished, and he commanded him to tell his wish freely. So Pythius, full of boldness, went on to say: "O my lord! thy servant has five sons; and it chances that all are called upon to join thee in this march against Greece. I beseech thee, have compassion upon my years; and let one of my sons, the eldest, remain behind, to be my prop and stay and the guardian of my wealth. Take with thee the other four; and when thou hast done all that is in thy heart, mayest thou come back in safety."

39. But Xerxes was greatly angered and replied to him: "Thou wretch, darest thou speak to me of thy son, when I am myself on the march against Greece with sons, and brothers, and kinsfolk, and friends? Thou, who art my bond-slave, and art in duty bound to follow me with all thy household, not excepting thy wife! Know that man's spirit dwelleth in his ears; and when it hears good things, straightway it fills all his body with delight; but no sooner does it hear the contrary than it heaves and swells with passion. As when thou didst good deeds and madest good offers to me, thou wert not able to boast of having out-done the king in bountifulness, so now when thou art changed and grown impudent, thou shalt not receive all thy deserts, but less. For thyself and four of thy five sons, the entertainment which I had of thee shall gain protection; but as for him to whom thou clingest above the rest, the forfeit of his life shall be thy punishment." Having thus spoken, forthwith he commanded those to whom such tasks were

assigned to seek out the eldest of the sons of Pythius and, having cut his body asunder, to place the two halves, one on the right, the other on the left of the great road, so that the army might march out between them.

D. The Battle of Thermopylae (Book VII)

The first major military engagement between the Greeks and Persians led by Xerxes occurred at a narrow pass in northern Greece called Thermopylae (the Hot Gates), where the much smaller forces of the Greeks had at least a reasonable chance to hold back the far larger army of the Persians, but the Persians eventually discovered an alternative route that enabled them to surround and annihilate the Greek defenders.

201. King Xerxes pitched his camp in the region of Malis called Trachinia, while on their side the Greeks occupied the narrows. These narrows the Greeks in general call Thermopylae (the Hot Gates); but the natives and those who dwell in the neighborhood call them Pylae (the Gates). Here then the two armies took their stand; the one master of all the region lying north of Trachis, the other of the country extending southward of that place to the verge of the continent.

202. The Greeks who at this spot awaited the coming of Xerxes were the following: from Sparta, three hundred men-at-arms; from Arcadia, a thousand Tegeans and Mantineans, five hundred of each people; a hundred and twenty Orchomenians, from the Arcadian Orchomenus; and a thousand from other cities: from Corinth, four hundred men; from Phlius, two hundred; and from Mycenae eighty. Such was the number from the Peloponnese. There were also present from Boeotia seven hundred Thespians and four hundred Thebans.

203. Besides these troops, the Locrians of Opus and the Phocians had obeyed the call of their countrymen and sent, the former all the force that they had, the latter a thousand men: for envoys had gone from the Greeks at Thermopylae among the Locrians and Phocians to call on them for assistance, and to say that "They were themselves but the vanguard of the host, sent to precede the main body, which might every day be expected to follow them. The sea was in good keeping,

watched by the Athenians, the Aeginetans, and the rest of the fleet. There was no cause why they should fear; for after all the invader was not a god but a man; and there never had been and never would be a man who was not liable to misfortunes from the very day of his birth, and those misfortunes greater in proportion to his own greatness. The assailant therefore, being only a mortal, must needs fall from his glory." Thus urged, the Locrians and the Phocians had come with their troops to Trachis.

204. The various nations had each captains of their own under whom they served; but the one to whom all especially looked up, and who had the command of the entire force, was the Spartan, Leonidas.... Leonidas had come to be king of Sparta quite unexpectedly.

205. Having two elder brothers, Cleomenes and Dorieus, he had no thought of ever mounting the throne. However, when Cleomenes died without male offspring, as Dorieus was likewise deceased, having perished in Sicily, the crown fell to Leonidas, who was older than Cleombrotus, the youngest of the sons of Anaxandridas, and, more-over, was married to the daughter of Cleomenes. He had now come to Thermopylae, accompanied by the three hundred men which the law assigned him, whom he had himself chosen from among the citizens, and who were all of them fathers with sons living....

206. The force with Leonidas was sent forward by the Spartans in advance of their main body in order that the sight of them might encourage the allies to fight and hinder them from going over to the Medes, as it was likely that they might have done, had they seen that Sparta was backward. They intended presently, when they had celebrated the Carneian festival, which was what now kept them at home, to leave a garrison in Sparta and to hasten in full force to join the army. The rest of the allies also intended to act similarly; for it happened that the Olympic festival fell exactly at this same period. None of them looked to see the contest at Thermopylae decided so speedily; where-fore they were content to send forward a mere advanced guard. Such accordingly were the intentions of the allies.

207. The Greek forces at Thermopylae, when the Persian army drew near to the entrance of the pass, were seized with fear; and a council was

held to consider about a retreat. It was the wish of the Peloponnesians generally that the army should fall back upon the Peloponnese and there guard the Isthmus. But Leonidas, who saw with what indignation the Phocians and Locrians heard of this plan, gave his voice for remaining where they were, while they sent envoys to the several cities to ask for help, since they were too few to make a stand against an army like that of the Medes.

208. While this debate was going on, Xerxes sent a mounted spy to observe the Greeks, to note how many they were, and to see what they were doing. He had heard, before he came out of Thessaly, that a few men were assembled at this place, and that at their head were certain Spartans under Leonidas, a descendant of Herakles. The horseman rode up to the camp and looked about him, but did not see the whole army; for such as were on the further side of the wall (which had been rebuilt and was now carefully guarded) it was not possible for him to behold; but he observed those on the outside, who were encamped in front of the rampart. It chanced that at this time the Spartans held the outer guard and were seen by the spy, some of them engaged in gymnastic exercises, others combing their long hair. At this the spy greatly marvelled, but he counted their number; and when he had taken accurate note of everything, he rode back quietly; for no one pursued after him, nor paid any heed to his visit. So he returned and told Xerxes all that he had seen.

209. Upon this, Xerxes, who had no means of surmising the truth—namely, that the Spartans were preparing to do or die manfully—but thought it laughable that they should be engaged in such employments, sent and called to his presence Demaratus the son of Ariston [a former Spartan king, now living in exile as an advisor to Xerxes], who still remained with the army. When he appeared, Xerxes told him all that he had heard, and he questioned him concerning the news, since he was anxious to understand the meaning of such behavior on the part of the Spartans. Then Demaratus said, "I spake to thee, o king, concerning these men long since, when we had but just begun our march upon Greece; thou, however, didst only laugh at my words, when I told thee of all this, which I saw would come to pass. Earnestly do I

struggle at all times to speak truth to thee, sire; and now listen to it once more. These men have come to dispute the pass with us; and it is for this that they are now making ready. It is their custom, when they are about to hazard their lives, to adorn their heads with care. Be assured, however, that if thou canst subdue the men who are here and the Spartans who remain in Sparta, there is no other nation in all the world which will venture to lift a hand in their defense. Thou hast now to deal with the first kingdom and town in Greece and with the bravest men." Then Xerxes, to whom what Demaratus said seemed altogether to surpass belief, asked further "how it was possible for so small an army to contend with his?" "O king!" Demaratus answered, "let me be treated as a liar, if matters fall not out as I say."

210. But Xerxes was not persuaded any the more. Four whole days he suffered to go by, expecting that the Greeks would run away. When, however, he found on the fifth that they were not gone, thinking that their firm stand was mere impudence and recklessness, he grew wroth and sent against them the Medes and Cissians with orders to take them alive and to bring them into his presence. Then the Medes rushed forward and charged the Greeks, but they fell in vast numbers: others, however, took the places of the slain and would not be beaten off, though they suffered terrible losses. In this way it became clear to all, and especially to the king, that though he had plenty of combatants, he had but very few warriors. The struggle, however, continued during the whole day.

211. Then the Medes, having met so rough a reception, withdrew from the fight; and their place was taken by the band of Persians under Hydarnes, whom the king called his "Immortals": they, it was thought, would soon finish the business. But when they joined battle with the Greeks, it was with no better success than the Median detachment. things went much as before: the two armies fighting in a narrow space, and the barbarians using shorter spears than the Greeks, and having no advantage from their numbers. The Spartans fought in a way worthy of note and showed themselves far more skillful in fight than their adversaries, often turning their backs and making as though they were all flying away, on which the barbarians would rush after them with

much noise and shouting, when the Spartans at their approach would wheel around and face their pursuers, in this way destroying vast numbers of the enemy. Some Spartans likewise fell in these encounters, but only a very few. At last the Persians, finding that all their efforts to gain the pass availed nothing, and that, whether they attacked by divisions or in any other way, it was to no purpose, withdrew to their own quarters.

212. During these assaults it is said that Xerxes, who was watching the battle, thrice leaped from the throne on which he sat in terror for his army. Next day, the combat was renewed, but with no better success on the part of the barbarians. The Greeks were so few that the barbarians hoped to find them disabled, by reason of their wounds, from offering any further resistance; and so they once more attacked them. But the Greeks were drawn up in detachments according to their cities and bore the brunt of the battle in turns, all except the Phocians, who had been stationed on the mountain to guard the pathway. So, when the Persians found no difference between that day and the preceding, they again retired to their quarters.

213. Now, as the king was in great strait and knew not how he should deal with the emergency, Ephialtes, the son of Eurydemus, a man of Malis, came to him and was admitted to a conference. Stirred by the hope of receiving a rich reward at the king's hands, he had come to tell him of the pathway which led across the mountain to Thermopylae; by which disclosure he brought destruction on the band of Greeks who had there withstood the barbarians. This Ephialtes afterwards, from fear of the Spartans, fled into Thessaly; and during his exile in an assembly of the Amphictyons held at Pylae a price was set upon his head by the Pylagorae. When some time had gone by, he returned from exile and went to Anticyra, where he was slain by Athenades, a native of Trachis....

215. Great was the joy of Xerxes on this occasion; and as he approved highly of the enterprise that Ephialtes undertook to accomplish, he forthwith sent upon the errand Hydarnes and the Persians under him. The troops left the camp about the time of the lighting of the lamps. The pathway along which they went was first discovered by the

Malians of these parts, who soon afterwards led the Thessalians by it to attack the Phocians, at the time when the Phocians fortified the pass with a wall and so put themselves under covert from danger. And ever since, the path has always been put to an ill use by the Malians....

217. The Persians took this path; and crossing the Asopus, they continued their march through the whole of the night, having the mountains of Oeta on their right hand, and on their left those of Trachis. At dawn of day they found themselves close to the summit. Now the hill was guarded, as I have already said, by a thousand Phocian men-at-arms, who were placed there to defend the pathway and at the same time to secure their own country. They had been given the guard of the mountain path, while the other Greeks defended the pass below, because they had volunteered for the service and had pledged themselves to Leonidas to maintain the post.

218. The ascent of the Persians became known to the Phocians in the following manner. During all the time that they were making their way up, the Greeks remained unconscious of it, inasmuch as the whole mountain was covered with groves of oak; but it happened that the air was very still, and the leaves which the Persians stirred with their feet made, as it was likely they would, a loud rustling; whereupon the Phocians jumped up and flew to seize their arms. In a moment the barbarians came in sight; and perceiving men arming themselves, they were greatly amazed; for they had fallen in with an enemy when they expected no opposition. Hydarnes, alarmed at the sight and fearing lest the Phocians might be Spartans, inquired of Ephialtes to what nation these troops belonged. Ephialtes told him the exact truth; whereupon he arrayed his Persians for battle. The Phocians, galled by the showers of arrows to which they were exposed and imagining themselves the special object of the Persian attack, fled hastily to the crest of the mountain and there made ready to meet death; but while their mistake continued, the Persians, with Ephialtes and Hydarnes, not thinking it worth their while to delay on account of Phocians, passed on and descended the mountain with all possible speed.

219. The Greeks at Thermopylae received the first warning of the destruction which the dawn would bring on them from the seer Megistias,

who read their fate in the victims as he was sacrificing. After this deserters came in and brought the news that the Persians were marching around by the hills: it was still night when these men arrived. Last of all, the scouts came running down from the heights and brought in the same accounts, when the day was just beginning to break. Then the Greeks held a council to consider what they should do, and here opinions were divided: some were strong against quitting their post, while others contended to the contrary. So when the council had broken up, part of the troops departed and went their ways homeward to their several states; part, however, resolved to remain and to stand by Leonidas to the last.

220. It is said that Leonidas himself sent away the troops who departed, because he tendered their safety, but he thought it unseemly that either he or his Spartans should quit the post which they had been especially sent to guard. For my own part, I incline to think that Leonidas gave the order, because he perceived the allies to be out of heart and unwilling to encounter the danger to which his own mind was made up. He therefore commanded them to retreat, but he said that he himself could not draw back with honor, knowing that if he stayed, glory awaited him, and that Sparta in that case would not lose her prosperity....

222. So, the allies, when Leonidas ordered them to retire, obeyed him and forthwith departed....

223. At sunrise Xerxes made libations, after which he waited until the time when the marketplace is wont to fill, and then he began his advance. Ephialtes had instructed him thus, as the descent of the mountain is much quicker and the distance much shorter than the way around the hills and the ascent. So, the barbarians under Xerxes began to draw nigh; and the Greeks under Leonidas, as they now went forth determined to die, advanced much further than on previous days, until they reached the more open portion of the pass. Hitherto they had held their station within the wall and from this had gone forth to fight at the point where the pass was the narrowest. Now they joined battle beyond the defile and carried slaughter among the barbarians, who fell in heaps. Behind them the captains of the squadrons, armed with

whips, urged their men forward with continual blows. Many were thrust into the sea and there perished; a still greater number were trampled to death by their own soldiers; no one heeded the dying: for the Greeks, reckless of their own safety and desperate, since they knew that, as the mountain had been crossed, their destruction was nigh at hand, exerted themselves with the most furious valor against the barbarians.

224. By this time the spears of the greater number were all shivered, and with their swords they hewed down the ranks of the Persians; and here, as they strove, Leonidas fell fighting bravely, together with many other famous Spartans, whose names I have taken care to learn on account of their great worthiness, as indeed I have those of all the three hundred. There fell too at the same time very many famous Persians: among them, two sons of Darius, Abrocomes and Hyperanthes, his children by Phratagune, the daughter of Artanes. Artanes was brother of King Darius, being a son of Hystaspes, the son of Arsames; and when he gave his daughter to the king, he made him heir likewise of all his substance; for she was his only child.

225. Thus two brothers of Xerxes here fought and fell. And now there arose a fierce struggle between the Persians and the Spartans over the body of Leonidas, in which the Greeks four times drove back the enemy, and at last by their great bravery they succeeded in bearing off the body. This combat was scarcely ended when the Persians with Ephialtes approached; and the Greeks, informed that they drew nigh, made a change in the manner of their fighting. Drawing back into the narrowest part of the pass and retreating even behind the cross wall, they posted themselves upon a hillock, where they stood all drawn up together in one close body, except only the Theban. The hillock whereof I speak is at the entrance of the straits, where the stone lion stands which was set up in honor of Leonidas. Here they defended themselves to the last, such as still had swords using them, and the others resisting with their hands and teeth; till the barbarians, who in part had pulled down the wall and attacked them in front, in part had gone around and now encircled them upon every side, overwhelmed and buried the remnant which was left beneath showers of missile weapons....

E. The Battle of Salamis (Book VIII)

Although the Greek cause had suffered a major setback at Thermopylae, the heroic stand of those who had died there galvanized the Greeks to defend their homeland. The Greek navy now took up a position in a confined area formed by the small island of Salamis and Attica. Like Thermopylae, this confined space favored the smaller Greek navy and offered the larger Persian fleet no real advantage, but luckily for the Greeks, Persian overconfidence prompted them to attack the Greeks near Salamis. The result was a smashing victory for the Greeks. Salamis therefore proved decisive in destroying the Persians' best chance to subdue Greece. Then in the following year (479 B.C.), as described in Book IX of Herodotus, the Persian invasion ended catastrophically when Mardonius was defeated and killed in a major land battle at Plataea, just north of Athens in Boeotia. The failure of Xerxes' invasion of Greece marked the halt of Persian expansion and paved the way for the confidence that characterized Greek culture during its Classical Period.

68. Mardonius [Xerxes' cousin and son-in-law] accordingly went around the entire assemblage, beginning with the Sidonian monarch, and asked this question; to which all gave the same answer, advising to engage the Greeks, except only Artemisia [queen of Herodotus' hometown of Halicarnassus], who spake as follows: "Say to the king, Mardonius, that these are my words to him: I was not the least brave of those who fought at Euboea, nor were my achievements there among the meanest; it is my right, therefore, o my lord, to tell thee plainly what I think to be most for thy advantage now. This then is my advice. Spare thy ships, and do not risk a battle; for these people are as much superior to thy people in seamanship, as men to women. What so great need is there for thee to incur hazard at sea? Art thou not master of Athens, for which thou didst undertake thy expedition? Is not Greece subject to thee? Not a soul now resists thy advance. They who once resisted were handled even as they deserved. Now learn how I expect that affairs will go with thy adversaries. If thou art not over-hasty to engage with them by sea, but wilt keep thy fleet near the land, then whether thou abidest as thou art, or marchest forward towards the Peloponnese, thou wilt easily accomplish all for which

thou art come hither. The Greeks cannot hold out against thee very long; thou wilt soon part them asunder and scatter them to their several homes. In the island where they lie, I hear that they have no food in store; nor is it likely, if thy land force begins its march towards the Peloponnese, that they will remain quietly where they are, at least such as come from that region. Of a surety they will not greatly trouble themselves to give battle on behalf of the Athenians. On the other hand, if thou art hasty to fight, I tremble lest the defeat of thy sea force bring harm likewise to thy land army. This, too, thou shouldst remember, o king; good masters are apt to have bad servants, and bad masters good ones. Now, as thou art the best of men, thy servants must needs be a sorry set. These Egyptians, Cyprians, Cilicians, and Pamphylians, who are counted in the number of thy subject-allies, of how little service are they to thee!"

69. As Artemisia spake, they who wished her well were greatly troubled concerning her words, thinking that she would suffer some hurt at the king's hands, because she exhorted him not to risk a battle; they, on the other hand, who disliked and envied her, favored as she was by the king above all the rest of the allies, rejoiced at her declaration, expecting that her life would be the forfeit. But Xerxes, when the words of the several speakers were reported to him, was pleased beyond all others with the reply of Artemisia; and whereas, even before this, he had always esteemed her much, he now praised her more than ever. Nevertheless, he gave orders that the advice of the greater number should be followed; for he thought that at Euboea the fleet had not done its best, because he himself was not there to see, whereas this time he resolved that he would be an eye-witness of the combat.

70. Orders were now given to stand out to sea; and the ships proceeded towards Salamis and took up the stations to which they were directed without let or hindrance from the enemy. The day, however, was too far spent for them to begin the battle, since night already approached. So, they prepared to engage upon the morrow....

84. The [Greek] fleet had scarce left the land when they were attacked by the barbarians. At once most of the Greeks began to back water and were about touching the shore, when Ameinias of Palline, one of

the Athenian captains, darted forth in front of the line and charged a ship of the enemy. The two vessels became entangled and could not separate; whereupon the rest of the fleet came up to help Ameinias and engaged with the Persians. Such is the account which the Athenians give of the way in which the battle began; but the Aeginetans maintain that the vessel which had been to Aegina for the Aeacidae [sacred images of their heroes] was the one that brought on the fight. It is also reported that a phantom in the form of a woman appeared to the Greeks, and in a voice that was heard from end to end of the fleet she cheered them on to the fight; first, however, rebuking them and saying, "Strange men, how long are ye going to back water?"

85. Against the Athenians, who held the western extremity of the line towards Eleusis, were placed the Phoenicians; against the Spartans, whose station was eastward towards the Piraeus, the Ionians. Of these last a few only followed the advice of Themistocles to fight backwardly; the greater number did far otherwise. I could mention here the names of many trierarchs who took vessels from the Greeks, but I shall pass over all excepting Theomestor, the son of Androdamas, and Phylacus, the son of Histiaeus, both Samians. I show this preference to them, inasmuch as for this service Theomestor was made tyrant of Samos by the Persians, whereas Phylacus was enrolled among the king's benefactors and presented with a large estate in land. In the Persian tongue the king's benefactors are called Orosangs.

86. Far the greater number of the Persian ships engaged in this battle were disabled, either by the Athenians or by the Aeginetans: for as the Greeks fought in order and kept their line, while the barbarians were in confusion and had no plan in anything that they did, the issue of the battle could scarce be other than it was. Yet, the Persians fought far more bravely here than at Euboea and indeed surpassed themselves; each did his utmost through fear of Xerxes; for each thought that the king's eye was upon himself.

87. What part the several nations, whether Greek or barbarian, took in the combat, I am not able to say for certain; Artemisia, however, I know, distinguished herself in such a way as raised her even higher than she stood before in the esteem of the king: for after confusion

had spread throughout the whole of the king's fleet, and her ship was closely pursued by an Athenian trireme, she, having no way to fly, since in front of her were a number of friendly vessels, and she was nearest of all the Persians to the enemy, resolved on a measure which in fact proved her safety. Pressed by the Athenian pursuer, she bore straight against one of the ships of her own party, a Calyndian, which had Damasithymus, the Calyndian king, himself on board. I cannot say whether she had had any quarrel with the man while the fleet was at the Hellespont, or no; neither can I decide whether she of set purpose attacked his vessel, or whether it merely chanced that the Calyndian ship came in her way; but certain it is that she bore down upon his vessel and sank it, and that thereby she had the good fortune to procure herself a double advantage: for the commander of the Athenian trireme, when he saw her bear down on one of the enemy's fleet, thought immediately that her vessel was a Greek or else had deserted from the Persians and was now fighting on the Greek side; he therefore gave up the chase and turned away to attack others.

88. Thus in the first place she saved her life by the action and was enabled to get clear off from the battle, while, further, it fell out that in the very act of doing the king an injury, she raised herself to a greater height than ever in his esteem: for as Xerxes beheld the fight, he marked (it is said) the destruction of the vessel; whereupon the bystanders observed to him, "Seest thou, master, how well Artemisia fights, and how she has just sunk a ship of the enemy?" Then Xerxes asked if it were really Artemisia's doing; and they answered, "Certainly;" for they knew her ensign: while all made sure that the sunken vessel belonged to the opposite side. Everything, it is said, conspired to prosper the queen. It was especially fortunate for her that not one of those on board the Calyndian ship survived to become her accuser. Xerxes, they say, in reply to the remarks made to him observed, "My men have behaved like women, my women like men!"

89. There fell in this combat Ariabignes, one of the chief commanders of the fleet, who was son of Darius and brother of Xerxes; and with him perished a vast number of men of high repute: Persians, Medes, and allies. Of the Greeks there died only a few; for, as they were able to

swim, all those that were not slain outright by the enemy escaped from the sinking vessels and swam across to Salamis. But on the side of the barbarians more perished by drowning than in any other way, since they did not know how to swim. The great destruction took place when the ships which had been first engaged began to fly; for they who were stationed in the rear, anxious to display their valor before the eyes of the king, made every effort to force their way to the front and thus became entangled with such of their own vessels as were retreating.

90. In this confusion the following event occurred. Certain Phoenicians belonging to the ships which had thus perished made their appearance before the king and laid the blame of their loss on the Ionians, declaring that they were traitors and had wilfully destroyed the vessels. But the upshot of this complaint was that the Ionian captains escaped the death which threatened them, while their Phoenician accusers received death as their reward: for it happened that, exactly as they spoke, a Samothracian vessel bore down on an Athenian and sank it, but it was attacked and crippled immediately by one of the Aeginetan squadron. Now the Samothracians were expert with the javelin and aimed their weapons so well that they cleared the deck of the vessel which had disabled their own, after which they sprang on board and took it. This saved the Ionians. Xerxes, when he saw the exploit, turned fiercely on the Phoenicians (he was ready in his extreme vexation to find fault with anyone) and ordered their heads to be cut off to prevent them, he said, from casting the blame of their own misconduct upon braver men. During the whole time of the battle Xerxes sat at the base of the hill called Aegaleos over against Salamis; and whenever he saw any of his own captains perform any worthy exploit, he inquired concerning him; and the man's name was taken down by his scribes, together with the names of his father and his city. Ariaramnes too, a Persian, who was a friend of the Ionians and present at the time whereof I speak, had a share in bringing about the punishment of the Phoenicians.

91. When the rout of the barbarians began, and they sought to make their escape to Phalerum, the Aeginetans, awaiting them in the channel,

performed exploits worthy to be recorded. Through the whole of the confused struggle the Athenians employed themselves in destroying such ships as either made resistance or fled to shore, while the Aeginetans dealt with those which endeavored to escape down the strait, so that the Persian vessels were no sooner clear of the Athenians than forthwith they fell into the hands of the Aeginetan squadron....

96. As soon as the sea-fight was ended, the Greeks drew together to Salamis all the wrecks that were to be found in that quarter and prepared themselves for another engagement, supposing that the king would renew the fight with the vessels which still remained to him. Many of the wrecks had been carried away by a westerly wind to the coast of Attica, where they were thrown upon the strip of shore called Colias....

97. Xerxes, when he saw the extent of his loss, began to be afraid lest the Greeks might be counselled by the Ionians, or without their advice might determine to sail straight to the Hellespont and break down the bridges there; in which case he would be blocked up in Europe and run great risk of perishing. He therefore made up his mind to fly; but as he wished to hide his purpose alike from the Greeks and from his own people, he set to work to carry a mound across the channel to Salamis, and at the same time he began fastening a number of Phoenician merchant ships together to serve at once for a bridge and a wall. He likewise made many warlike preparations, as if he were about to engage the Greeks once more at sea. Now, when these things were seen, all grew fully persuaded that the king was bent on remaining and intended to push the war in good earnest. Mardonius, however, was in no respect deceived; for long acquaintance enabled him to read all the king's thoughts. Meanwhile, Xerxes, though engaged in this way, sent off a messenger to carry intelligence of his misfortune to Persia....

113. King Xerxes and his army waited but a few days after the sea-fight and then withdrew into Boeotia by the road which they had followed on their advance. It was the wish of Mardonius to escort the king a part of the way; and as the time of year was no longer suitable for carrying on war, he thought it best to winter in Thessaly and wait for the

spring before he attempted the Peloponnese. After the army was come into Thessaly, Mardonius made choice of the troops that were to stay with him....

115. Xerxes, after this, left Mardonius in Thessaly and marched away himself at his best speed toward the Hellespont. In five-and-forty days he reached the place of passage, where he arrived with scarce a fraction, so to speak, of his former army. All along their line of march, in every country where they chanced to be, his soldiers seized and devoured whatever grain they could find belonging to the inhabitants; while, if no grain was to be found, they gathered the grass that grew in the fields and stripped the trees, whether cultivated or wild, alike of their bark and of their leaves and so fed themselves. They left nothing anywhere, so hard were they pressed by hunger. Plague too and dysentery attacked the troops while still upon their march and greatly thinned their ranks. Many died; others fell sick and were left behind in the different cities that lay upon the route, the inhabitants being strictly charged by Xerxes to tend and feed them. Of these some remained in Thessaly, others in Siris of Paeonia, others again in Macedon. Here Xerxes, on his march into Greece, had left the sacred car and steeds of Zeus, which upon his return he was unable to recover: for the Paeonians had disposed of them to the Thracian; and when Xerxes demanded them back, they said that the Thracian tribes who dwelt about the sources of the Strymon had stolen the mares as they pastured.

READING 32
FROM DELIAN LEAGUE
TO ATHENIAN EMPIRE

Thucydides devotes the first of his eight-book history of the Peloponnesian War to describing in great detail the events involving Corcyra, Epidamnus, Corinth, Athens, and Potidaea that prompted Sparta to decide that Athens had violated its treaty with Sparta and the Peloponnesian League. After narrating the debate in Sparta and the Spartan assembly voting that the treaty had been broken, Thucydides digresses from his chronological description of events and sets forth a brief account of how in the aftermath of Xerxes' invasion of Greece Athens had become the leader of the Delian League and succeeded in converting it into their naval empire over the Aegean area. This digression (ss.89-118) is our single most important source of information for the nearly fifty-year period (479-431 B.C.) between the end of Herodotus' account of the Persian Wars and the beginning of Thucydides' history of the Peloponnesian War.

(Taken from Book I of The History of Thucydides, translated by Richard Crawley, Oxford 1866, revised by Gary Forsythe)

89. The way in which Athens came to be placed in the circumstances under which her power grew was this. After the Medes had returned from Europe, defeated by sea and land by the Hellenes, and after those of them who had fled with their ships to Mycale had been destroyed, Leotychides, king of the Lacedaemonians, the commander

of the Hellenes at Mycale, departed home with the allies from Peloponnese. But the Athenians and the allies from Ionia and Hellespont,
who had now revolted from the King, remained and laid siege to Ses-
tos, which was still held by the Medes. After wintering before it, they
became masters of the place on its evacuation by the barbarians; and
after this they sailed away from Hellespont to their respective cities.
Meanwhile, the Athenian people, after the departure of the barbarian
from their country, at once proceeded to carry over their children and
wives, and such property as they had left, from the places where they
had deposited them; and they prepared to rebuild their city and their
walls: for only isolated portions of the circumference had been left
standing, and most of the houses were in ruins, though a few remained, in which the Persian grandees had taken up their quarters....

93. In this way the Athenians walled their city in a little while. To this day
the building shows signs of the haste of its execution. The foundations
are laid of stones of all kinds, and in some places not wrought or fitted,
but placed just in the order in which they were brought by the different hands; and many columns, too, from tombs and sculptured stones
were put in with the rest: for the bounds of the city were extended at
every point of the circumference; and so they laid hands on everything
without exception in their haste. Themistocles also persuaded them
to finish the walls of Piraeus, which had been begun before in his year
of office as archon, being influenced alike by the fineness of a locality
that has three natural harbors, and by the great start which the Athenians would gain in the acquisition of power by becoming a naval people: for he first ventured to tell them to stick to the sea and forthwith
began to lay the foundations of the empire. It was by his advice, too,
that they built the walls of that thickness which can still be discerned
around Piraeus, the stones being brought up by two wagons meeting
each other. Between the walls thus formed there was neither rubble
nor mortar, but great stones hewn square and fitted together, cramped
to each other on the outside with iron and lead. About half the height
that he intended was finished. His idea was by their size and thickness
to keep off the attacks of an enemy; he thought that they might be
adequately defended by a small garrison of invalids, and the rest be

freed for service in the fleet: for the fleet claimed most of his attention. He saw, as I think, that the approach by sea was easier for the king's army than that by land. He also thought Piraeus more valuable than the upper city. Indeed, he was always advising the Athenians that if a day should come when they were hard pressed by land, to go down into Piraeus and defy the world with their fleet. Thus, therefore, the Athenians completed their wall and commenced their other buildings immediately after the retreat of the Mede.

94. Meanwhile, Pausanias, son of Cleombrotus, was sent out from Lacedaemon as commander-in-chief of the Hellenes with twenty ships from Peloponnese. With him sailed the Athenians with thirty ships and a number of the other allies. They made an expedition against Cyprus and subdued most of the island, and afterwards against Byzantium, which was in the hands of the Medes; and they compelled it to surrender. This event took place while the Spartans were still supreme.

95. But the violence of Pausanias had already begun to be disagreeable to the Hellenes, particularly to the Ionians and the newly liberated populations. These resorted to the Athenians and requested them as their kinsmen to become their leaders and to stop any attempt at violence on the part of Pausanias. The Athenians accepted their overtures and determined to put down any attempt of the kind and to settle everything else as their interests might seem to demand....

96. The Athenians, having thus succeeded to the supremacy by the voluntary act of the allies through their hatred of Pausanias, fixed which cities were to contribute money against the barbarian, which ships: their professed object being to retaliate for their sufferings by ravaging the King's country. Now was the time that the office of "Treasurers for Hellas" was first instituted by the Athenians. These officers received the tribute, as the money contributed was called. The tribute was first fixed at four hundred and sixty talents. The common treasury was at Delos, and the congresses were held in the temple.

97. Their supremacy commenced with independent allies who acted on the resolutions of a common congress. It was marked by the following undertakings in war and in administration during the interval between

the Median and the present war: against the barbarian, against their own rebel allies, and against the Peloponnesian powers which would come in contact with them on various occasions.... The history of these events contains an explanation of the growth of the Athenian empire.

98. First the Athenians besieged and captured Eion on the Strymon from the Medes, and they made slaves of the inhabitants, being under the command of Cimon, son of Miltiades. Next they enslaved Scyros, the island in the Aegean, containing a Dolopian population; and they colonized it themselves. This was followed by a war against Carystus, in which the rest of Euboea remained neutral, and which was ended by surrender on conditions. After this Naxos left the confederacy, and a war ensued; and she had to return after a siege. This was the first instance of the engagement being broken by the subjugation of an allied city, a precedent which was followed by that of the rest in the order that circumstances prescribed.

99. Of all the causes of defection, that connected with arrears of tribute and vessels, and with failure of service, was the chief; for the Athenians were very severe and exacting and made themselves offensive by applying the screw of necessity to men who were not used to and in fact not disposed for any continuous labor. In some other respects the Athenians were not the old popular rulers that they had been at first; and if they had more than their fair share of service, it was correspondingly easy for them to reduce any that tried to leave the confederacy. For this the allies had themselves to blame: the wish to get off service making most of them arrange to pay their share of the expense in money instead of in ships, and so to avoid having to leave their homes. Thus, while Athens was increasing her navy with the funds that they contributed, a revolt always found them without resources or experience for war.

100. Next we come to the actions by land and by sea at the river Eurymedon between the Athenians with their allies and the Medes, when the Athenians won both battles on the same day under the conduct of Cimon, son of Miltiades, and they captured and destroyed the whole Phoenician fleet, consisting of two hundred vessels. Some time

afterwards occurred the defection of the Thasians, caused by disagreements about the market centers on the opposite coast of Thrace and about the mine in their possession. Sailing with a fleet to Thasos, the Athenians defeated them at sea and effected a landing on the island. About the same time they sent ten thousand settlers of their own citizens and the allies to settle the place then called Ennea Hodoi or Nine Ways, now Amphipolis. They succeeded in gaining possession of Ennea Hodoi from the Edonians; but on advancing into the interior of Thrace, they were cut off in Drabescus, a town of the Edonians, by the assembled Thracians, who regarded the settlement of the place Ennea Hodoi as an act of hostility.

101. Meanwhile, the Thasians, being defeated in the field and suffering siege, appealed to Lacedaemon and desired her to assist them by an invasion of Attica. Without informing Athens, she promised and intended to do so, but was prevented by the occurrence of the earthquake, accompanied by the secession of the Helots and the Thuriats and Aethaeans of the Perioikoi to Ithome. Most of the Helots were the descendants of the old Messenians who were enslaved in the famous war; and so all of them came to be called Messenians. So, the Lacedaemonians being engaged in a war with the rebels in Ithome, the Thasians in the third year of the siege obtained terms from the Athenians by razing their walls, delivering up their ships, and arranging to pay the moneys demanded at once, and tribute in future, giving up their possessions on the continent together with the mine.

102. The Lacedaemonians, meanwhile, finding the war against the rebels in Ithome likely to last, invoked the aid of their allies, and especially of the Athenians, who came in some force under the command of Cimon. The reason for this pressing summons lay in their reputed skill in siege operations. A long siege had taught the Lacedaemonians their own deficiency in this art, else they would have taken the place by assault. The first open quarrel between the Lacedaemonians and Athenians arose out of this expedition. The Lacedaemonians, when assault failed to take the place, apprehensive of the enterprising and revolutionary character of the Athenians and, further, looking upon them as of alien extraction, began to fear that if they remained, they

might be tempted by the besieged in Ithome to attempt some polit-ical changes. They accordingly dismissed them alone of the allies without declaring their suspicions, but merely saying that they had now no need of them. But the Athenians, aware that their dismissal did not proceed from the more honorable reason of the two, but from suspicions which had been conceived, went away deeply of-fended and conscious of having done nothing to merit such treatment from the Lacedaemonians. And as soon as they returned home, they broke off the alliance which had been made against the Mede, and they allied themselves with Sparta's enemy, Argos: each of the con-tracting parties taking the same oaths and making the same alliance with the Thessalians.

103. Meanwhile, the rebels in Ithome, unable to prolong further a ten years' resistance, surrendered to Lacedaemon, the conditions being that they should depart from Peloponnese under safe conduct and should never set foot in it again: anyone who might hereafter be found there was to be the slave of his captor. It must be known that the Lacedaemonians had an old oracle from Delphi, to the effect that they should let go the suppliant of Zeus at Ithome. So, they went forth with their children and their wives; and being received by Athens from the hatred that she now felt for the Lacedaemonians, they were lo-cated at Naupactus, which she had lately taken from the Ozolian Locrians. The Athenians received another addition to their confed-eracy in the Megarians, who left the Lacedaemonian alliance, annoyed by a war about boundaries forced on them by Corinth. The Athenians occupied Megara and Pegae and built the Megarians their long walls from the city to Nisaea, in which they placed an Athenian garrison. This was the principal cause of the Corinthians conceiving such a deadly hatred against Athens....

105. ... Subsequently, war broke out between Aegina and Athens, and there was a great battle at sea off Aegina between the Athenians and Aegine-tans, each being aided by their allies, in which victory remained with the Athenians, who took seventy of the enemy's ships, landed in the country, and commenced a siege under the command of Leocrates, son of Stroebus. Upon this the Peloponnesians, desirous of aiding the

Aeginetans, threw into Aegina a force of three hundred hoplites, who had before been serving with the Corinthians and Epidaurians....

107. About this time the Athenians began to build the long walls to the sea: that towards Phalerum, and that towards Piraeus. Meanwhile, the Phocians made an expedition against Doris, the old home of the Lacedaemonians, containing the towns of Boeum, Kitinium, and Erineum. They had taken one of these towns, when the Lacedaemonians under Nicomedes, son of Cleombrotus, commanding for King Pleistoanax, son of Pausanias, who was still a minor, came to the aid of the Dorians with fifteen hundred hoplites of their own and ten thousand of their allies. After compelling the Phocians to restore the town on conditions, they began their retreat. The route by sea across the Crissaean Gulf exposed them to the risk of being stopped by the Athenian fleet; that across Geraneia seemed scarcely safe, the Athenians holding Megara and Pegae: for the pass was a difficult one and was always guarded by the Athenians; and in the present instance the Lacedaemonians had information that they meant to dispute their passage. So, they resolved to remain in Boeotia and to consider which would be the safest line of march. They had also another reason for this resolve. Secret encouragement had been given them by a party in Athens, who hoped to put an end to the reign of democracy and the building of the Long Walls. Meanwhile, the Athenians marched against them with their whole levy and a thousand Argives and the respective contingents of the rest of their allies. Altogether they were fourteen thousand strong. The march was prompted by the notion that the Lacedaemonians were at a loss how to effect their passage, and also by suspicions of an attempt to overthrow the democracy. Some cavalry also joined the Athenians from their Thessalian allies; but these went over to the Lacedaemonians during the battle.

108. The battle was fought at Tanagra in Boeotia. After heavy loss on both sides, victory declared for the Lacedaemonians and their allies. After entering the Megarid and cutting down the fruit trees, the Lacedaemonians returned home across Geraneia and the isthmus. Sixty-two days after the battle the Athenians marched into Boeotia under the command of Myronides, defeated the Boeotians in battle at

Oenophyta, and became masters of Boeotia and Phocis. They dismantled the walls of the Tanagraeans, took a hundred of the richest men of the Opuntian Locrians as hostages, and finished their own long walls. This was followed by the surrender of the Aeginetans to Athens on conditions. They pulled down their walls, gave up their ships, and agreed to pay tribute in future. The Athenians sailed around Peloponnese under Tolmides, son of Tolmaeus, burned the arsenal of Lacedaemon, took Chalcis, a town of the Corinthians, and in a descent upon Sicyon defeated the Sicyonians in battle....

112. Three years afterwards [451 B.C.] a truce was made between the Peloponnesians and Athenians for five years. Released from Hellenic war, the Athenians made an expedition to Cyprus with two hundred vessels of their own and their allies under the command of Cimon. Sixty of these were detached to Egypt at the instance of Amyrtaeus, the king in the marshes [in a rebellion against the Persians]; the rest laid siege to Kitium, from which, however, they were compelled to retire by the death of Cimon and by scarcity of provisions. Sailing off Salamis in Cyprus, they fought with the Phoenicians, Cyprians, and Cilicians by land and sea; and being victorious on both elements, they departed home and with them the returned squadron from Egypt. After this the Lacedaemonians marched out on a sacred war; and becoming masters of the temple at Delphi, they placed it in the hands of the Delphians. Immediately after their retreat the Athenians marched out, became masters of the temple, and placed it in the hands of the Phocians.

113. Some time after this, Orchomenus, Chaeronea, and some other places in Boeotia being in the hands of the Boeotian exiles, the Athenians marched against the above-mentioned hostile places with a thousand Athenian hoplites and the allied contingents under the command of Tolmides, son of Tolmaeus. They took Chaeronea and made slaves of the inhabitants; and leaving a garrison, they commenced their return. On their road they were attacked at Coronea by the Boeotian exiles from Orchomenus along with some Locrians and Euboean exiles, and others who were of the same way of thinking. The Athenians were defeated in battle, and some killed, others taken captive. The Athenians

evacuated all Boeotia by a treaty providing for the recovery of the men; and the exiled Boeotians returned, and with all the rest they regained their independence.

114. This was soon afterwards followed by the revolt of Euboea from Athens [446 B.C.]. Pericles had already crossed over with an army of Athenians to the island, when news was brought to him that Megara had revolted, that the Peloponnesians were on the point of invading Attica, and that the Athenian garrison had been cut off by the Megarians with the exception of a few who had taken refuge in Nisaea. The Megarians had introduced the Corinthians, Sicyonians, and Epidaurians into the town before they revolted. Meanwhile, Pericles brought his army back in all haste from Euboea. After this the Peloponnesians marched into Attica as far as Eleusis and Thrius, ravaging the country under the conduct of King Pleistoanax, the son of Pausanias; and without advancing further they returned home. The Athenians then crossed over again to Euboea under the command of Pericles and subdued the whole of the island. All but Histiaea was settled by convention. The Histiaeans they expelled from their homes and occupied their territory themselves.

115. Not long after their return from Euboea, they made a truce with the Lacedaemonians and their allies for thirty years, giving up the posts which they occupied in Peloponnese: Nisaea, Pegae, Troezen, and Achaia. In the sixth year of the truce [440 B.C.] war broke out between the Samians and Milesians about Priene. Worsted in the war, the Milesians came to Athens with loud complaints against the Samians. In this they were joined by certain private persons from Samos itself, who wished to revolutionize the government. Accordingly, the Athenians sailed to Samos with forty ships, set up a democracy, took hostages from the Samians (fifty boys and as many men), and lodged them in Lemnos; and after leaving a garrison in the island, they returned home. But some of the Samians had not remained in the island, but had fled to the continent. Making an agreement with the most powerful of those in the city and an alliance with Pissuthnes, son of Hystaspes, the then satrap of Sardis, they got together a force of seven hundred mercenaries, and under cover of night they crossed over to

Samos. Their first step was to rise on the commons, most of whom they secured; their next was to steal their hostages from Lemnos, after which they revolted, gave up the Athenian garrison left with them and its commanders to Pissuthnes, and instantly prepared for an expedition against Miletus. The Byzantines also revolted with them.

116. As soon as the Athenians heard the news, they sailed with sixty ships against Samos. Sixteen of these went to Caria to look out for the Phoenician fleet, and to Chios and Lesbos carrying around orders for reinforcements, and so never engaged; but forty-four ships under the command of Pericles with nine colleagues gave battle off the island of Tragia to seventy Samian vessels, of which twenty were transports, as they were sailing from Miletus. Victory remained with the Athenians. Reinforced afterwards by forty ships from Athens and twenty-five Chian and Lesbian vessels, the Athenians landed; and having the superiority by land, they invested the city with three walls. It was also invested from the sea. Meanwhile, Pericles took sixty ships from the blockading squadron and departed in haste for Caunus and Caria, intelligence having been brought in of the approach of the Phoenician fleet to the aid of the Samians. Indeed, Stesagoras and others had left the island with five ships to bring them.

117. But in the meantime, the Samians made a sudden sally and fell on the camp, which they found unfortified. Destroying the look-out vessels and engaging and defeating such as were being launched to meet them, they remained masters of their own seas for fourteen days and carried in and carried out what they pleased. But on the arrival of Pericles, they were once more shut up. Fresh reinforcements afterwards arrived: forty ships from Athens with Thucydides, Hagnon, and Phormio; twenty with Tlepolemus and Anticles, and thirty vessels from Chios and Lesbos. After a brief attempt at fighting, the Samians, unable to hold out, were reduced after a nine months' siege and surrendered on conditions. They razed their walls, gave hostages, delivered up their ships, and arranged to pay the expenses of the war by instalments. The Byzantines also agreed to be subject as before.

READING 33
THE WORKINGS
OF THE ATHENIAN EMPIRE

One of our most important sources of information for the nuts-and-bolts workings of Athenian domination of the Delian League before the outbreak of the Peloponnesian War is a series of inscriptions recording Athenian public decisions concerning aspects of their rule. The following readings are a selection of the more important and more informative of these inscriptions.

> (Taken from pp. 7-9, 11-12, 13-14, and 15-16 of Greek Historical Documents, The Fifth Century B.C., by Naphtali Lewis, published by A. M. Hakkert, Toronto, copyright 1971, reprinted with the permission of the publisher)

A. Athenian Decree Concerning Erythrae

Erythrae, an Ionian city on the coast opposite Chios, was one of the original members of the Delian League. This decree, probably belonging to the period 470-450 B.C., illustrates how Athens infringed on the sovereignty of the allied cities: imposing democratic constitutions, increasingly requiring that major cases be tried in Athens, and substituting Athena for Apollo as the principal tutelary divinity for all member cities.

[The prescript is lost.] The Erythraeans shall bring to the Great Panathenaic Festival food worth not less than 3 minas, and to the Erythraeans attending the overseer of rites shall distribute the meat, a drachma's worth to each. If they bring less than 3 minas' worth, food for the rites shall be purchased according to their obligations, the amount of the deficiency shall be entered in a record of debt against the government, and anyone of the Erythraeans so desiring may see to it. Erythrae shall have a council of 120 men chosen by lot. The council shall examine (the qualifications of) each man so chosen: an alien may not be a councilor, nor anyone under 30 years of age, and violators (of this provision) shall be liable to prosecution. No one shall be a councilor twice within four years. The present council shall be drawn by lot and constituted by the (Athenian) overseers and garrison commander, in future by the council itself and the commander not less than thirty days before the council goes out of office. They shall swear by Zeus, Apollo, and Demeter, imprecating utter destruction upon those who swear false and utter destruction upon their children. They shall swear the oath over burning sacrifices; the council shall burn sacrifices of not less than oxen or else shall be liable to a fine of 1,000 drachmas; and when the assembly swears, the assembly shall burn no less.

The council oath is as follows: "To the best and truest of my ability I will serve as councilor for the people of Erythrae and Athens and the allies. I will not revolt against the people of Athens or against the allies of Athens, either of my own accord or at the behest of another; and I will not defect, either of my own accord or at the behest of any other person at all. Of the exiles (i.e., of those who fled to the Medes) I will never receive back a single one, either of my own accord or at the behest of another, without (the authorization of) the council and assembly of Athens, nor of those who remain will I drive any out without (the authorization of) the council and assembly of Athens."

If any Erythraean kills another Erythraean, he shall be put to death if convicted; if he is condemned to exile, he shall be banished from the entire Athenian alliance, and his property shall be confiscated by Erythrae. If anyone is convicted of acting to betray the city of Erythrae to tyrants, he himself may be put to death with impunity, and also the children born of him; but if the children born of him are shown to be supporters of the government of Erythrae and that of Athens, they shall be spared; and after forfeiting all his property, they shall receive back half, and half shall be confiscated.

[The rest of the inscription is fragmentary.]

B. The Coinage Decree

In Aristophanes' play entitled Birds, produced in 414 B.C., the Seller of Decrees proclaims that "the people of Cloudcuckooland shall use the same measures, weights, and coinage as the Olophyxians" (verses 1040-41). Behind this spoof we recognize a reference to an actual law imposed by Athens on the cities of the Confederacy c.450 B.C. Fragments of the law have been found at Aphytis, Cos, Smyrna, Siphnos, and Cyme, reflecting the provision of the decree that a copy was to be set up in every city of the Athenian empire. Different scholars have proposed various restorations of the missing portions of the text. The following translation is based for the most part on the text of Meiggs and Lewis, A Selection of Greek Historical Inscriptions to the End of the Fifth Century B.C., Oxford University Press 1969 #45.

[The beginning is too fragmentary for restoration.] If any citizen or foreigner in the cities, other than the (Athenian) governors, acts contrary to this decree, he shall be disfranchised, and his property shall be confiscated, a tithe going to the goddess. If there are no Athenian governors, the magistrates of the respective cities shall carry out the provisions of the decree; and if they act contrary to the decree, a prosecution for disfranchisement shall be instituted at Athens against such magistrates. -Receiving the (foreign) money in the mint (at Athens), the managers shall convert not less than half into (Athenian) coin ... exacting in each case a fee of three(?) drachmas per mina; the other half....

[Here another portion is too broken for continuous sense.] If anyone moves or votes to decree that it be lawful to use or make a loan in foreign coinage, he shall immediately be denounced to the Eleven [officials in charge of the prison in Athens], and the Eleven shall punish him with death; if he disputes the charge, they shall bring him to trial.

The assembly shall choose heralds and send them to the cities to announce the (present) decree: one herald to the Islands, one to Ionia, one to the Hellespont, and one to the settlements in Thrace. The generals shall dispatch them... and if not, each (general) shall be fined ten thousand drachmas. The governors in the cities shall have this decree inscribed on a stone stele and erect it in the agora of each city, and (at Athens) the managers (shall erect it) in front of the mint. Athens shall carry this out if the said persons are recalcitrant, but the herald who goes shall ask them to do what Athens bids.

The secretary of the council shall in future add the following to the oath of the council: "If anyone coins silver money in the cities and does not use Athenian coins or measures or weights but foreign coins and measures and weights, I will vote the penalty and punishment in accordance with the previous decree moved by Clearchus."

Anyone is permitted to turn in the foreign money that he has and exchange it on these same terms whenever he wishes, and the city will give him Athenian coinage in exchange; each shall bring his own to Athens and deposit it at the mint. The (mint) managers shall ... recording ... in front of the mint for anyone so desiring to inspect ... [The rest is lost.]

C. Measures for Collecting the Tribute

These regulations, aimed at assuring the receipt of all the tribute due from the cities of the Confederacy, were decreed by Athens c.447 B.C. The fluctuations in the number of cities in the surviving annual quota lists and the recurrence of incomplete and double payments in the early forties show that Athens could not rely on receiving every year all the tribute that was due to her. This decree is an attempt to improve discipline, and the measures approved by the assembly are to be the responsibility of the boule, with the co-operation of Athenian officials overseas, travelling commissioners, and resident officials, both of whom are found in other decrees of the 450s and 440s.

Gods. The council and the assembly decree (the tribe) Oineis was in prytany, Spoudias was secretary, —-on was president, Kleinias moved.

The council and the (Athenian) governors, as well as the visiting overseers, shall see to it that the tribute is collected each year and is brought to Athens. They shall issue seals to the cities, so that it will not be possible for those bringing the tribute to perpetrate fraud. The city shall write on a tablet the tribute that it is sending, mark it with the seal, and send it to Athens. Those bringing it shall deliver the tablet in the council for verification when they deliver the tribute. The prytaneis shall hold an assembly after the Dionysia for the Hellenotamiae [treasurers of the Delian League] to disclose to the Athenians the cities that have delivered the tribute in full and, separately, those falling short, if any. The Athenians shall choose four men to send to the cities to give receipts for the tribute delivered, and to exact the undelivered tribute from those falling short: two men shall sail on swift triremes to the cities in the Islands and Ionia, and two to the cities in Hellespont and Thrace. The prytaneis shall bring this matter before the council and the assembly immediately after the Dionysia, and they shall deliberate on this matter uninterruptedly until it is accomplished.

[The decree continues with provisions for filing and hearing complaints of irregularities or malfeasance. The final portion of the inscription is too fragmentary for restoration.]

D. Settlement of Affairs in Chalcis

In 446/5 B.C., after suppressing the secession of Euboea, Athens decreed new charters for the cities of the island. Euboea had been crushed; but its cities, except Histiaea, were to remain separate, autonomous states, members of the League, though more clearly than before controlled by Athens. The nature of that control is shown by the terms of the treaty with Chalcis, especially the last clause.

The council and assembly decree, (the tribe) Antiochis was in prytany, Drakontides presided, Diognetos moved.

The council (of 500) and the jurors of the Athenians shall take an oath as follows: "I will not expel the Chalcidians from Chalcis or destroy their city; I will not (vote to) disfranchise, punish with exile, arrest, put to death, or confiscate the property of any private citizen without trial, unless (authorized) by the government of Athens; nor will I without a formal summons take a vote either against the community of Chalcis or against any private citizen. If an embassy comes when I am prytanis, I will present it before the council and assembly within ten days insofar as possible.' I will uphold these provisions for the Chalcidians so long as they are obedient to the government of Athens."

An embassy coming from Chalcis shall, together with the (Athenian) commissioners of oaths, administer the oath to the Athenians and shall record (the names of) those who take the oath. The generals shall see to it that all take the oath.

The Chalcidians shall take an oath as follows: "I will not revolt against the government of Athens by any manner or means either in word or in deed, nor will I follow anyone revolting; and if anyone incites to revolt, I will denounce him to the Athenians. I will pay to the Athenians whatever tribute I may convince the Athenians (to assess). I will be the best and truest ally possible; I will aid and defend the government of Athens if anyone wrongs the government of Athens, and I will be obedient to the government of Athens."

All Chalcidians who are of age shall take the oath; any man who does not take the oath shall be disfranchised, his property shall be confiscated, and a tithe of his property shall be consecrated (in Chalcis) to Olympian Zeus. An embassy of Athenians coming to Chalcis shall, together with the commissioners of oaths in Chalcis, administer the oath and shall record (the names of) the Chalcidians who take the oath.

Antikles moved.

With the good fortune of the Athenians: The Athenians and the Chalcidians shall ratify the oath just as the government of Athens ordered in the case of the Eretrians. The generals shall see to it that this is done as soon as possible. The assembly shall choose immediately five men who shall go to Chalcis and administer the oath. Concerning the hostages, the answer to the Chalcidians shall be that for now the Athenians have decided to leave matters as already decreed; but whenever it shall seem appropriate, they will reconsider and will make such changes as may seem advantageous for Athens and Chalcis. All aliens residing in Chalcis, who do not pay taxes to Athens and have not been granted tax exemption by the government of Athens, shall pay taxes to Chalcis just like the other Chalcidians.

The secretary of the council shall, at the expense of the Chalcidians, inscribe this decree and the oath at Athens on a stone stele and shall erect it on the Acropolis, and in Chalcis the council of the Chalcidians shall inscribe and erect (a copy) in the temple of Olympian Zeus.

Such shall be the decree for the Chalcidians. And three men whom the council shall choose from among themselves shall, as soon as possible, together with Hierokles, offer the sacrifices in accordance with the oracles regarding Euboea. The generals shall assist in seeing to it that the sacrifices are offered as soon as possible, and shall provide the money therefor.

Archestratos moved.

In addition to Antikles' motion, the Chalcidians shall have the right to pass sentence against their own (people) at Chalcis just as the Athenians (have) at Athens, except for exile, death, and disfranchisement; concerning these there shall be an appeal to Athens to the court of the Thesmothetae according to government decree. Concerning the garrison of Euboea, the generals shall see to the best of their ability that it serves the best interests of Athens.

READING 34
THE OLD OLIGARCH

As the result of Athens' rise to naval supremacy in the Aegean following Xerxes' invasion of Greece, the Greek city-states of the Aegean world (with few exceptions) were eventually divided into one of two camps: the Peloponnesian League headed by Sparta, and the Delian League that Athens transformed into its naval empire. Moreover, since Sparta encouraged their allies to have governments based upon a citizenry with a hoplite census, whereas Athens, whenever possible, established among their allied communities governments in imitation of their own democracy, the internal politics of many Greek city-states became polarized between those who supported Athenian-style democracy and those who favored a less inclusive type of government. The following passage exemplifies this political division, which became further exacerbated during the Peloponnesian War and resulted in actual civil war between pro-Athenian democrats and pro-Spartan oligarchs within many city-states. Although the author of this little pamphlet is not known, modern scholars have come to call him "The Old Oligarch." He was apparently an Athenian of the upper class who strongly disapproved of the democracy, and who wrote this work in order to explain to his fellow aristocrats in other states (often with humorous irony and sarcasm) the rationale of the Athenian democracy.

(From Xenophon's *Constitution of the Athenians*, taken from *The Works of Xenophon*, Volume II, translated by Henry Graham Dakyns, MacMillan, London 1892, revised by Gary Forsythe)

1. Now, as concerning the polity of the Athenians, and the type or manner of constitution which they have chosen, I praise it not, insofar as the very choice involves the welfare of the baser folk as opposed to that of the better class. I repeat, I withhold my praise so far; but, given the fact that this is the type agreed upon, I propose to show that they set about its preservation in the right way; and that those other transactions in connection with it, which are looked upon as blunders by the rest of the Hellenic world, are the reverse.

In the first place, I maintain, it is only just that the poorer classes and the People of Athens should be better off than the men of birth and wealth, seeing that it is the people who man the fleet and put around the city her girdle of power. The steersman, the boatswain, the lieutenant, the look-out-man at the prow, the shipright—these are the people who engird the city with power far rather than her heavy infantry and men of birth of quality. This being the case, it seems only just that offices of state should be thrown open to everyone both in the ballot and the show of hands, and that the right of speech should belong to anyone who likes without restriction: for, observe, there are many of these offices which, according as they are in good or in bad hands, are a source of safety or of danger to the People, and in these the People prudently abstains from sharing; as, for instance, it does not think it incumbent on itself to share in the functions of the general or of the commander of cavalry. The sovereign People recognizes the fact that in forgoing the personal exercise of these offices, and leaving them to the control of the more powerful citizens, it secures the balance of advantage to itself. It is only those departments of government which bring emolument and assist the private estate that the People cares to keep in its own hands.

In the next place, in regard to what some people are puzzled to explain—the fact that everywhere greater consideration is shown to the base, to poor people, and to common folk than to persons of good quality—so far from being a matter of surprise, this, as can be shown, is the keystone of the preservation of the democracy. It is these poor people, this common folk, this riffraff, whose prosperity, combined with the growth of their numbers, enhances the democracy. Whereas, a shifting of fortune to the advantage of the wealthy and the better classes implies the establishment on the part of the commonalty of a strong power in opposition to itself. In fact, all the world over, the cream of society is in opposition to the democracy. Naturally, since the smallest amount of intemperance and injustice, together with the highest scrupulousness in the pursuit of excellence, is to be found in the ranks of the better class, while within the ranks of the People will be found the greatest amount of ignorance, disorderliness, rascality—poverty acting as a stronger incentive to base conduct, not to speak of lack of education and ignorance, traceable to the lack of means which afflicts the average of mankind.

The objection may be raised that it was a mistake to allow the universal right of speech and a seat in council. These should have been reserved for the cleverest, the flower of the community. But here, again, it will be found that they are acting with wise deliberation in granting to even the baser sort the right of speech: for supposing only the better people might speak or sit in council, blessings would fall to the lot of those like themselves, but to the commonalty the reverse of blessings. Whereas now, anyone who likes, any base fellow, may get up and discover something to the advantage of himself and his equals. It may be retorted: "And what sort of advantage either for himself or for the People can such a fellow be expected to hit upon?" The answer to which is, that in their judgment the ignorance and baseness of this fellow, together with his goodwill, are worth a great deal more to them than your superior person's virtue and wisdom, coupled with animosity. What it comes to, therefore, is that a state founded upon such institutions will not be the best state; but, given a democracy, these are the right means to procure its preservation. The People, it must be borne in mind, does not demand that the city should be well governed and itself a slave. It desires to be free and to be master. As to bad legislation, it does not concern itself about that. In fact, what you believe to be bad legislation is the very source of the People's strength and freedom. But if you seek for good legislation, in the first place, you will see the cleverest members of the community laying down the laws for the rest. And in the next place, the better class will curb and chastise the lower orders; the better class will deliberate in behalf of the state and not suffer crack-brained fellows to sit in council or to speak or vote in assembly. No doubt; but under the weight of such blessings the People will in a very short time be reduced to slavery.

Another point is the extraordinary amount of license granted to slaves and resident aliens at Athens, where a blow is illegal, and a slave will not step aside

to let you pass him in the street. I will explain the reason of this peculiar custom. Supposing it were legal for a slave to be beaten by a free citizen, or for a
resident alien or freedman to be beaten by a citizen, it would frequently happen
that an Athenian might be mistaken for a slave or an alien and receive a beating, since the Athenian People is no better clothed than the slave or alien, nor
in personal appearance is there any superiority. Or if the fact itself that slaves
in Athens are allowed to indulge in luxury and, indeed, in some cases to live
magnificently, be found astonishing, this too, it can be shown, is done of set
purpose. Where you have a naval power dependent upon wealth, we must per-
force be slaves to our slaves in order that we may get in our slave- rents and
let the real slave go free. Where you have wealthy slaves, it ceases to be advantageous that my slave should stand in awe of you. In Lacedaemon my slave
stands in awe of you. But if your slave is in awe of me, there will be a risk of
his giving away his own moneys to avoid running a risk in his own person. It
is for this reason then that we have established an equality between our slaves
and free men, and again between our resident aliens and full citizens, because
the city stands in need of her resident aliens to meet the requirements of such
a multiplicity of arts and for the purposes of her navy. That is, I repeat, the
justification for the equality conferred upon our resident aliens....

To speak next of the allies, and in reference to the point that emissaries
from Athens come out and, according to common opinion, calumniate and vent
their hatred upon the better sort of people, this is done on the principle that
the ruler cannot help being hated by those whom he rules; but that if wealth
and respectability are to wield power in the subject cities, the empire of the
Athenian People has but a short lease of existence. This explains why the better
people are punished with infamy, robbed of their money, driven from their
homes, and put to death, while the baser sort are promoted to honor. On the
other hand, the better Athenians throw their aegis over the better class in the
allied cities. And why? Because they recognize that it is to the interest of their
own class at all times to protect the best element in the cities. It may be urged
that if it comes to strength and power, the real strength of Athens lies in the
capacity of her allies to contribute their money quota. But to the democratic
mind it appears a higher advantage still for the individual Athenian to get hold
of the wealth of the allies, leaving them only enough to live upon and to cultivate their estates, but powerless to harbor treacherous designs.

Again, it is looked upon as a mistaken policy on the part of the Athenian democracy to compel her allies to voyage to Athens in order to have their cases tried. On the other hand, it is easy to reckon up what a number of advantages the Athenian People derive from the practice impugned. In the first place, there is the steady receipt of salaries throughout the year derived from the court fees. Next, it enables them to manage the affairs of the allied states while seated at home without the expense of naval expeditions. Thirdly, they thus preserve the partisans of the democracy and ruin her opponents in the law courts. Whereas, supposing the several allied states tried their cases at home, being inspired by hostility to Athens, they would destroy those of their own citizens whose friendship to the Athenian People was most marked. But besides all this, the democracy derives the following advantages from hearing the cases of her allies in Athens. In the first place, the one percent levied in Piraeus is increased to the profit of the state; again, the owner of a lodging- house does better and so, too, the owner of a pair of beasts, or of slaves to be let out on hire; again, heralds and criers are a class of people who fare better due to the sojourn of foreigners at Athens. Further still, supposing the allies had not to resort to Athens for the hearing of cases, only the official representative of the imperial state would be held in honor, such as the general, or trierarch, or am-bassador; whereas now every single individual among the allies is forced to pay flattery to the People of Athens, because he knows that he must betake himself to Athens and win or lose his case at the bar, not of any stray set of judges, but of the sovereign People itself, such being the law and custom at Athens. He is compelled to behave as a suppliant in the courts of justice; and when some ju-ryman comes into court, he is obliged to grasp his hand. For this reason, there-fore, the allies find themselves more and more in the position of slaves to the People of Athens.

Furthermore, due to the possession of property beyond the limits of Attica and the exercise of magistracies which take them into regions beyond the fron-tier, they and their attendants have insensibly acquired the art of navigation. A man who is perpetually voyaging is forced to handle the oar, he and his do-mestics alike, and to learn the terms familiar in seamanship. Hence, a stock of skillful mariners is produced, bred upon a wide experience of voyaging and practice. They have learned their business: some in piloting a small craft, oth-ers a merchant vessel, while others have been drafted off from these for service on a ship-of-war, so that the majority of them are able to row the moment they set foot on board a vessel, having been in a state of preliminary practice all their lives.

2   ... And as to the states subject to Athens which are not islanders, but situated on the continent, the larger are held in check by need and the small ones absolutely by fear, since there is no state in existence which does not depend upon imports and exports; and these she will forfeit if she does not lend a willing ear to those who are masters by sea. In the next place, a power dominant by sea can do certain things which a land power is debarred from doing: as, for instance, ravage the territory of a superior, since it is always possible to coast along to some point, where either there is no hostile force to deal with or merely a small body; and in case of an advance in force on the part of the enemy, they can take to their ships and sail away. Such a perform-ance is attended with less difficulty than that experienced by the re-lieving force on land. Again, it is open to a power so dominating by sea to leave its own territory and sail off on as long a voyage as you please; whereas the land power cannot place more than a few days' journey between itself and its own territory: for marches are slow af-fairs; and it is not possible for an army on the march to have food sup-plies to last for any great length of time. Such an army must either march through friendly territory, or it must force a way by victory in battle. The voyager, meanwhile, has it in his power to disembark at any point where he finds himself in superior force, or, at the worst, to coast by until he reaches either a friendly district or an enemy too weak to resist. Again, those diseases to which the fruits of the earth are liable as visitations from heaven fall severely on a land power, but are scarcely felt by the naval power: for such sicknesses do not visit the whole earth everywhere at once, so that the ruler of the sea can get in supplies from a thriving district. And if one may descend to more trifling particulars, it is to this same lordship of the sea that the Athenians owe the discovery, in the first place, of many of the luxuries of life through intercourse with other countries. Thus, the choice things of Sicily and Italy, of Cyprus and Egypt and Lydia, of Pontus

or Peloponnese, or wheresoever else it be, are all swept, as it were, into one center, and all due, as I say, to their maritime empire. And again, in process of listening to every form of speech, they have selected this from one place and that from another for themselves, so much so that while the rest of the Hellenes employ each pretty much their own peculiar mode of speech, habit of life, and style of dress, the Athenians have adopted a composite type, to which all sections of Hellas and the foreigner alike have contributed....

As to wealth, the Athenians are exceptionally placed with regard to Hellenic and foreign communities alike in their ability to hold it. For, given that some state or other is rich in timber for shipbuilding, where is it to find a market for the product except by persuading the ruler of the sea? Or, suppose the wealth of some state or other to consist of iron, or may be of bronze, or of linen yarn, where will it find a market except by permission of the supreme maritime power? Yet, these are the very things, you see, which I need for my ships. Timber I must have from one, and from another iron, from a third bronze, from a fourth linen yarn, from a fifth wax, etc. Besides which, they will not suffer their antagonists in those parts to carry these products elsewhither, or they will cease to use the sea. Accordingly, I, without one stroke of labor, extract from the land and possess all these good things, thanks to my supremacy on the sea, while not a single other state possesses the two of them—not timber, for instance, and yarn together, the same city. But where yarn is abundant, the soil will be light and devoid of timber. And in the same way bronze and iron will not be products of the same city. And so for the rest, never two, or at best three, in one state, but one thing here and another thing there. Moreover, above and beyond what has been said, the coastline of every mainland presents either some jutting promontory or adjacent island or narrow strait of some sort, so that those who are masters of the sea can come to moorings at one of these points and wreak vengeance on the inhabitants of the mainland....

Further, states oligarchically governed are forced to ratify their alliances and solemn oaths; and if they fail to abide by their contracts, the offense, by whomsoever committed, lies nominally at the door of the oligarchs who entered upon the contract. But in the case of engagements entered into by a democracy, it is open to the People to throw the blame on the single individual who spoke in favor of some measure or put it to the vote, and to maintain to the rest of the world, "I was not present, nor do I approve of the terms of the agreement." Inquiries are made in a full meeting of the People; and should any of these things be disapproved of, it can at once discover ten thousand excuses to avoid doing whatever they do not wish. And if any mischief should spring out of any resolutions which the People has passed in council, the People can readily shift the blame from its own shoulders. "A handful of oligarchs acting against the interests of the People have ruined us." But if any good result ensue, they, the People, at once take the credit of that to themselves.

In the same spirit it is not allowed to caricature on the comic stage or otherwise libel the People, because they do not care to hear themselves ill spoken of. But if anyone has a desire to satirize his neighbor, he has full leave to do so. And this because they are well aware that, as a general rule, this person caricatured does not belong to the People or the masses. He is more likely to be some wealthy or well-born person or man of means and influence. In fact, but few poor people and of the popular stamp incur the comic lash; or if they do, they have brought it on themselves by excessive love of meddling or some covetous self-seeking at the expense of the People, so that no particular annoyance is felt at seeing such folk satirized.

What, then, I venture to assert is, that the People of Athens has no difficulty in recognizing which of its citizens are of the better sort and which the opposite. And so recognizing those who are serviceable and advantageous to itself, even though they be base, the People loves them; but the good folk they are disposed rather to hate. This virtue of theirs, the People holds, is not engrained in their nature for any good to itself, but rather, for its injury. In direct opposition to this, there are some persons who, being born of the People, are yet by natural instinct not commoners. For my part I pardon the People its own democracy, as, indeed, it is pardonable in anyone to do good to himself. But the man who, not being himself one of the People, prefers to live in a state democratically governed rather than in an oligarchical state may be said to smooth his own path towards iniquity. He knows that a bad man has a better chance of slipping through the fingers of justice in a democratic than in an oligarchical state.

3. I repeat that my position concerning the polity of the Athenians is this: the type of polity is not to my taste, but given that a democratic form of government has been agreed upon, they do seem to me to go the right way to preserve the democracy by the adoption of the particular type which I have set forth....

There is another point in which it is sometimes felt that the Athenians are ill advised: in their adoption, namely, of the less respectable party in a state divided by faction. But if so, they do it advisedly. If they chose the more respectable, they would be adopting those whose views and interests differ from their own: for there is no state in which the best element is friendly to the people. It is the worst element which in every state favors the democracy on the principle that like favors like. It is simple enough then. The Athenians choose what is most akin to themselves. Also, on every occasion on which they have attempted to side with the better classes, it has not fared well with them, but within a short interval the democratic party has been enslaved, as, for instance, in Boeotia; or, as when they chose the aristocrats of the Milesians, and within a short time these revolted and cut the people to pieces; or, as when they chose the Lacedaemonians as against the Messenians, and within a short time the Lacedaemonians subjugated the Messenians and went to war against Athens.

READING 35
THUCYDIDES AND
THE PELOPONNESIAN WAR

With the rise of Athenian naval power in the aftermath of Xerxes' invasion of Greece and Athens' conversion of the Delian League into the Athenian Empire, most Greek states of the Aegean world found themselves aligned either with Sparta or Athens. Eventually, minor conflicts between parties of these two groups sparked off a tremendous war that involved all parties in a desperate struggle for victory. This war, which lasted for 27 years (431-404 B.C.) and did much to destroy the prosperity of Classical Greece, is known as the Peloponnesian War. We owe our knowledge of this war to Thucydides, an Athenian, who lived during this conflict and wrote an extremely detailed historical account of this war. He is generally recognized as the greatest historian of ancient Greece and one of the greatest historians of all time. Besides chronicling the events of this particular war in detail, Thucydides succeeded in portraying these human actions in universal terms, showing how intelligence, chance, boldness, miscalculations, lack of resolve, etc. affected the outcome of events, and how the pressures of war eroded public morality of all parties involved.

(Taken from The History of Thucydides, translated by Richard Crawley, Oxford 1866, revised by Gary Forsythe)

A. Thucydides' Methods of Research and Writing History (Book I)

1. Thucydides, an Athenian, wrote the history of the war between the

Peloponnesians and the Athenians, beginning at the moment that it broke out, and believing that it would be a great war and more worthy of relation than any that had preceded it. This belief was not without its grounds. The preparations of both the combatants were in every department in the last state of perfection; and he could see the rest of the Hellenic race taking sides in the quarrel: those who delayed doing so at once having it in contemplation....

22. With reference to the speeches in this history, some were delivered before the war began, others while it was going on; some I heard myself, others I got from various quarters; it was in all cases difficult to carry them word for word in one's memory. So, my habit has been to make the speakers say what was in my opinion demanded of them by the various occasions, of course, adhering as closely as possible to the general sense of what they really said. And with reference to the narrative of events, far from permitting myself to derive it from the first source that came to hand, I did not even trust my own impressions, but it rests partly on what I saw myself, partly on what others saw for me, the accuracy of the report being always tried by the most severe and detailed tests possible. My conclusions have cost me some labor from the want of coincidence between accounts of the same occurrences by different eye-witnesses, arising sometimes from imperfect memory, sometimes from undue partiality for one side or the other. The absence of romance in my history will, I fear, detract somewhat from its interest; but if it be judged useful by those inquirers who desire an exact knowledge of the past as an aid to the interpretation of the future, which in the course of human things must resemble if it does not reflect it, I shall be content. In fine, I have written my work not as an essay which is to win the applause of the moment, but as a possession for all time....

B. Sparta Declares War on Athens (Book I)

After some of Sparta's Peloponnesian allies complained to Sparta of Athenian aggression, the Spartans held an assembly of their adult male citizens to hear both their allies' complaints and the Athenians' reply. Then they debated what should be done. After listening to speeches made by one of their two kings (Archidamus) and one of their five annually elected ephors (Sthenelaidas), the Spartan assembly decided that the Athenians were guilty of breaking their treaty with Sparta; and Sparta was now ready to wage war upon Athens.

79. Such were the words of the Athenians. After the Spartans had heard the complaints of the allies against the Athenians, and the observations of the latter, they made all withdraw and consulted by themselves on the question before them. The opinions of the majority all led to the same conclusion: the Athenians were open aggressors, and war must be declared at once. But Archidamus, the Spartan king, came forward, who had the reputation of being at once a wise and a moderate man; and he made the following speech:

80. "I have not lived so long, Spartans, without having had the experience of many wars; and I see those among you of the same age as myself, who will not fall into the common misfortune of longing for war from inexperience or from a belief in its advantage and its safety. This, the war on which you are now debating, would be one of the greatest magnitude on a sober consideration of the matter. In a struggle with Peloponnesians and neighbors our strength is of the same character, and it is possible to move swiftly on the different points. But a struggle with a people who live in a distant land, who have also an extraordinary familiarity with the sea, and who are in the highest state of preparation in every other department with wealth private and public, with ships, and horses, and hoplites, and a population such as no one other Greek place can equal, and lastly a number of tributary allies, what can justify us in rashly beginning such a struggle? Wherein is our trust that we should rush on it unprepared? Is it in our ships? There we are inferior, while if we are to practise and become a match for them, time must intervene.

81 Is it in our money? There we have a far greater deficiency. We neither have it in our treasury, nor are we ready to contribute it from our private funds. Confidence might possibly be felt in our superiority in hoplites and population, which will enable us to invade and devastate their lands. But the Athenians have plenty of other land in their empire, and

they can import what they want by sea. Again, if we are to attempt an insurrection of their allies, these will have to be supported with a fleet, most of them being islanders. What then is to be our war? For unless we can either beat them at sea or deprive them of the revenues which feed their navy, we shall meet with little but disaster. Meanwhile, our honor will be pledged to keeping on, particularly if it be the opinion that we began the quarrel: for let us never be elated by the fatal hope of the war being quickly ended by the devastation of their lands. I fear rather that we may leave it as a legacy to our children; so improbable is it that the Athenian spirit will be the slave of their land, or Athenian experience be cowed by war.

82. Not that I would bid you be so unfeeling as to suffer them to injure your allies and to refrain from unmasking their intrigues; but I do bid you not to take up arms at once, but to send and remonstrate with them in a tone not too suggestive of war, nor again too suggestive of submission, and to employ the interval in perfecting our own preparations. The means will be, first, the acquisition of allies, Greek or barbarian it matters not, so long as they are an accession to our strength, naval or pecuniary. I say Greek or barbarian, because the odium of such an accession to all who, like us, are the objects of the designs of the Athenians is taken away by the law of self-preservation; and secondly, the development of our home resources. If they listen to our embassy, so much the better; but if not, after the lapse of two or three years our position will have become materially strengthened, and we can then attack them if we think proper. Perhaps by that time the sight of our preparations, backed by language equally significant, will have disposed them to submission, while their land is still untouched, and while their counsels may be directed to the retention of advantages as yet undestroyed: for the only light in which you can view their land is that of a hostage in your hands, a hostage the more valuable the better it is cultivated. This you ought to spare as long as possible and not make them desperate and so increase the difficulty of dealing with them: for if while still unprepared, hurried away by the complaints of our allies, we are induced to lay it waste, have a care that we do not bring deep disgrace and deep perplexity upon

Peloponnese. Complaints, whether of communities or individuals, it is possible to adjust; but war undertaken by a coalition for sectional interests, whose progress there is no means of foreseeing, does not easily admit of creditable settlement.

83. And none need think it cowardice for a number of confederates to pause before they attack a single city. The Athenians have allies as numerous as our own, and allies that pay tribute; and war is a matter not so much of arms as of money, which makes arms of use. And this is more than ever true in a struggle between a continental and a maritime power. First, then, let us provide money, and not allow ourselves to be carried away by the talk of our allies before we have done so, since we shall have the largest share of responsibility for the consequences, be they good or bad. We have also a right to a tranquil inquiry respecting them.

84. And the slowness and procrastination, the parts of our character that are most assailed by their criticism, need not make you blush. If we undertake the war without preparation, we should by hastening its commencement only delay its conclusion. Further, a free and a famous city has through all time been ours. The quality which they condemn is really nothing but a wise moderation; thanks to its possession, we alone do not become insolent in success and give way less than others in misfortune; we are not carried away by the pleasure of hearing ourselves cheered on to risks that our judgment condemns; nor, if annoyed, are we any the more convinced by attempts to exasperate us by accusation. We are both warlike and wise, and it is our sense of order that makes us so. We are warlike, because self-control contains honor as a chief constituent, and honor bravery. And we are wise, because we are educated with too little learning to despise the laws, and with too severe a self-control to disobey them; and we are brought up not to be too knowing in useless matters, such as the knowledge which can give a specious criticism of an enemy's plans in theory, but fails to assail them with equal success in practice; but we are taught to consider that the schemes of our enemies are not dissimilar to our own, and that the freaks of chance are not determinable by calculation. In practice we always base our preparations against an enemy on the

assumption that his plans are good. Indeed, it is right to rest our hopes not on a belief in his blunders, but on the soundness of our provisions. Nor ought we to believe that there is much difference between man and man, but to think that the superiority lies with him who is reared in the severest school.

85. These practices, then, which our ancestors have delivered to us, and by whose maintenance we have always profited, must not be given up. And we must not be hurried into deciding in a day's brief space a question which concerns many lives and fortunes and many cities, and in which honor is deeply involved. But we must decide calmly. This our strength peculiarly enables us to do. As for the Athenians, send to them on the matter of Potidaea, send on the matter of the alleged wrongs of the allies, particularly as they are prepared with legal satisfaction; and to proceed against one who offers arbitration as against a wrongdoer, law forbids. Meanwhile, do not omit preparation for war. This decision will be the best for yourselves, the most terrible to your opponents." Such were the words of Archidamus. Last came forward Sthenelaidas, one of the ephors for that year, and spoke to the Spartans as follows:

86. "The long speech of the Athenians I do not pretend to understand. They said a good deal in praise of themselves, but nowhere denied that they are injuring our allies and Peloponnese. And yet, if they behaved well against the Persians then, but ill towards us now, they deserve double punishment for having ceased to be good and for having become bad. We, meanwhile, are the same then and now, and shall not, if we are wise, disregard the wrongs of our allies or put off till tomorrow the duty of assisting those who must suffer today. Others have much money, ships, and horses; but we have good allies whom we must not give up to the Athenians, nor by lawsuits and words decide the matter, as it is anything but in word that we are harmed, but render instant and powerful help. And let us not be told that it is fitting for us to deliberate under injustice; long deliberation is rather fitting for those who have injustice in contemplation. Vote therefore, Spartans, for war, as the honor of Sparta demands; and neither allow the further aggrandizement of Athens, nor betray our allies to ruin, but with the gods let us advance against the aggressors."

87. With these words he, as ephor, himself put the question to the assembly of the Spartans. He said that he could not determine which was the loudest acclamation (their mode of decision is by acclamation not by voting)—the fact being that he wished to make them declare their opinion openly and thus to increase their ardor for war. Accordingly, he said: "All Spartans who are of opinion that the treaty has been broken, and that Athens is guilty, leave your seats and go there," pointing out a certain place; "all who are of the opposite opinion, there." They accordingly stood up and divided; and those who held that the treaty had been broken were in a decided majority. Summoning the allies, they told them that their opinion was that Athens had been guilty of injustice, but that they wished to convoke all the allies and put it to the vote in order that they might make war, if they decided to do so, on a common resolution.

C. Pericles' Last Speech (Book II)

This passage dates to the second year of the Peloponnesian War (430 B.C.) and shows how the outbreak of the plague in Athens and the Peloponnesian invasions of Attica weakened Athenian resolve so much that they were willing to consider making peace with Sparta. They took out their misery and anger upon Pericles, whose advice they had followed a short time before in not making any concessions to the Spartans, thus making the outbreak of war inevitable. But after being reproved by Pericles, the Athenians regained their resolve to continue on with the war. The passage ends with Thucydides' considered judgment of Pericles as a statesman and Thucydides' very insightful analysis of how the Athenian democracy fared under the leadership of Pericles' successors.

59. After the second invasion [of Attica] of the Peloponnesians [in 430 B.C.] a change came over the spirit of the Athenians. Their land had now been twice laid waste; and war and pestilence at once pressed heavy upon them. They began to find fault with Pericles, as the author of the war and the cause of all their misfortunes, and they became eager to come to terms with Lacedaemon and actually sent ambassadors thither, who did not, however, succeed in their mission. Their

despair was now complete and all vented itself upon Pericles. When he saw them exasperated at the present turn of affairs and acting exactly as he had anticipated, he called an assembly, being (it must be remembered) still general, with the double object of restoring confidence and of leading them from these angry feelings to a calmer and more hopeful state of mind. He accordingly came forward and spoke as follows:

60. "I was not unprepared for the indignation of which I have been the object, as I know its causes; and I have called an assembly for the purpose of reminding you upon certain points, and of protesting against your being unreasonably irritated with me, or cowed by your sufferings. I am of opinion that national greatness is more for the advantage of private citizens than any individual well-being is coupled with public humiliation. A man may be personally ever so well off; and yet, if his country be ruined, he must be ruined with it; whereas a flourishing commonwealth always affords chances of salvation to unfortunate individuals. Since then a state can support the misfortunes of private citizens, while they cannot support hers, it is surely the duty of everyone to be forward in her defense and not, like you, to be so confounded with your domestic afflictions as to give up all thoughts of the common safety, and to blame me for having counselled war and yourselves for having voted it. And yet, if you are angry with me, it is with one who, as I believe, is second to no man either in knowledge of the proper policy or in the ability to expound it, and who is, moreover, not only a patriot but an honest one. A man possessing that knowledge without that faculty of exposition might as well have no idea at all on the matter: if he had both these gifts, but no love for his country, he would be but a cold advocate for her interests; while, were his patriotism not proof against bribery, everything would go for a price. So, if you thought that I was even moderately distinguished for these qualities when you took my advice and went to war, there is certainly no reason now why I should be charged with having done wrong.

61. For those, of course, who have a free choice in the matter and whose fortunes are not at stake, war is the greatest of follies. But if the only choice was between submission with loss of independence, and danger

with the hope of preserving that independence, in such a case it is he who will not accept the risk that deserves blame, not he who will. I am the same man and do not alter. It is you who change, since in fact you took my advice while unhurt, and waited for misfortune to repent of it; and the apparent error of my policy lies in the infirmity of your resolution, since the suffering that it entails is being felt by everyone among you, while its advantage is still remote and obscure to all; and a great and sudden reverse having befallen you, your mind is too much depressed to persevere in your resolves: for before what is sudden, unexpected, and least within calculation, the spirit quails; and putting all else aside, the plague has certainly been an emergency of this kind. Born, however, as you are, citizens of a great state and brought up, as you have been, with habits equal to your birth, you should be ready to face the greatest disasters and still to keep unimpaired the luster of your name: for the judgment of mankind is as relentless to the weakness that falls short of a recognized renown, as it is jealous of the arrogance that aspires higher than its due. Cease then to grieve for your private afflictions, and address yourselves instead to the safety of the commonwealth.

62. If you shrink before the exertions which the war makes necessary, and if you fear that after all they may not have a happy result, you know the reasons by which I have often demonstrated to you the groundlessness of your apprehensions. If those are not enough, I will now reveal an advantage arising from the greatness of your dominion, which, I think, has never yet suggested itself to you, which I never mentioned in my previous speeches, and which has so bold a sound that I should scarce venture it now, were it not for the unnatural depression which I see around me. You perhaps think that your empire extends only over your allies. I will declare to you the truth. The visible field of action has two parts: land and sea. In the whole of one of these you are completely supreme, not merely as far as you use it at present, but also to what further extent you may think fit. In fine, your naval resources are such that your vessels may go where they please without the [Persian] King or any other nation on earth being able to stop them, so that although you may think it a great privation to lose

the use of your land and houses, still, you must see that this power is something widely different; and instead of fretting on their account, you should really regard them in the light of the gardens and other accessories that embellish a great fortune, and as, in comparison, of little moment. You should know too that liberty preserved by your efforts will easily recover for us what we have lost, while, the knee once bowed, even what you have will pass from you. Your fathers, receiving these possessions not from others, but from themselves, did not let slip what their labor had acquired, but delivered them safe to you; and in this respect at least you must prove yourselves their equals, remembering that to lose what one has got is more disgraceful than to be balked in getting; and you must confront your enemies not merely with spirit, but with disdain. Confidence indeed a blissful ignorance can impart, ay! even to a coward's breast; but disdain is the privilege of those who, like us, have been assured by reflection of their superiority to their adversary. And where the chances are the same, knowledge fortifies courage by the contempt which is its consequence, its trust being placed not in hope, which is the prop of the desperate, but in a judgment grounded upon existing resources, whose anticipations are more to be depended upon.

63. Again, your country has a right to your services in sustaining the glories of her position. These are a common source of pride to you all, and you cannot decline the burdens of empire and still expect to share its honors. You should remember also that what you are fighting against is not merely slavery as an exchange for independence, but also loss of empire and danger from the animosities incurred in its exercise. Besides, to recede is no longer possible, if indeed any of you in the alarm of the moment has become enamored of the honesty of such an unambitious part: for what you hold is, to speak somewhat plainly, a tyranny; to take it perhaps was wrong, but to let it go is unsafe. And men of these retiring views, making converts of others, would quickly ruin a state. Indeed, the result would be the same if they could live independent by themselves; for the retiring and unambitious are never secure without vigorous protectors at their side. In fine, such qualities are useless to an imperial city, though they may help a dependency to an unmolested servitude.

64. But you must not be seduced by citizens like these, or be angry with me, who, if I voted for war, only did as you did yourselves, in spite of the enemy having invaded your country and done what you could be certain that he would do, if you refused to comply with his demands; and although, besides what we counted for, the plague has come upon us, the only point indeed at which our calculation has been at fault. It is this, I know, that has had a large share in making me more unpopular than I should otherwise have been, quite undeservedly, unless you are also prepared to give me the credit of any success with which chance may present you. Besides, the hand of heaven must be borne with resignation, that of the enemy with fortitude; this was the old way at Athens, and do not you prevent it being so still. Remember, too, that if your country has the greatest name in all the world, it is because she never bent before disaster, because she has expended more life and effort in war than any other city and has won for herself a power greater than any hitherto known, the memory of which will descend to the latest posterity. Even if now, in obedience to the general law of decay, we should ever be forced to yield, still it will be remembered that we held rule over more Hellenes than any other Hellenic state, that we sustained the greatest wars against their united or separate powers, and inhabited a city unrivalled by any other in resources or magnitude. These glories may incur the censure of the slow and unambitious; but in the breast of energy they will awake emulation, and in those who must remain without them an envious regret. Hatred and unpopularity at the moment have fallen to the lot of all who have aspired to rule others; but where odium must be incurred, true wisdom incurs it for the highest objects. Hatred also is short-lived; but that which makes the splendor of the present and the glory of the future remains for ever unforgotten. Make your decision, therefore, for glory then and honor now, and attain both objects by instant and zealous effort. Do not send heralds to Lacedaemon, and do not betray any sign of being oppressed by your present sufferings, since they, whose minds are least sensitive to calamity, and whose hands are most quick to meet it, are the greatest men and the greatest communities."

65. Such were the arguments by which Pericles tried to cure the Athenians of their anger against him and to divert their thoughts from their immediate afflictions. As a community he succeeded in convincing them. They not only gave up all idea of sending to Lacedaemon, but applied themselves with increased energy to the war. Still, as private individuals they could not help smarting under their sufferings, the common people having been deprived of the little that they were possessed, while the higher orders had lost fine properties with costly establishments and buildings in the country, and, worst of all, had war instead of peace. In fact, the public feeling against him did not subside until he had been fined. Not long afterwards, however, according to the way of the multitude, they again elected him general and committed all their affairs to his hands, having now become less sensitive to their private and domestic afflictions, and understanding that he was the best man of all for the public necessities: for as long as he was at the head of the state during the peace, he pursued a moderate and conservative policy; and in his time its greatness was at its height. When the war broke out, here also he seems to have rightly gauged the power of his country. He outlived its commencement two years and six months, and the correctness of his forecasts respecting it became better known by his death. He told them to wait quietly, to pay attention to their seapower, to attempt no new conquests, and to expose the city to no hazards during the war; and doing this, he promised them a favorable result. What they did was the very contrary, allowing private ambitions and private interests, in matters apparently quite foreign to the war, to lead them into projects unjust both to themselves and to their allies, projects whose success would only conduce to the honor and advantage of private persons, and whose failure entailed certain disaster on the country in the war. The causes of this are not far to seek. Pericles indeed by his rank, ability, and known integrity was able to exercise an independent control over the multitude: in short, to lead them instead of being led by them; for as he never sought power by improper means, he was never compelled to flatter them, but, on the contrary, he enjoyed so high an estimation that he could afford to anger them by contradiction. Whenever he saw them

unseasonably and insolently elated, he would with a word reduce them to alarm; on the other hand, if they fell victims to a panic, he could at once restore them to confidence. In short, what was nominally a democracy became in his hands government by the first citizen. With his successors it was different. More on a level with one another, and each grasping at supremacy, they ended by committing even the conduct of state affairs to the whims of the multitude. This, as might have been expected in a great and sovereign state, produced a host of blunders, and among them the Sicilian expedition; though this failed not so much through a miscalculation of the power of those against whom it was sent, as through a fault in the senders in not taking the best measures afterwards to assist those who had gone out, but choosing rather to occupy themselves with private cabals for the leadership of the commons, by which they not only paralysed operations in the field, but also first introduced civil discord at home. Yet, after losing most of their fleet besides other forces in Sicily, and with faction already dominant in the city, they could still for three years make head against their original adversaries, joined not only by the Sicilians, but also by their own allies nearly all in revolt, and at last by the [Persian] King's son, Cyrus, who furnished the funds for the Peloponnesian navy. Nor did they finally succumb till they fell the victims of their own intestine disorders. So superfluously abundant were the resources from which the genius of Pericles foresaw an easy triumph in the war over the unaided forces of the Peloponnesians.

D. Athens Decides the Fate of Mytilene (Book III)

In the fourth year of the war (428 B.C.) one of Athens' major subjects, the city-state of Mytilene in the island of Lesbos, attempted to revolt and join the side of Sparta. Athens, however, learned of these plans before the revolt was fully in operation; and as a result, swift and decisive Athenian intervention prevented the revolt from succeeding. The Athenians were then faced with how and to what extent the people of Mytilene should be punished. After debating this matter in the citizen assembly, they initially decided by a slim majority vote to kill all adult males and to enslave all women and children of Mytilene so as to terrorize all their other subjects to keep them from contemplating similar actions. But given the extreme harshness of their decision, the matter was re-opened for a second debate, and a less harsh decision was taken toward Mytilene. In the following passage Thucydides shows how the Athenians wrestled with these difficult issues in an open public debate.

35. Arrived at Mytilene, Paches [the Athenian general] reduced Pyrrha and Eresus [two of the other four towns in the island]; and finding the Spartan, Salaethus, in hiding in the town, he sent him off to Athens, together with the Mytilenians whom he had placed in Tenedos, and any other persons whom he thought concerned in the revolt. He also sent back the greater part of his forces, remaining with the rest to settle Mytilene and the rest of Lesbos as he thought best.

36. Upon the arrival of the prisoners with Salaethus, the Athenians at once put the latter to death, although he offered among other things to procure the withdrawal of the Peloponnesians from Plataea, which was still under siege; and after deliberating as to what they should do with the former, in the fury of the moment they determined to put to death not only the prisoners at Athens, but the whole adult male population of Mytilene, and to make slaves of the women and children. It was remarked that Mytilene had revolted without being, like the rest, subjected to the empire; and what above all swelled the wrath of the Athenians was the fact of the Peloponnesian fleet having ventured over to Ionia to her support, a fact which was held to argue a long meditated rebellion. They accordingly sent a trireme to communicate the decree to Paches, commanding him to lose no time in dispatching the Mytilenians. The morrow brought repentance with it and reflection on the horrid cruelty of a decree, which condemned a whole city to the fate merited only by the guilty. This was no sooner perceived by the Mytilenian ambassadors at Athens and their Athenian supporters, than they moved the authorities to put the question again to the vote; which they the more easily consented to do, since they themselves plainly saw that most of the citizens wished someone to give them an opportunity for reconsidering the matter. An assembly was therefore at once called; and after much expression of opinion upon both sides, Cleon, son of Cleaenetus, the same who had carried the

314

former motion of putting the Mytilenians to death, the most violent man at Athens, and at that time by far the most powerful with the commons, came forward again and spoke as follows:

37. "I have often before now been convinced that a democracy is incapable of empire, and never more so than by your present change of mind in the matter of Mytilene. Fears or plots being unknown to you in your daily relations with each other, you feel just the same with regard to your allies, and you never reflect that the mistakes into which you may be led by listening to their appeals, or by giving way to your own compassion, are full of danger to yourselves and bring you no thanks for your weakness from your allies; entirely forgetting that your empire is a despotism and your subjects disaffected conspirators, whose obedience is ensured not by your suicidal concessions, but by the superiority given you by your own strength and not their loyalty. The most alarming feature in the case is the constant change of measures with which we appear to be threatened, and our seeming ignorance of the fact that bad laws which are never changed are better for a city than good ones that have no authority; that unlearned loyalty is more serviceable than quick-witted insubordination; and that ordinary men usually manage public affairs better than their more gifted fellows. The latter are always wanting to appear wiser than the laws and to overrule every proposition brought forward, thinking that they cannot show their wit in more important matters; and by such behavior too often they ruin their country, while those who mistrust their own cleverness are content to be less learned than the laws and less able to pick holes in the speech of a good speaker; and being fair judges rather than rival athletes, they generally conduct affairs successfully. These we ought to imitate, instead of being led on by cleverness and intellectual rivalry to advise your people against our real opinions.

38. For myself, I adhere to my former opinion and wonder at those who have proposed to reopen the case of the Mytilenians, and who are thus causing a delay which is all in favor of the guilty by making the sufferer proceed against the offender with the edge of his anger blunted; although where vengeance follows most closely upon the wrong, it

best equals it and most amply requites it. I wonder also who will be the man who will maintain the contrary, and who will pretend to show that the crimes of the Mytilenians are of service to us, and our misfortunes injurious to the allies. Such a man must plainly either have such confidence in his rhetoric as to venture to prove that what has been once for all decided is still undetermined, or be bribed to try to delude us by elaborate sophisms. In such contests the state gives the rewards to others and takes the dangers for herself. The persons to blame are you who are so foolish as to institute these contests, who go to see an oration as you would to see a sight, who take your facts on hearsay, judge of the practicability of a project by the wit of its advocates, and trust for the truth as to past events, not to the fact which you saw more than to the clever strictures which you heard—the easy victims of new-fangled arguments, unwilling to follow received conclusions, slaves to every new paradox, despisers of the commonplace—the first wish of every man being that he could speak himself, the next to rival those who can speak by seeming to be quite up with their ideas by applauding every hit almost before it is made, and by being as quick in catching an argument as you are slow in foreseeing its consequences; asking, if I may so say, for something different from the conditions under which we live, and yet comprehending inadequately those very conditions; very slaves to the pleasure of the ear, and more like the audience of a rhetorician than the council of a city.

39. In order to keep you from this, I proceed to show that no one state has ever injured you as much as Mytilene. I can make allowance for those who revolt because they cannot bear our empire, or who have been forced to do so by the enemy. But for those who possessed an island with fortifications, who could fear our enemies only by sea, who had there their own force of triremes to protect them, who were independent and held in the highest honor by you—to act as these have done, this is not revolt; revolt implies oppression; it is deliberate and wanton aggression; an attempt to ruin us by siding with our bitterest enemies; a worse offense than a war undertaken on their own account in the acquisition of power. The fate of those of their neighbors who had already rebelled and had been subdued was no lesson to them;

their own prosperity could not dissuade them from affronting danger; but blindly confident in the future, and full of hopes beyond their power though not beyond their ambition, they declared war and made their decision to prefer might to right, their attack being determined not by provocation but by the moment which seemed propitious. The truth is that great good fortune coming suddenly and unexpectedly tends to make a people insolent. In most cases it is safer for mankind to have success in reason than out of reason; and it is easier for them, one may say, to stave off adversity than to preserve prosperity. Our mistake has been to distinguish the Mytilenians as we have done. Had they been long ago treated like the rest, they never would have so far forgotten themselves, human nature being as surely made arrogant by consideration as it is awed by firmness. Let them now therefore be punished as their crime requires; and do not, while you condemn the aristocracy, absolve the people. This is certain, that all attacked you without distinction, although they might have come over to us and been now again in possession of their city. But no, they thought it safer to throw in their lot with the aristocracy and so joined their rebellion! Consider therefore: if you subject to the same punishment the ally who is forced to rebel by the enemy, and him who does so by his own free choice, which of them, think you, is there that will not rebel upon the slightest pretext, when the reward of success is freedom, and the penalty of failure nothing so very terrible? We, meanwhile, shall have to risk our money and our lives against one state after another; and if successful, we shall receive a ruined town from which we can no longer draw the revenue upon which our strength depends; while if unsuccessful, we shall have an enemy the more upon our hands and shall spend the time that might be employed in combating our existing foes in warring with our own allies.

40. No hope, therefore, which rhetoric may instil or money purchase, of the mercy due to human infirmity must be held out to the Mytilenians. Their offense was not involuntary, but of malice and deliberate; and mercy is only for unwilling offenders. I therefore, now, as before, persist against your reversing your first decision or giving way to the three failings most fatal to empire: pity, sentiment, and indulgence.

Compassion is due to those who can reciprocate the feeling, not to those who will never pity us in return, but who are our natural and necessary foes. The orators who charm us with sentiment may find other less important arenas for their talents in the place of one where the city pays a heavy penalty for a momentary pleasure, themselves receiving fine acknowledgments for their fine phrases; while indulgence should be shown towards those who will be our friends in future, instead of towards men who will remain just what they were, and as much our enemies as before. To sum up shortly, I say that if you follow my advice, you will do what is just towards the Mytilenians, and at the same time expedient; while by a different decision you will not oblige them so much as pass sentence upon yourselves: for if they were right in rebelling, you must be wrong in ruling. However, if, right or wrong, you decide to rule, you must carry out your principle and punish the Mytilenians as your interest requires; or else you must give up your empire and cultivate honesty without danger. Make up your minds, therefore, to give them like for like; and do not let the victims who escaped the plot be more insensible than the conspirators who hatched it; but reflect what they would have done if victorious over you, especially they were the aggressors. It is they who wrong their neighbor without a cause, who pursue their victim to the death because of the danger which they foresee in letting their enemy survive: for the object of a wanton wrong is more dangerous, if he escape, than an enemy who has not this to complain of. Do not, therefore, be traitors to yourselves, but recall as nearly as possible the moment of suffering and the supreme importance which you then attached to their reduction; and now pay them back in their turn without yielding to present weakness or forgetting the peril that once hung over you. Punish them as they deserve, and teach your other allies by a striking example that the penalty of rebellion is death. Let them once understand this, and you will not have so often to neglect your enemies while you are fighting with your own confederates."

41. Such were the words of Cleon. After him Diodotus, son of Eucrates, who had also in the previous assembly spoken most strongly

against putting the Mytilenians to death, came forward and spoke as follows:

42. "I do not blame the persons who have reopened the case of the Mytilenians, nor do I approve the protests which we have heard against important questions being frequently debated. I think that the two things most opposed to good counsel are haste and passion; haste usually goes hand in hand with folly, passion with coarseness and narrowness of mind. As for the argument that speech ought not to be the exponent of action, the man who uses it must be either senseless or interested: senseless if he believes it possible to treat of the uncertain future through any other medium; interested if, wishing to carry a disgraceful measure and doubting his ability to speak well in a bad cause, he thinks to frighten opponents and hearers by well-aimed calumny. What is still more intolerable is to accuse a speaker of making a display in order to be paid for it. If ignorance only were imputed, an unsuccessful speaker might retire with a reputation for honesty, if not for wisdom; while the charge of dishonesty makes him suspected, if successful, and thought, if defeated, not only a fool but a rogue. The city is no gainer by such a system, since fear deprives it of its advisors; although in truth, if our speakers are to make such assertions, it would be better for the country if they could not speak at all, since we should then make fewer blunders. The good citizen ought to triumph not by frightening his opponents but by beating them fairly in argument; and a wise city, without over-distinguishing its best advisors, will nevertheless not deprive them of their due; and far from punishing an unlucky counsellor, it will not even regard him as disgraced. In this way successful orators would be least tempted to sacrifice their convictions to popularity in the hope of still higher honors, and unsuccessful speakers to resort to the same popular arts in order to win over the multitude.

43. This is not our way. And besides, the moment that a man is suspected of giving advice, however good, from corrupt motives, we feel such a grudge against him for the gain which after all, we are not certain, he will receive that we deprive the city of its certain benefit. Plain good advice has thus come to be no less suspected than bad; and the advocate of the most monstrous measures is not more obliged to use deceit

to gain the people than the best counsellor is to lie in order to be believed. The city and the city only, owing to these refinements, can never be served openly and without disguise. He who does serve it openly is always suspected of serving himself in some secret way in return. Still, considering the magnitude of the interests involved and the position of affairs, we orators must make it our business to look a little farther than you who judge offhand; especially as we, your advisors, are responsible, while you, our audience, are not so: for if those who gave the advice, and those who took it, suffered equally, you would judge more calmly. As it is, you visit the disasters into which the whim of the moment may have led you upon the single person of your advisor, not upon yourselves, his numerous companions in error.

44. However, I have not come forward either to oppose or to accuse in the matter of Mytilene. Indeed, the question before us as sensible men is not their guilt, but our interests. Though I prove them ever so guilty, I shall not, therefore, advise their death, unless it be expedient; nor though they should have claims to indulgence, shall I recommend it, unless it be clearly for the good of the country. I consider that we are deliberating for the future more than for the present; and where Cleon is so positive as to the useful deterrent effects that will follow from making rebellion capital, I, who consider the interests of the future quite as much as he, as positively maintain the contrary. And I require you not to reject my useful considerations for his specious ones. His speech may have the attraction of seeming the more just in your present temper against Mytilene; but we are not in a court of justice, but in a political assembly; and the question is not justice, but how to make the Mytilenians useful to Athens.

45. Now, of course, communities have enacted the penalty of death for many offenses far lighter than this. Still, hope leads men to venture, and no one ever yet put himself in peril without the inward conviction that he would succeed in his design. Again, was there ever a city rebelling that did not believe that it possessed either in itself or in its alliances resources adequate to the enterprise? All, states and individuals, are alike prone to err, and there is no law that will prevent them; or why should men have exhausted the list of punishments in

search of enactments to protect them from evildoers? It is probable that in early times the penalties for the greatest offenses were less severe, and that as these were disregarded, the penalty of death has been by degrees in most cases arrived at, which is itself disregarded in like manner. Either then some means of terror more terrible than this must be discovered, or it must be owned that this restraint is useless; and that as long as poverty gives men the courage of necessity, or plenty fills them with the ambition which belongs to insolence and pride, and the other conditions of life remain each under the thraldom of some fatal and master passion, so long will the impulse never be wanting to drive men into danger. Hope also and cupidity, the one leading and the other following, the one conceiving the attempt, the other suggesting the facility of succeeding, cause the widest ruin; and although invisible agents, they are far stronger than the dangers that are seen. Fortune, too, powerfully helps the delusion; and by the unexpected aid that she sometimes lends, she tempts men to venture with inferior means; and this is especially the case with communities, because the stakes played for are the highest: freedom or empire. And when all are acting together, each man irrationally magnifies his own capacity. In fine, it is impossible to prevent, and only great simplicity can hope to prevent, human nature doing what it has once set its mind upon, by force of law or by any other deterrent force whatsoever.

46. We must not, therefore, commit ourselves to a false policy through a belief in the efficacy of the punishment of death, or exclude rebels from the hope of repentance and an early atonement of their error. Consider a moment. At present, if a city that has already revolted perceive that it cannot succeed, it will come to terms while it is still able to refund expenses and pay tribute afterwards. In the other case, what city, think you, would not prepare better than is now done, and would hold out to the last against its besiegers, if it is all one whether it surrender late or soon? And how can it be otherwise than hurtful to us to be put to the expense of a siege, because surrender is out of the question; and if we take the city, to receive a ruined town from which we can no longer draw the revenue which forms our real strength

against the enemy? We must not, therefore, sit as strict judges of the offenders to our own prejudice, but rather, see how by moderate chastisements we may be enabled to benefit in future by the revenue-producing powers of our dependencies; and we must make up our minds to look for our protection not to legal terrors but to careful administration. At present we do exactly the opposite. When a free community, held in subjection by force, rises, as is only natural, and asserts its independence, it is no sooner reduced than we fancy ourselves obliged to punish it severely, although the right course with freemen is not to chastise them rigorously when they do rise, but rigorously to watch them before they rise, and to prevent their ever entertaining the idea and, the insurrection suppressed, to make as few responsible for it as possible.

47. Only consider what a blunder you would commit in doing as Cleon recommends. As things are at present, in all the cities the people is your friend and either does not revolt with the oligarchy, or, if forced to do so, becomes at once the enemy of the insurgents, so that in the war with the hostile city you have the masses on your side. But if you butcher the people of Mytilene, who had nothing to do with the revolt, and who, as soon as they got arms, of their own motion surrendered the town, first you will commit the crime of killing your benefactors; and next you will play directly into the hands of the higher classes, who, when they induce their cities to rise, will immediately have the people on their side through your having announced in advance the same punishment for those who are guilty and for those who are not. On the contrary, even if they were guilty, you ought to seem not to notice it in order to avoid alienating the only class still friendly to us. In short, I consider it far more useful for the preservation of our empire voluntarily to put up with injustice than to put to death, however justly, those whom it is our interest to keep alive. As for Cleon's idea that in punishment the claims of justice and expediency can both be satisfied, facts do not confirm the possibility of such a combination.

48. Confess, therefore, that this is the wisest course. And without conceding too much either to pity or to indulgence, by neither of which

motives do I any more than Cleon wish you to be influenced, upon the plain merits of the case before you, be persuaded by me to try calmly those of the Mytilenians whom Paches sent off as guilty, and to leave the rest undisturbed. This is at once best for the future and most terrible to your enemies at the present moment, inasmuch as good policy against an adversary is superior to the blind attacks of brute force."

49. Such were the words of Diodotus. The two opinions thus expressed were the ones that most directly contradicted each other. And the Athenians, notwithstanding their change of feeling, now proceeded to a division, in which the show of hands was almost equal, although the motion of Diodotus carried the day. Another trireme was at once sent off in haste for fear that the first might reach Lesbos in the interval, and the city be found destroyed, the first ship having about a day and a night's start. Wine and barley-cakes were provided for the vessel by the Mytilenian ambassadors, and great promises made if they arrived in time; which caused the men to use such diligence upon the voyage that they took their meals of barley-cakes kneaded with oil and wine as they rowed, and they only slept by turns while the others were at the oar. Luckily, they met with no contrary wind; and the first ship making no haste upon so horrid an errand, while the second pressed on in the manner described, the first arrived so little before them that Paches had only just had time to read the decree and to prepare to execute the sentence, when the second put into port and prevented the massacre. The danger of Mytilene had indeed been great.

50. The other party whom Paches had sent off as the prime movers in the rebellion, were upon Cleon's motion put to death by the Athenians, the number being rather more than a thousand. The Athenians also demolished the walls of the Mytilenians and took possession of their ships. Afterwards tribute was not imposed upon the Lesbians; but all their land, except that of the Methymnians, was divided into three thousand allotments, three hundred of which were reserved as sacred for the gods, and the rest assigned by lot to Athenian shareholders, who were sent out to the island. With these the Lesbians agreed to pay a rent of two minae a year for each allotment, and they

cultivated the land themselves. The Athenians also took possession of the towns on the continent belonging to the Mytilenians, which thus became for the future subject to Athens. Such were the events that took place at Lesbos....

E. The Melian Dialogue (Book V)
The corrosive effects of the war upon morality and decency are best illustrated by how the Athenians treated the population of the small island of Melos in 416 B.C. Until then the islanders had been neutral parties, but the Athenians now decided that their neutral status represented an embarrassment to Athenian naval power. Thucydides' account of the dialogue between the Athenians and the Melians, as well as the annihilation of the latter by the former, is one of the most chilling illustrations of the doctrine of "might makes right" in the realm of warfare.

84. During the next summer Alcibiades sailed with twenty ships to Argos and seized the suspected persons still left of the Spartan faction to the number of three hundred, whom the Athenians forthwith lodged in the neighboring islands of their empire. The Athenians also made an expedition against the isle of Melos with thirty ships of their own, six Chian, and two Lesbian vessels, sixteen hundred hoplites, three hundred archers, and twenty mounted archers from Athens, and about fifteen hundred hoplites from the allies and the islanders. The Melians are a colony of Sparta that would not submit to the Athenians like the other islanders, and at first they remained neutral and took no part in the struggle. But afterwards upon the Athenians using violence and plundering their territory, they assumed an attitude of open hostility. Cleomedes, son of Lycomedes, and Tisias, son of Tisimachus, the generals, encamping in their territory with the above armament, before doing any harm to their land, sent envoys to negotiate. These the Melians did not bring before the people, but bade them state the object of their mission to the magistrates and the few; upon which the Athenian envoys spoke as follows:

85. Athenians: "Since the negotiations are not to go on before the people in order that we may not be able to speak straight on without interruption and deceive the ears of the multitude by seductive arguments

which would pass without refutation (for we know that this is the meaning of our being brought before the few), what if you who sit there were to pursue a method more cautious still? Make no set speech yourselves, but take us up at whatever you do not like, and settle that before going any farther. And first tell us if this proposition of ours suits you."

86. The Melian commissioners answered: "To the fairness of quietly instructing each other as you propose there is nothing to object; but your military preparations are too far advanced to agree with what you say, since we see that you are come to be judges in your own cause, and that all we can reasonably expect from this negotiation is war, if we prove to have right on our side and refuse to submit, and in the contrary case, slavery."

87. Athenians: "If you have met to reason about presentiments of the future or for anything else than to consult for the safety of your state upon the facts that you see before you, we will give over; otherwise, we will go on."

88. Melians: "It is natural and excusable for men in our position to turn more ways than one, both in thought and utterance. However, the question in this conference is, as you say, the safety of our country; and the discussion, if you please, can proceed in the way which you propose."

89. Athenians: "For ourselves, we shall not trouble you with specious pretences, either of how we have a right to our empire because we overthrew the Persians, or we are now attacking you because of wrong that you have done us, and make a long speech which would not be believed; and in return we hope that you, instead of thinking to influence us by saying that you did not join the Spartans, although their colonists, or that you have done us no wrong, will aim at what is feasible, holding in view the real sentiments of us both, since you know as well as we do that right, as the world goes, is only in question between equals in power, while the strong do what they can, and the weak suffer what they must."

90. Melians: "As we think, at any rate, it is expedient—we speak as we are obliged, since you enjoin us to let right alone and talk only of interest—that you should not destroy what is our common protection, the

privilege of being allowed in danger to invoke what is fair and right, and even to profit by arguments not strictly valid if they can be got to pass current. And you are as much interested in this as any, as your fall would be a signal for the heaviest vengeance and an example for the world to meditate upon."

91. Athenians: "The end of our empire, if end it should, does not frighten us: a rival empire like Sparta, even if Sparta was our real antagonist, is not so terrible to the vanquished as subjects who by themselves attack and overpower their rulers. This, however, is a risk that we are content to take. We will now proceed to show you that we are come here in the interest of our empire, and that we shall say what we are now going to say, for the preservation of your country, as we would fain exercise that empire over you without trouble and see you preserved for the good of us both."

92. Melians: "And how, pray, could it turn out as good for us to serve as for you to rule?"

93. Athenians: "Because you would have the advantage of submitting before suffering the worst, and we should gain by not destroying you."

94. Melians: "So that you would not consent to our being neutral, friends instead of enemies, but allies of neither side?"

95. Athenians: "No; for your hostility cannot so much hurt us as your friendship will be an argument to our subjects of our weakness, and your enmity of our power."

96. Melians: "Is that your subjects' idea of equity: to put those who have nothing to do with you in the same category with peoples that are most of them your own colonists, and some conquered rebels?"

97. Athenians: "As far as right goes, they think that one has as much of it as the other, and that if any maintain their independence, it is because they are strong, and that if we do not molest them, it is because we are afraid, so that besides extending our empire, we should gain in security by your subjection: the fact that you are islanders and weaker than others rendering it all the more important that you should not succeed in baffling the masters of the sea."

98. Melians: "But do you consider that there is no security in the policy which we indicate? For here again, if you debar us from talking about

justice and invite us to obey your interest, we also must explain ours and try to persuade you, if the two happen to coincide. How can you avoid making enemies of all existing neutrals who shall look at our case and take from it that one day or another you will attack them? And what is this but to make greater the enemies that you have already, and to force others to become so who would otherwise have never thought of it?"

99. Athenians: "Why, the fact is that continentals generally give us but little alarm. The liberty which they enjoy will long prevent their taking precautions against us. It is rather islanders like yourselves, outside our empire, and subjects smarting under the yoke, who would be the most likely to take a rash step and lead themselves and us into obvious danger."

100. Melians: "Well then, if you risk so much to retain your empire, and your subjects to get rid of it, it were surely great baseness and cowardice in us who are still free not to try everything that can be tried, before submitting to your yoke."

101. Athenians: "Not if you are well advised, the contest not being an equal one, with honor as the prize and shame as the penalty, but a question of self-preservation and of not resisting those who are far stronger than you are."

102. Melians: "But we know that the fortune of war is sometimes more impartial than the disproportion of numbers might lead one to suppose. To submit is to give ourselves over to despair, while action still preserves for us a hope that we may stand erect."

103. Athenians: "Hope, danger's comforter, may be indulged in by those who have abundant resources, if not without loss at all events without ruin; but its nature is to be extravagant, and those who go so far as to put their all upon the venture see it in its true colors only when they are ruined. But so long as the discovery would enable them to guard against it, it is never found wanting. Let not this be the case with you, who are weak and hang on a single turn of the scale; nor be like the vulgar, who, abandoning such security as human means may still afford, when visible hopes fail them in extremity, turn to invisible, to prophecies and oracles, and other such inventions that delude men with hopes to their destruction."

104. Melians: "You may be sure that we are as well aware as you of the difficulty of contending against your power and fortune, unless the terms be equal. But we trust that the gods may grant us fortune as good as yours, since we are just men fighting against unjust, and that what we want in power will be made up by the alliance of the Spartans, who are bound, if only for very shame, to come to the aid of their kindred. Our confidence, therefore, after all is not so utterly irrational."

105. Athenians: "When you speak of the favor of the gods, we may as fairly hope for that as yourselves; neither our pretensions nor our conduct being in any way contrary to what men believe of the gods or practise among themselves. Of the gods we believe, and of men we know, that by a necessary law of their nature they rule wherever they can. And it is not as if we were the first to make this law or to act upon it when made. We found it existing before us and shall leave it to exist for ever after us. All that we do is to make use of it, knowing that you and everybody else, having the same power as we have, would do the same as we do. Thus, as far as the gods are concerned, we have no fear and no reason to fear that we shall be at a disadvantage. But when we come to your notion about the Spartans, which leads you to believe that shame will make them help you, here we bless your simplicity but do not envy your folly. The Spartans, when their own interests or their country's laws are in question, are the worthiest men alive; of their conduct towards others much might be said, but no clearer idea of it could be given than by shortly saying that of all the men whom we know, they are most conspicuous in considering what is agreeable honorable, and what is expedient just. Such a way of thinking does not promise much for the safety which you now unreasonably count upon."

106. Melians: "But it is for this very reason that we now trust to their respect for expediency to prevent them from betraying the Melians, their colonists, and thereby losing the confidence of their friends in Greece and helping their enemies."

107. Athenians: "Then you do not adopt the view that expediency goes with security, while justice and honor cannot be followed without danger; and danger the Spartans generally court as little as possible."

108. Melians: "But we believe that they would be more likely to face even danger for our sake and with more confidence than for others, since our nearness to Peloponnese makes it easier for them to act; and our common blood ensures our fidelity."

109. Athenians: "Yes, but what an intending ally trusts to is not the good-will of those who ask his aid, but a decided superiority of power for action; and the Spartans look to this even more than others. At least, such is their distrust of their home resources that it is only with numerous allies that they attack a neighbor. Now is it likely that while we are masters of the sea, they will cross over to an island?"

110. Melians: "But they would have others to send. The Cretan Sea is a wide one, and it is more difficult for those who command it to intercept others than for those who wish to elude them to do so safely. And should the Spartans miscarry in this, they would fall upon your land and upon those left of your allies whom Brasidas [a successful Spartan general] did not reach; and instead of places which are not yours, you will have to fight for your own country and your own confederacy."

111. Athenians: "Some diversion of the kind of which you speak you may one day experience, only to learn, as others have done, that the Athenians never once yet withdrew from a siege for fear of any. But we are struck by the fact that after saying that you would consult for the safety of your country, in all this discussion you have mentioned nothing which men might trust in and think to be saved by. Your strongest arguments depend upon hope and the future, and your actual resources are too scanty, as compared with those arrayed against you, for you to come out victorious. You will therefore show great blindness of judgment, unless, after allowing us to retire, you can find some counsel more prudent than this. You will surely not be caught by that idea of disgrace, which in dangers that are disgraceful and at the same time too plain to be mistaken, proves so fatal to mankind, since in too many cases the very men who have their eyes perfectly open to what they are rushing into, let the thing called disgrace, by the mere influence of a seductive name, lead them on to a point at which they become so enslaved by the phrase as in fact to fall wilfully into hopeless disaster and incur disgrace more disgraceful as the companion of

error, than when it comes as the result of misfortune. This, if you are well advised, you will guard against; and you will not think it dishonorable to submit to the greatest city in Greece, when it makes you the moderate offer of becoming its tributary ally without ceasing to enjoy the country that belongs to you; nor when you have the choice given you between war and security, will you be so blinded as to choose the worse. And it is certain that those who do not yield to their equals, who keep terms with their superiors and are moderate towards their inferiors, on the whole succeed best. Think over the matter, therefore, after our withdrawal; and reflect once and again that it is for your country that you are consulting, that you have not more than one, and that upon this one deliberation depends its prosperity or ruin."

112. The Athenians now withdrew from the conference; and the Melians, left to themselves, came to a decision corresponding with what they had maintained in the discussion, and they answered: "Our resolution, Athenians, is the same as it was at first. We will not in a moment deprive of freedom a city that has been inhabited these seven hundred years; but we put our trust in the fortune by which the gods have preserved it until now, and in the help of men, that is, of the Spartans; and so we will try to save ourselves. Meanwhile, we invite you to allow us to be friends to you and foes to neither party, and to retire from our country after making such a treaty as shall seem fit to us both."

113. Such was the answer of the Melians. The Athenians now departing from the conference said: "Well, you alone, as it seems to us, judging from these resolutions, regard what is future as more certain than what is before your eyes, and what is out of sight in your eagerness as already coming to pass; and as you have staked most on and trusted most in the Spartans, your fortune and your hopes, so will you be most completely deceived."

114. The Athenian envoys now returned to the army; and the Melians showing no signs of yielding, the generals at once betook themselves to hostilities and drew a line of circumvallation around the Melians, dividing the work among the different states. Subsequently, the Athenians returned with most of their army, leaving behind them a certain

number of their own citizens and of the allies to keep guard by land and sea. The force thus left stayed on and besieged the place.

115. About the same time the Argives invaded the territory of Phlius and lost eighty men cut off in an ambush by the Phliasians and Argive exiles. Meanwhile, the Athenians at Pylos took so much plunder from the Spartans that the latter, although they still refrained from breaking off the treaty and going to war with Athens, yet proclaimed that any of their people who chose might plunder the Athenians. The Corinthians also commenced hostilities with the Athenians for private quarrels of their own; but the rest of the Peloponnesians stayed quiet. Meanwhile, the Melians attacked by night and took the part of the Athenian lines over against the market; and they killed some of the men, brought in grain and all else that they could find useful to them, and so returned and kept quiet, while the Athenians took measures to keep better guard in future.

116. Summer was now over. In the next winter the Spartans intended to invade the Argive territory; but arriving at the frontier, they found the sacrifices for crossing unfavorable and went back again. This intention of theirs gave the Argives suspicions of certain of their fellow citizens, some of whom they arrested; others, however, escaped them. About the same time the Melians again took another part of the Athenian lines which were but feebly garrisoned. Reinforcements afterwards arriving from Athens in consequence under the command of Philocrates, son of Demeas, the siege was now pressed vigorously; and some treachery taking place inside, the Melians surrendered at discretion to the Athenians, who put to death all the grown men whom they took, sold the women and children for slaves, subsequently sent out five hundred colonists, and inhabited the place themselves.

F. Nicias' Letter to the Athenian Democracy (Book VII)

This passage dates to the year 414 B.C. and pertains to the Athenian expedition in Sicily. At that point, Nicias, who had opposed the expedition in the first place, was the only one of the original three commanders sent out to lead Athens' large force to conquer the island; and the nature of the letter that he sends to Athens to inform the state of their present precarious situation offers us clues as to the difficulty that leaders often had in dealing with the Athenian democracy.

8. Nicias, perceiving this and seeing the strength of the enemy and his own difficulties daily increasing, himself also sent to Athens. He had before sent frequent reports of events as they occurred; and he felt it especially incumbent upon him to do so now, since he thought that they were in a critical position, and that, unless speedily recalled or strongly reinforced from home, they had no hope of safety. He feared, however, that the messengers, either through inability to speak, or through failure of memory, or from a wish to please the multitude, might not report the truth, and so thought it best to write a letter to ensure that the Athenians should know his own opinion without its being lost in transmission and should be able to decide upon the real facts of the case. His emissaries, accordingly, departed with the letter and the requisite verbal instructions; and he attended to the affairs of the army, making it his aim now to keep on the defensive and to avoid any unnecessary danger....

10. Summer was now over. The winter ensuing [late 414 B.C.], the persons sent by Nicias, reaching Athens, gave the verbal messages which had been entrusted to them and answered any questions that were asked them; and they delivered the letter. The clerk of the city now came forward and read out to the Athenians the letter, which was as follows:

11. "Our past operations, Athenians, have been made known to you by many other letters. It is now time for you to become equally familiar with our present condition and to take your measures accordingly. We had defeated in most of our engagements with them the Syracusans, against whom we were sent, and we had built the works which we now occupy, when Gylippus arrived from Lacedaemon with an army obtained from Peloponnese and from some of the cities in Sicily. In our first battle with him we were victorious. In the battle on the following day we were overpowered by a multitude of cavalry and darters and were compelled to retire within our lines. We have now,

therefore, been forced by the numbers of those opposed to us to discontinue the work of circumvallation and to remain inactive, being unable to make use even of all the force that we have, since a large portion of our hoplites is absorbed in the defense of our lines. Meanwhile, the enemy have carried a single wall past our lines, thus making it impossible for us to invest them in future, until this cross wall be attacked by a strong force and captured. So, the besieger in name has become, at least from the land side, the besieged in reality, since we are prevented by their cavalry from even going for any distance into the country.

12. Besides this, an embassy has been dispatched to Peloponnese to procure reinforcements, and Gylippus has gone to the cities in Sicily, partly in the hope of inducing those that are at present neutral to join him in the war, partly of bringing from his allies additional contingents for the land forces and material for the navy: for I understand that they contemplate a combined attack upon our lines with their land forces and with their fleet by sea. You must, none of you, be surprised that I say by sea also. They have discovered that the length of the time which we have now been in commission has rotted our ships and wasted our crews, and that with the entireness of our crews and the soundness of our ships, the pristine efficiency of our navy has departed: for it is impossible for us to haul our ships ashore and careen them, because, the enemy's vessels being as many or more than our own, we are constantly anticipating an attack. Indeed, they may be seen exercising, and it lies with them to take the initiative; and not having to maintain a blockade, they have greater facilities for drying their ships.

13. This we should scarcely be able to do, even if we had plenty of ships to spare and were freed from our present necessity of exhausting all our strength upon the blockade: for it is already difficult to carry in supplies past Syracuse; and were we to relax our vigilance in the slightest degree, it would become impossible. The losses which our crews have suffered and still continue to suffer arise from the following causes. Expeditions for fuel and for forage, and the distance from which water has to be fetched, cause our sailors to be cut off by the

Syracusan cavalry; the loss of our previous superiority emboldens our slaves to desert; our foreign seamen are impressed by the unexpected appearance of a navy against us and the strength of the enemy's resistance; such of them as were pressed into the service take the first opportunity of departing to their respective cities; such as were originally seduced by the temptation of high pay and expected little fighting and large gains, leave us either by desertion to the enemy or by availing themselves of one or other of the various facilities of escape which the magnitude of Sicily affords them. Some even engage in trade themselves and prevail upon the captains to take Hyccaric slaves on board in their place; thus they have ruined the efficiency of our navy.

14. Now I need not remind you that the time during which a crew is in its prime is short, and that the number of sailors who can start a ship on her way and keep the rowing in time is small. But by far my greatest trouble is that holding the post which I do, I am prevented by the natural indocility of the Athenian seaman from putting a stop to these evils; and that meanwhile, we have no source from which to recruit our crews, which the enemy can do from many quarters, but we are compelled to depend both for supplying the crews in service and for making good our losses upon the men whom we brought with us: for our present confederates, Naxos and Catana, are incapable of supplying us. There is only one thing more wanting to our opponents, I mean the defection of our Italian markets. If they were to see you neglecting to relieve us from our present condition, and if they were to go over to the enemy, famine would compel us to evacuate, and Syracuse would finish the war without a blow. "I might, it is true, have written to you something different and more agreeable than this, but nothing certainly more useful, if it is desirable for you to know the real state of things here before taking your measures. Besides, I know that it is your nature to love to be told the best side of things and then to blame the teller if the expectations which he has raised in your minds are not answered by the result; and I therefore thought it safest to declare to you the truth.

15. Now you are not to think that either your generals or your soldiers have ceased to be a match for the forces originally opposed to them.

But you are to reflect that a general Sicilian coalition is being formed against us; that a fresh army is expected from Peloponnese, while the force which we have here is unable to cope even with our present antagonists; and you must promptly decide either to recall us or to send out to us another fleet and army as numerous again with a large sum of money and someone to succeed me, since a disease in the kidneys unfits me for retaining my post. I have, I think, some claim on your indulgence, since while I was in my prime, I did you much good service in my commands. But whatever you mean to do, do it at the commencement of spring and without delay, since the enemy will obtain his Sicilian reinforcements shortly, those from Peloponnese after a longer interval; and unless you attend to the matter, the former will be here before you, while the latter will elude you as they have done before."

G. Athenian Utter Defeat in Sicily (Book VII)

After squandering their initial element of surprise against Syracuse due to the three commanders (Nicias, Alcibiades, and Lamachus not being able to agree), the Athenians eventually succeeded in bringing Syracuse to its knees and nearly investing it with earthworks and fortifications; but just as the Athenians were about to complete their encirclement of the city, a hard-fought night battle, resulting in Syracusan victory, prevented the Athenians from closing the noose; and the Athenians eventually found themselves blockaded by the Syracusans. In order to break the blockade, the Athenians fought a desperate naval battle in the Great Harbor of Syracuse; but when they were defeated, the Athenian force attempted to escape by fleeing overland, but they were forced to surrender, and many of the captives died miserable deaths in the Syracusan stone quarries.

72. The sea-fight having been a severe one, and many ships and lives having been lost on both sides, the victorious Syracusans and their allies now picked up their wrecks and dead, sailed off to the city, and set up a trophy. The Athenians, overwhelmed by their misfortune, never even thought of asking leave to take up their dead or wrecks, but they wished to retreat that very night. Demosthenes, however, went to

Nicias and gave it as his opinion that they should man the ships which they had left and make another effort to force their passage out next morning, saying that they still had left more ships fit for service than the enemy, the Athenians having about sixty remaining as against less than fifty of their opponents. Nicias was quite of his mind; but when they wished to man the vessels, the sailors refused to go on board, being so utterly overcome by their defeat as no longer to believe in the possibility of success.

73. Accordingly, they all now made up their minds to retreat by land. Meanwhile, the Syracusan Hermocrates—suspecting their intention, and impressed by the danger of allowing a force of that magnitude to retire by land, to establish itself in some other part of Sicily, and thence to renew the war—went and stated his views to the authorities and pointed out to them that they ought not to let the enemy get away by night, but that all the Syracusans and their allies should at once march out and block up the roads and seize and guard the passes. The authorities were entirely of his opinion and thought that it ought to be done, but on the other hand, they felt sure that the people, who had given themselves over to rejoicing and were taking their ease after a great battle at sea, would not be easily brought to obey; besides, they were celebrating a festival, having on that day a sacrifice to Heracles, and most of them in their rapture at the victory had fallen to drinking at the festival and would probably consent to anything sooner than to take up their arms and march out at that moment. For these reasons the thing appeared impracticable to the magistrates; and Hermocrates, finding himself unable to do anything further with them, had now recourse to the following stratagem of his own. What he feared was that the Athenians might quietly get the start of them by passing the most difficult places during the night; and he therefore sent, as soon as it was dusk, some friends of his own to the camp with some horsemen who rode up within earshot and called out to some of the men, as though they were well-wishers of the Athenians,

74. and told them to tell Nicias (who had in fact some correspondents who informed him of what went on inside the town) not to lead off the army by night, since the Syracusans were guarding the roads, but

to make his preparations at his leisure and to retreat by day. After saying this, they departed; and their hearers informed the Athenian generals, who put off going for that night on the strength of this message,
not doubting its sincerity. Since after all they had not set out at once,
they now determined to stay also the following day to give time to
the soldiers to pack up as well as they could the most useful articles
and, leaving everything else behind, to start only with what was strictly
necessary for their personal subsistence. Meanwhile, the Syracusans
and Gylippus marched out and blocked up the roads through the
country by which the Athenians were likely to pass; and they kept
guard at the fords of the streams and rivers, posting themselves so as
to receive them and stop the army where they thought best, while
their fleet sailed up to the beach and towed off the ships of the Athenians. Some few were burned by the Athenians themselves as they had
intended; the rest the Syracusans lashed on to their own at their
leisure as they had been thrown up on shore without anyone trying
to stop them, and they conveyed them to the town.

75. After this, Nicias and Demosthenes now thinking that enough had
been done in the way of preparation, the removal of the army took
place upon the second day after the sea-fight. It was a lamentable
scene, not merely from the single circumstance that they were retreating after having lost all their ships, their great hopes gone, and themselves and the state in peril; but also in leaving the camp there were
things most grievous for every eye and heart to contemplate. The
dead lay unburied; and each man, as he recognized a friend among
them, shuddered with grief and horror, while the living whom they
were leaving behind, wounded or sick, were to the living far more
shocking than the dead, and they were more to be pitied than those
who had perished. These fell to entreating and bewailing until their
friends knew not what to do, begging them to take them and loudly
calling to each individual comrade or relative whom they could see,
hanging upon the necks of their tent-fellows in the act of departure,
and following as far as they could and, when their bodily strength
failed them, calling again and again upon heaven and shrieking aloud
as they were left behind, so that the whole army, being filled with tears

and distracted after this fashion, found it not easy to go, even from an enemy's land, where they had already suffered evils too great for tears and in the unknown future before them feared to suffer more. Dejection and self-condemnation were also rife among them. Indeed, they could only be compared to a starved-out town, and that no small one, escaping—the whole multitude upon the march being not less than forty thousand men. All carried anything that they could which might be of use; and the hoplites and troopers, contrary to their wont, while under arms, carried their own victuals: in some cases for want of servants, in others through not trusting them, since they had long been deserting and now did so in greater numbers than ever. Yet, even thus they did not carry enough, since there was no longer food in the camp. Moreover, their disgrace generally and the universality of their sufferings, however to a certain extent alleviated by being borne in company, were still felt at the moment a heavy burden, especially when they contrasted the splendor and glory of their setting out with the humiliation in which it had ended: for this was by far the greatest reverse that ever befell an Hellenic army. They had come to enslave others and were departing in fear of being enslaved themselves. They had sailed out with prayer and paeans; and now they started to go back with omens directly contrary; travelling by land instead of by sea, and trusting not in their fleet but in their hoplites. Nevertheless, the greatness of the danger still impending made all this appear tolerable.

76. Nicias, seeing the army dejected and greatly altered, passed along the ranks and encouraged and comforted them as far as was possible under the circumstances, raising his voice still higher and higher as he went from one company to another in his earnestness and in his anxiety that the benefit of his words might reach as many as possible....

78. As he made this address, Nicias went along the ranks and brought back to their place any of the troops whom he saw straggling out of the line, while Demosthenes did as much for his part of the army, addressing them in words very similar. The army marched in a hollow square, the division under Nicias leading, and that of Demosthenes

following, the hoplites being outside and the baggage-carriers and the bulk of the army in the middle. When they arrived at the ford of the river Anapus, there they found drawn up a body of the Syracusans and allies; and routing these, they made good their passage and pushed on, harassed by the charges of the Syracusan horse and by the missiles of their light troops. On that day they advanced about four miles and a half, halting for the night upon a certain hill. On the next they started early and got on about two miles further; and they descended into a place in the plain and there encamped in order to procure some eatables from the houses, since the place was inhabited, and to carry on with them water thence, since for many furlongs in front in the direction in which they were going, it was not plentiful. The Syracusans, meanwhile, went on and fortified the pass in front, where there was a steep hill with a rocky ravine on each side of it, called the Acraean Cliff. On the next day the Athenians advancing found themselves impeded by the missiles and charges of the horse and darters, both very numerous, of the Syracusans and allies; and after fighting for a long while, at length they retired to the same camp, where they had no longer provisions as before, it being impossible to leave their position by reason of the cavalry.

79. Early on the next morning they started afresh and forced their way to the hill, which had been fortified, where they found before them the enemy's infantry drawn up many shields deep to defend the fortification, the pass being narrow. The Athenians assaulted the work, but they were greeted by a storm of missiles from the hill, which told with the greater effect through its being a steep one; and unable to force the passage, they retreated again and rested. Meanwhile, there occurred some claps of thunder and rain, as often happens towards autumn, which still further disheartened the Athenians, who thought all these things to be omens of their approaching ruin. While they were resting, Gylippus and the Syracusans sent a part of their army to throw up works in their rear on the way by which they had advanced. However, the Athenians immediately sent some of their men and prevented them, after which they retreated more towards the plain and halted for the night. When they advanced the next day, the

Syracusans surrounded and attacked them on every side and disabled many of them, falling back if the Athenians advanced, and coming on if they retired, and in particular assaulting their rear in the hope of routing them in detail and thus striking a panic into the whole army. For a long while the Athenians persevered in this fashion, but after advancing for four or five furlongs, they halted to rest in the plain, the Syracusans also withdrawing to their own camp.

80. During the night Nicias and Demosthenes, seeing the wretched condition of their troops now in want of every kind of necessary, and numbers of them disabled in the numerous attacks of the enemy, determined to light as many fires as possible and to lead off the army, no longer by the same route as they had intended, but towards the sea in the opposite direction to that guarded by the Syracusans. The whole of this route was leading the army not to Catana but to the other side of Sicily, towards Camarina, Gela, and the other Hellenic and barbarian towns in that quarter. They accordingly lit a number of fires and set out by night. Now all armies, and the greatest most of all, are liable to fears and alarms, especially when they are marching by night through an enemy's country and with the enemy near; and the Athenians falling into one of these panics, the leading division, that of Nicias, kept together and got on a good way in front, while that of Demosthenes, comprising rather more than half the army, got separated and marched on in some disorder. By morning, however, they reached the sea; and getting into the Helorine road, they pushed on in order to reach the river Cacyparis and to follow the stream up through the interior, where they hoped to be met by the Sicels whom they had sent for. Arrived at the river, they found there also a Syracusan party engaged in barring the passage of the ford with a wall and a palisade; and forcing this guard, they crossed the river and went on to another called the Erineus, according to the advice of their guides.

81. Meanwhile, when day came, and the Syracusans and allies found that the Athenians were gone, most of them accused Gylippus of having let them escape on purpose; and hastily pursuing by the road which they had no difficulty in finding that they had taken, they overtook them about dinner-time. They first came up with the troops under

Demosthenes, who were behind and marching somewhat slowly and in disorder due to the night panic above referred to. And at once they attacked and engaged them, the Syracusan horse surrounding them with more ease now that they were separated from the rest, and hemming them in on one spot. The division of Nicias was five or six miles on in front, since he led them more rapidly, thinking that under the circumstances their safety lay not in staying and fighting, unless obliged, but in retreating as fast as possible, and only fighting when forced to do so. On the other hand, Demosthenes was, generally speaking, harassed more incessantly, as his post in the rear left him the first exposed to the attacks of the enemy; and now, finding that the Syracusans were in pursuit, he omitted to push on in order to form his men for battle; and so, he lingered until he was surrounded by his pursuers and himself and the Athenians with him placed in the most distressing position, being huddled into an enclosure with a wall all around it, a road on this side and on that, and olive-trees in great number, where missiles were showered in upon them from every quarter. This mode of attack the Syracusans had with good reason adopted in preference to fighting at close quarters, since to risk a struggle with desperate men was now more for the advantage of the Athenians than for their own. Besides, their success had now become so certain that they began to spare themselves a little in order not to be cut off in the moment of victory, thinking too that, as it was, they would be able in this way to subdue and capture the enemy.

82. In fact, after plying the Athenians and allies all day long from every side with missiles, they at length saw that they were worn out with their wounds and other sufferings; and Gylippus, the Syracusans, and their allies made a proclamation, offering their liberty to any of the islanders who chose to come over to them; and some few cities went over. Afterwards a capitulation was agreed upon for all the rest with Demosthenes: to lay down their arms on condition that no one was to be put to death either by violence or imprisonment or want of the necessaries of life. Upon this they surrendered to the number of six thousand in all, laying down all the money in their possession, which filled the hollows of four shields, and they were immediately conveyed

by the Syracusans to the town. Meanwhile, Nicias with his division arrived that day at the river Erineus, crossed over, and posted his army upon some high ground upon the other side.

83. On the next day the Syracusans overtook him and told him that the troops under Demosthenes had surrendered; and they invited him to follow their example. Incredulous of the fact, Nicias asked for a truce to send a horseman to see. And upon the return of the messenger with the tidings that they had surrendered, he sent a herald to Gylippus and the Syracusans, saying that he was ready to agree with them on behalf of the Athenians to repay whatever money the Syracusans had spent upon the war if they would let his army go; and he offered until the money was paid to give Athenians as hostages, one for every talent. The Syracusans and Gylippus rejected this proposition and attacked this division as they had the other, standing all around and plying them with missiles until the evening. Food and necessaries were as miserably wanting to the troops of Nicias as they had been to their comrades. Nevertheless, they watched for the quiet of the night to resume their march. But as they were taking up their arms, the Syracusans perceived it and raised their paean, upon which the Athenians, finding that they were discovered, laid them down again, except about three hundred men who forced their way through the guards and went on during the night as they were able.

84. As soon as it was day, Nicias put his army in motion, pressed, as before, by the Syracusans and their allies, pelted from every side by their missiles, and struck down by their javelins. The Athenians pushed on for the Assinarus, impelled by the attacks made upon them from every side by a numerous cavalry and the swarm of other arms, fancying that they should breathe more freely if once across the river, and driven on also by their exhaustion and craving for water. Once there, they rushed in, and all order was at an end, each man wanting to cross first, and the attacks of the enemy making it difficult to cross at all. Forced to huddle together, they fell against and trod down one another, some dying immediately upon the javelins, others getting entangled together and stumbling over the articles of baggage without being able to rise again. Meanwhile, the opposite bank, which was

steep, was lined by the Syracusans, who showered missiles down upon the Athenians, most of them drinking greedily and heaped together in disorder in the hollow bed of the river. The Peloponnesians also came down and butchered them, especially those in the water, which was thus immediately spoiled, but which they went on drinking just the same, mud and all, bloody as it was, most even fighting to have it.

85. At last, when many dead now lay piled one upon another in the stream, and part of the army had been destroyed at the river, and the few who escaped thence cut off by the cavalry, Nicias surrendered himself to Gylippus, whom he trusted more than he did the Syracusans, and told him and the Lacedaemonians to do what they liked with him, but to stop the slaughter of the soldiers. Gylippus, after this, immediately gave orders to make prisoners; upon which the rest were brought together alive, except a large number secreted by the soldiery, and a party was sent in pursuit of the three hundred who had got through the guard during the night, and who were now taken with the rest. The number of the enemy collected as public property was not considerable; but that secreted was very large, and all Sicily was filled with them, no convention having been made in their case as for those taken with Demosthenes. Besides this, a large portion were killed outright, the carnage being very great, and not exceeded by any in this Sicilian war. In the numerous other encounters upon the march not a few also had fallen. Nevertheless, many escaped, some at the moment, others served as slaves and then ran away subsequently. These found refuge at Catana.

86. The Syracusans and their allies now mustered, took up the spoils and as many prisoners as they could, and went back to the city. The rest of their Athenian and allied captives were deposited in the quarries, this seeming the safest way of keeping them; but Nicias and Demosthenes were butchered against the will of Gylippus, who thought that it would be the crown of his triumph if he could take the enemy's generals to Lacedaemon. One of them, as it happened, Demosthenes, was one of her greatest enemies, on account of the affair of the island [Sphacteria in 424 B.C.] and of Pylos; while the other, Nicias, was for the same reasons one of her greatest friends due to his exertions to

procure the release of the prisoners by persuading the Athenians to make peace. For these reasons the Lacedaemonians felt kindly towards him; and it was in this that Nicias himself mainly confided when he surrendered to Gylippus. But some of the Syracusans who had been in correspondence with him were afraid, it was said, of his being put to the torture and troubling their success by his revelations; others, especially the Corinthians, of his escaping, since he was wealthy, by means of bribes and living to do them further mischief; and these persuaded the allies and put him to death. This or the like was the cause of the death of a man who, of all the Hellenes in my time, least deserved such a fate, seeing that the whole course of his life had been regulated with strict attention to virtue.

87. The prisoners in the quarries were at first harshly treated by the Syracusans. Crowded in a narrow hole without any roof to cover them, the heat of the sun and the stifling closeness of the air tormented them during the day, and then the nights, which came on autumnal and chilly, made them ill by the violence of the change. Besides, since they had to do everything in the same place for want of room, and the bodies of those who died of their wounds or from the variation in the temperature, or from similar causes, were left heaped together one upon another, intolerable stenches arose; while hunger and thirst never ceased to afflict them, each man during eight months having only half a pint of water and a pint of grain given him daily. In short, no single suffering to be apprehended by men thrust into such a place was spared them. For some seventy days they thus lived all together, after which all, except the Athenians and any Siceliots or Italiots who had joined in the expedition, were sold. The total number of prisoners taken it would be difficult to state exactly, but it could not have been less than seven thousand. This was the greatest Hellenic achievement of any in this war, or, in my opinion, in Hellenic history: at once most glorious to the victors, and most calamitous to the conquered. They were beaten at all points and altogether; all that they suffered was great; they were destroyed, as the saying is, with a total destruction. Their fleet, their army, everything was destroyed, and few out of many returned home. Such were the events in Sicily.

Book VIII

1. When the news was brought to Athens, for a long while they disbe-
lieved even the most respectable of the soldiers who had themselves
escaped from the scene of action and clearly reported the matter, a
destruction so complete not being thought credible. When the conviction was forced upon them, they were angry with the orators who
had joined in promoting the expedition, just as if they had not themselves voted it; and they were enraged also with the reciters of oracles,
soothsayers, and all other omen-mongers of the time who had encouraged them to hope that they should conquer Sicily. Already distressed at all points and in all quarters, after what had now happened,
they were seized by a fear and consternation quite without example.
It was grievous enough for the state and for every man in his proper
person to lose so many hoplites, cavalry, and able-bodied troops and
to see none left to replace them; but when they saw, also, that they
had not sufficient ships in their docks, or money in the treasury, or
crews for the ships, they began to despair of salvation. They thought
that their enemies in Sicily would immediately sail with their fleet
against Piraeus, inflamed by so signal a victory, while their adversaries
at home, redoubling all their preparations, would vigorously attack
them by sea and land at once, aided by their own revolted confederates. Nevertheless, with such means as they had, it was determined to
resist to the last, to provide timber and money, to equip a fleet as they
best could, to take steps to secure their confederates and above all Euboea, to reform things in the city upon a more economical footing,
and to elect a board of elders to advise upon the state of affairs as occasion should arise. In short, as is the way of a democracy, in the panic
of the moment they were ready to be as prudent as possible.

READING 36
THE THIRTY TYRANTS OF ATHENS

When Athens was forced to surrender to Sparta at the end of the Peloponnesian War in the spring of 404 B.C., one condition imposed upon Athens by
Sparta was the termination of the democracy and the establishment of a new
form of government. To bring about this transition, a group of thirty Athenian
aristocrats (soon termed the thirty tyrants) was appointed to form a committee,
whose purpose was to draw up a new constitution. But rather than carrying
out their appointed function, the thirty instead attempted to establish themselves permanently in power; and under the leadership of their most extreme
member, Critias, they employed ruthless means to destroy all opposition to
their rule. Many Athenians fled into exile and eventually organized themselves
into an opposing military force. Meanwhile, Theramenes, one of the thirty,
attempted to oppose the lawlessness of his colleagues; but as the following passage describes, he failed and was executed. Following his death, the Athenian
exiles invaded Attica and eventually succeeded in bringing about the downfall
of the thirty and the reestablishment of the democracy.

The following passage is taken from The Hellenica of Xenophon. Thucydides, of course, had taken on the task of writing a history of the Peloponnesian
War, but he died before finishing the work. His account ends with the events
of 411 B.C. Xenophon, another Athenian, carried forward the narration of
Greek affairs in the Aegean world for the period 411-362 B.C., and this narrative is known as The Hellenica. Xenophon was born in 431 B.C., the year
in which the Peloponnesian War began; and he lived until 354 B.C. Although his abilities as a historian are less than those of both Herodotus and

Thucydides, he was an intelligent and well-informed contemporary of the events that he described. The following passage is one of the more dramatic and vivid episodes in his historical account; and it is likely that Xenophon was an eye-witness to the trial of Theramenes.

(From Book II of Xenophon's Hellenica, taken from The Works of Xenophon, Volume I, translated by Henry Graham Dakyns, MacMillan, London 1890, revised by Gary Forsythe)

The Thirty had been chosen almost immediately after the long walls and the fortifications around Piraeus had been razed. They were chosen for the express purpose of compiling a code of laws for the future constitution of the state. The laws were always on the point of being published, yet they were never forthcoming; and the thirty compilers contented themselves meanwhile with appointing a boule and the other magistracies as suited their fancy best. That done, they turned their attention, in the first instance, to such persons as were well known to have made their living as informers under the democracy and to be thorns in the side of all respectable people. These they laid hold on and prosecuted on the capital charge. The new boule gladly recorded its vote of condemnation against them; and the rest of the world, conscious of bearing no resemblance to them, seemed scarcely vexed.

But the Thirty did not stop there. Presently they began to deliberate by what means they could get the city under their absolute control, in order that they might work their will upon it. Here again they proceeded tentatively. In the first instance, they sent two of their number, Aeschines and Aristoteles, to Sparta and persuaded Lysander to support them in getting a Spartan garrison despatched to Athens. They only needed it until they had got the "malignants" out of the way and had established the constitution; and they would undertake to maintain these troops at their own cost. Lysander was not deaf to their per-suasions, and by his co-operation their request was granted. A bodyguard with Callibius as governor was sent. And now that they had got the garrison, they fell to flattering Callibius with all servile flattery, in order that he might give countenance to their doings. Thus they prevailed on him to allow some of the guards, whom they selected, to accompany them, while they proceeded to lay hands on whom they would, no longer confining themselves to base folk and people of no account, but boldly laying hands on those who, they felt sure, would least easily brook being thrust aside, or, if a spirit of opposition seized them, could command the largest number of partisans. These were early days; as yet Critias was of one mind with Theramenes, and the two were friends. But the time came when, in proportion as Critias was ready to rush headlong into wholesale carnage, like one who thirsted for the blood of the democracy, which had banished him, Theramenes balked and thwarted him. It was barely reasonable, he argued, to put people to death, who had never done a thing wrong to respectable people in their lives, simply because they had enjoyed influence and honor under the democracy. "Why, you and I, Critias," he would add, "have said and done many things ere now for the sake of popularity." To which the other (for the terms of friendly intimacy still subsisted) would retort, "There is no choice left to us, since we intend to take the lion's share, but to get rid of those who are best able to hinder us. If you imagine, because we are thirty instead of one, our government requires one whit the less careful guarding than an actual tyranny, you must be very innocent."

So things went on. Day after day the list of persons put to death for no just reason grew longer. Day after day the signs of resentment were more significant in the groups of citizens banding together and forecasting the character of this future constitution, till at length Theramenes spoke again, protesting: There was no help for it but to associate with themselves a sufficient number of persons in the conduct of affairs, or the oligarchy would certainly come to an end. Critias and the rest of the Thirty, whose fears had already converted Theramenes into a dangerous popular idol, proceeded at once to draw up a list of three thousand citizens, fit and proper persons, to have a share in the conduct of affairs. But Theramenes was not wholly satisfied, indeed, he must say, for himself, he regarded it as ridiculous that in their effort to associate the better classes with themselves in power they should fix on just that particular number, three thousand, as if that figure had some necessary connection with the exact number of gentlemen in the state, making it impossible to discover any respectability outside or rascality within the magic number. "And in the second place," he continued, "I see that we are trying to do two things diametrically opposed: we are manufacturing a government, which is based on force, and at the same time inferior in strength to those whom we propose to govern."

That was what he said, but what his colleagues did was to institute a military inspection or review. The Three Thousand were drawn up in the Agora; and the rest of the citizens, who were not included in the list, elsewhere in various quarters of the city. The order to take arms was given; but while the men's backs were turned, at the bidding of the Thirty the Spartan guards with those of the citizens, who shared their views, appeared on the scene and took away the arms of all except the Three Thousand, carried them up to the Acropolis, and safely deposited them in the temple. The ground being thus cleared, as it were, and feeling that they had it in their power to do what they pleased, they embarked on a course of wholesale butchery, to which many were sacrificed to the merest hatred, many to the accident of possessing riches.

Presently the question arose. How were they to get money to pay their guards? To meet this difficulty, a resolution was passed, empowering each of the committee to seize on one of the resident aliens apiece, to put his victim to death, and to confiscate his property. Theramenes was invited, or rather, was told to seize someone or other. "Choose whom you will, only let it be done." To which he made answer, it hardly seemed to him a noble or worthy course on the part of those who claimed to be the elite of society to go beyond the informers in injustice. "Yesterday they, today we: with this difference, the victim of the informer must live as a source of income; our innocents must die that we may get their wealth. Surely their method was innocent in comparison with ours."

The rest of the Thirty, who had come to regard Theramenes as an obstacle to any course that they might wish to adopt, proceeded to plot against him. They addressed themselves to the members of the boule in private, here a man and there a man, and denounced him as harming the constitution. Then they issued an order to the young men, picking out the most audacious characters whom they could find, to be present, each with a dagger hidden in the hollow of the armpit; and so, they called a meeting of the boule. When Theramenes had taken his place, Critias stood up and addressed the meeting.

"If," said he, "any member of this council, here seated, imagines that an undue amount of blood has been shed, let me remind him that with changes of constitution such things cannot be avoided. It is the rule everywhere, but more particularly at Athens it was inevitable that there should be found a specially large number of persons sworn foes to any constitutional change in the direction of oligarchy, and this for two reasons. First, because the population of this city, compared with other Hellenic cities, is enormously large; and again, due to the length of time during which the people has battened upon liberty. Now, as to two points we are clear. The first is that democracy is a form of government detestable to persons like ourselves—to us and to you; the next is that the people of Athens could never be got to be friendly to our friends and saviors, the Spartans. But on the loyalty of the better classes the Spartans can count. And that is our reason for establishing an oligarchical constitution with their concurrence. That is why we do our best to rid us of everyone whom we perceive to be opposed to the oligarchy; and in our opinion, if one of ourselves should elect to undermine this constitution of ours, he would deserve punishment. Do you not agree?

And the case," he continued, "is no imaginary one. The offender is here present—Theramenes. And what we say of him is that he is bent upon destroying yourselves and us by every means in his power. These are not baseless charges; but if you will consider it, you will find them amply established in this unmeasured censure of the present posture of affairs, and his persistent opposition to us, his colleagues, if ever we seek to get rid of any of these demagogues. Had this been his guiding principle of action from the beginning, in spite of hostility, at least he would have escaped all imputation of villainy. Why, this is the very man who originated our friendly and confidential relations with Sparta. This is the very man who authorised the abolition of the democracy, who urged us on to inflict punishment on the earliest batch of prisoners brought before us. But today all is changed; now you and we are out of odor with the people, and he accordingly has ceased to be pleased with our proceedings. The explanation is obvious. In case of a catastrophe, how much pleasanter for him once again to light upon his legs and to leave us to render account for our past performances. I contend that this man is fairly entitled to render his account also, not only as an ordinary enemy, but as a traitor to yourselves and us. And let us add. Not only is treason more formidable than open war in proportion as it is harder to guard against a hidden assassin than an open foe, but it bears the impress of a more enduring hostility, inasmuch as men fight their enemies and come to terms with them again and are fast friends; but whoever heard of reconciliation with a traitor? There he stands unmasked. He has forfeited our confidence for evermore.

But to show you that these are no new tactics of his, to prove to you that he is a traitor in grain, I will recall to your memories some points in his past history. He began by being held in high honor by the democracy; but taking a leaf out of his father Hagnon's book, he next showed a most headlong anxiety to transform the democracy into the Four Hundred. And in fact, for a time he held the first place in that body. But presently, detecting the formation of rival power to the oligarchs, around he shifted; and we find him next a ringleader of the popular party in assailing them. It must be admitted that he has well earned his nickname 'Buskin' [a boot worn by actors that fitted both feet]. Yes, Theramenes! clever you may be, but the man who deserves to live should not show his cleverness in leading on his associates into trouble; and when some obstacle presents itself, at once veer around; but like a pilot on shipboard, he ought then to redouble his efforts, until the wind is fair. Else, how in the name of wonderment are those mariners to reach the haven? Where would they be if at the first contrary wind or tide they turn about and sail in the opposite di-rection? Death and destruction are concomitants of constitutional changes and revolution, no doubt. But you are such an impersonation of change that as you twist and turn and double, you deal destruction on all sides. At one swoop you are the ruin of a thousand oligarchs at the hands of the people, and at another of a thousand democrats at the hands of the better classes. Why, sirs, this is the man to whom the orders were given by the generals in the sea-fight off Lesbos [Arginusae in 406 B.C.] to pick up the crews of the disabled vessels; and who, neglecting to obey orders, turned around and accused the generals; and to save himself he murdered them! What, I ask you, of a man who so openly studied the art of self-seeking, deaf alike to the pleas of honor and to the claims of friendship? Would not leniency towards such a creature be mis-placed? Can it be our duty at all to spare him? Ought we not rather, when we know the doublings of his nature, to guard against them, lest we enable him presently to practise on ourselves? The case is clear. We therefore hereby cite this man before you as a conspirator and traitor against yourselves and us.

The reasonableness of our conduct one further reflection may make clear. No one, I take it, will dispute the splendor, the perfection of the Laconian constitution. Imagine one of the ephors there in Sparta in lieu of devoted obe-dience to the majority, taking on himself to find fault with the government and to oppose all measures. Do you not think that the ephors themselves, and the whole commonwealth besides, would hold this renegade worthy of condign punishment? So, too, by the same token, if you are wise, do you spare yourselves, not him: for what does the alternative mean? I will tell you. His preservation will cause the courage of many who hold opposite views to your own to rise. His destruction will cut off the last hopes of all your enemies, whether within or without the city."

With these words he sat down, but Theramenes arose and said: "Sirs, with your permission I will first touch upon the charge against me which Critias has mentioned last. The assertion is that as the accuser of the generals I was their murderer. Now I presume that it was not I who began the attack upon them, but it was they who asserted that in spite of the orders given me I had neglected to pick up the unfortunates in the sea-fight off Lesbos. All that I did was to defend myself. My defense was that the storm was too violent to permit any vessel to ride at sea, much more therefore to pick up the men, and this defense was accepted by my fellow citizens as highly reasonable, while the generals seemed to be condemned out of their own mouths: for while they kept on asserting that it was possible to save the men, the fact still remained that they abandoned them to their fate, set sail, and were gone. However, I am not surprised, I confess, at this grave misconception on the part of Critias: for at the time of these occurrences he was not in Athens. He was away in Thessaly, laying the foundations of a democracy with Prometheus, and arming the Penestae [Helot-like serfs] against their masters. Heaven forbid that any of his transactions there should be re-enacted here. However, I must say, I do heartily concur with him on one point. Whoever desires to exclude you from the government or to strengthen the hands of your secret foes, deserves and ought to meet with condign punishment; but who is most capable of so doing? That you will best discover, I think, by looking a little more closely into the past and the present conduct of each of us.

Well, then! up to the moment at which you were formed into a boule, when the magistracies were appointed, and certain notorious 'informers' were brought to trial, we all held the same views. But later on, when our friends yonder began to hale respectable honest folk to prison and to death, I, on my side, began to differ from them. From the moment when Leon of Salamis, a man of high and well-deserved reputation, was put to death, though he had not committed the shadow of a crime, I knew that all his equals must tremble

for themselves and, so trembling, be driven into opposition to the new constitution. In the same way, when Niceratus, the son of Nicias, was arrested, a
wealthy man, who, no more than his father, had never done anything that
could be called popular or democratic in his life, it did not require much in-
sight to discover that his compeers would be converted into our foes. But to
go a step further: when it came to Antiphon falling at our hands—Antiphon,
who during the war contributed two fast-sailing men-of-war out of his own
resources, it was then plain to me that all who had ever been zealous and pa-
triotic must eye us with suspicion. Once more I could not help speaking out
in opposition to my colleagues when they suggested that each of us ought to
seize some one resident alien: for what could be more certain than that their
death-warrant would turn the whole resident foreign population into enemies
of the constitution.

I spoke out again when they insisted on depriving the populace of their
arms, it being no part of my creed that we ought to take the strength out of
the city; nor, indeed, so far as I could see, had the Spartans stepped between
us and destruction merely that we might become a handful of people, powerless to aid them in the day of need. Had that been their object, they might
have swept us away to the last man. A few more weeks, or even days, would
have sufficed to extinguish us quietly by famine. Nor, again, can I say that the
importation of mercenary foreign guards was altogether to my taste, when it
would have been so easy for us to add to our own body a sufficient number of
fellow citizens to ensure our supremacy as governors over those whom we es-
sayed to govern. But when I saw what an army of malcontents this government
had raised up within the city walls, besides another daily increasing host of exiles without, I could not but regard the banishment of people like Thrasybulus,
Anytus, and Alcibiades as impolitic. Had our object been to strengthen the
rival power, we could hardly have set about it better than by providing the
populace with the competent leaders whom they needed, and the would-be
leaders themselves with an army of willing adherents. I ask then, is the man
who tenders such advice in the full light of day justly to be regarded as a traitor
and not as a benefactor? Surely, Critias, the peacemaker, the man who hinders
the creation of many enemies, whose counsels tend to the acquisition of yet
more friends, cannot be accused of strengthening the hands of the enemy.
Much more truly may the imputation be retorted on those who wrongfully

appropriate their neighbors' goods and put to death those who have done no wrong. These are they who cause our adversaries to grow and multiply, and who in very truth are traitors, not to their friends only, but to themselves, spurred on by sordid love of gain.

I might prove the truth of what I say in many ways, but I beg you to look at the matter thus. With which condition of affairs here in Athens do you think will Thrasybulus, Anytus, and the other exiles be the better pleased? That which I have pictured as desirable, or that which my colleagues yonder are producing? For my part, I cannot doubt but that as things now are, they are saying to themselves, 'Our allies muster thick and fast.' But were the real strength, the pith and fiber of this city, kindly disposed to us, they would find it an uphill task even to get a foothold anywhere in the country.

Then, with regard to what he said of me and my propensity to be for ever changing sides, let me draw your attention to the following facts. Was it not the people itself, the democracy, who voted the constitution of the Four Hundred? This they did, because they had learned to think that the Spartans would trust any other form of government rather than a democracy. But when the efforts of Sparta were not a whit relaxed, when Aristoteles, Melanthius, Aristarchus, and the rest of them, acting as generals, were plainly minded to construct an intrenched fortress on the mole for the purpose of admitting the enemy [the Spartans in 411 B.C. during the brief rule of the 400], and so getting the city under the power of themselves and their associates; because I got wind of these schemes and nipped them in the bud, is that to be a traitor to one's friends? Then he threw in my teeth the nickname 'Buskin,' as descriptive of an endeavor on my part to fit both parties. But what of the man who pleases neither? What in heaven's name are we to call him? Yes! you—Critias? Under the democracy you were looked upon as the most ardent hater of the people, and under the aristocracy you have proved yourself the bitterest foe of everything respectable. Yes! Critias, I am, and ever have been, a foe of those who think that a democracy cannot reach perfection until slaves and those who from poverty would sell the city for a drachma, can get their drachma a day [paid by the previous democracy as daily jury duty]. But not less am I, and ever have been, a pronounced opponent of those who do not think that there can possibly exist a perfect oligarchy until the state is subjected to the despotism of a few. On the contrary, my own ambition has been to combine with those who are rich enough to possess a horse and shield and to use them for the benefit of the state. That was my ideal in the old days, and I still hold to it without a shadow of turning. If you can imagine when and where, in conjunction with despots or demagogues, I have set my hand to depriving honest gentlefolk of their citizenship, pray speak. If you can convict me of such crimes at present or can prove my perpetration of them in the past, I admit that I deserve to die, and by the worst of deaths."

With these words he ceased, and the loud murmur of the applause that followed marked the favorable impression produced upon the boule. It was plain to Critias that if he allowed his adversary's fate to be decided by formal voting, Theramenes would escape, and life to himself would become intolerable. Accordingly, he stepped forward and spoke a word or two in the ears of the Thirty. This done, he went out and gave an order to the attendants with the daggers to stand close to the bar in full view of the boule. Again he entered and addressed the boule thus:

"I hold it to be the duty of a good president, when he sees the friends about him being made the dupes of some delusion, to intervene. That at any rate is what I propose to do. Indeed, our friends here standing by the bar say that if we propose to acquit a man so openly bent upon the ruin of the oligarchy, they do not mean to let us do so. Now there is a clause in the new code forbidding any of the Three Thousand to be put to death without your vote; but the Thirty have power of life and death over all outside that list. Accordingly," he proceeded, "I herewith strike this man, Theramenes, off the list; and this with the concurrence of my colleagues. And now," he continued, "we condemn him to death."

Hearing these words, Theramenes sprang upon the altar of Hestia, exclaiming: "And I, sirs, supplicate you for the barest forms of law and justice. Let it not be in the power of Critias to strike off either me or anyone of you whom he will. But in my case, in what may be your case, if we are tried, let our trial be in accordance with the law that they have made concerning those on the list. I know," he added, "but too well that this altar will not protect me; but I will make it plain that these men are as impious towards the gods as they are nefarious towards men. Yet, I do marvel, good sirs and honest gentlemen: for so you are, that you will not help yourselves, and that too when you must see that the name of everyone of you is as easily erased as mine."

But when he had got so far, the voice of the herald was heard giving the order to the Eleven [men in charge of prisoners] to seize Theramenes. They at that instant entered with their satellites—at their head Satyrus, the boldest and most shameless of the body—and Critias exclaimed, addressing the Eleven, "We deliver over to you Theramenes yonder, who has been condemned according to the law. Do you take him and lead him away to the proper place, and do there with him what remains to do." As Critias uttered the words, Satyrus laid hold upon Theramenes to drag him from the altar, and the attendants lent their aid. But he, as was natural, called upon gods and men to witness what was happening. The boule meanwhile kept silence, seeing the companions of Satyrus at the bar, and the whole front of the boule-house crowded with the foreign guards. Nor did they need to be told that there were daggers in reserve among those present. And so Theramenes was dragged through the Agora, in vehement and loud tones proclaiming the wrongs that he was suffering.

One word, which is said to have fallen from his lips, I cite. It is this: Satyrus bade him be silent, or he would rue the day; to which he made answer, "And if I be silent, shall I not rue it?" Also, when they brought him the hemlock, and the time was come to drink the fatal draught, they tell how he playfully jerked out the dregs from the bottom of the cup, like one who plays "Cotta-bos," with the words, "This to the lovely Critias." These are but utterances too trivial, it may be thought, to find a place in history. Yet, I must deem it an admirable trait in this man's character, if at such a moment, when death confronted him, neither his wits forsook him, nor could the child-like sportiveness vanish from his soul.

READING 37
THEBES LIBERATED FROM SPARTA

Sparta's victory in the Peloponnesian War resulted in large measure from the efforts and sacrifices made by its allies, the two most important of which were Corinth and Thebes. But since the latter two states did not share in the spoils of victory, Corinth and Thebes soon became unfriendly toward Sparta and joined both Athens and Argos in challenging Spartan hegemony during the so-called Corinthian War (394-386 B.C.). But when Sparta emerged from this war victorious with the backing of Persia, it proceeded systematically to undermine the power of states hostile to Sparta. The most important of these enemies was Thebes. In 382 B.C., as a Spartan commander (Phoebidas) was marching with reinforcements through central Greece on his way to Thrace to Sparta's war against the Chalcidian League, pro-Spartan leaders in Thebes plotted with the Spartan commander and betrayed to him the citadel (Cadmea) in Thebes. For the next three years a Spartan force in the Cadmea kept Thebes subservient, but then during the winter of 379/8 B.C., a small group of Theban exiles succeeded in assassinating the pro-Spartan leaders in Thebes and then rallied the Theban population to expel the Spartan force holding the Cadmea. Over the next several years Thebes, principally under the leadership of Epaminondas and Pelopidas, succeeded in uniting the other ten small communities of Boeotia into a federation that finally ended the Spartan hegemony in the battle of Leuctra in 371 B.C.

The following passage, which recounts the liberation of Thebes during the winter of 379/8 B.C., is taken from Plutarch's Life of Pelopidas, one of the fifty biographies of famous Greeks and Romans written by Plutarch, a native of the small western Boeotian town of Chaeronea.

(Taken from Plutarch's Life of Pelopidas: Plutarch's Lives, translated by Arthur Hugh Clough, published by Little, Brown and Co., Boston 1859, revised by Gary Forsythe)

5. After this the Lacedaemonians pretended to be friends to Thebes, but in truth they looked with jealous suspicions on the designs and power of the city, and they chiefly hated the party of Ismenias and Andro-clides, in which Pelopidas also was an associate, as tending to liberty and the advancement of the commonalty. Therefore Archias, Leon-tidas, and Philip, all rich men of oligarchical principles and immod-erately ambitious, urged Phoebidas the Spartan, as he was on his way past the city with a considerable force, to surprise the Cadmea and, banishing the contrary faction, to establish an oligarchy and by that means to subject the city to the supremacy of the Spartans. He, ac-cepting the proposal, at the festival of Demeter unexpectedly fell on the Thebans and made himself master of the citadel. Ismenias was taken, carried to Sparta, and in a short time murdered; but Pelopidas, Pherenicus, Androclides, and many more who fled were publicly pro-claimed outlaws. Epaminondas stayed at home, being not much looked after, as one whom philosophy had made inactive and poverty incapable.

6. The Lacedaemonians cashiered Phoebidas and fined him one hun-dred thousand drachmas, yet still kept a garrison in the Cadmea; which made all Greece wonder at their inconsistency, since they pun-ished the doer, but approved the deed. And though the Thebans, hav-ing lost their polity, and being enslaved by Archias and Leontidas, had no hopes to get free from this tyranny, which they saw guarded by the whole military power of the Spartans, and had no means to break the yoke, unless these could be deposed from their command of sea and land; yet, Leontidas and his associates, understanding that the exiles lived at Athens in favor with the people and with honor from all the good and virtuous, formed secret designs against their lives. And sub-orning some unknown fellows, they despatched Androclides, but were not successful on the rest. Letters, besides, were sent from Sparta to the Athenians, warning them neither to receive nor countenance the

exiles, but to expel them as declared common enemies of the confederacy. But the Athenians—from their natural hereditary inclination to be kind, and also to make a grateful return to the Thebans, who had very much assisted them in restoring their democracy [at the time of the Thirty Tyrants], and had publicly enacted that if any Athenian would march armed through Boeotia against the tyrants, no Boeotian should either see or hear it—did the Thebans no harm.

7. Pelopidas, though one of the youngest, was active in privately exciting each single exile and often told them at their meetings that it was both dishonorable and impious to neglect their enslaved and engarrisoned country and, lazily contented with their own lives and safety, to depend on the decree of the Athenians, and through fear to fawn on every smooth-tongued orator who was able to work upon the people: no, they must venture for this great prize, taking as their example the bold courage of Thrasybulus [the Athenian military leader against the Thirty Tyrants], and how he had advanced from Thebes and had broken the power of the Athenian tyrants, so they should march from Athens and free Thebes. When by this method he had persuaded them, they privately despatched some persons to those friends whom they had left at Thebes, and acquainted them with their designs. Their plans being approved, Charon, a man of the greatest distinction, offered his house for their reception; Phillidas contrived to get himself made secretary to Archias and Philip, who then held the office of polemarch or chief captain; and Epaminondas had already inflamed the youth: for in their exercises he had encouraged them to challenge and wrestle with the Spartans; and again, when he saw them puffed up with victory and success, he sharply told them that it was the greatest shame to be such cowards as to serve those whom in strength they so much excelled.

8. The day of action being fixed, it was agreed upon by the exiles that Pherenicus with the rest should stay at the Thriasian plain [Athenian land bordering on Boeotia], while some few of the younger men tried the first danger by endeavoring to get into the city; and if they were surprised by their enemies, the others should take care to provide for their children and parents. Pelopidas first offered to undertake the

business. He was then joined by Melon, Damoclides, and Theopompus, men of noble families, who, in other things loving and faithful to one another, were constant rivals only in glory and courageous exploits. They were twelve in all; and having taken leave of those who stayed behind, they sent a messenger to Charon and went forward, clad in short coats, and carrying hounds and hunting-poles with them in order that they might be taken for hunters beating over the fields, and prevent all suspicion in those who met them on the way. When the messenger came to Charon and told him that they were approaching, he did not change his resolution at the sight of danger, but being a man of his word, he offered them his house. But one Hipposthenidas—a man of no ill principles, a lover of his country and a friend to the exiles, but not of as much resolution as the shortness of time and the character of the action required, being as it were dizzied at the greatness of the approaching enterprise, and beginning now for the first time to comprehend that relying on that weak assistance which could be expected from the exiles, they were undertaking no less a task than to shake the government and to overthrow the whole power of Sparta—went privately to his house and sent a friend to Melon and Pelopidas, desiring them to forbear for the present, to return to Athens, and to wait for a better opportunity. The messenger's name was Chlidon, who, going home in haste and bringing out his horse, asked for the bridle. But his wife did not know where it was; and when it could not be found, she told him that she had lent it to a friend. First they began to chide, then to curse one another; and his wife wished that the journey might prove ill to him and those who sent him, insomuch that Chlidon's passion made him waste a great part of the day in this quarrelling. And then, looking on this chance as an omen, he laid aside all thoughts of his journey and went away to some other business. So nearly had these great and glorious designs, even in their very birth, lost their opportunity.

9. But Pelopidas and his companions, dressing themselves like countrymen, separated. And while it was yet day, they entered at different quarters of the city. It was, besides, a windy day; and now it just began to snow, which contributed much to their concealment, because most

people were gone indoors to avoid the weather. Those, however, who were concerned in the design received them as they came, and they conducted them to Charon's house, where the exiles and others made up forty-eight in number. The tyrant's affairs stood thus: the secretary, Phillidas, as I have already observed, was an accomplice in and privy to all the contrivance of the exiles; and he some time before had invited Archias with others to an entertainment on that day to drink freely and to meet some women of the town with the purpose that when they were drunk and given up to their pleasures, he might deliver them over to the conspirators. But before Archias was thoroughly heated, notice was given him that the exiles were privately in the town: a true report indeed, but obscure, and not well confirmed. Nevertheless, though Phillidas endeavored to divert the discourse, Archias sent one of his guards to Charon and commanded him to attend immediately. It was evening, and Pelopidas and his friends with him in the house were putting themselves into a fit posture for action, having their breastplates on already, and their swords girt. But at the sudden knocking at the door, one stepped forth to inquire the matter, learned from the officer that Charon was sent for by the polemarch, returned in great confusion, and acquainted those within; and immediately he conjectured that the whole plot was discovered, and that they should be cut in pieces before so much as achieving any action to do credit to their bravery. Yet, all agreed that Charon should obey and attend the polemarch to prevent suspicion. Charon was, indeed, a man of courage and resolution in all dangers. Yet, in this case he was extremely concerned, lest any should suspect that he was the traitor, and that the death of so many brave citizens be laid on him. Therefore, when he was ready to depart, he brought his son out of the women's apartment, a little boy as yet, but one of the best looking and strongest of all those of his age; and he delivered him to Pelopidas with these words: "If you find me a traitor, treat the boy as an enemy without any mercy." The concern which Charon showed drew tears from many; but all protested vehemently against his supposing that anyone of them was so mean-spirited and base at the appearance of approaching danger as to suspect or blame him; and they therefore desired him not to involve his son, but to set him out of harm's way, so that he, perhaps escaping the tyrant's power, might live to revenge the city and his friends. Charon, however, refused to remove him and asked, "What life, what safety could be more honorable than to die bravely with his father and such generous companions?" Thus, imploring the protection of the gods, and saluting and encouraging them all, he departed, considering with himself and composing his voice and countenance in order that he might look as little like as possible to what in fact he really was.

10. When he was come to the door, Archias with Phillidas came out to him and said, "I have heard, Charon, that there are some men just come and are lurking in the town, and that some of the citizens are resorting to them." Charon was at first disturbed, but asked, "Who are they? and who conceals them?" And finding that Archias did not thoroughly understand the matter, he concluded that none of those privy to the design had given this information; and he replied, "Do not disturb yourselves for an empty rumor. I will look into it, however: for no report in such a case is to be neglected." Phillidas, who stood by, commended him, led back Archias, and got him deep in drink, still prolonging the entertainment with the hopes of the women's company at last. But when Charon returned and found the men prepared not as if they hoped for safety and success, but to die bravely and with the slaughter of their enemies, he told Pelopidas and his friends the truth, but pretended to others in the house that Archias talked to him about something else, inventing a story for the occasion. This storm was just blowing over when fortune brought another; for a messenger came with a letter from one Archias, the Hierophant at Athens, to his namesake Archias, who was his friend and guest. This did not merely contain a vague conjectural suspicion, but, as it appeared afterwards, it disclosed every particular of the design. The messenger being brought in to Archias, who was now pretty well drunk, and delivering the letter, said to him, "The writer of this desired that it might be read at once. It is on urgent business." Archias with a smile replied, "Urgent business tomorrow." And so receiving the letter, he put it under his pillow and returned to what

he had been speaking of with Phillidas; and these words of his are a proverb to this day among the Greeks.

11. Now when the opportunity seemed convenient for action, they set out in two companies. Pelopidas and Damoclides with their party went against Leontidas and Hypates, who lived near together; Charon and Melon against Archias and Philip, having put on women's apparel over their breastplates and thick garlands of fir and pine to shade their faces; and so, as soon as they came to the door, the guests clapped and gave an huzza, supposing them to be the women whom they expected. But when the conspirators had looked about the room and carefully marked all who were at the entertainment, they drew their swords; and making at Archias and Philip among the tables, they disclosed who they were. Phillidas persuaded some few of his guests to sit still, and those who rose up and endeavored to assist the polemarch, being drunk, were easily despatched. But Pelopidas and his party met with a harder task, since they attempted Leontidas, a sober and formidable man. When they came to his house, they found his door shut, he being already gone to bed. They knocked a long time before anyone would answer, but at last a servant who heard them, came out and unbarred the door. As soon as the gate gave way, they rushed in, overpowered the man, and made all haste to Leontidas' chamber. But Leontidas, guessing at the matter by the noise and running, leaped from his bed and drew his dagger, but he forgot to put out the lights and by that means to make them fall foul of one another in the dark. As it was, being easily seen by reason of the light, he received them at his chamber door and stabbed Cephisodorus, the first man who entered. On his falling, the next whom he engaged was Pelopidas; and the passage being narrow and Cephisodorus' body lying in the way, there was a fierce and dangerous conflict. At last Pelopidas prevailed; and having killed Leontidas, he and his companions went in pursuit of Hypates; and in the same manner they broke into his house. He perceived the design and fled to his neighbors; but they closely followed, caught, and killed him.

12. This done, they joined Melon and sent to hasten the exiles whom they had left in Attica; and they called upon the citizens to maintain their

liberty; and taking down the spoils from the porches and breaking open all the armorers' shops that were near, they equipped those who came to their assistance. Epaminondas and Gorgidas came in already armed with a gallant train of young men and the best of the old. Now the city was in a great excitement and confusion, a great noise and hurry, lights set up in every house, men running here and there; however, the people did not as yet gather into a body, but amazed at the proceedings and not clearly understanding the matter, they waited for the day. Therefore, the Spartan officers were thought to have been in fault for not falling on them at once, since their garrison consisted of about fifteen hundred men, and many of the citizens ran to them; but alarmed with the noise, the fires, and the confused running of the people, they kept quietly within the Cadmea. As soon as day appeared, the exiles from Attica came in armed, and there was a general assembly of the people. Epaminondas and Gorgidas brought forth Pelopidas and his party, surrounded by the priests, who held out garlands and exhorted the people to fight for their country and their gods. The assembly at their appearance rose up in a body and with shouts and acclamations received the men as their deliverers and benefactors.

13. Then Pelopidas, being chosen chief captain of Boeotia, together with Melon and Charon, proceeded at once to blockade the citadel and stormed it on all sides, being extremely desirous to expel the Lacedaemonians and to free the Cadmea before an army could come from Sparta to their relief. And he just so narrowly succeeded that they, having surrendered on terms and departed, on their way home met Cleombrotus [one of the two Spartan kings] at Megara marching towards Thebes with a considerable force. The Spartans condemned and executed Herippidas and Arcissus, two of their governors at Thebes; and Lysanoridas, the third, being severely fined, fled to Peloponnesus. This action, so closely resembling that of Thrasybulus in the courage of the actors, the danger, the encounters, and equally crowned with success, was called the sister of it by the Greeks: for we can scarcely find any other examples in which so small and weak a party of men by bold courage overcame such numerous and powerful enemies, or brought greater blessings to their country by so doing.

But the subsequent change of affairs made this action the more famous: for the war, which forever ruined the pretensions of Sparta to command and put an end to the supremacy that she then exercised alike by sea and by land, proceeded from that night, in which Pelopidas, not surprising any fort or castle or citadel, but coming as the twelfth man to a private house, loosed and broke, if we may speak truth in metaphor, the chains of the Spartan sway, which before seemed of adamant and indissoluble.

READING 38
PHILIP OF MACEDON

During the century and a half before Philip became king of Macedonia (510-360 B.C.) the Macedonians were the poorer and much weaker cousins of the Greeks to the north. After first being vassals to the Persians during the reigns of Darius I and Xerxes, they were obliged to be acquiescent to the superior naval power of the Athenians, who needed to have a compliant Macedonia in order to obtain Macedonian timber for the building and maintenance of their triremes. Then following the demise of the Athenian empire, the Chalcidic League centered about Olynthus posed a major threat to the Macedonians until the league was humbled by Sparta in 380 B.C. Moreover, during the forty years before Philip's reign (400-360 B.C.) Macedonia continued to be weak as the result of conspiracies and assassinations within the royal house and serious foreign threats posed by the neighboring Thracians and Illyrians.

A. Philip's Astonishing Accession to the Throne

When Philip succeeded his older brother Perdiccas as king, it looked as if Macedonia's previous history of weakness and turmoil would continue. But as the following passage shows, Philip within two years or so completely reversed this course of affairs. After neutralizing simultaneous threats from the Paeonians, Thracians, and Athenians, he put together a major military force and succeeded in turning the tables on the Illyrians. Indeed, as Diodorus here seems to suggest, it may have been at the very beginning of his reign that Philip carried out his revolutionary military reform that for the first time equipped the Macedonian kingdom with a formidable infantry force, the famous Macedonian phalanx of pikemen.

(Taken from Book XVI of Diodorus Siculus, translated by Gary Forsythe)

2.   ... Philip, the son of Amyntas and the father of Alexander who defeated the Persians, took over the kingdom of the Macedonians for the following reasons. When Amyntas had been defeated by the Illyrians and was forced to pay tribute to the victors, the Illyrians took Philip, the youngest of his sons, as a hostage and placed him in the care of the Thebans; and they placed the youth in the care of the father of Epaminondas and instructed him to watch over his ward carefully and to supervise his upbringing and education. Since Epaminondas had a Pythagorean philosopher as his instructor, Philip was raised with him and shared much in the Pythagorean sayings. As both students displayed both a nature and a fondness for hard work, each distinguished himself in excellence. By undergoing great contests and dangers Epaminondas, contrary to expectation, bestowed upon his country the leadership of Greece; whereas Philip, employing the same assets, did not fall short of Epaminondas' fame: for following Amyntas' death, Alexander, his oldest son, received the rule; but Ptolemy, the son of Alorus, assassinated him and took over the kingdom; and likewise, Perdiccas did away with him and was king. But when he fell in a great battle and was killed by the Illyrians, his brother Philip, having run off from being a hostage, received the kingdom that was in disarray: for more than four thousand Macedonians had been lost in the battle; and the survivors, beaten down, greatly feared the forces of the Illyrians and had no heart to fight. At the same time the Paeonians, neighbors of Macedonia, were plundering their land in contempt for the Macedonians; and the Illyrians were gathering large forces and were preparing to invade Macedonia; and a certain Pausanias of the royal lineage was plotting to enter Macedonia through the aid of the king of the Thracians. Likewise, the Athenians, hostile to Philip, were attempting to restore Argaeus to the kingdom

and had sent out their general Mantias with three thousand hoplites and a respectable naval force.

3. Due to their misfortunes in battle and the magnitude of the dangers being brought against them, the Macedonians were in the greatest state of consternation. Yet, with so many fears and dangers standing over them, Philip was not panic-stricken at the magnitude of the expected perils. But by convening the Macedonians in assemblies continuously, and by encouraging them with the power of his speech, he emboldened them to courage; and having rectified the military ranks for the better, and having equipped the men with shields suitable for war, he continuously held reviews and competitive exercises. He even devised the compactness and equipment of the phalanx, imitating the interlocking shields of the heroes at Troy; and he was the first to organize the Macedonian phalanx. He was courteous in groups, and he induced the multitudes to the greatest good cheer through his gifts and promises; and he cleverly counteracted the multitude of dangers being brought against them. Observing that the Athenians were bringing all their ambition on repossessing Amphipolis and for this reason were bringing Argaeus back to the kingdom, he voluntarily withdrew from the city and left it autonomous. Having sent an embassy to the Paeonians, he corrupted some with gifts and persuaded others with generous promises, and he agreed with them to live at peace for the present time. Similarly, he also prevented Pausanias from returning by persuading with gifts the king who intended to restore him. Mantias, the general of the Athenians, after sailing to Methone, remained there and sent Argaeus on to Aegae [capital of Macedonia] with the mercenaries. On arriving before the city, he called upon those in Aegae to welcome his restoration and to be founders of his kingship. But when no one paid attention to him, he withdrew back to Methone. Philip, appearing with soldiers and engaging in battle, killed many of the mercenaries and released the others under a truce, after they had taken refuge on a hill; and he received from them the exiles. Therefore, by winning this first battle Philip made the Macedonians bolder for the successive contests. While these things were being done, the Thasians settled the place called

Crenides, which the king later named Philippi from himself and filled with settlers. Of writers, Theopompus of Chios began his history of Philip from this point and composed 58 books, of which five are lost.

4. ... Philip sent ambassadors to Athens and persuaded the people to make peace with him by agreeing never to claim Amphipolis for himself. Released from the war with the Athenians, and learning that Agis, king of the Paeonians had died, he conjectured that it was the time to set upon the Paeonians. He therefore marched into Paeonia, overcame the barbarians in battle, and compelled the nation to submit to the Macedonians. Since the Illyrians were hostile, he was ambitious to defeat them too. He therefore immediately summoned an assembly, encouraged his soldiers for the war with his words, and marched into the land of the Illyrians with no less than ten thousand infantry and six hundred cavalry. On learning of the presence of the enemy, Bardylis, the king of the Illyrians, first sent out ambassadors for a settlement, on condition that both sides be masters of the cities that they possessed. But when Philip said that he was eager for peace, but would not agree to this one unless the Illyrians withdrew from all the Macedonian cities, the ambassadors returned, having accomplished nothing. Bardylis, trusting in his previous victories and in the bravery of the Illyrians, met the enemy with a force of ten thousand chosen infantry and up to five hundred cavalry. When the armies drew near to one another and closed in battle with much shouting, Philip, holding the right wing with the best of the Macedonians fighting with him, ordered the cavalry to ride alongside and to attack the barbarians on the flank. He himself fell upon the enemy from the front and commenced a stout battle. The Illyrians, forming themselves into a square, strongly entered the danger. At first for a long time the battle was equally poised because of the extraordinary bravery on both sides. As many were being killed and still more wounded, the danger tipped the scales this way and that, constantly swayed by the bravery of the combatants. Afterwards, as the cavalry forced themselves on the flank and rear, and as Philip with the best men struggled heroically, the multitude of the Illyrians was forced to take to flight. After a pursuit over much ground with many killed in flight, Philip halted

the Macedonians by trumpet, erected a trophy, and buried his own dead. The Illyrians sent out ambassadors, withdrew from all the Macedonian cities, and obtained peace. In this battle there were lost more than seven thousand Illyrians.

B. Demosthenes and The Battle of Chaeronea

Through two decades of constant warfare and shrewd diplomacy Philip succeeded in establishing Macedonian hegemony over the neighboring Epirotes, Illyrians, and Thracians and even over many Greek city-states to the south. As Macedonia gradually emerged as the leading power in the northern Aegean, it posed a major threat to Athens, because the latter wished to retain naval supremacy in the Aegean in order to maintain its steady importation of grain from the Black Sea for feeding Athens' large population. Consequently, it was virtually inevitable that Macedonia and Athens someday would come into conflict. Some Athenian politicians advocated peaceful coexistence with Macedonia, but others regarded Macedonian power as a threat that must be opposed. The leading figure in the latter camp was Demosthenes, Athens' greatest public speaker. He eventually succeeded in rallying other Greek states to join Athens in opposing Macedonian domination; but when the Greek coalition went down in defeat at Chaeronea in the summer of 338 B.C., Macedonian hegemony over Greece was secure and allowed Philip to formalize his supremacy by organizing the League of Corinth, whose representatives from the various Greek states soon declared war on Persia and voted Philip as their commander in chief for the enterprise.

(Taken from Plutarch's Life of Demosthenes: Plutarch's Lives, translated by Arhtur Hough Clough, published by Little, Brown and Co., Boston 1859, revised by Gary Forsythe)

17. But when things came at last to war, Philip on the one side being not able to live in peace, and the Athenians on the other side being stirred up by Demosthenes, the first action that he put them upon was the reducing of Euboea, which by the treachery of the tyrants was brought under subjection to Philip. And on Demosthenes' proposal the decree was voted, and the Athenians crossed over thither and chased the

Macedonians out of the island. The next was the relief of the Byzantines and Perinthians, whom the Macedonians at that time were attacking. Demosthenes persuaded the Athenian people to lay aside
their enmity against these cities, to forget the offenses committed by
them in the Social War [355-353 B.C.], and to send them such assistance as eventually saved and secured them. Not long after, he undertook an embassy through the states of Greece, which he solicited and
so far incensed against Philip that, a few only excepted, he brought
them all into a general league, so that, besides the forces composed
of the citizens themselves, there was an army consisting of fifteen
thousand foot and two thousand horse; and the money to pay these
strangers was levied and brought in with great cheerfulness. On this
occasion it was, says Theophrastus, on the allies requesting that their
contributions for the war might be ascertained and stated, Crobylus,
the orator, made use of the saying, "War cannot be fed at so much a
day." Now was all Greece up in arms and in great expectation what
would be the outcome. The Euboeans, the Achaeans, the Corinthians,
the Megarians, the Leucadians, and Corcyraeans, their people and
their cities, were all joined together in a league. But the hardest task
yet remained. It was left for Demosthenes to draw the Thebans into
this confederacy with the rest. Their country bordered next upon Attica. They had great forces for the war, and at that time they were ac-
counted the best soldiers of all Greece, but it was no easy matter to
make them break with Philip, who by many good offices had so lately
obliged them in the Phocian war, especially considering how the subjects of dispute and variance between the two cities were continually
renewed and exasperated by petty quarrels, arising out of the prox-
imity of their frontiers.

18. But after Philip, being now grown high and puffed up with his good
success at Amphissa, on a sudden surprised Elatea and possessed himself of Phocis, and the Athenians were in a great consternation, none
dared to venture to rise up to speak. No one knew what to say. All
were at a loss, and the whole assembly was in silence and perplexity.
In this extremity of affairs Demosthenes was the only man who appeared, his counsel to them being alliance with the Thebans. And

having in other ways encouraged the people, and, as his manner was, raised their spirits up with hopes, he with some others was sent as ambassador to Thebes. To oppose him, as Aresyas says, Philip also sent thither his envoys, Amyntas and Clearchus, two Macedonians, besides Daochus, a Thessalian, and Thrasydaeus. Now the Thebans in their consultations were well enough aware what suited best with their own interest, but everyone had before his eyes the terrors of war, and their losses in the Phocian troubles were still recent. But such was the force and power of the orator, fanning up, as Theopompus says, their courage, and firing their emulation, that casting away every thought of prudence, fear, or obligation, in a sort of divine possession they chose the path of honor, to which his words invited them. And this success, thus accomplished by an orator, was thought to be so glorious and of such consequence that Philip immediately sent heralds to treat and petition for a peace. All Greece was aroused and up in arms to help. And the commanders-in-chief, not only of Attica, but of Boeotia, applied themselves to Demosthenes and observed his directions. He managed all the assemblies of the Thebans no less than those of the Athenians. He was beloved both by the one and by the other, and he exercised the same supreme authority with both: and that not by unfair means or without just cause, as Theopompus professes, but indeed it was no more than was due to his merit.

19. But there was, it would seem, some divinely ordered fortune commissioned in the revolution of things to put a period at this time to the liberty of Greece, which opposed and thwarted all their actions and by many signs foretold what should happen. Such were the sad predictions uttered by the Pythian priestess, and this old oracle cited out of the Sibyl's verses: "The battle on Thermodon that shall be safe at a distance I desire to see, far, like an eagle, watching in the air. Conquered shall weep, and conqueror perish there." This Thermodon, they say, is a little rivulet here in our country in Chaeronea, running into the Cephisus. But we know of none that is so called at the present time, and we can only conjecture that the streamlet which is now called Haemon [Blood] and runs by the Temple of Herakles, where the Grecians were encamped, might perhaps in those days have been

called Thermodon, and after the fight, being filled with blood and dead bodies, upon this occasion, as we guess, might have changed its old name for that which it now bears. Yet, Duris says that this Thermodon was no river, but that some of the soldiers, as they were pitching their tents and digging trenches about them, found a small stone statue, which by the inscription appeared to be the figure of Thermodon, carrying a wounded Amazon in his arms; and that there was another oracle current about it, as follows: "The battle on Thermodon that shall be, fail not, black raven, to attend and see. The flesh of men shall there abound for thee."

20. In fine, it is not easy to determine what is the truth. But of Demosthenes it is said that he had such great confidence in the Grecian forces and was so excited by the sight of the courage and resolution of so many brave men ready to engage the enemy that he would by no means endure that they should give any heed to oracles or hearken to prophecies, but he gave out that he suspected even the prophetess herself, as if she had been tampered with to speak in favor of Philip. The Thebans he put in mind of Epaminondas, the Athenians of Pericles, who always took their own measures and governed their actions by reason, looking upon things of this kind as mere pretexts for cowardice. Thus far, therefore, Demosthenes acquitted himself like a brave man. But in the fight he did nothing honorable, nor was his performance answerable to his speeches: for he fled, deserting his place disgracefully, and throwing away his arms, not ashamed, as Pytheas observed, to belie the inscription written on his shield in letters of gold, "With good fortune." In the meantime, Philip in the first moment of victory was so transported with joy that he grew extravagant; and going out after he had drunk largely to visit the dead bodies, he chanted the first words of the decree that had been passed on the motion of Demosthenes, "The motion of Demosthenes, Demosthenes' son," dividing it metrically into feet and marking the beats. But when he came to himself and had well considered the danger under which he had lately been, he could not forbear from shuddering at the wonderful ability and power of an orator who had made him hazard his life and empire on the issue of

a few brief hours. The fame of it also reached even to the court of Persia; and the king sent letters to his lieutenants, commanding them to supply Demosthenes with money and to pay every attention to him, as the only man of all the Grecians who was able to keep Philip occupied and to find employment for his forces near home in the troubles of Greece. This afterwards came to the knowledge of Alexander by certain letters of Demosthenes, which he found at Sardis, and by other papers of the Persian officers, stating the large sums which had been given him.

21. At this time, however, upon the ill-success which now happened to the Grecians, those of the contrary faction in the commonwealth fell foul upon Demosthenes and took the opportunity to frame several informations and indictments against him. But the people not only acquitted him of these accusations, but they continued towards him their former respect and even invited him as a man who meant well to take a part in public affairs insomuch that when the bones of those who had been slain at Chaeronea were brought home to be solemnly interred, Demosthenes was the man whom they chose to make the funeral oration. They did not show under the misfortunes that had befallen them a base or ignoble mind, as Theopompus writes in his exaggerated style, but on the contrary, by the honor and respect paid to their counsellor they made it appear that they were in no way dissatisfied with the counsels that he had given them. The speech, therefore, was spoken by Demosthenes. But the subsequent decrees he would not allow to be passed in his own name, but he made use of those of his friends, one after another, looking upon his own as unfortunate and inauspicious, till at length he took courage again after the death of Philip, who did not long outlive his victory at Chaeronea. And this, it seems, was that which was foretold in the last verse of the oracle: "Conquered shall weep, and conqueror perish there."

C. Philip's Polygamy and Last Disastrous Marriage

The following brief passage illustrates how Philip used marriages with women from conquered peoples to cement his growing power. But after he had finally succeeded in establishing Macedonian hegemony, he decided for the first time to marry a Macedonian woman, and this marriage introduced major turmoil into the Macedonian court and was soon followed by Philip's assassination.

(Taken from Athenaeus, Deipnosophistai XIII. 557B-E, translated by Gary Forsythe)

Philip the Macedonian did not bring his wives to his wars, as did Darius, the one defeated by Alexander, who, when waging war for everything, took around with him 360 concubines, as Dicaearchus records in the third book of his Life of Greece. But Philip always married in wartime. Thus, in 22 years during which he was king, as Satyrus says in his biography of him, he married Audata of Illyria and had by her a daughter, Cynna. He also married Phila, sister of Derdas and Machatas; and wishing to claim for himself the nation of the Thessalians, he had children by two Thessalian women. One was Nicesipolis of Pherae, who bore to him Thessalonice; and the other was Philinna of Larissa, by whom he begot Arrhidaeus. He also took possession of the kingdom of the Molossians by marrying Olympias, by whom he had Alexander and Cleopatra. And when he took Thrace, there came to him Cothelas, the king of the Thracians, bringing his daughter Meda and many gifts. Having married her, he brought her also in alongside Olympias. In addition to all of them, he married and fell in love with Cleopatra, the sister of Hippostratus and the niece of Attalus; and by bringing her in alongside of Olympias he threw his entire life into confusion: for straightway at the wedding itself Attalus said, "Now indeed legitimate and not bastard kings shall be born." On hearing this, Alexander threw at Attalus the goblet that he held in his hands, and the other threw at him his drinking cup. After that Olympias fled to the Molossians, and Alexander to the Illyrians. Cleopatra bore to Philip a daughter, the one called Europa.

D. Philip's Assassination
The following passage is our most detailed account of Philip's assassination. Although Diodorus portrays the assassin Pausanias as having acted alone, other ancient sources regarded him as only the frontman of a larger conspiracy, and they variously speculated that the conspiracy was headed by Olympias, Alexander, Demosthenes, or the Persians. Thus, in the modern scholarship on ancient Greece Philip's assassination has become a much discussed "who done it."

(Taken from Book XVI of Diodorus Siculus, translated by Gary Forsythe)

91.   ... In this year King Philip, elected hegemon by the Greeks and initiating the war against the Persians, sent ahead into Asia Attalus and Parmenion with part of the forces and with orders to free the Greek states, while he himself, being eager to conduct the war with the approval of the gods, asked the Pythia if he would overcome the king of the Persians; and she gave him the following oracle: "Wreathed is the bull; the end is at hand, and there is the one to do the sacrificing." Now then Philip, though the oracle was devious, received the saying according to his advantage: that the sacred prophecy was foretelling that the Persian would be sacrificed in a fashion. But in doing so he did not grasp its truth, but it was signaling the opposite, that at a festival and sacrifices of the gods Philip would be slaughtered like a garlanded bull. Yet, thinking that the gods were allied to him, he was greatly cheered that Asia would be won by the Macedonians. He therefore ordered splendid sacrifices to the gods and finalized the marriage of his daughter Cleopatra, born of Olympias. He had matched her with Alexander, king of Epirus and Olympias' full brother. Besides honoring the gods, he wished as many Greeks as possible to participate in the celebration; and he prepared splendid musical contests and illustrious banquets for his friends and guests. Accordingly, he summoned from all Greece his own personal guest-friends and commanded his friends to receive from abroad as many notables as possible: for he was extremely ambitious to be kind toward the Greeks and to repay with appropriate entertainments the honors granted him for the whole leadership.

92.   At last, many poured in from everywhere to the festival, and the games and the marriage were performed at Aegae in Macedonia. Not only did individual distinguished persons crown him with gold crowns, but also so did many of the noteworthy states, including Athens; and when this crowning was announced through a herald, the last thing said was this: if anyone plotted against Philip and fled to Athens, he would be handed over. Through this spontaneous utterance, as if by

divine foresight, the divinity hinted at the plot immediately forth-coming for Philip. Following these, there were even other utterances that seemed divinely inspired and making clear the destruction of the king. At the royal banquet Philip ordered the tragic actor Neoptole-mus, excelling in his great voice and fame, to present well-received lines and especially those relating to the expedition against the Per-sians. The artist, judging that the lines would be taken to refer to Philip's crossing, and wishing to chastise the prosperity of the Persian king, though great and well known, so that he might someday fall into the opposite by fortune, began to recite the following lines: "You pon-der higher than the sky and fields of great plains. You ponder homes surpassing homes, guiding your life thoughtlessly afar. But the one creeping in shadow ensnares the quick-footed, and suddenly, going unseen, takes away our distant hopes: Hades, the one of many woes for mortals." He continued these things in their order, all bearing on the same thought. Philip was pleased with the message and was fully and completely borne away with the thought of the Persian king's overthrow; and at the same time he recalled the Pythian oracle having a thought similar to what the tragic actor had said. Finally, the ban-quet ended. Since the contests had their beginning on the following day, the multitude, although it was still night, rushed into the theater; and at daylight, when the parade began, with the other splendid arrangements there was a parade of statues of the twelve gods, wrought exceedingly with workmanship and amazingly ornamented with the brilliance of wealth. With these there was paraded a thir-teenth of Philip himself, a godlike statue, the king displaying himself as enthroned with the twelve gods.

93. The theater was full, and Philip himself went along, clad in a white garment and having ordered his spear-bearers to follow a long way off from himself: for he intended to show everyone that since he was preserved by the general goodwill of the Greeks, he had no need of the protection of his spear-bearers. But though the pomp surrounding him was so great, and while everyone was praising and blessing the man, there appeared against the king a deadly attack, totally unex-pected and contrary to expectation. In order that the story concerning

these things be clear, we shall set forth the reasons for the attack. Pausanias was a Macedonian from Orestis and was a bodyguard of the king; and because of his handsomeness he became Philip's friend. This man, on seeing another Pausanias (by the same name as himself) being loved by the king, used most abusive words against him, saying that he was a man-woman, and that he readily welcomed lovers from whoever wished. Though not enduring the insult of the abuse, he kept silent for the present; but after confiding to a certain Attalus among his friends concerning what he intended to do, he voluntarily and unexpectedly ended his own life: for a few days later, while Philip was contending with Pleurias, king of the Illyrians, he stood in front of the king, received on his own body all the blows being brought against him, and thus died. When the deed had been noised abroad, Attalus, being one of those at court and of those very powerful with the king, invited Pausanias to dinner; and after filling him with much unmixed wine, he handed his body over to his muleteers for outrage and drunken violence. After recovering from his drunkenness and being very aggrieved at the outrage to his body, he accused Attalus before the king. Philip was incensed at the lawlessness of the deed; but because of his relationship with Attalus and his usefulness for the time being, he was unwilling to punish him: for Attalus was a nephew of the Cleopatra married by the king and had been hand-picked as a general for the force sent ahead into Asia; and he was brave in warlike contests. Accordingly, wishing to soothe Pausanias' justified anger for his suffering, the king apportioned him noteworthy gifts and promoted him honorably to the bodyguard.

94. Pausanias, nursing his anger relentlessly, was eager to take revenge not only from the perpetrator, but from the one who did not avenge him; and the sophist Hermocrates especially encouraged this decision: for while Pausanias studied with him and inquired during his instruction how one might become most illustrious, the sophist replied, if he eliminated the one who had done the greatest things, because the one who had eliminated him would be encompassed by the remembrance surrounding him. He related the saying to his own anger and made no change of his mind due to his feeling; and he organized the

plot for the proposed contests themselves in the following manner. After stationing horses at the gates, he came to the entrances into the theater with a concealed Celtic dagger. After Philip had urged the friends following alongside him to enter the theater ahead of him, and his spear-bearers were at a distance, he saw that the king was isolated; and he ran to him, delivered blows through his ribs, and stretched the king out dead, while he himself ran toward the gates and the horses prepared for his escape. Immediately, some of the bodyguard ran to the king's body, and others poured out against the perpetrator of the murder. Among the latter were Leonnatus, Perdiccas, and Attalus. By being ahead of the pursuit, Pausanias would have mounted his horse unapprehended, except he fell when his boot became entangled in a vine. Accordingly, those with Perdiccas overtook him as he was standing up from the ground, and they killed him with javelins.

95. Philip therefore received this sort of destruction to his life, having become the greatest of the kings in Europe in his time, and through the magnitude of his rule he numbered himself as enthroned with the twelve gods. He ruled 24 years. This king seems to have received the smallest assets for the monarchy, but came to possess the greatest of monarchies among the Greeks, and he increased his leadership not so much through courage in arms as through negotiation [lit., the interchange in words] and geniality. They say that Philip himself placed more value on his understanding as a general and on his successes through negotiation rather than on his bravery in battles, because all those who served in the army shared in the successes in the contests, but of those successes obtained through diplomacy he alone took the credit.

READING 39
ALEXANDER THE GREAT

When Alexander became king of Macedonia at the age of twenty, he inherited from his father the finest and most experienced military machine at that time in the Mediterranean area and western Asia. As a result, some modern scholars have regarded his conquest of the Persian Empire as virtually inevitable and as a phenomenon to which Alexander himself contributed rather little militarily, so that Philip, rather than Alexander, should be given the lion's share of the glory. On the contrary, Alexander's earliest military exploits suggest that for him there was no such thing as a learning curve in military matters. Having grown up during his father's reign and rise to power, Alexander is likely to have acquired an incomparable military education; and the combination of his own military genius and the extraordinary ability of his army made the two unbeatable.

A. The Smartness and Effectiveness of the Macedonian Army
Following Philip's unexpected death by assassination, the young Alexander had to spend almost two years in securing both his position on the Macedonian throne and the mastery over the various areas that his father had conquered. The following passage describes one episode in his first campaign as Macedonian king and displays his superb talents as a commander in the field.

> (Taken from Book I of The Anabasis of Alexander by Arrian of Nicomedia, translated by Edward James Cinnock, published by Hodder and Stoughton, London 1884, revised by Gary Forsythe)

5. He [Alexander] then advanced into the land of the Agrianians and Paeonians, where messengers reached him, who reported that Cleitus, son of Bardylis, had revolted, and that Glaucias, king of the Taulantians, had gone over to him. They also reported that the Autariatians intended to attack him on his way. He accordingly resolved to commence his march without delay. But Langarus, king of the Agrianians, who in the lifetime of Philip had been an open and avowed friend of Alexander, and had gone on an embassy to him in his private capacity, at that time also came to him with the finest and best armed of the shield-bearing troops, which he kept as a bodyguard. When this man heard that Alexander was inquiring who the Autariatians were, and what was the number of their men, he said that he need take no account of them, since they were the least warlike of the tribes of that district; and that he would himself make an inroad into their land, so that they might have too much occupation about their own affairs to attack others. Accordingly, at Alexander's order he made an attack upon them; and not only did he attack them, but he swept their land clean of captives and booty. Thus the Autariatians were indeed occupied with their own affairs. Langarus was rewarded by Alexander with the greatest honors and received from him the gifts which were considered most valuable in the eyes of the king of the Macedonians. Alexander also promised to give him his sister Cyna in marriage when he arrived at Pella. But Langarus fell ill and died on his return home. After this, Alexander marched along the river Erigon and proceeded to the city of Pelium; for Cleitus had seized this city, since it was the strongest in the country. When Alexander arrived at this place and had encamped near the river Eordaicus, he resolved to make an assault upon the wall on the next day. But Cleitus held the mountains which encircled the city and commanded it from their height; moreover, they were covered with dense thickets. His intention was to fall upon the Macedonians from all sides, if they assaulted the city. But Glaucias, king of the Taulantians, had not yet joined him. Alexander, however, led his forces towards the city; and the enemy, after sacrificing three boys, an equal number of girls, and three black rams, sallied forth for the purpose of receiving the Macedonians in a

hand-to-hand conflict. But as soon as they came to close quarters, they left the positions which they had occupied, strong as they were, in such haste that even their sacrificial victims were captured still lying on the ground. On this day he shut them up in the city; and encamping near the wall, he resolved to intercept them by a circumvallation; but on the next day Glaucias, king of the Taulantians, arrived with a great force. Then, indeed, Alexander gave up the hope of capturing the city with his present force, since many warlike troops had fled for refuge into it, and Glaucias with his large army would be likely to follow him up closely if he assailed the wall. But he sent Philotas on a foraging expedition with the beasts of burden from the camp and a sufficient body of cavalry to serve as a guard. When Glaucias heard of the expedition of Philotas, he marched out to meet him and seized the mountains which surrounded the plain, from which Philotas intended to procure forage. As soon as Alexander was informed that his cavalry and beasts of burden would be in danger if night overtook them, taking the shield-bearing troops, the archers, the Agrianians, and about four hundred cavalry, he went with all speed to their aid. The rest of the army he left behind near the city in order to prevent the citizens from hastening forth to form a junction with Glaucias (as they would have done), if all the Macedonian army had withdrawn. Directly, when Glaucias perceived that Alexander was advancing, he evacuated the mountains; and Philotas and his forces returned to the camp in safety. But Cleitus and Glaucias still imagined that they had caught Alexander in a disadvantageous position; for they were occupying the mountains, which commanded the plain by their height, with a large body of cavalry, javelin-throwers, and slingers, besides a considerable number of heavy-armed infantry. Moreover, the men who had been beleaguered in the city were expected to pursue the Macedonians closely if they made a retreat. The ground also through which Alexander had to march was evidently narrow and covered with wood; on one side it was hemmed in by a river, and on the other there was a very lofty and craggy mountain, so that there would not be room for the army to pass, even if only four shield-bearers marched abreast.

6. Then Alexander drew up his army in such a way that the depth of the phalanx was 120 men; and stationing 200 cavalry on each wing, he ordered them to preserve silence in order to receive the word of command quickly. Accordingly, he gave the signal to the heavy-armed infantry in the first place to hold their spears erect, and then to couch them at the concerted sign; at one time to incline their spears to the right, closely locked together, and at another time towards the left. He then set the phalanx itself into quick motion forward and marched it towards the wings, now to the right, and then to the left. After thus arranging and rearranging his army many times very rapidly, he at last formed his phalanx into a sort of wedge and led it towards the left against the enemy, who had long been in a state of amazement at seeing both the order and the rapidity of his evolutions. Consequently, they did not sustain Alexander's attack, but quitted the first ridges of the mountain. Upon this, Alexander ordered the Macedonians to raise the battle cry and to make a clatter with their spears upon their shields; and the Taulantians, being still more alarmed at the noise, led their army back to the city with all speed. Since Alexander saw only a few of the enemy still occupying a ridge, along which lay his route, he ordered his bodyguards and personal companions to take their shields, mount their horses, and to ride to the hill; and when they reached it, if those who had occupied the position awaited them, he said that half of them were to leap from their horses and to fight as foot-soldiers, being mingled with the cavalry. But when the enemy saw Alexander's advance, they quitted the hill and retreated to the mountains in both directions. Then Alexander with his companions seized the hill and sent for the Agrianians and archers, who numbered 2,000. He also ordered the shield-bearing guards to cross the river, and after them the regiments of Macedonian infantry, with instructions that, as soon as they had succeeded in crossing, they should draw out in rank towards the left, so that the phalanx of men crossing might appear compact at once. He himself in the vanguard was all the time observing from the ridge the enemy's advance. They, seeing the force crossing the river, marched down the mountains to meet them with the purpose of attacking Alexander's rear in its retreat. But as they

were just drawing near, Alexander rushed forth with his own division, and the phalanx raised the battle-cry, as if about to advance through the river. When the enemy saw all the Macedonians marching against them, they turned and fled. Upon this, Alexander led the Agrianians and archers at full speed towards the river and succeeded in being himself the first man to cross it. But when he saw the enemy pressing upon the men in the rear, he stationed his engines of war upon the bank and ordered the engineers to shoot from them as far forward as possible all sorts of projectiles which are usually shot from military engines. He directed the archers, who had also entered the water, to shoot their arrows from the middle of the river. But Glaucias did not dare to advance within range of the missiles, so that the Macedonians passed over in such safety that not one of them lost his life in the retreat. Three days after this, Alexander discovered that Cleitus and Glaucias lay carelessly encamped; that neither were their sentinels on guard in military order, nor had they protected themselves with a rampart or ditch, as if they imagined that he had withdrawn through fear; and that they had extended their line to a disadvantageous length. He therefore crossed the river again secretly at the approach of night, leading with him the shield-bearing guards, the Agrianians, the archers, and the brigades of Perdiccas and Coenus, after having given orders for the rest of the army to follow. As soon as he saw a favorable opportunity for the attack, without waiting for all to be present, he despatched the archers and Agrianians against the foe. These, being arranged in phalanx, fell unawares with the most furious charge upon their flank, where they were likely to come into conflict with their weakest point, and he slew some of them still in their beds, others being easily caught in their flight. Accordingly, many were there captured and killed, as were many also in the disorderly and panic-stricken retreat which ensued. Not a few, moreover, were taken prisoners. Alexander kept up the pursuit as far as the Taulantian mountains; and as many of them as escaped, preserved their lives by throwing away their arms. Cleitus first fled for refuge into the city, which, however, he set on fire, and withdrew to Glaucias in the land of the Taulantians.

B. Alexander's Visit to Siwah

When Alexander landed in Anatolia to begin his campaign against the Persians, he first visited the site of Troy and paid homage to Achilles, the greatest Greek warrior of the Trojan War, and from whom Alexander traced his descent through his mother Olympias and the royal house of the Molossians of Epirus. In addition, throughout his youth Alexander had been an avid reader of the Homeric poems. It seems likely that Alexander's string of unbroken victories soon began to transform his notion of heroic heritage into heroic destiny. Moreover, although he had begun his Asian campaign as king of Macedonia and leader of the Greeks in a war of vengeance against the detested Persians, his encounter with other notions of kingship (especially Egyptian and Persian) gradually led him to redefine his position as monarch; and this redefinition eventually created considerable friction between himself and his Macedonians, because many of the latter insisted upon him being a purely Macedonian king and with them to lord it over Asia.

The earliest major incident that caused Alexander to begin rethinking his self-image seems to have been his visit to the oracle of Zeus Ammon at Siwah, located in one of the desert oases west of the Nile. Ancient sources record various things about this visit, what Alexander asked the oracle, and what responses he received. Many of these claims are obvious later fictions, but the following passage from the Greek geographer Strabo is based upon the contemporary account of Callisthenes, a nephew of Aristotle, who accompanied Alexander in order to serve as the official historian of the campaign.

(Taken from Volume III of The Geography of Strabo, translated by H. C. Hamilton and W. Falconer, published in three volumes by H. G. Bohn of London 1854-1857)

Book XVII.1.43: Hence the oracle of Ammon, which was formerly held in great esteem, is now nearly deserted. This appears chiefly from the historians who have recorded the actions of Alexander, adding, indeed, much that has the appearance of flattery, but yet relating what is worthy of credit. Callisthenes, for instance, says that Alexander was ambitious of the glory of visiting the oracle, because he knew that Perseus and Herakles had before performed the journey thither. He set out from Paraetonium, although the south winds were blowing; and he succeeded in his undertaking by vigor and perseverance. When out of his way on the road, he escaped being overwhelmed in a sandstorm by a fall of rain, and by the guidance of two crows, which directed his course. These things are stated by way of flattery, as also what follows: that the priest permitted the king alone to pass into the temple in his usual dress, whereas the others changed theirs; that all heard the oracles on the outside of the temple, except Alexander, who was in the interior of the building; that the answers were not given, as at Delphi and at Branchidae in words, but chiefly by nods and signs, as in Homer [quoting Book I of The Iliad]; "the son of Kronos nodded with his sable brows," the prophet imitating Zeus. This, however, the man told the king, in express terms, that he was the son of Zeus. Callisthenes adds (after the exaggerating style of tragedy) that when Apollo had deserted the oracle among the Branchidae, on the temple being plundered by the Branchidae (who espoused the party of the Persians in the time of Xerxes), and the spring had failed, it then reappeared (on the arrival of Alexander); that the ambassadors also of the Milesians carried back to Memphis numerous answers of the oracle respecting the descent of Alexander from Zeus, as well as the future victory which he should obtain at Arbela [i.e., Gaugamela], the death of Darius, and the political changes at Sparta. He says also that the Erythraean Athenais, who resembled the ancient Erythraean Sibyl, had declared the high descent of Alexander. Such are the accounts of historians.

C. Alexander before the Battle of Gaugamela

The following brief passage is also derived from Callisthenes and suggests that already by the time of the battle of Gaugamela in the autumn of 331 B.C., Alexander was declaring himself to be the son of Zeus.

> (Taken from Plutarch's Life of Alexander: Plutarch's Lives, translated by Arhtur Hough Clough, published by Little, Brown and Co., Boston 1859, revised by Gary Forsythe)

33. He made the longest address that day to the Thessalians and other Greeks, who answered him with loud shouts, desiring him to lead them on against the barbarians, upon which he shifted his lance into his left hand, and with his right lifted up towards heaven he besought

the gods, as Callisthenes tells us, that if he was of a truth the son of Zeus, they would be pleased to assist and strengthen the Grecians.

D. The Murder of Cleitus

During the summer of 328 B.C., while Alexander was engaged in his conquest of Sogdiana, located on the northeastern edge of the Persian Empire, the following event occurred at the satrapal capital of Maracanda (modern Samarkand in Uzbekistan). The quarrel between Alexander and Cleitus that culminated in the murder of the latter by the former illustrates the growing tension between Alexander and some of his Macedonians, who disapproved of his claims of divine sonship and his adoption of Persian royal dress.

(Taken from Plutarch's Life of Alexander: Plutarch's Lives, translated by Arhtur Hough Clough, published by Little, Brown and Co., Boston 1859, revised by Gary Forsythe)

50. Not long after this happened, there occurred the deplorable end of Cleitus, which, to those who barely hear the matter, may seem more inhuman than that of Philotas; but if we consider the story with its circumstance of time and weigh the cause, we shall find it to have occurred rather through a sort of mischance of the king's, whose anger and over-drinking offered an occasion to the evil genius of Cleitus. The king had a present of Grecian fruit brought him from the seacoast, which was so fresh and beautiful that he was surprised at it and called Cleitus to him to see it and to give him a share of it. Cleitus was then sacrificing, but he immediately left off and came, followed by three sheep, on whom the drink-offering had been already poured preparatory to sacrificing them. Alexander, being informed of this, told his diviners, Aristander and Cleomantis the Lacedaemonian; and he asked them what it meant; on whose assuring him it was an ill omen, he commanded them in all haste to offer sacrifices for Cleitus' safety, forasmuch as three days before he himself had seen a strange vision in his sleep: of Cleitus all in mourning, sitting by Parmenion's sons who were dead. Cleitus, however, stayed not to finish his devotions, but he came straight to supper with the king, who had sacrificed

to Castor and Pollux. And when they had drunk pretty hard, some of the company fell to singing the verses of one Pranichus or, as others say, of Pierion, which were made upon those captains who had been lately worsted by the barbarians, on purpose to disgrace and turn them to ridicule. This gave offense to the older men who were there, and they upbraided both the author and the singer of the verses, though Alexander and the younger men about him were much amused to hear them and encouraged them to go on, till at last Cleitus, who had drunk too much and was besides of a forward and willful temper, was so nettled that he could hold no longer, saying that it was not well done to expose the Macedonians before the barbarians and their enemies, since though it was their misfortune to be overcome, yet they were much better men than those who laughed at them. And when Alexander remarked that Cleitus was pleading his own cause, giving cowardice the name of misfortune, Cleitus started up: "This cowardice, as you are pleased to term it," said he to him, "saved the life of a son of the gods, when in flight from Spithridates' sword [at the battle of the Granicus]; it is by the expense of Macedonian blood and by these wounds that you are now raised to such a height as to be able to disown your father Philip and to call yourself the son of Ammon."

51. "Thou base fellow," said Alexander, who was now thoroughly exasperated, "dost thou think to utter these things everywhere of me, and stir up the Macedonians to sedition, and not be punished for it?" "We are sufficiently punished already," answered Cleitus, "if this be the recompense of our toils, and we must esteem theirs a happy lot who have not lived to see their countrymen scourged with Median rods and forced to sue to the Persians to have access to their king." While he talked thus at random, and those near Alexander got up from their seats and began to revile him in turn, the elder men did what they could to compose the disorder. Alexander, in the meantime, turning about to Xenodochus, the Cardian, and to Artemius, the Colophonian, asked them if they were not of opinion that the Greeks in comparison with the Macedonians behaved themselves like so many demigods among wild beasts. But Cleitus for all this would not give over, desiring Alexander to speak out if he had anything more to say,

or else why did he invite men who were freeborn and accustomed to speak their minds openly without restraint to sup with him. He had better live and converse with barbarians and slaves who would not scruple to bow the knee to his Persian girdle and his white tunic. These words so provoked Alexander that not able to suppress his anger any longer, he threw one of the apples that lay upon the table at him and hit him, and then he looked about for his sword. But Aristophanes, one of his bodyguards, had hid that out of the way; and others came about him and besought him, but in vain: for, breaking from them, he called out aloud to his guards in the Macedonian language, which was a certain sign of some great disturbance in him; and he commanded a trumpeter to sound, giving him a blow with his clenched fist for not instantly obeying him, though afterwards the same man was commended for disobeying an order which would have put the whole army into tumult and confusion. Cleitus, still refusing to yield, was with much trouble forced by his friends out of the room. But he came in again immediately at another door, very irreverently and confidently singing the verses out of Euripides' Andromache "In Greece, alas! how ill things ordered are!" Upon this, at last, Alexander, snatching a spear from one of the soldiers, met Cleitus as he was coming forward and was pushing aside the curtain that hung before the door; and he ran him through the body. He fell at once with a cry and a groan. Thereat the king's anger immediately vanishing, he came perfectly to himself; and when he saw his friends about him all in a profound silence, he pulled the spear out of the dead body and would have thrust it into his own throat, if the guards had not held his hands and by main force carried him away into his chamber.

52. There all that night and the next day he wept bitterly, till being quite spent with lamenting and exclaiming, he lay as it were speechless, only fetching deep sighs. His friends, apprehending some harm from his silence, broke into the room, but he took no notice of what any of them said, till Aristander putting him in mind of the vision that he had seen concerning Cleitus, and of the prodigy that followed, as if all had come to pass by an unavoidable fatality, he then seemed to moderate his grief. They now brought to him Callisthenes and

Anaxarchus of Abdera, the former being the philosopher and near friend of Aristotle. Callisthenes used moral language and gentle and soothing means, hoping to find access for words of reason and to get a hold upon the passion. But Anaxarchus, who had always taken a course of his own in philosophy and had a name for despising and slighting his contemporaries, as soon as he came in, cried aloud, "Is this the Alexander whom the whole world looks to, lying here weeping like a slave for fear of the censure and reproach of men, to whom he himself ought to be a law and measure of equity, if he would use the right that his conquests have given him as supreme lord and governor of all, and not be the victim of a vain and idle opinion? Do not you know," said he, "that Zeus is represented to have Justice and Law at each of his hands to signify that all the actions of a conqueror are lawful and just?" With these and the like speeches Anaxarchus indeed allayed the king's grief, but withal he corrupted his character, rendering him more audacious and lawless than he had been. Nor did he fail by these means to insinuate himself into his favor and to make Callisthenes' company, which was not very acceptable at all times because of his austerity, more uneasy and disagreeable to him.

E. Mutiny and Reconciliation

During the summer of 324, one year or less before his death, and after he and his army had returned from the Indus Valley to the heartland of the Persian Empire, Alexander decided to discharge and send back to Macedonia many of the veterans who had accompanied him on his extraordinary campaign and had survived all its vicissitudes. At the meeting for announcing this decision many Macedonians vociferously expressed their unhappiness with this decision, as if they were now being cast aside when their services were no longer needed; and they further expressed their resentment at Alexander's adoption of persian court ceremonial and the inclusion of Persians into the army and among his circle of trusted nobles. Following this tumultuous meeting, Alexander staged a formal reconciliation by presiding over a massive banquet at Opis on the Tigris, in which he brought together both Macedonians and Persians, and he prayed for their concord and their sharing the rule of his new empire.

(Taken from Book VII of The Anabasis of Alexander by Arrian of Nicomedia, translated by Edward James Cinnock,
published by Hodder and Stoughton, London 1884, revised
by Gary Forsythe)

8. When he arrived at Opis, he collected the Macedonians and announced that he intended to discharge from the army those who were
useless for military service either from age or from being maimed in
the limbs; and he said that he would send them back to their own
abodes. He also promised to give those who went back as much as
would make them special objects of envy to those at home and would
arouse in the other Macedonians the wish to share similar dangers
and labors. Alexander said this, no doubt, for the purpose of pleasing
the Macedonians; but on the contrary, they were, not without reason,
offended by the speech which he delivered, thinking that now they
were despised by him and deemed to be quite useless for military service. Indeed, throughout the whole of this expedition they had been
offended at many other things: for his adoption of the Persian dress,
thereby exhibiting his contempt for their opinion, caused them grief,
as did also his equipping the foreign soldiers called Epigonoi in the
Macedonian style, and the mixing of the alien horsemen among the
ranks of the Companions. They therefore could not remain silent and
control themselves, but urged him to dismiss all of them from his
army; and they advised him to prosecute the war in company with his
father, deriding Ammon by this remark. When Alexander heard this
(for at that time he was more hasty in temper than heretofore, and no
longer, as of old, indulgent to the Macedonians from having a retinue
of foreign attendants), leaping down from the platform with his officers around him, he ordered the most conspicuous of the men who
had tried to stir up the multitude to sedition to be arrested. He himself
pointed out with his hand to the shield-bearing guards those whom
they were to arrest, to the number of thirteen; and he ordered these
to be led away to execution. When the rest, stricken with terror, became silent, he mounted the platform and spoke as follows....

[In this speech, as recorded by Arrian, Alexander played down his divine sonship from Zeus Ammon and instead stressed the accomplishments of his father Philip along with what Alexander and his fellow Macedonians had accomplished in their years of campaigning.]

11. Having thus spoken, he leaped down quickly from the platform and entered the palace, where he paid no attention to the decoration of his person, nor was any of his Companions admitted to see him. Not even on the morrow was anyone of them admitted to an audience; but on the third day he summoned the select Persians within, and among them he distributed the commands of the brigades and made the rule that only those whom he had proclaimed his kinsmen, should have the honor of greeting him with a kiss. But the Macedonians who heard the speech were thoroughly astonished at the moment and remained there in silence near the platform; nor when he retired did any of them accompany the king, except his personal Companions and the confidential body-guards. Though they remained, most of them had nothing to do or say; and yet they were unwilling to retire. But when the news was reported to them about the Persians and Medes, that the military commands were being given to Persians, that the foreign soldiers were being selected and divided into companies, that a Persian foot-guard, Persian foot Companions, a Persian regiment of men with silver shields, as well as the cavalry Companions, and another royal regiment of cavalry distinct from these, were being called by Macedonian names, they were no longer able to restrain themselves; but running in a body to the palace, they cast their weapons there in front of the gates as a sign of supplication to the king. Standing in front of the gates, they shouted, beseeching to be allowed to enter, and saying that they were willing to surrender the men who had been the instigators of the disturbance on that occasion, and those who had begun the clamor. They also declared that they would not retire from the gates either day or night, unless Alexander would take some pity upon them. When he was informed of this, he came out without delay; and seeing them lying on the ground in humble guise, and

hearing most of them lamenting with loud voice, tears began to flow also from his own eyes. He made an effort to say something to them, but they continued their importunate entreaties. At length one of them, Callines by name, a man conspicuous both for his age and because he was captain of the Companion cavalry, spoke as follows: "O king, what grieves the Macedonians is that thou hast already made some of the Persians kinsmen to thyself, and that Persians are called Alexander's kinsmen and have the honor of greeting thee with a kiss; whereas none of the Macedonians have as yet enjoyed this honor." Then Alexander, interrupting him, said: "But all of you without exception I consider my kinsmen, and so from this time I shall call you." When he had said this, Callines advanced and greeted him with a kiss, and so did all those who wished to greet him. Then they took up their weapons and returned to the camp, shouting and singing a song of thanksgiving to Apollo. After this Alexander offered sacrifice to the gods to whom it was his custom to sacrifice, and he gave a public banquet, over which he himself presided, with the Macedonians sitting around him; and next to them the Persians; after whom came the men of the other nations, honored for their personal rank or for some meritorious action. The king and his guests drew wine from the same bowl and poured out the same libations, both the Greek prophets and the Magi commencing the ceremony. He prayed for other blessings, and especially that harmony and sharing of rule might exist between the Macedonians and Persians. The common account is that those who took part in this banquet were 9,000 in number, that all of them poured out one libation, and after it sang a song of thanksgiving to Apollo.

12. Then those of the Macedonians who were unfit for service on account of age or any other misfortune went back of their own accord, to the number of about 10,000. To these Alexander gave the pay not only for the time which had already elapsed, but also for that which they would spend in returning home. He also gave to each man a talent in addition to his pay. If any of them had children by Asiatic wives, he ordered them to leave them behind with him, lest they should introduce into Macedonia a cause of discord, taking with them children by

foreign women who were of a different race from the children whom they had left behind at home born of Macedonian mothers. He promised to take care that they should be brought up as Macedonians, educating them not only in general matters, but also in the art of war. He also undertook to lead them into Macedonia when they arrived at manhood, and to hand them over to their fathers. These uncertain and obscure promises were made to them as they were departing; and he thought that he was giving a most indubitable proof of the friendship and affection that he had for them by sending with them, as their guardian and the leader of the expedition, Craterus, the man most faithful to him, and whom he valued equally with himself. Then, having saluted them all, he with tears dismissed them likewise weeping from his presence. He ordered Craterus to lead these men back and, when he had done so, to take upon himself the government of Macedonia, Thrace, and Thessaly, and to preside over the freedom of the Greeks. He also ordered Antipater to bring to him the Macedonians of manly age as successors to those who were being sent back.

SUGGESTED MODERN READINGS

Given the vast chronological span covered in this book, it has seemed advantageous to organize this bibliography into three distinct sections. The first one includes works on the civilizations of western Asia and the eastern Mediterranean down to the end of the Late Bronze Age. The second section covers the three great empires of the ancient Near East following the end of the Bronze Age, as well as Hebrew history and religion. The third section encompasses the Archaic and Classical Periods of Greece.

A. Before 1100 B.C.

Assmann, Jan. The Search for God in Ancient Egypt, tr. David Lorton, Ithaca NY 2001.

Astour, Michael C. "New Evidence on the Last Days of Ugarit," American Journal of Archaeology 69 (1965) 253-258.

Barber, Elizabeth Wayland. Women's Work, The First 20,000 Years: Women, Cloth, and Society in Early Times, New York 1994.

Bass, George F. Cape Gelidonya: A Bronze Age Shipwreck, Transactions of the American Philosophical Society, New Series 57, Part 8, Philadelphia 1967.

Beckman, Gary M.; Trevor R. Bryce; and Eric H. Cline (editors). The Ahhiyawa Texts, Leiden 2012.

Blegen, Carl W. Troy and the Trojans, New York 1963.

Bottero, Jean. Religion in Ancient Mesopotamia, tr. Teresa Lavender Pagan, Chicago 2001.

Bryce, Trevor R. "Madduwatta and Hittite Policy in Western Anatolia,"

Historia 35 (1986) 1-12.

——. The Kingdom of the Hittites, Oxford 1998.

——. Life and Society in the Hittite World, Oxford 2002.

——. Letters of the Great Kings of the Ancient Near East: The Royal Correspondence of the Late Bronze Age, London 2003.

——. The Trojans and Their Neighbours: The Secrets of Troy, London 2006.

Chadwick, John. The Decipherment of Linear B, Cambridge 1959.

——. The Mycenaean World, Cambridge 1976.

Chavalas, Mark W. (editor). Ancient Near East: Historical Sources in Translation, London 2006.

Chiera, Edward. They Wrote on Clay: The Babylonian Tablets Speak Today, Chicago 1938.

Cline, Eric H. 1177 B.C.: The Year Civilization Collapsed, Princeton 2014.

Cooper, J. S. Reconstructing History from Ancient Inscriptions: The Lagash-Umma Border Conflict, Malibu CA 1983.

Craigie, Peter G. Ugarit and the Old Testament, Grand Rapids MI 1983.

Drews, Robert. The Coming of the Greeks: Indo-European Conquests in the Aegean and the Near East, Princeton 1988.

——. The End of the Bronze Age: Changes in Warfare and the Catastrophe ca. 1200 B.C., Princeton 1993.

——. Early Riders: The Beginnings of Mounted Warfare in Asia and Europe, New York and London 2004.

Finley, Moses I., et al. "The Trojan War," Journal of Hellenic Studies 84 (1964) 1-20.

Forsyth, Phyllis Young. Thera in the Bronze Age, New York 1997.

Frankfort, Henri, et al. The Intellectual Adventure of Ancient Man: An Essay on Speculative Thought in the Ancient Near East, Chicago 1946.

——. Kingship and the Gods: A Study of Ancient Near Eastern Religion as the Integration of Society and Nature, Chicago 1950.

——. The Birth of Civilization in the Near East, Bloomington IN 1954.

Garstang, John, and O. R. Gurney. The Geography of the Hittite Empire, London 1959.

Guterbock, Han Gustav. "The Deeds of Suppiluliuma as told by his Son, Mursili II," Journal of Cuneiform Studies 10 (1956) 41-68, 75-98, and 107-130.

Gurney, O. R. The Hittites, London 1999.

Hornung, Eric. History of Ancient Egypt, An Introduction, tr. David Lorton, Ithaca NY 1999.

Horwitz, Silvia L. The Find of a Lifetime: Sir Arthur Evans and the Discovery of Knossos, New York 1981.

Jacobsen, Thorkild. "Primitive Democracy in Ancient Mesopotamia," Journal of Near Eastern Studies 2 (1943) 159-172.

Kemp, Mary J. Ancient Egypt: Anatomy of a Civilization, Second Edition, London 2006.

Kitchen, K. A. Pharaoh Triumphant: The Life and Times of Ramesses II, King of Egypt, Warminster UK 1982.

Kramer, Samuel Noah. "New Light on the Early History of the Ancient Near East," American Journal of Archaeology 52 (1948) 156-164.

———-. "Gilgamesh and Agga with Comments by Thorkild Jacobsen," American Journal of Archaeology 53 (1949) 1-22.

———-. The Sumerians: Their History, Culture, and Character, Chicago 1963.

———-. History Begins at Sumer: 39 Firsts Recorded in History, Third Revised Edition, Philadelphia 1981.

Kuhrt, Amelie. The Ancient Near East C. 3000-330 B.C., Two Volumes, London 1995.

Latacz, Joachim. Troy and Homer: Towards a Solution of an Old Mystery, tr. Kevin Windle and Rosh Ireland, Oxford 2004.

Leick, Gwendolyn. Mesopotamia: The Invention of a City, Penguin Books 2002.

Moorehead, Caroline. Lost and Found: The 9,000 Treasures of Troy, Heinrich Schliemann, and the Gold That Got Away, Penguin Books 1996.

Oppenheim, A. L. Ancient Mesopotamia: Portrait of a Dead Civilization, Revised Edition Completed by Erica Reiner, Chicago 1977.

Page, Denys L. History and the Homeric Iliad, Berkeley 1966.

Pettinato, Giovanni. Ebla: A New Look at History, tr. C. Faith Richardson, Baltimore 1991.

Redman, Charles L. The Rise of Civilization from Early Farmers to Urban Society in the Ancient Near East, San Francisco 1978.

Roux, Georges. Ancient Iraq, New Edition, Penguin Books 1992.

Sandars, Nancy K. The Sea Peoples: Warriors of the Ancient Mediterranean 1250-1150 B.C., London 1978.

Taylor, John H. Death and Afterlife in Ancient Egypt, Chicago 2001.

Tyldesley, Joyce A. Daughters of Isis: Women of Ancient Egypt, Penguin Books 1995.

——-. Hatshepsut: The Female Pharaoh, Penguin Books 1996.

——-. Nefertiti: Egypt's Sun Queen, Penguin Books 1999.

——-. Ramesses, Egypt's Greatest Pharaoh, Penguin Books 2000.

Van De Mieroop, Marc. Cuneiform Texts and the Writing of History, London 1999.

——-. A History of the Ancient Near East, ca. 3000 to 323 B.C., London 2004.

——-. A History of Ancient Egypt, London 2011.

Vernus, Pascal. Affairs and Scandals in Ancient Egypt, tr. David Lorton, Ithaca NY 2003.

Wilkinson, Richard H. (editor). Tausret, Forgotten Queen and Pharaoh of Egypt, Oxford 2012.

Weeks, Kent R. The Lost Tomb, New York 1998.

Wilson, John A. The Culture of Ancient Egypt, Chicago 1956.

Wood, Michael. In Search of the Trojan War, Berkeley 1996.

Woodard, Roger. D. (editor). The Ancient Languages of Mesopotamia, Egypt, and Aksum, Cambridge 2008.

——-. The Ancient Languages of Asia Minor, Cambridge 2008.

Woolley, Sir Charles Leonard. Ur of the Chaldees, New York 1952.

Yuon, M. The Royal City of Ugarit on the Tell of Ras Shamra, Winona Lake IN 2006.

B. The Great Empires and the Hebrews

Adkins, Lesley. Empires of the Plain: Henry Rawlinson and the Lost Languages of Babylon, London 2003.

Albright, William Foxwell. From the Stone Age to Christianity, Garden

City NY 1957.

———-. The Biblical Period from Abraham to Ezra, New York 1963.

Briant, Pierre. From Cyrus to Alexander: A History of the Persian Empire, Winona Lake IN 2002.

Bright, John. A History of Israel, Third Edition, Philadelphia 1981.

Bryce, Trevor R. The World of the Neo-Hittite Kingdoms: A Political and Military History, Oxford 2012.

Carleton, James; and Joachim Schaper (editors). The New Cambridge History of The Bible, Volume 1: From the Beginnings to 600, Cambridge 2013.

Cheyne, T. K. Founders of Old Testament Criticism, London 1893.

Cross, Frank M. Canaanite Myth and Hebrew Epic, Cambridge MA 1973.

Friedman, Richard E. Who Wrote the Bible, Englewood Cliffs NJ 1987.

Grant, Robert M. A Short History of the Interpretation of The Bible, New York 1948.

Gray, Edward M. Old Testament Criticism, New York 1923.

Habel, Norman C. Literary Criticism of The Old Testament, Philadelphia 1971.

Kuhrt, Amelie. The Ancient Near East C. 3000-330 B.C., Two Volumes, London 1995.

———-. The Persian Empire: A Corpus of Sources from the Achaemenid Period, London 2009.

Liverani, Mario. The Ancient Near East: History, Society, and Economy, tr. Soraia Tabatabai, London 2014.

Mendenhall, G. E. Law and Covenant in Israel and the Ancient Near East, Pitsburgh PA 1955.

Olmstead, A. T. History of Assyria, New York 1923.

———-. History of the Persian Empire, Chicago 1948.

Van De Mieroop, Marc. A History of the Ancient Near East, ca. 3000 to 323 B.C., London 2004.

———-. A History of Ancient Egypt, London 2011.

Waters, Matt. Ancient Persia: A Concise History of the Achaemenid Empire 550-330 BCE, Cambridge 2013.

Williamson, H. G. M. Israel in the Books of Chronicles, Cambridge 1977.

C. Archaic and Classical Greece

Adcock, F. E. The Greek and Macedonian Art of War, Berkeley 1957.

Adkins, Arthur W. H. Moral Values and Political Behavior in Ancient Greece: From Homer to the End of the Fifth Century, New York 1972.

Anderson, J. K. Military Theory and Practice in the Age of Xenophon, Berkeley 1970.

Andrewes, A. The Greek Tyrants, London 1966.

Ascheri, David; Alan Lloyd; and Aldo Corcella. A Commentary on Herodotus Books I-IV, Oxford 2007.

Badian, Ernst. "Alexander the Great and the Unity of Mankind," Historia 7 (1958) 425-444.

——. From Plataea to Potidaea, Baltimore 1993.

Billows, Richard. Marathon: The Battle That Changed Western Civilization, New York 2011.

Boardman, John. The Greeks Overseas, New and Enlarged Edition, Baltimore 1980.

Borza, Eugene N. In the Shadow of Olympus, Princeton 1990.

Bosworth, A. B. Conquest and Empire: The Reign of Alexander the Great, Cambridge 1988.

Buckler, John. The Theban Hegemony, Cambridge MA 1980.

——. Philip II and the Sacred War, Leiden 1989.

——. Aegean Greece in the Fourth Century B.C., Leiden 2003.

Burkert, Walter. The Orientalizing Revolution: Near Eastern Influence on Greek Culture in the Early Archaic Age, Cambridge MA 1992.

Burn, A. R. Persia and the Greeks: The Defense of the West, c. 546-478 B.C., New York 1962.

Bury, J. B. The Ancient Greek Historians, London 1909.

Cargill, Jack. The Second Athenian League: Empire or Free Alliance? Berkeley 1981.

Carney, Elizabeth D. Women and Monarchy in Macedonia, Norman OK 2000.

——. "The Politics of Polygamy: Olympias, Alexander and the Murder of Philip," Historia 41 (1992) 169-189.

Cartledge, Paul. Sparta and Lakonia: A Regional History, 1300 to 362

B.C., London 1979.

——-. Agesilaus and the Crisis of Sparta, Baltimore 1987.

——-. The Spartans: An Epic History, London 2002.

——-. The Spartans: The World of the Warrior-Heroes of Ancient Greece, From Utopia to Crisis and Collapse, Woodstock NY 2003.

——-. Thermopylae: The Battle that Changed the World, New York 2007.

——-. After Thermopylae: The Oath of Plataea and the End of the Greco-Persian Wars, Oxford 2013.

Casson, Lionel. Ships and Seafaring in Ancient Times, Boston 1994.

Cawkwell, George L. Philip of Macedon, London 1978.

De Ste. Croix, G. E. M. The Origins of the Peloponnesian War, Ithaca NY 1972.

Donlan, Walter. The Aristocratic Ideal in Ancient Greece: Attitudes of Superiority From Homer to the End of the Fifth Century B.C., Lawrence KA 1980.

Drews, Robert. "The First Tyrants in Greece," Historia 21 (1972) 129-144.

——-. Greek Accounts of Eastern History, Cambridge MA 1973.

Dunbabin, T. J. The Western Greeks, Oxford 1948.

——-. The Greeks and their Eastern Neighbours: Studies in the Relations between Greece and the Countries of the Near East in the Eighth and Seventh Centuries B.C., London 1957.

Ehrenberg, Victor. From Solon to Socrates: Greek History and Civilization during the Sixth and Fifth Centuries B.C., New York 1973.

Ellis, J. R. Philip II and Macedonian Imperialism, Princeton 1976.

Engels, Donald W. Alexander the Great and the Logistics of the Macedonian Army, Berkeley 1978.

Fink, Dennis L. The Battle of Marathon in Scholarship: Research, Theories, and Controversies since 1850, Jefferson NC 2014.

Finley, Moses I. The World of Odysseus, New York 1982.

Forrest, W. G. A History of Sparta, 950-192 B.C., London 1968.

Gomme, A. W. A Historical Commentary on Thucydides, Five Volumes, Oxford 1945-1981.

Gorman, Vanessa B. Miletos, The Ornament of Ionia: A History of the

City to 400 B.C.E., Ann Arbor MI 2001.

Graham, A. John. Colony and Mother City in Ancient Greece, New York 1964.

Green, Peter. Armada from Athens, New York 1970.

——-. Alexander of Macedon, 356-323 B.C.: A Historical Biography, Berkeley 1992.

Grundy, G. B. The Great Persian War and its Preliminaries: A Study of the Evidence, Literary and Topographical, London 1901.

Hale, John R. Lords of the Sea: The Epic Story of the Athenian Navy and the Birth of Democracy, Penguin Books 2009.

Hamilton, Charles. Sparta's Bitter Victories: Politics and Diplomacy in the Corinthian War, Ithaca NY 1979.

Hanson, Victor Davis. "Epaminondas, the Battle of Leuctra, and a Revolution in Greek Battle Tactics," Classical Antiquity 7 (1988) 190-207.

—— (editor). Hoplites: The Ancient Greek Battle Experience, London 1991.

——-. The Western Way of War: Infantry Battle in Classical Greece, Second Edition, Berkeley 1998.

——-. The Other Greeks, Second Edition, Berkeley 1999.

——-. A War Like No Other: How the Athenians and Spartans Fought the Peloponnesian War, New York 2005.

Hignett, Charles. A History of the Athenian Constitution to the End of the Fifth Century B.C., Oxford 1952.

——-. Xerxes' Invasion of Greece, Oxford 1963.

Holland, Tom. Persian Fire: Empire and the Battle for the West, New York and London 2005

Hooker, J. T. The Ancient Spartans, London 1980.

Hornblower, Simon. A Commentary on Thucydides, Two Volumes, Oxford 1990-1996.

How, W. W.; and J. Wells. A Commentary on Herodotus, Two Volumes, Oxford, first published 1912, reprinted with corrections 1936.

Kagan, Donald. The Outbreak of the Peloponnesian War, Ithaca NY 1969.

——-. The Archidamian War, Ithaca NY 1974.

——-. The Peace of Nicias and the Sicilian Expedition, Ithaca NY 1981.

————. The Fall of the Athenian Empire, Ithaca NY 1987.

————. The Peloponnesian War, New York 2003.

Krentz, Peter. The Battle of Marathon, New Haven CT 2010.

Lazenby, J. F. The Spartan Army, Warminster UK 1985.

————. The Defense of Greece 490-479 B.C., Warminster UK 1993.

————. The Peloponnesian War, A Military History, London 2004.

McGregor, Malcolm F. The Athenians and their Empire, Vancouver BC 1987.

Meiggs, Russell. The Athenian Empire, Oxford 1972.

Morrison, J. S.; J. E. Coates; and N. B. Rankov. The Athenian Trireme: The History and Reconstruction of an Ancient Greek Warship, Cambridge 2000.

Murray, Oswyn. Early Greece, Second Edition, Cambridge MA 1993.

Osborne, Robin. Greece in the Making, 1200-479 B.C., London 1996.

Pearson, Lionel. Early Ionian Historians, Oxford 1939.

————. The Lost Histories of Alexander the Great, Stanford 1960.

Pritchett, W. Kendrick. The Greek States at War, Five Volumes, Berkeley 1971-1991.

Robinson, Eric W. Democracy beyond Athens: Popular Government in Classical Greece, Cambridge MA 2011.

Rusch, Scott. Sparta at War: Strategy, Tactics, and Campaigns, 550-362 B.C., London 2011.

Shipley, G.; and John Rich (editors). Warfare and Society in the Greek World, London 1993.

Strauss, Barry. The Battle of Salamis: The Naval Encounter that Saved Greece and Western Civilization, New York 2004.

Tarn, W. W. Alexander the Great, Two Volumes, Cambridge 1948.

Ure, Percy N. The Origin of Tyranny, London 1922.

Westlake, H. D. Individuals in Thucydides, Cambridge 1968.

Wilcken, Ulrich. Alexander the Great, tr. by G. C. Richards with an introduction by Eugene Borza, New York 1967.

Worthington, Ian. Philip II of Macedonia, New Haven CT 2008.

————. By the Sear: Philip II, Alexander the Great, and the Rise and Fall of the Macedonian Empire, Oxford 2014.

Zimmern, A. E. The Greek Commonwealth, Oxford 1924.

CPSIA information can be obtained
at www.ICGtesting.com
Printed in the USA
LVHW011924020820
662196LV00017B/1604

9 781480 954250